PRICING ANALYTICS

The theme of this book is simple. The price – the number someone puts on a product to help consumers decide to buy that product – comes from data. Specifically, it comes from statistically modeling the data.

This book gives the reader the statistical modeling tools needed to get the number to put on a product. But statistical modeling is not done in a vacuum. Economic and statistical principles and theory conjointly provide the background and framework for the models. Therefore, this book emphasizes two interlocking components of modeling: economic theory and statistical principles.

The economic theory component is sufficient to provide understanding of the basic principles for pricing, especially about elasticities, which measure the effects of pricing on key business metrics. Elasticity estimation is the goal of statistical modeling, so attention is paid to the concept and implications of elasticities.

The statistical modeling component is advanced and detailed covering choice (conjoint, discrete choice, MaxDiff) and sales data modeling. Experimental design principles, model estimation approaches, and analysis methods are discussed and developed for choice models. Regression fundamentals have been developed for sales model specification and estimation and expanded for latent class analysis.

Walter R. Paczkowski, Ph.D., worked at AT&T, AT&T Bell Labs, and AT&T Labs. He founded Data Analytics Corp., a statistical consulting company, in 2001. Dr. Paczkowski is also a part-time lecturer of economics at Rutgers University. He published *Market Data Analysis Using JMP* in 2016.

PRICING ANALYTICS

Models and Advanced Quantitative Techniques for Product Pricing

Walter R. Paczkowski

Routledge
Taylor & Francis Group

LONDON AND NEW YORK

First published 2019
by Routledge
2 Park Square, Milton Park, Abingdon, Oxon OX14 4RN

and by Routledge
711 Third Avenue, New York, NY 10017

Routledge is an imprint of the Taylor & Francis Group, an informa business

© 2019 Walter R. Paczkowski

The right of Walter R. Paczkowski to be identified as author of this work has been asserted by him in accordance with sections 77 and 78 of the Copyright, Designs and Patents Act 1988.

British Library Cataloguing-in-Publication Data
A catalogue record for this book is available from the British Library

Library of Congress Cataloging-in-Publication Data
Names: Paczkowski, Walter R., author.
Title: Pricing analytics : models and advanced quantitative
techniques for product pricing / Walter R. Paczkowski.
Description: 1 Edition. | New York : Routledge, 2018.
Identifiers: LCCN 2018004869 | ISBN 9781138036758 (hardback)
Subjects: LCSH: Pricing. | Quantitative research–Computer programs.
Classification: LCC HF5416.5 .P33 2018 | DDC 658.8/16–dc23
LC record available at https://lccn.loc.gov/2018004869

ISBN: 978-1-138-03675-8 (hbk)
ISBN: 978-1-138-62393-4 (pbk)
ISBN: 978-1-315-17834-9 (ebk)

Typeset in Bembo
by Out of House Publishing

CONTENTS

PART II
Stated preference models   65

FIGURES

TABLES

PREFACE

I run a small consulting firm primarily focused on supporting organizations doing market research. I perform their statistical analysis and modeling. Since I have a Ph.D. in economics, I am frequently drawn into pricing studies. Clients often ask how they could determine the "optimal" price for a good or service, whether it is an existing one, a line extension, or something new to the world. At the heart of answering this question is the price sensitivity, or what economists call the *price elasticity*. The purpose of this book is to explain, develop, and illustrate methodologies for estimating price elasticities.

Quite often I am frustrated with the marketing pricing literature. Much of it focuses on strategies, or the top ten pricing secrets to winning customers, or the five things not to do, or something else along these lines. Modeling issues and techniques are buried in the econometrics literature with casual mention every now and then about prices, so I needed to translate the econometrics literature to have a marketing pricing focus. This book reflects my attempts at these translations.

Theme of this book

The theme of this book is that the price – the *number* someone puts on a tag that goes on a product that helps a consumer decide whether or not to buy that product – can only come from *data*; specifically, from statistically modeling data. This book will give you tools for doing the statistical modeling to get the number to put on the tag you put on your product.

Possible approaches to writing this book

There are various ways I could have approached writing this book. I could have written a book for a business manager or executive who just wants an overview of what is quantitatively possible so he or she could understand the analysts and consultants who build pricing models. Such a book would be long on ideas but short on techniques. Buzzwords would dominate. It would, in short, be just another management book.

Alternatively, I could have written a book that provides technical details targeted to the analysts who build pricing models. This is what I chose to do. The target audience consists of those analysts charged, like me in my consulting practice, with actually estimating elasticities or somehow deriving or calculating the "optimal" price.

Specifically, I wrote this book with two analyst audiences in mind. The first consists of the analysts (whether economists, statisticians, or market researchers) who have to estimate the optimal price for a product or service. They need more than a superficial understanding of techniques. The ones who either need or want a superficial understanding typically only want to be able to read a report written by the analysts or comprehend a presentation on pricing so they can make a logical, consistent, and coherent decision; they are typically the decision makers and not the doers. These people would have marginal benefit from this book. Those who want a depth of understanding are the doers who actually work with data and build pricing models. They will benefit from this book. The second audience consists of students and some academics (e.g., professors teaching an econometrics or pricing course), whether in economics, statistics, or market research. The students, and their professors, need a guide to these techniques. These students could be upper-level majors in one of these disciplines or beginning graduate students.

Depth of material

I had to be realistic in how deep I could go into modeling. For some readers, the material in this book may be just a good review. For others, it may raise more questions and issues than it addresses. Detailed information is provided in the references for the methodologies and techniques discussed here.

Book structure

This book has 12 chapters divided into four parts. The first part is the background, consisting of three chapters dealing with a framework for quantitatively determining prices, a consumer demand theory review, and the role and importance of elasticities.

The second part begins the discussion of how to estimate elasticities from survey data in which people state their preferences for products and product attributes. Hence, this family of techniques is called *stated preference modeling*. The main estimation methodology is the regression *family* of statistical techniques, which is a broad family. One member of the family is the ordinary least squares (OLS) regression model, which is a special case usually taught in basic statistics and econometrics classes.

The third part is concerned with price segmentation. The previous part dealt with a single market and a single price for that market. This assumes that consumers are homogeneous. Businesses, however, typically segment markets in order to tailor products and messages to different groups. They recognize that consumers are heterogeneous. Prices, as part of the marketing mix, should also be tailored to different groups. This is price segmentation.

The last part of the book deals with preferences that are revealed in the market by the actual purchase decisions people make. Transaction data are collected into and maintained in large databases called data warehouses and data marts. This is Big Data. Working with Big Data is a challenge because of the magnitude of the databases. This part begins with a discussion of the issues. Modeling is then discussed within this context. The models developed here are purely econometric, although technically all the models in this book are econometric. It is just that the models developed here look like models you may have seen in an econometrics or regression analysis class. Finally, because of the use of transaction data, nonlinear pricing is included in this part. Pricing in the previous parts (actually, in all but the last chapter) dealt with linear prices: prices that are proportional to quantity sales. Nonlinear prices vary by sales. There are many issues associated with nonlinear prices and a discussion of these is what closes the book.

Required background

This book is technical, but not so technical that you need a Ph.D. to read it. An undergraduate background in statistics through regression analysis and perhaps an econometrics course is all that is needed. It is thus assumed that basic statistics, probability theory, and regression analysis are known. Design of experiments plays a big role in Part II. Since this is not typically taught at the level needed here, the principles of design will be developed as needed.

Caveats

My background is mostly in consumer products. I have done a lot of work in food, beverages, jewelry, pharmaceuticals, high tech, finance, and publishing, to mention a few, so some of my examples will come from these areas. Also, I will write about "products" because I am too lazy to use the tedious phrase "goods and services." Whatever I discuss, it can be applied equally well to services and non-consumer goods.

Before we start

Finally, although there are many econometric issues that are not covered here, I hope this book will be a start for those charged with modeling for pricing, the people I call the *doers*.

ACKNOWLEDGEMENTS

What can I possibly say about all the help and support I received from my wonderful wife, Gail, my two daughters, Kristin and Melissa, and my son-in-law David? My wife encouraged me to sit down and just write, especially when I did not want to, while my daughters provided those extra sets of eyes I needed to make this perfect. I would also like to say something about my two grandsons who, at two and six, obviously did not contribute to this book, but who, I hope, will look at it in their adult years and say, "My grandpa wrote this."

PART I
Background

There is an old Chinese proverb most are familiar with: "A journey of a thousand miles begins with a single step."[1] This first part is that first step. It sets the stage for the remainder of the book by discussing the importance of pricing and getting the "right" price. There are many ways to set the price of a product or service. In fact, there is probably an infinite number of ways, one for each marketing or pricing manager who has to wrestle with the issue of what to charge. Each manager brings his or her own biases and experiences to the pricing table. That does not mean that the methods are correct or good. Often, pure judgement is used, summarized in the pithy statement: "I know what the price should be." This reflects the art of pricing.

Getting the price right is also a science just as much as it is an art. There are statistical and econometric tools – well-developed and sophisticated *quantitative* tools – that complement and support the art side of pricing. These tools cannot be overlooked or ignored solely in favor of the art. That would court business disaster.

What exactly do the tools do? Most of them, but not all, provide elasticities, an economic concept that is at the heart of pricing. An elasticity tells you quantitatively how much sales will change (in percentage terms) when you change the price (also in percentage terms). This is vital to know because, while you may believe that lowering price will stimulate sales, the amount of stimulation could be insufficient to offset the revenue loss of the lower price, resulting in a decrease in revenue. The art side of pricing will not tell you this, but the science side, summarized by the elasticities, will.

This first part of the book is divided into three chapters. The first gives an overall perspective of pricing and the importance of a quantitative approach, one that actually produces a number to go on the product's price tag. This chapter highlights the art side of pricing, but then makes the case for the science or quantitative side.

The second chapter reviews and develops the elasticity concept. This could be skipped by those very familiar with basic economic concepts, especially consumer demand theory, up through a typical intermediate microeconomic theory course. For those readers, I recommend skimming through this chapter just to pick up the notation used elsewhere in the book.

The third chapter discusses how elasticities are used in pricing. It does not mean much to say (as in Chapter 2) that elasticities are important. They have to be shown to be important. This third chapter illustrates their use in different market structures. At the end of this chapter, you will be prepared to tackle the remaining chapters of the book in order to learn how to estimate elasticities from market data.

Note

1 Attributed to the Chinese philosopher, Laozi (c.604–c.531 BC) in the *Tao Te Ching*, Chapter 64, as noted in http://en.wiktionary.org/wiki/a_journey_of_a_thousand_miles_begins_with_a_single_step. Last accessed November 5, 2013.

1

INTRODUCTION

Each day, business managers answer a number of questions: legal, personnel, regulatory, and the list goes on. There is one question they must answer – the *Key Business Question* – that ultimately drives the business: "*What do I charge?*" They need a number to put on the tag that goes on their product so a consumer can decide whether or not to buy the product. That price, that number, has to be the "best" one to capture the most consumers and make the most sales. Otherwise, the business manager will be out of a job and the business may no longer exist. A lot rests on that price, that number.

What to charge, how to price the product, is the most difficult of the business questions to handle because it is often unclear how much people are willing and able to pay for a product. This holds true for existing products as well as new products. For the former, the current market price may not be the best one. It may be too low so money is "left on the table" (that is, higher revenue could be earned without changing the cost structure for the product) or it may be too high so that sales are needlessly lost. For the case of a new product, there is often a lack of information regarding where to begin setting the price and so new product pricing offers unique challenges.

Marketing professionals base their marketing plans on the "*P*s" of marketing, a clever mnemonic for the key tools available for marketing.[1] The *P*s are:

Product: The item to be sold as defined by its characteristics and features; that is, its attributes.
Place: Where the product is to be sold.
Position: The product space location where the product will lie relative to competitor products (e.g., as a premium or a bargain product).
Promotion: How potential consumers of the product will learn about it (i.e., how they will gain the information needed to make a purchase decision).
Price: How much consumers will be asked to pay for the product.

Pricing is different from the other *P*s in a number of respects. The price, or a change in the price, is the only marketing factor that goes directly to the bottom-line of the income statement. Change the price and the revenue side of the income statement changes immediately. Also, the price can be changed almost instantly. Within a matter of minutes, a store can raise or lower its price merely by posting a sign or, in our increasingly technological world, by changing a statement in a computer program that controls an electronic price display such as the ones gas stations now use.

The other marketing *P*s also affect the bottom-line, but not so directly and immediately. They require time to implement and "spread the word." Take promotion, for example. Once it is decided that a new promotional campaign is needed, perhaps a new in-store display or a flyer mailed to consumers, then a lengthy process is set in motion to develop and deploy the new promotion. The development is not cost free. Creative designers and writers are needed who are usually high-priced professionals. In addition, the optimal mix of magazines, newspapers, TV and radio spots, and in-store displays has to be chosen, which also requires time and expensive market research. So, in addition to potentially improving the bottom-line, a promotion may also hurt it by increasing the cost side of the accounts. Any increase in net income from increased sales due to the promotional campaign could be partially, if not completely, offset by the costs of the campaign. A price change, on the other hand, only affects the revenue side.[2]

This chapter is divided into eight sections. This first outlines issues associated with answering the *Key Business Question* by using one of two classes of pricing strategies. Section 2 introduces the importance of a price effect measure, basically the price elasticity. Section 3 discusses approaches to pricing research, while the following two sections, 4 and 5, discuss each in depth. The use of a simulator to study the results of quantitative research is mentioned in Section 6, while Section 7 highlights the role of elasticities. Section 8 is a summary.

1.1   Answering the *Key Business Question*

Business managers typically begin addressing the *Key Business Question* by focusing on a pricing strategy. A strategy is a statement of the key actions that will be taken by the business. Consider the following example of a pricing strategy statement for a fashion product: "It is optimal to price high at the beginning of a fashion season to attract price-insensitive, fashion-forward consumers and then lower prices over time to price discriminate to reach the more price-sensitive customers."[3] This statement clearly articulates how prices will be changed, and to whom the specific prices will be targeted. What is lacking is the specific price point – the number to be charged and changed.

1.1.1   Uniform pricing strategy

A uniform pricing strategy is one that uses a simple, single price for all units sold to all buyers. This is an almost naive pricing strategy because it assumes that all consumers are homogeneous and there is only one product without variations due to quality. Since the price applies to all units sold, no consideration is given to order size (i.e., quantity discounts) or order composition (i.e., bundling). Prices are then linear rather than nonlinear.

1.1.2   Price discrimination strategy

A price discrimination strategy as in the above strategy statement is basically a strategy to sell products (identical or not) to different people at different prices. There are three basic forms, or *degrees*, of price discrimination:

First-degree: Price varies by how much each consumer is willing and able to pay for the product.

Second-degree: Price varies with the amount purchased. This is a form of nonlinear pricing in which the pricing schedule is a nonlinear function of the quantity. This is typically used by electric utilities, but it also applies to quantity discounts, bundling, and product-line pricing.

Third-degree: Price varies by consumer segments. Segments may be defined by age, gender, location, and status (e.g., students vs. non-students, senior citizens vs. non-seniors). This is a common form of price discrimination.

The fashion example is a *third-degree price discrimination* form because consumers are divided into two segments: fashion-forward and non-fashion-forward. The former must have the latest fashion trends as soon as they become available to be ahead of the fashion curve, while the latter wait to see what everyone else is wearing and what is in fashion before they buy. The former would be more inelastic, while the latter would be more elastic. Therefore, the fashion-forward buyers would be charged a high price, as the strategy statement says, and the non-fashion-forward buyers would be charged a lower price.

Whatever the form, price discrimination as a pricing strategy is widely used. I will return to the theoretical issues of determining the price for a price discrimination strategy in Chapter 3.

1.1.3   Strategy parts

The fashion-forward example illustrates that a pricing strategy has two parts:

Price structure: A high price at the beginning of the fashion season and a low price at the end to target consumers based on their price sensitivities or *elasticities*.

Price level: The price that actually will be charged (which is not mentioned in the fashion strategy statement).

A pricing strategy statement simultaneously expresses both structure and level as is clearly done in the fashion example. The *Key Business Question*, however, is about the second part of a strategy statement: the *number* for the level. What is the number and where does it come from?

There are many books on pricing structures and strategies. [53] and [56] are two excellent examples. In this book, I will focus on the *level* because that is the number that goes on the tag that is on the product that must be sold. Chapter 6, however, will deviate from this by discussing ways to gain insight into structure.

1.2 Price effect

Just as important as the price level is the price *effect*. All too often, managers just think of "stimulating demand" by lowering the price, as in the fashion-forward example. But this is too narrow and simplistic a focus. Thinking more broadly, what effect will a different price level have on a key business metric such as:

- Revenue?
- Contribution?
- Customer acquisition?
- Customer retention?
- Market share?

If a price decrease results in a decrease in revenue, then is the new price level the correct one to use? No.

The level part of the answer to the *Key Business Question*, therefore, is subdivided into two parts: a level – or number – answer and an effect assessment answer. This is illustrated in Figure 1.2.1. Both level and effect are determined simultaneously by *pricing analytics*.

The remainder of this chapter is divided into six sections. The first section to follow, Section 1.3, discusses two approaches – qualitative and quantitative – a pricing manager could use to set the price level. This section sets the stage for the

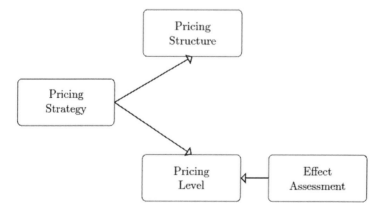

FIGURE 1.2.1 The basic pricing framework most marketing professionals use has two components: strategy and level. Most of the emphasis by marketers is on the strategy part. But the level part, along with the effect assessment, cannot be ignored.

next two sections that discuss the qualitative and quantitative approaches in more detail. The remainder of the book, of course, focuses on the quantitative.

Sections 1.4 and 1.5 discuss in more detail the two approaches and argue for the use of a quantitative approach to pricing. Section 1.5 also introduces a framework for doing *pricing analytics*. This framework will be followed throughout the book to answer the *Key Business Question*.

Sections 1.6 and 1.7 introduce simulators as a tool for pricing analytics and the economist's notion of a price elasticity. This is a very brief introduction as befitting an introductory chapter. This important concept is more fully discussed and applied in Chapters 2 and 3. The final section, Section 1.8, is a summary.

1.3   Pricing research approaches

In this section, I will discuss two broad approaches for pricing research: qualitative and quantitative research (see Figure 1.3.1).

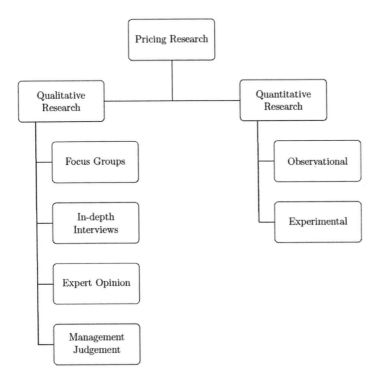

FIGURE 1.3.1 There are two major approaches analysts have used for pricing: qualitative and quantitative. This book is concerned with the quantitative approach using observational and experimental data. We can observe consumers' purchase behaviors that reveal their preferences and build econometric models to estimate elasticities, but you can also ask them to state their preferences using an experimental design and then build econometric models to estimate elasticities.

Qualitative research is largely opinion based and unscientific. Sampling methodologies and statistical tools are not used to determine the price level or even to assess effect – they cannot because qualitative research does not rely on data per se. This is not meant to disparage or condemn qualitative research, because it does have a valid role to play in determining a price level and assessing effect, but that role is not a sole or primary one. Qualitative research is discussed in Section 1.4.

Quantitative research consists of data analysis and statistical modeling using either observational or experimental data and founded on the basic economic paradigm of consumer demand. The data analysis, aside from what is fundamentally used in model building, includes methods to find data anomalies, correlations, patterns, and trends. Statistical models based on observational data – data measuring actual consumer purchase behavior that reveal preferences (and, hence, are called *revealed preference data*) – are usually regression models of varying complexity.[4] Statistical models based on experimental data – data collected via an experimental design in which consumers state their preferences (and, hence, are called *stated preference data*) – are either conjoint or discrete choice models. Quantitative research is discussed in Section 1.5.

Going forward, observational data will be referred to as "revealed preference data" and experimental data as "stated preference data."

Qualitative and quantitative research can be done to support one another at different stages of the overall research process. Qualitative research done before the quantitative work can provide information and insight into factors other than price that drive or determine the demand for a product, which can then be used in the quantitative research. It can also be done after the quantitative research to give support or credibility to the quantitative results by using, for example, expert assessments. Likewise, quantitative research can be used to give credibility to qualitative research results or to support or bolster expert or managerial opinion or judgement.

Although quantitative pricing research methodologies based on revealed or stated data will be discussed in this book, something should be said about qualitative research. This is done in the next section.

1.4 Qualitative pricing research

Qualitative research consists of focus groups, in-depth interviews, expert opinions, and managerial judgements, to mention a few possibilities.

Focus groups are popular for learning about consumer preferences. Led by a trained and experienced moderator, a well-thought-out and executed series of focus groups coupled with a detailed moderator guide can yield useful information about consumer preferences and buying intentions. This extends to pricing by asking consumers in the groups how much they would be willing to pay. This information, however, can only yield approximate prices, or, better yet, price ranges because the consumers in the focus groups, even though they are chosen

based on specific demographic and buying behavior criteria, are not a scientifically selected random sample. Insufficient sample size is always an issue because
focus groups tend to be small. What the focus group participants say cannot be
generalized to the market, but can only be used as guides and input into further
scientific and quantitative work – the quantitative branch of the pricing tree in
Figure 1.3.1.

A specialization of the focus group is the in-depth personal interview in which
a subject matter expert (SME) or key opinion leader (KOL) is questioned in detail
about some issue. The SMEs may talk to the sales force, which has a direct link
to retailers and customers, and the SMEs inform the sales force about what the
price should be. The SMEs may also talk to consultants who know the market and
understand dynamic market operations for the product's category. The KOLs write
blogs, lengthy industry reports, and columns in various trade press publications
prognosticating on the future of their industry or products. Although the information garnered is useful, it is still biased by the few interviews that can be conducted
and who is interviewed.

Management judgement plays a large role in retail pricing. [43] starts an article
on retail pricing by saying:

> A large department store wants to sell a "one-of-a-kind" designer gown.
> Although the manager has some idea about the price that the gown can
> command, there is generally some guesswork associated with the process.
> How should he choose his initial price?

Notice the focus on guesswork.

Management, or the management team, uses information from SMEs and
KOLs, plus their own instincts, to determine the best price or how prices should
be changed in an attempt to remove the guesswork. They do know something
independent of what statistics tells them. This information is called *prior information*,
or just a *prior*. The information, however, is personal to them, having been built
through years of experience with similar products and situations. They may have
developed a "sixth sense" or "gut feel" or a set of rules of thumb (ROTs) that guide
their decision. In seasonal retailing, for instance, managers often set prices high at
the beginning of the season and then lower them dramatically later in the season
just to sell or move merchandise because experience taught them about seasonal
effects (see [43]).

The use of prior information is the basis of Bayesian data analysis. This is a complex, highly technical area of statistics that is now used more frequently because of
great strides in software and algorithmic procedures, especially simulations with
Markov Chain Monte Carlo (MCMC) methods (see [60] for an excellent discussion). Bayesian issues will be discussed in Chapter 5 for the design of discrete choice
studies.

All the information gathered from the qualitative side of the pricing tree of
Figure 1.3.1, whether from the judgement or ROTs of managers, SMEs, KOLs, or

consumers in focus groups, has a place in pricing. In the early stage of new product pricing, before any quantitative work is or can be done, a rough approximation of prices may be needed for developing scenarios for a business case to prove or support the continuation of the development of the new product. If the product is in the conceptual development stage, there may not be enough product details to specify a quantitative study, yet the effects of price are needed to decide whether or not it is profitable to continue product development. This is illustrated in the next section.

1.4.1 Pharmaceuticals case study

Pharmaceutical new product development provides an excellent case study of pricing research issues and techniques. As background, new pharmaceutical products must pass a series of rigorous tests or checkpoints that collectively span several years before product launch. The tests are divided into phases[5]:

Phase I: Dose and administration testing; this is preceded by pre-clinical development and testing.
Phase II: Efficacy testing with a test and control group.
Phase III: Overall effectiveness testing in a large population.
Phase IV (optional): Tracking after launch.

Each phase can last several years. The total time for Phases I–III could be a decade, but the actual time depends on many factors.[6] Given the time span of these phases plus the time required to develop the new drug before the phase testing even begins, it should be clear that new drug development is a costly endeavor.

At each stage of this process, not only is the new drug tested, but its financial viability is also closely monitored through the *business case* process. A business case is a competitive market and financial assessment of the viability of a product. This process is illustrated in Figure 1.4.1.

The competitive assessment part of a business case considers the structure of the market (competitive, fragmented), entry barriers, regulatory restrictions, perceived attribute similarities (from the consumers' viewpoint), likely competitive reactions to marketing programs, and, of course, price structure and levels. The financial assessment part of a business case considers unit sales forecasts, expected average unit costs, and proposed price points to calculate an expected rate of return for the product. The goal is to determine if the product's estimated rate of return under these conditions would meet or exceed a management-mandated rate of return, or "hurdle rate."

Determining the optimal selling price a decade before the new product is launched, let alone developing it a year before launch, is an impossible task for obvious reasons. Nonetheless, a price point for the business case is needed. In the early business cases, it is best to use a price range of "most likely" prices, with a specific price point developed closer to actual launch. This is where qualitative

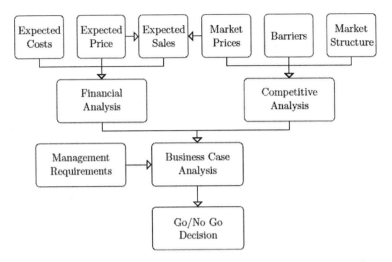

FIGURE 1.4.1 This schematic of the business case process is, of course, highly stylized. The actual process will vary across companies, but the key components and linkages will not differ much from what is shown here.

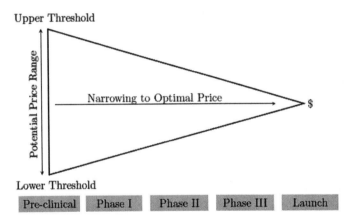

FIGURE 1.4.2 Due to the long time frame for new product development in the pharmaceutical industry, different levels of pricing are needed and are possible during the development process. Wide ranges are the best that can be developed in early stages. A price point, however, is needed at launch. The quantitative methodologies are different at the different stages. Adapted from [21].

research can play a big role. [21] recommends that KOLs be relied on. This should then be followed by quantitative research as the launch date comes closer, especially stated preference research, with a price range replaced by a price point by the day of launch. This is illustrated in Figure 1.4.2.

1.4.2 Cost-plus pricing

I would be remiss if I did not say something about cost-plus pricing. Cost-plus pricing is probably the most common pricing approach, typically among those companies that are "less sophisticated." Cost-plus pricing

> ... is used primarily because it is easy to calculate and requires little information. There are several varieties, but the common thread in all of them is that one first calculates the cost of the product, then includes an additional amount to represent profit. It is a way for companies to calculate how much profit they will make. Cost-plus pricing is often used on government contracts, and has been criticized as promoting wasteful expenditures.
>
> The method determines the price of a product or service that uses direct costs, indirect costs, and fixed costs whether related to the production and sale of the product or service or not. These costs are converted to per unit costs for the product and then a predetermined percentage of these costs is added to provide a profit margin.[7]

In essence, this approach to pricing involves finding the average cost of producing the product and then adding a markup over that cost. Cost-plus pricing has the appearance of a quantitative approach to pricing since costs, a quantitative concept, has a markup, another quantitative concept, applied to it. Adding a markup to costs is a financial issue, which is certainly quantitative. My position is that the markup itself, although a number, is actually based on management judgement about what is acceptable or required for the business to return to its owners as a profit and so falls into the realm of the qualitative approaches. The result of this qualitative action is quantitative, not the input. As such, it is outside the scope of this book.

Cost-plus pricing has many other issues (see [56], pp. 2–4 for a discussion). It has been pointed out that cost-plus pricing can even lead to perverse pricing in that a company could be led to increase prices in a weak market and have prices that are too low in a strong market. The central issues with cost-plus pricing is that the customers are not considered; only management's judgement about the size of the markup is considered. I advocate for the use of a strong quantitative approach focused on what the customer is willing and able to pay for a product or service. Estimates of demand elasticities are at the heart of this approach. Elasticities and their uses are discussed in detail in Chapters 2 and 3, respectively.

Although my position is that cost-plus pricing per se is strictly qualitative, you can, nonetheless, determine the percentage markup over average incremental cost using elasticities. The elasticities are quantitatively based so you can calculate the percentage markup. This is different, however, from *specifying* the markup, which is what cost-plus pricing per se usually entails.

1.4.3 Importance of qualitative information

Although qualitative pricing research is not emphasized in this book, it has an important role in pricing because it establishes prior information – information prior to the quantitative research – that helps guide the quantitative research. Qualitative research, however, does not and cannot lead to useful numbers. The best qualitative techniques can do is provide opinions.

As you will see later, discrete choice approaches to modeling can be greatly enhanced by using prior information (simply called *priors*). A basic recommendation is to use priors if they are available. I will discuss how later in this book.

1.5   Quantitative pricing research

The quantitative approach is more complicated than the qualitative because it involves three interconnected parts:

> *Theory foundation*: Establishes the underlying principles for the research.
> *Data analysis*: Supports a statistical model.
> *Statistical model*: Estimates elasticities for determining price level and effect.

These three parts address the *Key Business Question* ("What do I charge?") and form the basis for estimating price elasticities. We can represent these three parts as a triangle as shown in Figure 1.5.1.

The *theory foundation* highlights key variables or drivers of data collection and empirical model specification. For pricing, this is the economic theory of consumer demand. *Data analysis* supports theory development and statistical model specification, with graphs and transformations (e.g., logs) playing major roles. The *statistical model* estimates parameters consistent with the theory and directs data collection. The *data analysis* and the *statistical model* together form the *empirical stage of analysis*.

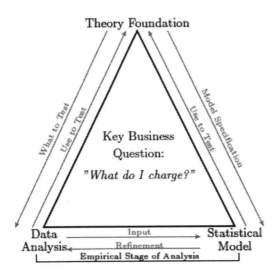

FIGURE 1.5.1 The pricing analytics framework is a stylized depiction of the research process, whether for pricing or any type of quantitative research. Here, the *Key Business Question* is the focus of the process.

At the center of the triangle is the *Key Business Question*, the driving motivation for the quantitative research study. The three vertices of the triangle revolve around, address, and support this *Key Business Question*. The triangle could be rotated in any direction and it would still stand on its own with no part dominating. They all work together to address the *Key Business Question*.

1.5.1 The role of theory

Theory plays a major role in any research because it is an organizing framework. Theories are designed to promote "systematic and organized methods of reasoning"[8] by allowing you to create artificial worlds to test ideas. The role of theory does not stop here. Theory helps you to avoid confusing causation and correlation, which people often think are one and the same – that they can be used interchangeably. Causation is distinct from correlation. Correlation means association, not causation. See [77] for some discussion of the importance of this distinction in the legal area.

Theory also helps you avoid spurious correlations in which a third, unexamined variable may be latent; it may be there and exert an influence, but you may not be able to identify it (yet) or measure it (yet). You may find, for example, a high positive correlation between the amount of ice cream sold at the Jersey shore in mid-July and the number of drownings at the Jersey shore also in mid-July. This is spurious because of the existence of another factor: the hot weather. This third unaccounted variable, the hot weather, is the reason for the supposed high correlation.

Let me pause to handle an issue about "theory" vs. hypotheses. Here is a popular quote from the British economist, John Maynard Keynes [39] (emphasis added):

> The ideas of economists and political philosophers, both when they are right and when they are wrong, are more powerful than is commonly understood. Indeed the world is ruled by little else. *Practical men, who believe themselves to be quite exempt from any intellectual influence, are usually the slaves of some defunct economist.*

The important part of this quote is the emphasized sentence on "Practical men." Economists develop theories about how the world works and, one way or another, usually through the infamous Economics 101 college course, those theories are learned, although often not well. Nonetheless, they are learned and applied, whether we know it or not. They influence us as part of our stock of knowledge and for empirical work they are our ultimate guide as to what we should do, whether we acknowledge it or not. So Keynes' economists are always there.

Despite these economic theories still having an influence, some people prefer not to acknowledge them and instead talk about "hypotheses." You could substitute the word "hypothesis" for "theory" and nothing would change. In some sense, all analytical work is hypothesis driven. Analytical work involves the use of data, data often too voluminous to wade through effectively without a guide. The guide for going through the data is the set of hypotheses.

Referring to the research triangle, theories or hypotheses, whichever word is preferred, guide what data you need to collect and tell you how you should analyze them. Here are some example pricing hypotheses:

- Setting our price at $4.50 for each unit will yield sales of 1000 units.
- Increasing price 1% will increase our profit margin.
- Male customers will be willing to pay $100 more for a convertible option.
- Customers over 45 years old are more price sensitive than younger customers.
- There are four price segments in our market, each with a different price elasticity.
- Our competitor's pricing strategy has little effect on our market share.

The statistical model should be founded on economic theory. After all, you are concerned with how people make decisions and economic theory is about economic decision making. Since you are trying to say something about people's behavior regarding prices – a definite economic concept – you should use economic theory (in particular, consumer demand theory) as the framework for the statistical model. Economic theory is the guide. If economic theory is not used to guide the development of a statistical model, then you would just have parameter estimates that are uninterpretable. I provide some background on consumer demand theory in Chapter 2.

1.5.2   The role of data and data analysis

Once the statistical model based on economic theory is specified, the model's parameters can be estimated. This means that data are needed. There are two types of data: observational and experimental. Once the model's parameters are estimated, elasticities can be calculated. Sometimes a simulator is built using the elasticities to estimate demand and other key business metrics (e.g., revenue, contribution) under different conditions or *scenarios*. The optimal price is determined by studying these scenarios to test the hypotheses.

Figure 1.5.2 is an expanded version of Figure 1.2.1 showing how the quantitative pieces of data, statistical model, and simulator are used.

Revealed preference data

Revealed preference data are data on consumer transactions that are usually maintained in a large database. The database typically has details on the items purchased, prices paid, characteristics of the consumers (e.g., demographics, shopping history), and sales and advertising history. For extremely large operations, the data may be stored in Hadoop clusters with very sophisticated software managing, querying, and analyzing the data. Some might say that these large databases approach "Big Data" status, especially if the company also stores web searches for products,

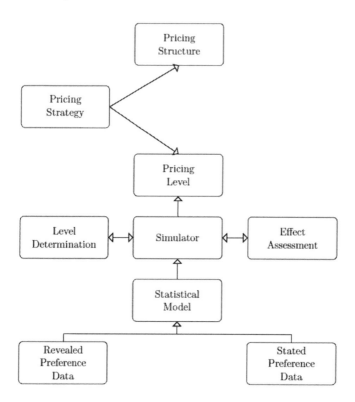

FIGURE 1.5.2 There are a number of steps in pricing research that feed into the price level part of a price strategy. The key component feeding into the level determination is the simulator, which in turn takes input from a statistical model. The types of models are discussed throughout this book.

customer online comments or reviews, emails, customer service rep interactions, and so forth. Internal customer databases are prime sources for much of the modeling done in pricing. For example, telecommunications companies gather detailed information on each subscriber regarding the number of minutes of a call, the type of call, the time of day and day of week of a call, where the call was placed to, and the consumers' calling plans. In addition, details on consumers are either maintained (e.g., address) or easily obtained either by sampling consumers in the database or by purchasing demographic data that map very closely to customer characteristics.

Pricing analysts typically build models, usually regression models, from internal databases such as a data warehouse or "data mart" organized into tables of customer purchases. A data mart is a specialized subset of a data warehouse for a business department or function. For example, the marketing department of a national seller of exercise equipment maintains a data mart of all the equipment sold to private gyms, schools, institutions, and households. The sales data are in tables called *Orders*, *Products*, and *Customers*. The Orders table contains data about each order with fields for an order number, order date, ship date, order quantity, product identification

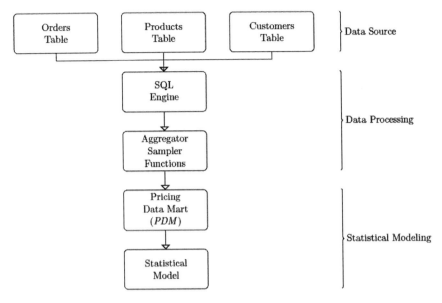

FIGURE 1.5.3 A typical pricing modeling framework using a data warehouse of revealed preference data. The pricing data mart (PDM) must be built before any statistical model can be estimated.

number (PID), and customer identification number (CID). The Products table has fields for linking PIDs, product description, current price, and maybe price change history. The Customers table has a linking CID, customer name, address, and maybe some demographics. By linking, filtering, and aggregating the tables, perhaps with Structured Query Language (SQL) commands, you can build a table of quantity ordered of a product, the relevant prices, and pertinent aggregate customer information. You could sample the records using an appropriate sampling technique such as simple random sampling or stratified random sampling and dividing the data into training, validation, and test tables. In the end, a pricing data mart (PDM) – a collection of data tables ready for modeling – will be produced. Figure 1.5.3 illustrates this process. Issues associated with working with Big Data plus more background on PDMs are discussed in Chapter 10.

Models based on revealed preference data in the PDM run straight into five difficult and challenging data issues:

1. Multicollinearity;
2. Lack of variation;
3. Timeliness;
4. Existence;
5. Self-selection.

See [57] for some discussion of these problems.

Multicollinearity

Many key drivers of purchases are highly correlated because of how markets work. This leads to the statistical problem known as *multicollinearity*. Simply put, some variables in the PDM are highly correlated, making them redundant. Software cannot identify which variables are effective in a regression estimation – the higher the correlation, the more the redundancy and the less able the software is to distinguish one variable from another.

Lack of variation

Some key drivers, such as price, may not vary in the market, especially for the period under study. Variation is important because statistical models work only if there is variation in the data – without variation there is nothing to estimate.

Timeliness

Observational data may be "old." If the data are, for example, monthly for five years, many of them may not reflect current market conditions, especially in rapidly changing markets such as computers and cell phones.

Existence

Since observational data are what actually exist (i.e., observed), the price levels product managers may want to test may not be reflected in the data. How can anyone say how customers would respond to prices they have never seen?

Self-selection

This is a subtle problem. The people in the data mart self-selected to be there. Self-selection means that people chose to be in the data mart because of their purchases. If they purchased elsewhere or chose not to purchase at all because the price was too high or the product quality too low, they would not be in the company's data mart as a buyer; there would be no record of them. Yet they are there because they liked the product features (including price) better than a competitor's product.

   For those in the data mart, all you know is what they bought and the price they paid. You do not know what they compared the product to in order to make their final purchase decision (basically, you do not know the competitive price and features they saw). For all those in the data mart who made a purchase decision, there are many others not in the data mart either because they chose not to buy anything or because they chose to buy the competitive product at a better price; you just do not know which one. In short, you do not know the true, total population of buyers.

You could argue that at least the competitive prices are known because a competitive assessment group in marketing tracks these data using input from the sales force, advertisements, and surveys, so this is not an issue. Unfortunately, just because you know the prices and features does not mean the customers (and non-customers) knew those same prices when they made their purchase decisions. Information about the market is said to be asymmetric. You also cannot say with certainty what prices people saw because you simply do not know.

Since people self-select to buy and thus appear in the data mart, any regression estimation (e.g., ordinary least squares; OLS) would be impacted. Basically, because of self-selection, the sample is not a random sample – it is biased. A random sample would provide a description of the entire purchasing population, not just the one in the company's data mart. OLS estimates will be inconsistent because the models fail to account for this self-selection; they are misspecified. To put it briefly, inconsistency means that if you could allow the sample size to become larger, the OLS estimates would not converge to the true parameter value, in our case the elasticities; they would be biased. Intuitively, you want the estimates to be consistent so that in very large samples you get the correct answer. With a non-random sample, no matter how large the sample, it will still not reflect the true population of buyers. If the estimated elasticities based on the non-random, self-selected sample are biased, then how can you make the correct pricing decision? The whole purpose of modeling is to take the raw and chaotic data and extract the information needed for pricing to "beat the competition" in a competitive market. But if the estimated elasticities are wrong, then how can you beat anyone? In fact, the competition will win if they use correctly (or better) specified models based on a random sample.

The model misspecification is due to two decisions. The first is a vendor choice decision (who they will buy from) and the second is a quantity decision (how much they will buy). The typical model focuses only on the second of the two decisions, the first being ignored. But the first cannot be ignored since the two decisions are not independent. They are functions, typically, of the same key drivers such as price and product attributes. There are two models! The vendor decision model can be summarized in a key ratio[9] that is incorporated into the quantity decision model. To ignore this new variable is to omit a relevant variable and thus to misspecify the model, and misspecified models lead to biased results.

This is a complicated problem, but there are two recommendations. First, recognize that a problem exists because of self-selection. This is not an insurmountable problem or a killer of data warehouses or data marts. Failure to recognize it or, worse, ignoring it is to help the competition win. Second, do not rely solely on data warehouses and data marts as *the* sources of all data. Aside from self-selection, the four other problems mentioned above still hold and have to be addressed. These are characteristics of observational data. Consider using discrete choice experiments in which these problems, including self-selection, are avoided. The self-selection problem, for example, is a non-issue because the sample used in an experiment is a random sample of all potential buyers. Discrete choice experiments are discussed in Chapter 5.

Stated preference data

Stated preference data are data on key drivers of purchases, especially price, which are collected and manipulated under controlled conditions determined by an experimental design. Conjoint and discrete choice studies are the main approaches used to collect and analyze data. Statistical models are estimated for stated preference data just as they are used for revealed preference data, but unlike revealed preference data, stated preference data do not have the five flaws. The stated preference designs ensure that key factors are not correlated and have sufficient variation. Also, by the nature of experimentation, hypothetical situations can be posed to customers to get their reactions, so timeliness and existence are not issues. Finally, both buyers and non-buyers can be included in the study, so self-selection is not an issue. In fact, people will actually state that they will not buy as part of the study. For many pricing studies, stated preference data approaches are far superior and highly recommended. The gold standard for pricing analytics should be stated preference analytics.

1.5.3   The role of statistical models

A statistical model – the third part of the research triangle – is necessary because the raw, almost chaotic data have to be organized and the important elements (i.e., information) extracted. That can only be done by estimating the key (unknown) parameters of a model.

The model is a statement of relationships you expect to learn about from the data. Without a model, you would just be searching (mining?) for relationships that seem plausible. Such searching is called *unsupervised learning*; using a model is called *supervised learning* (see [33] and [22] for an advanced discussion). This is not to say that unsupervised learning is not important – it is, in some cases. But this is to say that a structured approach to learning is better, especially in this case since you are looking for a particular numeric quantity – an elasticity – to help price a product. Fishing in a pool of data will not yield the number; it has to be calculated, and a model tells you how.

You should distinguish between a *mechanistic model* and a *statistical model* because there are similarities that may obfuscate the critical differences.

Mechanistic model

A mechanistic model is one for which you know exactly the value for a variable Y when you know a value for one or more other variables. The relationship is exact. You could refer to a mechanistic model as *deterministic* because of this exactness. A classic example from physics is Einstein's famous equation, $E = MC^2$. If you know the mass of an object, M, and the speed of light, C, then you know the amount of energy, E, and you know it exactly. Energy, E, is determined mechanically from this equation.

You can write any mechanistic model as

$$Y = f(X) \tag{1}$$

where Y is a variable to be explained, sometimes called the *dependent variable* or the *response variable*, and X is a vector of variables that explain or drive or determine Y. These variables are sometimes called *independent variables, key driver variables*, or *predictors*. They are non-random (C, the speed of light in Einstein's equation, is, after all, fixed by nature) and can be measured perfectly. The notation $f(\cdot)$ represents some function of the non-random X. For Einstein's equation, $f(\cdot)$ is a multiplicative function of two variables, M and C^2.

A common functional form is a linear model such as

$$Y = \beta_0 + \beta_1 X \tag{2}$$

where β_0 and β_1 are two (usually unknown) parameters. If you have two independent variables, you write

$$Y = \beta_0 + \beta_1 X_1 + \beta_2 X_2. \tag{3}$$

In general, for p independent variables, you write

$$Y = \beta_0 + \beta_1 X_1 + \beta_2 X_2 + \ldots + \beta_p X_p \tag{4}$$

$$= \sum_{i=0}^{p} \beta_i X_i \tag{5}$$

where $X_0 = 1$.

Einstein's equation is called *inherently linear* because it can be linearized by taking the log of both sides[10]:

$$\ln(E) = \ln(M) + 2 \times \ln(C) \tag{6}$$

which has the same form as (2). That is, you can write

$$\ln(E) = \beta_0 + \beta_1 \times \ln(M) + \beta_2 \times \ln(C) \tag{7}$$

with $\beta_0 = 0$, $\beta_1 = 1$, and $\beta_2 = 2$.

Mechanistic models have no role in pricing because they lack a stochastic element. Randomness is a part of the real economic world and that randomness must be accounted for. This is where a statistical model enters the picture. See [52] on the influence of randomness in our daily lives.

Statistical model

A statistical model is similar to a mechanistic model in mathematical form, but it differs in that it describes how one or more random variables are related to one or more other random variables. The model is statistical since the dependent and independent variables are not deterministically but *stochastically* related.[11] A simple statistical linear model is written as

$$Y = \beta_0 + \beta_1 X + \varepsilon$$

where ε is a stochastic or random variable that represents the factors that also drive Y but that are unknown. Since ε is a random variable, Y is also a random variable. Simple statistical modeling typically treats X as non-stochastic, although advanced econometrics recognizes the stochastic nature of X.

The random variable ε, called a *disturbance term*, has special significance in this model because it represents all the other factors that could drive Y but that are not our central focus or are unknown or unknowable. The X is our central focus and represents our *testable hypothesis* of how Y is determined. It is our hypothesis about what causes Y and it is testable because you can use data with statistical methods. The X is based on a theory, the top part of the research triangle, or solid intuition or experience of what drives or determines Y. A theory such as, for example, consumer demand theory in economics provides the foundation for identifying just those few special factors from the plethora of factors that determine quantity sold, the Y. These may be stated explicitly in the theory, with their relationships to Y well stated, or they may be derived by implication, as is typically the case. In either case, these are the ones you want to focus on and the theory tells you why. All other factors are subsumed in the ε. As a random variable, we usually assume that $\varepsilon \sim N(0, \sigma^2)$, although other specifications are possible, as you will see with discrete choice models in Chapter 5.

1.6 Simulators

The simulator in Figure 1.5.2 is a very important part of the pricing analytics process. This is where the results of the statistical model, in the form of the estimated parameters and elasticities, are pulled together to determine the optimal price level and the effects on the key business metrics. The simulator allows you to test different pricing scenarios and, depending on the quality of the simulator, also allows upper management to do the same if they wish.

The simulator should allow for the ability to flexibly change:

1. The business's own product price;
2. Any key competitor's price;
3. Key product attributes if the issue is new product pricing;
4. Average incremental cost;
5. Key promotional features.

The simulator should show the key business metrics such as revenue, total costs, contribution, and contribution margin. Figure 1.6.1 shows a screenshot of a simulator for an example developed in Chapter 8.

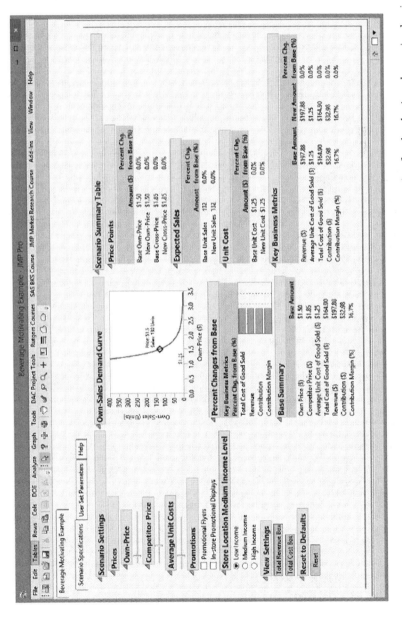

FIGURE 1.6.1 A pricing simulator allows the you to test different pricing scenarios for developing the optimal price point. This screenshot shows the interface for a simulator that allows you to test different prices in order to determine the effect on key business metrics such as revenue and contribution.

1.7 Price elasticities

The economic concept of a price elasticity, also sometimes referred to as *price sensitivity* or *price responsiveness*, is the key result of pricing analytics. Using the elasticities, you can propose a base or reference price (perhaps the existing market price) and then determine how sales would change as price deviates from this base case, but without actually changing the price in the market. The simulator, of course, is the tool to use for this analysis. Since revenue is merely price times quantity, the impact on revenue, or any other key business metric, can be quickly assessed.

Unfortunately, even in books on pricing, the concept of an elasticity is often given the back seat to discussions about strategies and tactics. In [56], for instance, elasticity is only introduced on page 109 (and in an appendix, at that) after financial issues have long been discussed. Yet being customer focused is the key message of [56]. Being customer focused means understanding how the customer will react to changes in his/her environment, with pricing being just one aspect of that environment. Elasticities summarize the customer's reaction to changes, whether the changes are the firm's actions or a competitor's actions. [53] discusses the elasticity concept, but at a rudimentary level. I devote Chapter 2 to a detailed examination of elasticities because of their importance, while in Chapter 3 I discuss how elasticities are used in pricing. The remainder of the current book focuses on estimating elasticities.

1.8 Summary

This book is concerned with the quantitative research methodologies for estimating price elasticities using observational or experimental data in statistical models. These elasticities are critical for determining the price – the number that goes on the product so that the consumer can make a rational decision whether to buy or not to buy. Pricing analytics is the process for using data to estimate or calculate the elasticities. Either revealed or stated preference data can be used, but revealed preference data have five problems that you must be aware of and handle. The rest of this book discusses the major models used in pricing analytics.

Notes

1 [49]. McCarthy introduced this framework with four Ps in 1960. Four is most common, although the list has expanded over the years. I prefer the five listed in the text. See the Wikipedia article on marketing mix (http://en.wikipedia.org/wiki/Talk:Marketing_mix#How_many_Ps.3F) for some discussion.
2 There may be minor implementation costs in deploying a new price. After all, computers have to be reprogrammed for the new price. But these costs are small compared to the price of an ad campaign.
3 [4]. Also see [43].
4 [61] originally proposed a theory of revealed preference as an alternative to utility theory. This has since generated much criticism, controversy, and a wide literature. See, for example, [71]. I am not concerned with the pure theory of revealed preference for this book.

5 A new phase, Phase 0, has been added. See the Wikipedia article "Clinical trial" at http://en.wikipedia.org/wiki/Clinical_trial.

6 See www.cancerresearchuk.org/cancer-help/about-cancer/cancer-questions/how-long-does-it-take-for-a-new-drug-to-go-through-clinical-trials.

7 See http://en.wikipedia.org/wiki/Cost-plus_pricing.

8 Cited in [16].

9 This is called the inverse Mills ratio and is used in a two-stage regression estimation to handle selection bias. See [25] and [24]. Also see [81], which develops a brand and quantity choice model. This is briefly described in Chapter 12.

10 Natural logs are typically used because they have useful mathematical properties, as you will see later.

11 See Wikipedia article "Statistical model" at https://en.wikipedia.org/wiki/Statistical_model.

2

ELASTICITIES – BACKGROUND AND CONCEPT

The cornerstone of pricing analytics is the estimation of price elasticities to measure the effect of a price change.[1] The effect is how much sales change for a given price change and how much revenue or another key business metric will change.

In this chapter, I will review the economic concept of an elasticity, describe the various types of elasticities relevant to pricing research, and discuss the factors that determine the magnitude of the elasticities. The latter are important to know because they can be used as a check on the values produced by formal statistical models. It is often insufficient to just produce estimates; they also have to make sense or be intuitive. Later chapters develop elasticity formulas specific to the model discussed in those chapters.[2] The concept and interpretation are based on material developed here.

This chapter has 12 sections. Sections 1–3 focus on basic consumer demand theory. These could be omitted on a first reading of the chapter if you believe you have enough understanding of this theory. Sections 4–7 discuss elasticity definitions and properties. You are urged to study these sections on a second reading because they will help you with the later chapters. Sections 8–11 extend the basic discussion of elasticities. Section 12 is the summary.

2.1 Economic concept

The starting point for a discussion of the elasticity concept is the consumer demand curve. It is certainly well known that the amount bought (i.e., quantity demanded) is inversely related to the price of the good.[3] This inverse relationship is derived by assuming that any consumer has a subjective function of, say, two goods. Two goods are the minimum since if there is only one there would not be much of a problem for the consumer; he or she would just have to buy all of it until income is exhausted. With two goods, however, he or she would have to trade off between each, consuming more of one and less of the other, because of a set income level.[4]

The notion of a trade-off is important for later chapters in this book where advanced methodologies for estimating elasticities and analyzing choice in general are developed. A mainstay of those methodologies is that consumers trade-off one good for another or one attribute of a good for another. The trade-offs are viewed as rational choice decisions all consumers must make and the models try to capture or mirror those choice decisions.

With two (or more) goods, the consumer subjectively trades off one for the other because the amount of satisfaction received from one is assumed to decline as more of that good is consumed. A function, called a *utility function*, shows the total level of satisfaction from the two goods and is assumed to reflect the subjective trade-off.

The utility function has been controversial, to say the least. For beginning students, it is useful to describe this function as measuring satisfaction or "a sensation, an introspective magnitude" [62]. This implies that it is a cardinal concept, something with a numeric value. Professional economists now view it solely as a means to express an ordinal ranking of goods showing preference (i.e., one good is preferred, equally preferred, or not preferred to another) without numeric magnitudes (i.e., by how much). This concept of preference ranking will be used in the chapters on conjoint and discrete choice, especially the latter. See [62] for a classic discussion of the utility concept.

Formally, let U_i be the level of utility or satisfaction consumer i, $i = 1,\ldots,n$, receives from two goods, Q_{i1} and Q_{i2}. The utility function for consumer i is written as

$$U_i = U_i\left(Q_{i1}, Q_{i2}\right) \tag{8}$$

where the function is assumed to be continuous and twice differentiable with

$$\frac{\partial U_i}{\partial Q_{ij}} > 0, \frac{\partial^2 U_i}{\partial Q_{ij}^2} < 0, j = 1, 2.$$

This holds for all consumers, $i = 1,\ldots,n$, in the market.

The first partial derivative is called the *marginal utility* of Q_{ij} (written as MU_{ij}) and shows the amount by which utility or satisfaction increases as Q_{ij} increases. This is the slope of the utility function. The MU_{ij} is the subjective value or worth to consumer i of good j. The second partial derivative reflects an assumption that the level of utility rises at a decreasing rate (diminishing marginal utility) so that each additional unit of the good adds less utility or satisfaction than the previous additional unit. The *Law of Diminishing Marginal Utility* is a fundamental concept in economics.[5] So marginal utility is positive but declining over some relevant range of consumption (see Figure 2.1.1).

This assumes, of course, that the goods Q_{ij} are infinitely divisible; that they are continuous. For some consumer goods, such as electricity and water, this is

MU_i

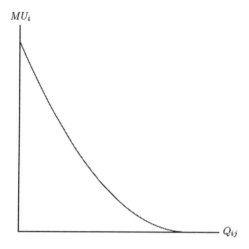

Q_{ij}

FIGURE 2.1.1 This is a typical textbook depiction of a marginal utility curve. It has a negative slope throughout the range of Q_{ij} reflecting diminishing utility from extra units consumed. In addition, the curve is convex to the origin, meaning that marginal utility declines more rapidly as extra units are consumed.

reasonable. For others, this may be just a good first approximation. For yet other goods (or services), this assumption is unrealistic because these goods are characterized by indivisibility; they are discrete. Examples are modes of transportation to work, colleges to attend, places to vacation, and jewelry styles to buy as a gift. The utility concept can still be used, but the framework has to be modified to handle the discrete situation. I will do this in Chapter 5. For now, I will assume perfect divisibility.

The utility function (8) is purely subjective for consumer i. The issue is the level of utility; that is, the amounts of Q_{ij} ($j = 1,2$) to consume. Without constraints, anyone would consume an unlimited amount of everything. There are constraints, however, primarily the objective constraint all consumers face: income. The goal is to choose levels of Q_{ij} so as to maximize utility subject to an income constraint, I_i. That is,

$$\text{Choose } Q_{i1}, Q_{i2} \text{ to} \tag{9}$$

$$\max U_i = U_i\left(Q_{i1}, Q_{i2}\right) \tag{10}$$

$$\text{Subject To } I_i = \sum_{j=1}^{2} P_j Q_{ij} \tag{11}$$

where P_j is the objectively determined market price for good j. Prices are objective because they are assumed to be fixed and observable for all goods in the market and the individual consumer has no influence on them. In reality, the marketing or pricing managers need to determine these prices given market constraints, which is the focus of this book. The prices are said to be uniform in that one price, P_j, applies to all units purchased. The price is fixed.

It is shown elsewhere[6] that maximization occurs where

$$\frac{MU_{i1}}{P_1} = \frac{MU_{i2}}{P_2} \tag{12}$$

where MU_{ij} is the marginal utility of the jth good for the ith consumer.

Each ratio is the consumer's subjective valuation of each good in the sense that it is the amount of extra utility received per dollar spent on the good. The equality says that no further expenditure on any one good will improve overall utility. The equality can be logically proven by assuming that the ratios are not equal. Suppose

$$\frac{MU_{i1}}{P_1} > \frac{MU_{i2}}{P_2} \tag{13}$$

Since more value per dollar spent on good 1 is received than per dollar spent on good 2, the consumer has an incentive to buy more of good 1. By the assumption of diminishing marginal utility, as more of good 1 is consumed, the marginal utility decreases so the term MU_{i1} / P_1 declines. At the same time, less of good 2 is consumed because of the budget constraint, so the ratio MU_{i2} / P_2 rises. Now if you assume

$$\frac{MU_{i1}}{P_1} < \frac{MU_{i2}}{P_2} \tag{14}$$

then the reverse occurs. The only place where there is no change, the definition of equilibrium, is where

$$\frac{MU_{i1}}{P_1} = \frac{MU_{i2}}{P_2} \tag{15}$$

Equation (12) can be rewritten as

$$\frac{MU_{i1}}{MU_{i2}} = \frac{P_1}{P_2}. \tag{16}$$

The ratio on the left-hand side is the *marginal rate of substitution* (MRS_i) and the ratio on the right-hand side is the relative price ratio. The MRS_i can be interpreted as the internal, subjective valuation of one extra unit of Q_{i1} taken on or consumed in terms of Q_{i2} units given up to hold utility constant. It shows how much the consumer is willing to give up of Q_{i2} to receive one more unit of Q_{i1}. It is the marginal utility of one extra unit of good 1 in terms of the marginal utility of one extra unit of good 2 that must be given up. The relative price ratio, based on the objectively

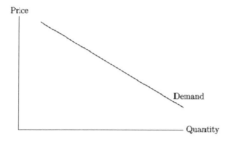

FIGURE 2.1.2 Straight line demand curve. This is a typical textbook depiction. Most analysts would use a convex function, as discussed later.

given prices in the market, can be interpreted as the external, objective valuation of an extra unit of Q_{i1} in terms of Q_{i2}. It shows how much the market asks the consumer to give up of Q_{i2} (that is, the price of Q_1) to receive one more unit of Q_{i1}. By (16), utility maximization occurs when the internal valuation equals the external valuation – when the value consumer i places on an extra unit of Q_{i1} equals the amount the market says someone should pay for an extra unit of Q_{i1}. See [17] for a good discussion.

Given the prices P_1 and P_2, you know the amounts of Q_{i1} and Q_{i2} consumer i will buy. By varying, say, P_1 while holding P_2 and income fixed, you can define other amounts of Q_{i1} and Q_{i2} the consumer will buy. These other amounts trace out a negative relationship between P_1 and Q_{i1}. This is shown graphically as a negatively sloped curve called a *demand curve* (see Figure 2.1.2).

The demand curve is typically depicted with the price of the good on the vertical axis, in this case P_1, making it seem as if demand is a function solely of P_1. But the demand curve was derived by changing P_1 relative to P_2. Clearly, as P_2 changes, a new demand curve for Q_{i1} is traced. Since there are only two goods, it is equally clear that the demand curve will shift to the left at each level of P_1 if P_2 decreases; Q_{i1} becomes more expensive relative to Q_{i2}, so less of Q_{i1} is consumed regardless of the value of P_1. The consumer substitutes out of Q_{i1} and into the now relatively less expensive Q_{i2}.

The placement of the demand curve in the price–quantity plane is determined by the level of income and the price of the other good – P_2 in our case. In general, higher levels of income place the curve further out in the plane than lower levels of income. In other words, as income rises, demand (the whole curve) shifts to the right at each price point for good 1.

The demand curve is also sometimes described as a function of tastes or fads. These directly reflect the utility function structure. In general, as tastes shift in favor of Q_{i1}, the demand curve shifts to the right at each price point.

The demand curve can be written as a function of the two prices and income as

$$Q_{ij} = f\left(P_1, P_2, I_i\right),$$

$j = 1, 2$, with

$$\frac{\partial Q_{ij}}{\partial P_k} < 0 \qquad k = j$$

$$\frac{\partial Q_{ij}}{\partial P_k} \lessgtr 0 \qquad k \neq j$$

$$\frac{\partial Q_{ij}}{\partial I_i} > 0.$$

The sign on $\partial Q_{ij} / \partial P_{ik}, k \neq j$, defines the two goods as substitutes or complements. If positive, then an increase in the price of good k increases the demand for good j, all else constant, making the two goods *substitutes*. Increasing the price of k reduces the consumption of k, forcing the consumer to consume more (substitute into) j. If the sign is negative, then the two goods are *complements*. See Section 2.7 for further discussion.

It can be shown that for the two-good case, it must be that

$$\frac{\partial Q_{ij}}{\partial Q_{ik}} < 0 \qquad k \neq j$$

(if you consume more of k, you must give up some of j, and vice versa). Therefore,

$$\frac{\partial Q_{ij}}{\partial P_k} \frac{\partial P_k}{\partial Q_{ik}} < 0.$$

The second term on the left-hand side is the inverse of the demand function and is negative. Therefore, the first term must be positive as contended: they are substitutes.

This framework can be generalized to any number of goods, Q_{ij}, $j = 1, 2, \ldots, J$, with their associated prices, P_j, $j = 1, 2, \ldots, J$. The individual's demand function is then

$$Q_{ij} = f\left(P_1, P_2, \ldots, P_J, I_i\right)$$

where $P_j, j = 1, \ldots, J$ is called the *own-price* of good j and the other prices are called the *cross-prices* of good j.

2.2   Consumer surplus

If there is a single market price at P_0 (i.e., the pricing strategy is a single uniform price and the price level is the market price P_0), then the individual consumer would buy Q_{i0} units as shown in Figure 2.2.1.

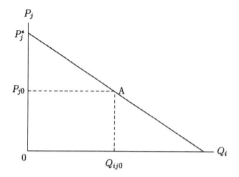

FIGURE 2.2.1 Demand curve with consumer surplus. The consumer surplus for consumer i is the triangular area $P_{j0}P_j^*A$. Consumer i's total expenditure is simply price times quantity, or the area $0P_{j0}AQ_{ij0}$. The area $0P_j^*AQ_{ij0}$ is the total value or worth to the consumer, which is the sum of the total expenditure (what the consumer will pay) and the consumer surplus.

The total area under the demand curve up to some quantity, say Q_{ij0} (that is, area $0P_j^*AQ_{ij0}$), is the total value or worth of the good to the consumer. This is the amount the consumer is willing to pay for the marginal unit Q_{ij0}. This area can be divided into two parts: $0P_{j0}AQ_{ij0}$ and $P_{j0}P_j^*A$.

The area $0P_{j0}AQ_{ij0}$ is the consumer's total expenditure on the good as

$$TE_{ij} = P_{j0} \times Q_{ij0}.$$

Since the amount the consumer spends is identical to the amount the business earns, this is also the firm's total revenue. This is the amount of the value the consumer pays to the firm. The area $P_{j0}P_j^*A$ is the amount of the value the consumer does not pay but retains. This is called the *consumer surplus*. The consumer would be willing and is able to pay this amount, but because of the uniform price structure in this market, he or she does not have to pay it. This value remains with him or her. The business's revenue can obviously be increased if this value can be captured by or transferred to the business. This is the goal of *price discrimination*. An essential part of a discriminatory price structure is the price elasticity, which is discussed below. So, a goal of setting a good pricing structure is a pricing strategy to capture as much, if not all, of the consumer surplus. The elasticity helps.

2.3 The market demand curve

We are usually not interested in the demand of a particular individual. It is the market demand, the aggregation of all demands, that is of primary concern. The individual demand functions are merely building blocks. This does not mean, however, that you should ignore the individual functions when developing the pricing structure part of a strategy. If you know the function for each individual, then you could develop a price for each individual and potentially increase revenue (and profits) by capturing all of the consumer surplus. This is first-degree price discrimination. Before the age of Big Data, it was believed that that this form of discrimination was impractical, since you would require too much information. Big Data databases may change this (see [64] and Section 3.5.4; also see Chapter 11 in this book).

The classic textbook treatment of consumer demand theory shows that market demand is just the sum of the individual demands at each price level. So,

$$Q_j(P_1, P_2, \ldots, P_J) = Q_j = \sum_{i=1}^{N} Q_{ij}$$
$$= \sum_{i=1}^{N} f\left(P_1, P_2, \ldots, P_J, I_i\right).$$

This is simplistic because it does not effectively account for the distribution of income in the market. Biases occur in any market analysis if the distribution is ignored, but this is an issue beyond the scope of this book. See [66] for a discussion. The market quantity, Q_j, will be used in all that follows.

2.4 Elasticity concept

A logical question to ask is: *How much does quantity demanded change when the own-price of the good changes?* This is the effect assessment mentioned in Chapter 1. A first guess of a measure is the inverse of the slope of the demand curve, since this is $1/\partial P_j / \partial Q_j$ for the conventionally drawn curve. As P_j changes, you move along the curve so Q_j changes. Further reflection, however, shows that this is not a good measure. Consider what happens if the units for good Q_j change. Let the original units be, say, pounds, which are then changed to ounces. This immediately changes the inverse of the slope by a factor of 16. The measure changed, yet the quantity is fundamentally the same, just measured differently. The situation is similar if the price changes from, say, dollars to cents. More formally, if our measure is the inverse of $\partial P_j^\star / \partial Q_j$ with $P_j^\star = k_p P_j$, k_p a constant, then you have $k_p\left(\partial P_j^\star / \partial Q_j\right)$. The same holds for a change in the units of Q_j.

A better measure is units free, a pure number so that no matter how the units of either quantity or price change, the measure remains the same. Yet the measure must maintain the notion of change in consumption and change in price. A candidate is a ratio of percentage changes: the percentage change in quantity demanded in response to a percentage change in its price. Each percentage change is units free; so is the ratio. The candidate measure is

$$\eta_{P_j}^{Q_j} = \frac{\dfrac{\partial Q_j}{Q_j}}{\dfrac{\partial P_j}{P_j}} \tag{17}$$

$$= \frac{P_j}{Q_j} \frac{\partial Q_j}{\partial P_j}, \tag{18}$$

or, using natural logarithmic differentiation,

$$\eta_{P_j}^{Q_j} = \frac{\partial \ln\left(Q_j\right)}{\partial \ln\left(P_j\right)} \tag{19}$$

The left-hand side is the elasticity of demand for good Q_j with respect to the good's own-price P_j. Price plays the role of the independent variable.

Referring to the previous discussion about multiplying price by a constant factor k_p, it is clear that if $P_j^* = k_p P_j$, then $\ln P_j^* = \ln\left(k_p P_j\right) = \ln k_p + \ln P_j$ and

$$\partial \ln P_j^* = \partial\left(\ln k_p + \ln P_j\right)$$

$$= \partial \ln P_j$$

so nothing changes since k_p is a constant. The same holds for quantity. Therefore, multiplying either Q_j or P_j by a constant factor does not change the elasticity.

This is a general definition of an elasticity. *Any* elasticity is defined as the ratio of the logarithmic derivative of the dependent variable (e.g., quantity consumed) to the logarithmic derivative of the independent variable (e.g., price).

For the demand elasticity, notice that

$$\eta_{P_j}^{Q_j} = \frac{P_j}{Q_j} \frac{Q_j}{\partial P_j}$$

$$= \frac{P_j}{Q_j} \frac{1}{slope_j},$$

so our elasticity is related to the demand curve's slope scaled by the factor P_j / Q_j. This multiplication factor is the slope of a ray from the origin (the first term) to a point on the demand curve (the second term). Also, for a downward sloping demand curve,

$$\eta_{P_j}^{Q_j} < 0.$$

This follows because the slope of the ray is positive (a ratio of two positive terms) and the slope of the demand curve is negative.

Finally, because the elasticity is a ratio of two percentage changes, its value and interpretation depend on the relative magnitudes of the numerator and denominator. Table 2.1 summarizes the possibilities.

TABLE 2.1 Elasticity values and interpretations.

Relative magnitude	Value of ratio	Label	Interpretation
$\left\|\partial \ln\left(Q_j\right)\right\| > \left\|\partial \ln\left(P_j\right)\right\|$	>1	Elastic	If P_j rises 1%, Q_j falls more than 1%
$\left\|\partial \ln\left(Q_j\right)\right\| = \left\|\partial \ln\left(P_j\right)\right\|$	=1	Unit elastic	If P_j rises 1%, Q_j falls exactly 1%
$\left\|\partial \ln\left(Q_j\right)\right\| < \left\|\partial \ln\left(P_j\right)\right\|$	<1	Inelastic	If P_j rises 1%, Q_j falls less than 1%

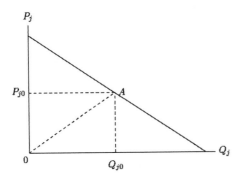

FIGURE 2.5.1 Straight line demand curve with a ray from the origin. The ray is the line $0A$, which has a slope $AQ_{j0}/0Q_{j0}$.

There are two special cases. The first occurs when $\partial \ln Q_j = 0$, so the demand curve is vertical at Q_j. Demand is said to be *perfectly inelastic*: a 1% change in price results in no change in the quantity demanded. The second case occurs when $\partial \ln Q_j \to \infty$ so that the demand curve is horizontal. Demand is said to be *perfectly elastic*: a 1% change in price produces an infinite change in quantity demanded. Most demand elasticities are between these two special cases.

2.5 Properties of elasticities

Consider a straight line demand curve as illustrated in Figure 2.5.1. The equation is

$$P_j = a + bQ_j, \qquad b < 0, \tag{20}$$

which can be rewritten as

$$Q_j = -\frac{a}{b} + \frac{1}{b}P_j \tag{21}$$

$$= a^* + b^*P_j \tag{22}$$

with $a^* = -a/b$ and $b^* = 1/b$. Then

$$\frac{dQ_j}{dP_j} = b^* = \frac{1}{b}$$

and

$$\eta_{P_j}^{Q_j} = \frac{P_j}{Q_j}\frac{dQ_j}{dP_j}$$
$$= \frac{P_j}{Q_j}\frac{1}{b} < 0. \tag{23}$$

Clearly, the elasticity changes as you move along the curve, with the changes being due to the ratio P_j/Q_j since $1/b$, the slope, is fixed by definition. The ratio P_j/Q_j is a ray drawn from the origin to a point A on the curve and has slope P_{j0}/Q_{j0}. The elasticity, therefore, is the product of two slopes: the slope of the demand curve itself (actually, its inverse) and the slope of a ray from the origin as I stated before. The slope of the ray can be interpreted as the average amount paid per unit purchased; it is the average price per unit, which is labeled AP_j. The average price per unit falls as more is consumed.

The slope of the demand curve shows the additional dollars spent per one extra unit of the good consumed. This is a marginal concept and I will label it MP_j for the marginal price per unit consumed. For the straight line demand curve, MP_j is constant and negative. The inverse of MP_j is

$$\frac{1}{MP_j} = \frac{1}{b} = \frac{dQ_j}{dP_j} < 0$$

and can be interpreted as the extra amount of consumption foregone per one dollar of a higher price.

The elasticity is

$$\eta_{P_j}^{Q_j} = \frac{P_j}{Q_j}\frac{dQ_j}{dP_j}$$
$$= \frac{AP_j}{MP_j} < 0.$$

The price elasticity of demand for good Q_j is the ratio of the average price per unit consumed to the marginal price per unit consumed. In fact, *all* elasticities are ratios of a marginal concept to an average concept, but the ratio is inverted for the demand curve because of the economist's convention of writing the price, the independent variable in this case, on the vertical axis (see [153]). In general, the elasticity of some function $F(x)$ evaluated at a point a is $[a/F(a)] \times F'(a)$, where $F'(a)$ is the marginal and $a/F(a)$ is the average.

If you draw the demand curve slightly differently, with the price on the horizontal axis to reflect its role as an independent variable and quantity on the vertical axis to reflect its role as a dependent variable, then $\partial Q_j / \partial P_j$ is the slope of this rendition of a demand curve and shows the marginal consumption per extra dollar spent. The ray from the origin is now $\partial Q_j / \partial P_j$ and shows the average consumption per dollar spent. The elasticity is still $\eta_{P_j}^{Q_j}$, but now it is the ratio of marginal consumption to average consumption.

A logical question to ask is: *How does the elasticity change as the slope of the ray changes?* That is, what happens to the elasticity as you move along the straight line demand curve? Consider the straight line demand curve in Figure 2.5.2. From basic plane geometry, you can quickly see some key angles such as

$$\angle P^*CO = \angle P^* AP_{j0} = \theta$$
$$\angle COA = \angle P_{j0} AO = \varphi.$$

Also, from basic trigonometry, you see that

$$\tan \varphi = \frac{AQ_{j0}}{OQ_{j0}} = \frac{OP_{j0}}{P_{j0}A}$$
$$\cot \theta = \frac{Q_{j0}C}{AQ_{j0}} = \frac{P_{j0}A}{P_{j0}P^*}$$
$$\cos \theta = \frac{Q_{j0}C}{AC} = \frac{P_{j0}A}{P^*A}.$$

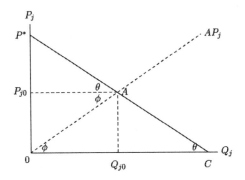

FIGURE 2.5.2 Straight line demand curve with an average price curve. Various angles have been labeled. For example, the slope of the average price curve, AP_j, is $\varphi = AQ_{j0}/OQ_{j0}$.

The slope of the ray from the origin is $\tan\phi$; that is, $\tan\phi = P/Q$. The $\cot\theta$ is the inverse of the slope of the demand curve; that is, $\cot\theta = \partial Q/\partial P$. Using these observations, you see that the elasticity is then

$$\eta_{P_j}^{Q_j} = \frac{P_j}{Q_j}\frac{dQ_j}{dP_j}$$
$$= \tan\phi \cdot \cot\theta$$
$$= \frac{AQ_{j0}}{OQ_{j0}} \cdot \frac{Q_{j0}C}{AQ_{j0}}$$
$$= \frac{Q_{j0}C}{OQ_{j0}}.$$

If $OQ_{j0} = Q_{j0}C$, then $\eta_{P_j}^{Q_j} = |1|$, so demand is unit elastic. If $OQ_{j0} > Q_{j0}C$, then $\eta_{P_j}^{Q_j} < |1|$, so demand is inelastic; otherwise, it is elastic. From the $\cos\theta$ you have

$$Q_{j0}C = AC\cos\theta$$

and

$$OQ_{j0} = P_{j0}A = P^{\star}A\cos\theta.$$

Therefore,

$$\eta_{P_j}^{Q_j} = \frac{AC\cos\theta}{P^{\star}A\cos\theta}$$
$$= \frac{AC}{P^{\star}A}.$$

The elasticity is the ratio of the relative lengths of segments of the demand curve, the lengths cut off by the ray from the origin; that is, the AP_j curve.[7] You can now quickly see that if $P^{\star}A = AC$, then $\eta_{P_j}^{Q_j} = |1|$ for a unit elastic demand; if $P^{\star}A > AC$, then $\eta_{P_j}^{Q_j} > |1|$ for an elastic demand; if $P^{\star}A < AC$, then $\eta_{P_j}^{Q_j} < |1|$ for an inelastic demand. Further, if $AC = 0$, then $\eta_{P_j}^{Q_j} = 0$ for a perfectly elastic demand, and if $P^{\star}A = 0$, then $\eta_{P_j}^{Q_j} \to \infty$ for a perfectly inelastic demand.

2.6 Parallel shifts in demand

Consider a parallel shift in the demand curve, say to the right from D_{j0} to D_{j1} as in Figure 2.6.1. The slope stays the same, just the intercept changes. Fix the price at P_{j0}. For D_{j0}, the ray from the origin is AP_{j0} with slope P_{j0}/Q_{j0}. But when the demand curve shifts to the right, the slope of the ray falls to AP_{j1} with slope

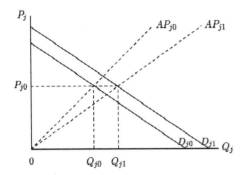

FIGURE 2.6.1 Effect of a parallel shift in demand. Let the demand at each price point increase from D_{j0} to D_{j1}. For a fixed price P_{j0}, the quantity rises from Q_{j0} to Q_{j1}. The ray from the origin falls from AP_{j0} to AP_{j1}.

$P_{j0}/Q_{j1} < P_{j0}/Q_{j0}$. Clearly, the elasticity has fallen, so the demand curve is less elastic the further the demand curve is to the right.

2.7 Cross-price elasticities

There are two prices (more for a general demand function) for every good: *own-price* and *cross-price*. The own-price is the price of the good in question, say P_1 for Q_1. If the demand function is for coffee, the own-price of coffee is merely the price of coffee. The cross-price is the price of another good, say Q_2. So, again, if the demand function is for coffee, a possible cross-price is the price of tea.

The other good is classified as either a *substitute* or a *complement*. Two goods are substitutes if an increase in the price of one causes an increase in the *demand* for the second. Notice that the demand changes, which means the entire demand curve shifts at each price level. The logic is that an increase in the price of the first good causes consumers to reduce their consumption of that good (recall the downward-sloping demand curve), but then increase their consumption of the second good so as to completely spend their income (i.e., to satisfy their budget constraint). The increased consumption of the second good is independent of the price of the second good; its demand curve shifts to the right at all prices. Two goods are complements if an increase in the price of the first good causes consumers to reduce their consumption of the second. As you will see shortly, in a simple two-good case, both goods must be substitutes to meet the budget constraint.

In the *J*-good case, the own-price elasticity for good *j* is

$$\eta_{P_j}^{Q_j} = \frac{\partial \ln(Q_j)}{\partial \ln(P_j)}, \qquad j = 1,\ldots,J \tag{24}$$

Clearly,

$$\eta_{P_j}^{Q_j} < 0$$

as before. The cross-price elasticity is

$$\eta_{P_k}^{Q_j} = \frac{\partial \ln(Q_j)}{\partial \ln(P_k)}, \qquad j = 1,\dots,J; k = 1,\dots,J; j \neq k. \tag{25}$$

This shows the percentage change in the rate of consumption of good j for a 1% change in the price of another good, k. If $\eta_{P_k}^{Q_j} < 0$, then goods j and k are *complements*. An increase in the price of good k reduces the rate of consumption of k (because of the downward-sloping demand curve for k) and also reduces the demand for good j. If $\eta_{P_k}^{Q_j} > 0$, then the two goods are *substitutes*.

2.7.1 Elasticity constraints

Consider an ordinary linear demand function for two goods, say Q_1 and Q_2, and the budget constraint relating the total expenditure on each to total real disposable income as

$$Y = P_1 Q_1 + P_2 Q_2 \tag{26}$$

Suppose only P_1 changes; P_2 and income are fixed. Take the total derivative of (26) with respect to P_1 to get

$$0 = P_1 \frac{dQ_1}{dP_1} + Q_1 + P_2 + \frac{dQ_2}{dP_1} \tag{27}$$

or

$$0 = P_1 Q_1 \frac{dQ_1}{dP_1} \frac{1}{Q_1} + Q_1 + P_2 Q_2 + \frac{dQ_2}{dP_1} \frac{1}{Q_1} \tag{28}$$

Multiplying through by P_1 and dividing through by Y fixed at $\overline{Y}$, you get

$$0 = \frac{P_1 Q_1}{\overline{Y}} \frac{dQ_1}{dP_1} \frac{P_1}{Q_1} + \frac{P_1 Q_1}{\overline{Y}} + \frac{P_2 Q_2}{\overline{Y}} \frac{dQ_2}{dP_1} \frac{P_1}{Q_2} \tag{29}$$

$$= \alpha_1 \eta_{P_1}^{Q_1} + \alpha_1 + \alpha_2 \eta_{P_1}^{Q_1} \tag{30}$$

where $\alpha_j = P_j Q_j / \overline{Y} > 0$ is the proportion of the budget spent on good Q_j, and

$$\sum_{j=1}^{2} \alpha_j = 1. \tag{31}$$

The proportions α_j are weights, so (30) can be written as

$$-\alpha_1 = \sum_{j=1}^{2} \alpha_j \eta_{P_j}^{Q_j}. \tag{32}$$

The sum of the weighted price elasticities is the negative of the own-weight for good Q_1, the good whose price changed. This places a constraint on the elasticities.

Notice that (30) can be written as

$$0 = \alpha_1 [1 + \eta_{P_1}^{Q_1}] + \alpha_2 \eta_{P_2}^{Q_2}. \tag{33}$$

If $\alpha_1 = 1.0$, so that 100% of the budget is spent on good Q_1, then $\alpha_2 = 0$ and $\eta_{P_1}^{Q_1} = -1$, so good 1 has a unit elastic demand. This makes sense since if total expenditure is on one good Q_1, then a 1% change in P_1 must be reflected exactly in a 1% change in consumption of Q_1.

2.7.2 Expenditures

Consider the term in brackets in (33). First, define the total expenditure on good Q_1 as

$$E_1 = P_1 Q_1.$$

This is, of course, a business's total revenue from the sale of Q_1. Then

$$\frac{\partial E_1}{\partial P_1} = Q_1 + P_1 \frac{\partial Q_1}{\partial P_1}.$$

Multiply through by P_1, divide through by E_1, and simplify to get

$$\frac{P_1}{E_1} \frac{\partial E_1}{\partial P_1} = 1 + \frac{P_1}{Q_1} \frac{\partial Q_1}{\partial P_1},$$

or

$$\eta_{P_1}^{E_1} = 1 + \eta_{P_1}^{Q_1}. \tag{34}$$

This is the expenditure elasticity of good Q_1 with respect to the price of good Q_1. If demand is unit elastic, then $\eta_{P_1}^{E_1} = 0$ and there is no change in total expenditures on good Q_1. The percentage decline in the rate of consumption of good Q_1 exactly matches the percentage increase in the price of good Q_1, so total expenditure does not change. If demand is elastic, then the expenditure elasticity is negative and expenditure declines if price rises. If demand is inelastic, then the expenditure elasticity is positive and expenditure rises. This is summarized in Table 2.2.

TABLE 2.2 Expenditure elasticity summary for an increase in the own-price of the good. If price is increased 1% and demand is elastic, then expenditures will fall because more is lost in sales than is gained by the price increase. This is equivalent to a loss in revenue.

Elasticity	Expenditure elasticity	Expenditure change
Inelastic	Positive	Rises
Unit elastic	Zero	No change
Elastic	Negative	Falls

Also notice that for good Q_2 you have

$$E_2 = P_2 Q_2$$

and

$$\frac{P_1}{E_2} \frac{\partial E_2}{\partial P_1} = \frac{P_1 P_2}{E_2} \frac{\partial Q_2}{\partial P_1}$$
$$= \frac{P_1}{Q_2} \frac{\partial Q_2}{\partial P_1}$$
$$= \eta_{P_1}^{Q_2}.$$

So (33) is

$$0 = \alpha_1 \eta_{P_1}^{E_1} + \alpha_2 \eta_{P_1}^{E_2}. \tag{35}$$

The sum of the weighted expenditure elasticities for a change in P_1 is zero.

To further explore the relationship between the own- and cross-price elasticities, consider the budget constraint one more time:

$$Y = \sum_j P_j Q_j.$$

Differentiate the budget constraint with respect to P_k, holding income and all other prices fixed, to get

$$\frac{\partial Y}{\partial P_k} = \sum_{j \neq k} P_j \frac{\partial Q_j}{\partial P_k} + Q_k = 0,$$

or

$$Q_k = -\sum_{j \neq k} P_j \frac{\partial Q_j}{\partial P_k}.$$

Dividing by Q_k and multiplying appropriately, you get

$$
\begin{aligned}
1 &= -\sum_{j \neq k} \frac{\partial Q_j}{\partial P_k} \frac{P_k}{Q_j} \frac{P_j}{P_k} \frac{Q_j}{Q_k} \\
&= -\sum_{j \neq k} \eta_{P_k}^{Q_j} \frac{E_j}{E_k}.
\end{aligned}
$$

Extracting good k from the summation, you see that

$$
1 = -\eta_{P_k}^{Q_k} - \sum_{\substack{j \\ j \neq k}} \eta_{P_k}^{Q_j} \frac{E_j}{E_k}.
$$

This implies that if good k is price elastic, so $\eta_{P_k}^{Q_k} < -1$, then the weighted average of the cross-price elasticities for the other $J - 1$ goods must be positive; the other goods are, on average, substitutes. See, for example, [18] for a discussion.

Also, from what you know about expenditure elasticities, you can see that

$$
\eta_{P_k}^{E_k} = 1 + \eta_{P_k}^{Q_k} \tag{36}
$$

$$
= -\sum_{\substack{j \\ j \neq k}} \eta_{P_k}^{Q_{ij}} \frac{E_j}{E_k}, \tag{37}
$$

so that if good k is price elastic, the expenditure on it falls ($\eta_{E_k}^{P_k} < 0$), so the expenditures on the other goods must, on average, increase to consume the entire budget constraint. Since $\eta_{E_k}^{P_k} = \eta_{P_k}^{Q_k}$, then (36) becomes

$$
\eta_{P_k}^{E_k} = -\beta_k \sum_{\substack{j \\ j \neq k}} \eta_{E_j}^{P_k}
$$

with $\beta_k = 1 - E_k / E_k > 0$. If the expenditure elasticity on good k is negative, then the expenditure elasticity on the other goods must be positive.

2.8 Income elasticities

Although I focus on pricing analytics and price elasticities in this book, I would be remiss if I did not discuss income elasticities. I already observed that a rightward shift of the demand curve decreases the price elasticity at a fixed price because the slope of the ray from the origin declines, and this ray represents the average price per unit consumed. This begs a question: *Why did the demand curve shift?* There are a host of possible reasons, a primary one being a change in income.

Recall from (9) that income is a constraint on the rate of consumption. You cannot consume more than you have.[8] Income has two effects. First, it places the demand curve in the P–Q plane; that is, the *level* of income determines the level of demand, along with other factors. Second, a *change* in income determines a change in demand. This section is concerned with the latter.

We can define an income elasticity in a manner similar to a price elasticity. The income elasticity of good Q_j with respect to income Y (that is, the amount by which demand for Q_j will change when Y changes) is

$$\eta_Y^{Q_j} = \frac{\partial \ln(Q_j)}{\partial \ln(Y)} > 0, \; < 0, \text{ or } = 0.$$

The size of the elasticity coefficient depends on the consumer's perception of the good. Generally, the sign is positive: an increase in income, all else constant, increases consumption. The goods are said to be *normal goods*.

Using the budget constraint for the two-good case, but now holding prices fixed so that $dP_1 = dP_2 = 0$, you get

$$1 = P_1 \frac{dQ_1}{dY} + P_2 \frac{dQ_2}{dY}.$$

Multiplying the terms on the right-hand side appropriately, you get

$$1 = \frac{P_1 Q_1}{Y} \frac{dQ_1}{dY} \frac{Y}{Q_1} + \frac{P_2 Q_2}{Y} \frac{dQ_2}{dY} \frac{Y}{Q_2}$$
$$= \alpha_1 \eta_Y^{Q_1} + \alpha_2 \eta_Y^{Q_2}$$

where α_1 and α_2 are the shares of the two goods in total income, with $\alpha_1 + \alpha_2 = 1$. These are weights.

For J goods, you have

$$1 = \sum_{j=1}^{J} \alpha_j \eta_Y^{Q_1}.$$

The sum of the weighted income elasticities is unity.

2.9 Elasticities and time

Until now, time has not been a factor in the demand equations. Elasticities, therefore, were not affected by time. Time, however, cannot be ignored, since most (if not all) economic processes take place in time. This is certainly true of demand for a good: consumers make purchases on a regular basis, say weekly as for groceries, perhaps out of habit or because of physical or technological constraints.

The notion of physical or technological constraints is important because they restrict the consumer from adjusting consumption after a price change. As time passes, however, the constraints are relaxed. In fact, you could argue that in the long run all constraints are relaxed (except income, of course, which is governed by your labor – unless you win a Powerball Lottery). A good example is the technological constraint of using your car as a mode of transportation to work. In the short run, you are unable to change your mode of transportation after a gasoline price increase because the only technology available for getting to work is your car. As time passes, however, other transportation modes become available (busses, for example), you can purchase a more fuel-efficient car, or other work possibilities can be introduced (telecommuting, for instance). These all have an effect on your gasoline consumption: consumption will not fall much, if at all, after the price increase, but it will fall more and more over time. The gasoline demand will be highly inelastic in the short run, but more elastic in the long run.

2.10   Some general demand function specifications

The demand functions described in this chapter have been linear. You are not restricted to just linear functions. In fact, most empirical work uses nonlinear functions. I describe these in this section, with their full use illustrated later in the book.

2.10.1 Isoelastic demand function

Consider the demand function

$$Q = aP^b. \tag{38}$$

The parameters a and b are constants. This can be written as

$$\ln(Q) = \ln(a) + b\ln(P), \tag{39}$$

so the demand function is now linear. This is called an *inherently linear demand function* or sometimes a *log-log function* because of the log term on both sides of the equation.

From (39), you can see that

$$
\begin{aligned}
b &= \frac{d\ln(Q)}{d\ln(P)} \\
&= \frac{P}{Q}\frac{dQ}{dP} \\
&= \eta_P^Q,
\end{aligned}
$$

which is fixed. Clearly, b, the price elasticity, is negative:

$$b = \left(\overset{+}{\frac{P}{Q}}\right) \times \left(\overset{-}{\frac{dQ}{dP}}\right) < 0.$$

TABLE 2.3 Several different demand models and their associated elasticities.

Model	Name	Elasticity
$Q = a + b \times P$	Linear	$(b \times P)/Q$
$Q = a + b \times ln(P)$	Linear-log	b/Q
$ln(Q) = a + b \times ln(P)$	Log-log	b
$ln(Q) = a + b \times P$	Log-linear	$b \times P$

The elasticity is constant for this demand function, unlike the straight line demand function, which has a varying elasticity. Equation (38) is sometimes called an *isoelastic demand function* and is frequently used in empirical work because of this constant elasticity property. This is the demand function used in later chapters.

2.10.2 Log-linear demand function

Another form of model is

$$Q = ae^{bP}.$$

Taking the natural log of both sides gives

$$ln(Q) = ln(a) + bP$$

and the elasticity is

$$\eta_P^Q = bP.$$

These elasticities are summarized in Table 2.3 along with several others (see [65] for details).

2.11 Qualitative statements about elasticities

You can qualitatively state what you expect an elasticity to be: inelastic, highly inelastic, elastic, highly elastic, etc. The usual list is shown in Table 2.4. See [56] for a discussion of these factors.

It is important to know these qualitative factors, not because they can absolve you from doing any empirical work (they do not), but because they can act as intuitive checks (sometimes called *sanity checks*) on the empirical work based on the tools developed in the rest of this book. All too often, analysts estimate a demand model (or any other kind of model) and then just take the results at face value (assuming the values are statistically significant) without asking if they make intuitive sense. Estimated parameters, in our case estimated elasticities, should be statistically significant, but also intuitive and plausible. Basically, can you accept what

TABLE 2.4 Qualitative elasticity statements about features of products and consumers that have implications for demand elasticities.

Qualitative statement	Probable elasticity
Many good substitutes	More elastic
Larger portion of the budget	More elastic
More time elapsed since price change	More elastic
Greater ability to pass price onto others	More inelastic

you just estimated? The qualitative statements listed in Table 2.4, while certainly not complete, can act as those checks. For example, if you estimate the elasticity for bottled water for a bottled water company you should expect a very elastic demand because there are many good substitutes for that firm's product: other water companies, water from the faucet, other beverages such as soda, etc. Yet if the estimated elasticity if very low (i.e., inelastic), then you should immediately suspect that something is wrong. At a minimum, you should be suspicious and thus examine your data and results.

2.12   Summary

Although this chapter borders on a detailed microeconomic treatment of demand, which to many may seem unnecessary, it does have a place in the empirical analysis of demand for pricing. Most textbook treatments of elasticities go only as far as defining the concept and then perhaps presenting some estimated elasticities to illustrate the concept. The purpose of this chapter is to extend the concept so that you will have a deeper understanding of elasticities. Elasticities are the key to effective pricing since they show the effect of a price change on sales and revenue, two key business metrics. Without knowing the elasticities, these effects cannot be determined short of actually changing a price to see what happens in the market – but then it may be too late.

The next chapter will show how the elasticity concept is used. Succeeding chapters will focus on measuring preferences to estimate elasticities.

Notes

1 The marketing literature often uses the terms *price sensitivity* or *price responsiveness*, while economists use *price elasticity*. I will use the economic phrase.
2 Not all the methodologies directly yield elasticity measures. This will be noted appropriately.
3 This entire discussion applies to services as well. Rather than repeatedly use the cumbersome phrase "goods and services," the word "goods" will simply be used.
4 The idea of a trade-off will be used extensively later when advanced methods called *conjoint* and *discrete choice experiments* are developed and discussed.

5 See the Wikipedia article "Marginal utility" at http://en.wikipedia.org/wiki/Marginal_ utility.

6 See, for example, [27], [30], [62], and [14] for a traditional mathematical development.

7 See [14] for a similar proof.

8 You can, of course, reduce your savings account or borrow, which effectively increase your income.

3

ELASTICITIES – THEIR USE IN PRICING

This short chapter develops the foundations for pricing a product based on elasticities. In a sense, it is a continuation of what I developed in the previous chapter by showing how elasticities are used. The estimation of elasticities is the subject of the rest of the book.

For those who have taken a microeconomics course, this chapter can be considered a review just like the previous one; otherwise, it will be new material. In either case, the review is brief, since it is not the intent of this book to be a microeconomic textbook. The foundations for pricing lie in microeconomic theory, so it is only fitting that it is used to understand what will come in succeeding chapters where the focus is on estimating elasticities. Chapter 2 was also a review of basic economic theory, primarily demand theory. So again, this chapter continues that discussion. Since the microeconomics literature of firm pricing is so extensive (in fact, there is even a subdivision called "industrial organization" that develops the pricing implications even further), this chapter should be short by necessity. It is meant to illustrate only a few uses of elasticities. There are many excellent books on microeconomic theory and industrial organization. See [3], [14], and [27] for the details of microeconomic theory and [67] for industrial organization.

This chapter has six sections. Section 1 reviews the basic market structures you may have to consider when doing your analyses. Section 2 presents material on classic profit maximization for different market situations. This is not meant to be a refresher on profit maximization methods, but to show you the importance of elasticities. Section 3 discusses pricing and market power, a concept often used in antitrust cases but that has wider applicability. The importance of elasticities is again emphasized. Section 4 introduces a more realistic market structure involving a dominant firm. My clients often say they are the market leader (no one ever says they are the laggard!). Their pricing is driven by elasticities, just as are the traditional firm structures of Section 1. Section 5 reviews the major form of pricing structure practiced by firms with some degree of market power: price discrimination. The forms of discrimination and the role of elasticities in one of the forms are highlighted. This section, however, also sets the stage in a small way for Part III of this book, where price segmentation is discussed, and then in Part IV, where modeling with Big Data is discussed. Section 6 is a summary.

3.1 The basics

The starting point for studying price setting by a firm is the structure of the market in which it operates. Classical economic theory defines a structure continuum with the end points being purely theoretical constructs with no (or almost no) real-world counterparts. Real markets lie between these points. The continuum, moving from left to right, progresses from a single firm, the pure monopoly, to a large number of firms, the perfectly competitive market with each firm in this market being a perfect competitor. Various degrees of oligopoly and monopolistic competition lie between the two extremes. This continuum is illustrated in Figure 3.1.1.

In the monopoly extreme, the sole firm's demand curve is the same as the market's demand curve. Contrary to popular belief, the monopolist does not have the ability to set whatever price it wishes. Its demand curve is downward sloping, so an increase in price produces a decrease in quantity demanded (i.e., sales), the degree of the decline dictated by the demand elasticity. Consumers can, motivated by the higher price, either drop out of the market and do without or switch to (i.e., substitute into) another product. This other product may not, and in fact is not, exactly the same as the monopolist's product (otherwise, the monopolist would not be a monopolist), but it will still serve the same purpose – maybe not perfectly, but the purpose can still be met. A simple, almost classic, example is electricity. If too high a price is charged by the local utility (ignoring regulatory issues), consumers could install their own generators or solar panels. In terms of elasticities, the monopolist's demand elasticity is identical to the market elasticity and the degree or magnitude of it is determined by the availability and quality of substitutes. The monopolist has the ability to set price, but it is limited by the downward-sloping demand curve.

Single Firm: One Product	Few Firms: Highly Differentiated Products	Many Firms: Less Differentiated Products	Many Firms Identical Products
Monopoly			Perfectly Competitive

FIGURE 3.1.1 Market structure continuum. All firms lie somewhere on this continuum. The end points – a monopoly firm and a perfectly competitive firm – are theoretical constructs used to anchor the continuum and establish logical comparison firms for the more realistic cases in the middle.

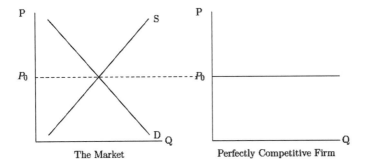

FIGURE 3.1.2 Relationship between the market price and the perfectly competitive firm's demand curve. The firm's price is determined by the market supply and demand in the left panel. P_0 is the market price, P_C is the competitive price, and $P_0 = P_C$.

In the perfectly competitive extreme, there are so many firms in the market selling an identical product that no firm can set a price that differs from the others, that price being the market price determined by supply and demand. If a firm set a slightly higher price, consumers would immediately stop buying from it and instead buy from another firm that has the identical product at a lower price. The firm that raised its price would immediately go out of business. Therefore, it has no incentive to raise its price. If, instead, the firm slightly lowered its price, then it would quickly find that it is losing revenue. It just has to raise its price back to the market price to gain more revenue. Therefore, it has no incentive to lower its price. Consequently, it will price at the current market price and, in fact, all firms will do the same. In this case, the perfectly competitive firm's demand curve is perfectly elastic. Based on the material in Chapter 2, this means the firm's demand curve has zero slope (i.e., perfectly horizontal) at the market price. This is illustrated in Figure 3.1.2.

The conclusion is that a monopolist has market power over price, while a perfectly competitive firm has none. All other types of firms are between these two extremes with some degree of market power, the extent of the power depending on their ability to differentiate their product.

3.2 Profit maximization

The question for both extremes and anything in between is the price point that maximizes profit. Economists view the problem from the output perspective: what is the output level that maximizes profit, the price being given by the demand function. This section considers the monopoly case first, followed by the perfectly competitive case. Economists typically first study the competitive case as the ideal, but I will reverse this because the result for the monopolist simplifies to the competitive result as a special case.

3.2.1 Monopoly firm profit maximization

Define the monopolist's profit as

$$\pi_M = P_M \times Q(P_M) - C(Q) \tag{40}$$

where $Q(P_M)$ is the market demand function as a function of the monopolist's price, P_M, and $C(Q)$ is the monopolist's cost function as a function of output, Q. The cost function is often written as the sum of two components: fixed and variable costs. I will subsume these two components into one function since my goal is a general statement for profit maximization. Besides, in the calculus to follow, fixed cost is a constant that drops out anyway.

I will assume that

$$\frac{dQ}{dP_M} < 0 \tag{41}$$

so that the demand curve is negatively sloped and

$$\frac{dC}{dQ} > 0 \tag{42}$$

so that the cost curve is positively sloped. This function, dC/dQ, is also a cost function called the *marginal cost* (MC). The marginal cost is the amount by which total cost increases for each additional unit of output produced. It is typically graphed as a positively sloped curve for (most of) the range of output in the cost–output plane. Finally, the product, $P_M \times Q(P_M)$, is the firm's revenue.

Profit is maximized when

$$\frac{d\pi_M}{dQ} = P_M + Q \times \frac{dP_M}{dQ} - \frac{dC}{dQ} = 0. \tag{43}$$

Collecting and rearranging terms gives

$$P_M \left[1 + \frac{Q}{P_M} \times \frac{dP_M}{dQ} \right] = \frac{dC}{dQ} \tag{44}$$

or

$$P_M \left[1 + \frac{1}{\eta_{P_M}^Q} \right] = MC \tag{45}$$

where $\eta_{P_M}^Q$ is the price elasticity of the monopolist's demand curve. The term on the left-hand side is the monopolist's *marginal revenue* (MR), the amount by which total revenue changes for each additional unit of output sold. Marginal revenue is a negatively sloped curve in the dollar–output plane. The condition (45) states that the monopolist's profits are maximized where $MR = MC$. This makes logical sense. If $MR > MC$, then increasing output adds more to revenue than cost, so the firm has an incentive to produce more output. If $MR < MC$, then increasing output adds more to cost than revenue, so the firm has an incentive to reduce output. The point where $MR = MC$ is the only point where it has no incentive to change output.

Note that marginal revenue is a function of the price elasticity from (45). Clearly,

$$MR < 0 \text{ when } -1 < \eta^Q_{P_M} < 0 \text{ (inelastic)}$$
$$MR = 0 \text{ when } \eta^Q_{P_M} = -1 \text{ (unit elastic)}$$
$$MR > 0 \text{ when } \eta^Q_{P_M} < -1 \text{ (elastic)}.$$

This immediately suggests that the monopolist will never produce in the inelastic portion of the demand curve: a slight increase in price (decrease in output) into the elastic portion will increase revenue by the amount of the marginal revenue.

Myopic monopolist price

Simple algebraic manipulation of (45) gives

$$P_M = \frac{\eta^Q_{P_M}}{1 + \eta^Q_{P_M}} \times MC \tag{46}$$

$$= \lambda \times MC \tag{47}$$

where λ is the price markup over cost. As long as the monopolist operates in the elastic portion of the demand curve, then $\lambda > 1$, $\lim_{\eta^Q_{P_M} \to -\infty} \lambda = 1$ and $\lambda \in R^+$.

Therefore, $P_M > MC$, but $P_M \to MC$ as λ approaches 1. The price P_M could be called the *myopic monopolist price* (see [4]).

The monopolist is myopic because it fails to consider the lifetime value (LTV) of a customer and the cost of acquiring and holding that customer. LTV is the present value of the expected future earnings from a customer. See [4] for a lengthy discussion of LTV. No firm wants a customer who just buys once and then disappears, because the firm would never know when the next customer would appear, let alone buy. The firm would always incur a search cost since it would always have to look (search) for new customers. Instead, it should want customers who repeatedly buy its product. Consulting firms, for instance, are certainly aware of these search costs since they look for "leads" by buying mailing lists, sending out email blasts, and placing ads on LinkedIn and Google. In addition, they hire vice-president executives in charge of business development whose sole function is to scout out new clients. If a firm could obtain and maintain a customer for a long time, it would have reasonable assurance of a revenue stream from repeat business with no search costs. There will be maintenance costs, however, in the form of keeping in touch through online services such as ConstantContact and making special offers (e.g., loyalty programs with special discounts and other rewards).

You can expand the pricing equation (46) to include a firm acquiring customers by looking at their future profitability. Not all new customers are equally profitable over their lifetime as customers. If the firm can identify or classify potential customers based on their projected profitability, then it can price discriminate by charging more (projected) profitable customers a lower *acquisition* price just to attract them as customers. Price discrimination is discussed in Section 3.5.

It can be shown (see [4]) that the acquisition price is

$$P_A = \frac{\eta_{P_A}^A}{1 + \eta_{P_A}^A} \times MC_A - \frac{\eta_{P_A}^A}{1 + \eta_{P_A}^A} \times \varphi$$

$$= P_M - \frac{\eta_{P_A}^A}{1 + \eta_{P_A}^A} \times \varphi$$

where

P_A = acquisition price (the cost of acquiring a customer)
P_M = myopic monopolist price
$\eta_{P_A}^A$ = elasticity of (the probability) of acquisition < 0
MC_A = the marginal (or incremental) acquisition cost
φ = expected LTV.

The higher the LTV of customers (the larger is φ), the lower the acquisition price compared to the myopic price to attract those customers. This is the basis for the price discrimination for the fashion example in Chapter 1: the fashion-forward people will keep coming back, so they will have a higher LTV. The more elastic the acquisition, the lower the price compared to the myopic price. If $LTV = 0$, then $P_A = P_M$.

This is impressive, but you need to know the elasticities!

3.2.2 Perfectly competitive firm profit maximization

Now consider the other extreme of a perfectly competitive firm. The firm is just one of many identical firms in the market, each selling an identical product. "Identical product" means that all the features, or attributes, of the product for one firm are exactly the same as for the product of another firm. This includes quality, post-sale service, and price (since price is an attribute). The price is identical for all firms because the demand curve facing any firm is a horizontal line at the price point set in the market; it is perfectly elastic. Therefore, $\eta_{P_C}^Q = -\infty$ where P_C is the competitive price. If you apply the profit maximization procedure to this case, you see immediately that the competitive firm maximizes profit where $P_C = MC$. This follows since if $\eta_{P_C}^Q = -\infty$, then $1/\eta_{P_C}^Q = 1/-\infty = 0$, so $\lambda = 1$ in (46). So there is really only one profit maximization equation, (45), that handles both extremes.

Economists typically use the perfectly competitive case as a benchmark for assessing welfare loss due to the lack of competition. The marginal cost, MC, can be interpreted as the cost society incurs from producing one more unit of the good; it is society's opportunity cost of one more unit. Price can be interpreted as society's assessment of the value of one more unit of the good; how much it is willing to pay for one more unit. Society's welfare is optimized if the amount it is willing to pay for one more unit just equals the opportunity cost of producing that unit. When price deviates from marginal cost, then social welfare is harmed, with the degree of deviance measuring the degree of harm. Monopolists are viewed as having the largest deviance: they can price above marginal cost, with the markup given by λ, and so therefore the largest social welfare loss is due to a monopoly market structure. The monopolist is said to have *market power*. There is no social welfare loss under perfect competition since $\lambda = 1$. The degree of market power is clearly a major focus of interest among economists. In fact, the degree of market power is at the heart of much antitrust literature and litigation because a firm with any degree of market power has the ability to set price. It must be stressed, however, that this ability is constrained by the market demand curve (see [3] for a discussion).

3.3 Pricing and market power

A measure, or index, of market power was proposed by [45]. The index, sometimes called the *Lerner Index* (*LI*), simply shows how much price deviates from marginal cost as a proportion of price:

$$LI = \frac{P - MC}{P}. \tag{48}$$

In the perfectly competitive case, $P = MC$, so $LI = 0$. For a monopolist, $P > MC$, so $LI > 0$. Therefore, you can state that $LI \geq 0$. You can go further. Using (48) and (45), you get, after some rearranging of terms,

$$LI = \frac{P - MC}{P} = -\frac{1}{\eta_P^Q}. \tag{49}$$

For the competitive case, $P_C = MC$, so $LI = 0$. For the monopolist case, $P_M = \lambda \times MC, \lambda > 1$, so $LI = 1 - 1/\lambda$. Then $\lim_{\lambda \to \infty} LI = 1$. So $0 \leq LI \leq 1$.

In terms of elasticities, for the competitive case $\eta_{P_C}^Q = -\infty$, so $LI = 0$ as before. For the monopoly case, $\eta_{P_M}^Q < -\infty$, but the monopolist will never price (i.e., operate) where $-1 < \eta_{P_M}^Q < 0$; that is, in the inelastic portion of the demand curve. At $\eta_P^Q = -1$, $LI = 1$.

The Lerner Index is often used in antitrust cases regarding the determination and assessment of market power (see [79] for a discussion).

3.4 Pricing by the dominant firm

A more realistic market structure arises when one firm dominates the market with all other firms in the industry playing a role, albeit a fringe role. The fringe firms are sometimes called the *competitive fringe*. A competitive fringe firm is assumed to be so small relative to the market that it has no market power. The fringe firms are effectively perfect competitors.

The dominant firm, however, is different. It sets the tone for the market, but it must still take account of the competitive fringe, especially when setting its price. In particular, the dominant firm supplies whatever the competitive fringe does not supply. The price it charges must account for this.

Figure 3.4.1 shows a typical presentation of the dominant firm model. The competitive fringe supplies S_{CF}, a typical upward-sloping supply curve, which is appropriate since the competitive fringe firms are assumed to be perfectly competitive firms. The dominant firm's demand is whatever demand is not satisfied by the competitive fringe. This demand, D_{DF}, sometimes called a *residual demand*, is given by

$$D_{DF} = D_M - S_{CF} \tag{50}$$

where D_M is the total market demand. These functions are all dependent on the market price, P.

Now

$$\frac{dD_{DF}}{dP} = \frac{dD_M}{dP} - \frac{dS_{CF}}{dP}. \tag{51}$$

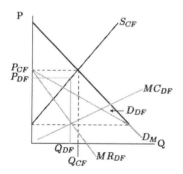

FIGURE 3.4.1 Relationship between the dominant firm and the competitive fringe. S_{CF} is the supply curve for the competitive fringe; D_M is the market demand; the line labeled D_{DF} is the dominant firm's demand curve with the appropriate marginal revenue curve (MR_{DF}); and MC_{DF} is the dominant firm's marginal cost curve. The price charged by the dominant firm is P_{DF} and it produces Q_{DF} where $MR_{DF} = MC_{DF}$. The competitive fringe sells Q_{CF} at P_{CF} based on supply and demand.

Multiplying both sides by P/D_{DF} gives

$$\frac{P}{D_{DF}} \times \frac{dD_{DF}}{dP} = \frac{P}{D_{DF}} \times \frac{dD_M}{dP} - \frac{P}{D_{DF}} \times \frac{dS_{CF}}{dP} \tag{52}$$

or

$$\eta_P^{DF} = \frac{P}{D_{DF}} \times \frac{dD_M}{dP} - \frac{P}{D_{DF}} \times \frac{dS_{CF}}{dP} \tag{53}$$

where η_P^{DF} is the price elasticity of the dominant firm. Multiplying the first term on the right by D_M/D_M, the second term by S_{CF}/S_{CF}, and rearranging gives

$$\eta_P^{DF} = \left(\frac{P}{D_M} \times \frac{dD_M}{dP} \right) \times \frac{D_M}{D_{DF}} - \left(\frac{P}{S_{CF}} \times \frac{dS_{CF}}{dP} \right) \times \frac{S_{CF}}{D_{DF}}. \tag{54}$$

Define $S = D_{DF}/D_M > 0$ as the dominant firm's market share. Then, noting that $S_{CF} = D_M - D_{DF}$, you get

$$\frac{S_{CF}}{D_{DF}} = \frac{S_{CF}}{D_M} \times \frac{D_M}{D_{DF}} \tag{55}$$

$$= \frac{1-S}{S} \tag{56}$$

which is the share of the competitive fringe relative to the share of the dominant firm. Our elasticity formula is then

$$\eta_P^{DF} = \eta_P^M \times \frac{1}{S} - \eta_P^{SCF} \times \frac{1-S}{S} < 0 \tag{57}$$

since $\eta_P^{DF} < 0$, $\eta_P^{SCF} > 0$, and $(1-S)/S > 0$. The Lerner Index for the dominant firm is

$$LI^{DF} = -\frac{1}{\eta_P^{DF}} \tag{58}$$

$$= -\frac{S}{\eta_P^M - \eta_P^{SCF} \times (1-S)} > 0. \tag{59}$$

Note that if the dominant firm is a monopolist, then $S = 1$ and $LI^{DF} = -1/\eta_P^M$ as before. If there is no dominant firm, just competitive firms, then $S = 0$ and $LI = 0$ also as before.

The dominant firm's price elasticity is not a simple expression. A firm in this position cannot simply assume that because it is the dominant firm its price elasticity is the same as the market elasticity. It must allow for the competitive fringe's supply elasticity and the respective market shares.

See [3] for a discussion of dominant firm models. Also see [42], which this derivation closely follows. Finally, see [79] for insights into the dominant firm model in antitrust analysis.

3.5   Pricing structures and elasticities

I emphasized in Chapter 1 that pricing strategies consist of structures and levels. The most common pricing structure is the universal class of *price discrimination*. Structures within this class can be used by any firm with some degree of market power; that is, $LI > 0$. Price discrimination includes, to mention a few[1]:

- Bundling;
- Tie-in sales;
- Discounts;
- Coupons;
- Premium pricing;
- Segmentation by age group, gender, student status, occupation, and employer;
- Retail and industrial buyer incentives;
- Versioning;
- Matching lowest price.

The following sections will review price discrimination to illustrate how price elasticities are used. The literature on price discrimination is huge, to say the least. Some useful references are [6] and [70], but also see [67].

3.5.1   Definition of price discrimination

The motivation for price discrimination is to capture as much consumer surplus as possible. In market situations without price discrimination (i.e., in which all consumers pay a uniform price), consumers retain all their consumer surplus while the firms only get their producer's surplus. The profit-maximizing firm can increase its profit if it can capture all or some of the consumer surplus. How can it do this? By price discrimination (see [70] and [67]).

The definition of price discrimination is unclear. The conventional definition is: *price discrimination is present when the same commodity is sold at different prices to different consumers.* There are problems with this definition, as noted by [70]: different prices charged to different consumers could simply reflect transportation costs or similar costs of selling the good. In addition, price discrimination could be present even when all consumers are charged the same price, as with a *uniform delivered price*, where customers do not pay the full delivery price for their product (see [70] for a full discussion).

3.5.2   Price discrimination family

Three forms of price discrimination were originally distinguished by [58], and these forms are still used and analyzed today and effectively define price discrimination. These were simply referred to as *first-*, *second-*, and *third-degree price discrimination*. For excellent review and summary articles, see [164] and [70].

First-degree price discrimination

For first-degree price discrimination, the firm with market power identifies the reservation price for each unit of a good for each consumer in the market. More importantly, the firm can charge the reservation price. Each consumer would gladly pay it, but no more, for each unit bought because, by definition, a reservation price is the maximum amount a consumer is willing and able to pay for each unit. By charging the reservation price, the firm captures all the consumer surplus from each consumer, thus increasing profits by the amount of the surplus. This is sometimes called perfect first-degree price discrimination. If there are n consumers in the market, there would be n demand curves and thus n price schedules.

Until recently, economists believed that perfect first-degree price discrimination is impossible to implement because of the amount of information needed to identify the reservation price for each unit of the good for each consumer. With modern Big Data, firms may be able to dynamically charge each consumer according to perfect first-degree price discrimination and thus capture each customer's consumer surplus (see [64] for a discussion).

Instead of perfect first-degree price discrimination, some firms use an imperfect version by charging a fixed fee (sometimes called a buy-in charge, access fee, entry fee, or cover charge) and then a per-use fee. The buy in is meant to capture the consumer surplus but not perfectly, since it is the same amount for all consumers. The schedule is called a two-part tariff expressed by the affine equation $T(Q) = A + P(Q)$, where A is the buy in (see [67]).

Second-degree price discrimination

For second-degree price discrimination, the firm with market power identifies or defines blocks of units of a good and charges a separate price for each block. The more blocks purchased, the lower the price for the marginal block. Electricity is priced this way. There will be one demand schedule. Nonlinear pricing falls into this category. See [74] for a treatment of nonlinear pricing.

Third-degree price discrimination

For third-degree price discrimination, the firm segments the market into at least two homogeneous parts or segments and charges a different price for each. The firm must know the price elasticities in each segment and so, with this knowledge, it will be able to set the price in each in accordance with these elasticities. To work, the market must be segmented so that arbitrage is impossible. Arbitrage is discussed in Section 3.5.3. Suppose there are s segments so that the total demand is $Q = \sum_{i=1}^{s} Q_i$. Also, assume that the cost of producing and selling the product is the same regardless of the market. This is a reasonable assumption. As an example, suppose a total grocery market in a local community consists of people 65 years old and older ("seniors") and all others ("non-seniors"). The cost of selling groceries to each segment should be the same. Why should a consumer's age matter?

For s segments, the total cost is $C(Q) = C \times \left(\sum_{i=1}^{s} Q_i \right)$ and the marginal cost, $\partial C / \partial Q$, is

$$\frac{\partial C}{\partial Q} = \frac{\partial C}{\partial Q_1} = \frac{\partial C}{\partial Q_2} = \cdots = \frac{\partial C}{\partial Q_s}.$$

Profit is the sum of the revenue from each segment less the total cost, or

$$\pi = \sum_{i=1}^{s} P_i \times Q_i(P_i) - C \times \left(\sum_{i=1}^{s} Q_i \right) \tag{60}$$

where $Q_i(P_i)$ is the demand in segment i as a function of the price charged in segment i, P_i. For profit maximization,

$$\frac{\partial \pi}{\partial Q_i} = P_i + Q_i \times \frac{\partial P_i}{\partial Q_i} - \frac{\partial C}{\partial Q} = 0 \tag{61}$$

for $i = 1, 2, \ldots, s$. Rearranging yields

$$P_i \times \left[1 + \frac{1}{\eta_{P_i}^{Q_i}} \right] = MC. \tag{62}$$

or

$$\frac{P_i - MC}{P_i} = -\frac{1}{\eta_{P_i}^{Q_i}}. \tag{63}$$

which is the Lerner Rule for segments. Then, similar to (46), $P_i = \lambda_i \times MC$. If $\eta_{P_i}^{Q_i} > \eta_{P_j}^{Q_j}$, $i \neq j$, so that i is relatively more inelastic (remember that the elasticities are negative), then $\lambda_i > \lambda_j$, so $P_i > P_j$. The difference in prices is $P_i - P_j = (\lambda_i - \lambda_j) \times MC$, so that if the elasticities are the same in the two segments, then there is no price differential. Otherwise, the firm with the ability to segment the market can price differently in each segment. The segment with the higher price elasticity (i.e., the relatively more elastic market) will have the lower price, while the one with the lower price elasticity (i.e., the more inelastic market) will have the higher price.

This makes intuitive sense. For the grocery example, you should intuitively expect that seniors would be more elastic (because of their fixed income, the grocery bill should be a larger portion of their [fixed] income), while non-seniors should be less elastic.[2] The seniors should be charged a lower price, while the non-seniors should be charged a higher price.[3]

3.5.3 Conditions for price discrimination

There are three conditions for effective price discrimination:

Market power: A firm must have market power, defined by the Lerner Index, to set price. A perfectly competitive firm has no market power – its Lerner Index is zero since $P = MC$, so it cannot capture any consumer surplus by manipulating price. A pure monopolist, on the other hand, has a high Lerner index, so it has the ability to set price and thus capture consumer surplus – it just needs the right price structure to do so. All other firms are between these two extremes with different values for their Lerner Indices.

No arbitrage: Arbitrage is the ability of a person (a consumer in this case) to buy a product at a low price in one market and resell it at a higher price in another. The difference in price is pocketed as profit. The keys to effective arbitrage are: (1) the guarantee of the price differential profit – the arbitrageur cannot lose on the arbitrage game – so that the arbitrage is riskless; and (2) the two markets have to be separated in time or space.

Arbitrage is frequently practiced in the financial markets (see [11] and [2] for some discussions). As an example of an arbitrage game in finance, suppose a Treasury T-Bond sells in New York for P_B^{NY} and in Chicago for P_B^{CH}. Assume $P_B^{NY} > P_B^{CH}$. The rational arbitrageur can buy the T-Bond in Chicago and quickly resell it in New York, making a profit of $P_B^{NY} - P_B^{CH}$. There is no chance for a loss since the price in New York is higher. This action is fundamentally a buy low/sell high strategy, but this is not the same as the oft-quoted strategy of "buy low, sell high" in which it is expected that the price of the asset will be higher tomorrow; this is a speculative strategy, as the price may not rise tomorrow. Arbitrage is not speculative – *it is a sure thing*. Economically, it works to eliminate a profit opportunity since only one investor (or agent) is needed to work the arbitrage game. Arbitrage is more primitive than the equilibrium concept in economics, which requires that all participants in the market act with any one person too small to impact the market. In arbitrage, only one participant is needed to act. The arbitrageur can repeat the arbitrage over and over to eliminate a profit opportunity if not successful the first time.

Arbitrage leads to only one price existing in the market for similar items. A single item (e.g., a bond) cannot have two prices at the same time. Arbitrage will drive the prices to equality, so this is sometimes called the *Law of One Price* (see [11] and [2]). Referring to the T-Bond example, buying the T-Bond in Chicago drives up price in Chicago by simple supply and demand.

Subsequently selling it in New York drives its price down in New York, also by supply and demand. As long as the New York price is higher, the arbitrageur will repeat this action until the price difference disappears. The result: $P_B^{NY} = P_B^{CH} = P_B$. Applying this to our two segments, i and j, it should be clear that with arbitrage $P_i = P_j = P$ by the *Law of One Price*.

Arbitrage is more complicated in real life compared to a textbook treatment. In the real world, there is the chance (i.e., risk) that prices will change adversely before the arbitrage is completed. The arbitrageur may suffer a loss if price differences narrow or close before he/she can act.

Heterogeneous consumers: The firm must be able to segment its consumer base into at least two groups, with each segment distinguished by different price elasticities. Segmentation is a large and active research area with many different techniques used to group consumers into different clusters. The "older" but still used method for segmentation is based on the multivariate statistical technique of cluster analysis, which involves looking at the distance between points and linking them together in some fashion. Statisticians tend to be leary of cluster analysis because it lacks formal models and there are few accepted methods for judging the quality of a cluster solution. Consequently, some recommend that clustering be used as an exploratory tool since different combinations of linkages and distance measures result in different solutions. To pin a firm's fortunes on a cluster analysis for segmentation for third-degree price discrimination is dangerous (see [69] and [44]).

A preferred method is based on latent class analysis. For an extensive discussion of cluster analysis, see [34], [13], and [73]. For latent class analysis, see [9].

Latent class segmentation is a regression-based method that simultaneously models consumers' responses to key measures (e.g., preferences, purchase intent, use) as a function of other variables or factors (i.e., independent variables called indicators). These indicator variables are explicitly incorporated into a model and the estimation process identifies which are statistically significant in explaining the key measure. The classes or segments the consumers belong to are levels of a *latent* or *hidden factor*, which is derived as part of the estimation process. In short, in a latent class segmentation model, the segments and the significant factors both contribute to explaining the key measure and are simultaneously determined.

The list of explicit factors usually includes attitudes, opinions, buying behaviors, and demographics. Those factors that are significant can be used to profile the segments. Hence, segment profiling is a natural by-product of the method.

Rather than allocating each consumer to one cluster as in older methods, the latent class approach determines the probability that every consumer belongs to every cluster. These probabilities can be used in other analyses.

Latent class segmentation is becoming the preferred way to segment markets because it uses key factors to both define the segments and profile them. This is much more efficient than older "tandem" procedures for segmentation in which consumers were clustered using a hierarchical clustering procedure and then the clusters profiled using a multivariate procedure such as discriminate analysis. Latent class segmentation is more accurate.

The main benefit of latent class segmentation is flexibility in terms of:

- The type of questions/variables used in the segmentation (nominal, categorical, ordinal, and counts).
- The underlying models used to define the segments.
- The ability to compare and assess the fit of different segmentation models, producing more robust and repeatable segmentations than other methods.
- Allowing consumers to assess a key measure (e.g., purchase intent) to focus the segmentation on the issue of greatest interest.

For more information on segmentation, see [73]. Clustering is discussed in Chapter 8 and latent class analysis in Chapter 9.

3.5.4 Price discrimination and Big Data

Section 3.5.3 listed several classic conditions for effective price discrimination. Another is the ability to sort (i.e., segment) customers so that different prices can be charged. In particular, a way is needed to sort customers by their willingness to pay (WTP). Second- and third-degree price discrimination allow customers to self-sort (second degree) or customers are easily sorted by visual inspection (e.g., gender, age) or by use of a government-sponsored ID (third degree). To effectively sort, information is needed on tastes, preferences, and WTP. Information, however, is costly to collect. The higher costs drive businesses to simpler discrimination structures if the returns from a more complex discrimination structure do not outweigh the information costs. Economists say that information is asymmetric: consumers know their own WTP (perhaps), but sellers do not. Third-degree price discrimination is the most widely used form because the information needed to implement it is minimal and easily obtained or identified in some cases. Information collection costs are minimal if segmentation is based on exogenous factors such as gender or age. Second-degree price discrimination is also widely practiced because customers provide the information through self-selection. The classic example is electric utility pricing mentioned above, where customers self-identify what rate block they are in by the amount of electricity they consume.

As noted above, economists until recently believed that first-degree price discrimination was impossible to implement because the amount of information needed to identify the reservation price for each unit of the good for each consumer would be too great (i.e., costly). With modern Big Data, however, firms may be able to dynamically charge each consumer according to first-degree price discrimination. Current pricing strategies, which are predominately discriminatory, can morph into first-degree price discrimination.

Unlike past purchases, WTP is not revealed in the market. If you know that a consumer bought a particular brand and type of shampoo on the past ten purchase occasions, you could then send a coupon or special offer for the next purchase. But the price paid does not tell you the *maximum* amount the consumer is willing to pay – the WTP. We need to *model* WTP. Using Big Data on similar consumers and purchase occasions, you can predict WTP based on characteristics of like individuals (demographics) and purchase occasions/habits (e.g., web activity). The types of models and modeling issues associated with Big Data are discussed in Chapters 10 and 11.

3.6 Summary

This chapter illustrated the importance of price elasticities by placing them in the context of market structure and profit maximization. You may feel that this material, like the material in Chapter 2, is too theoretical, but a review of it will help you with your pricing research.

Notes

1 See http://en.wikipedia.org/wiki/Price_discrimination for a discussion.
2 Especially those who are in their prime working and family years who have limited time to shop (i.e., search) for better prices. Seniors have more time and inclination to price search and so will be more price elastic.
3 I say "should" from the purely economic perspective of the grocery store maximizing profits, not a moralistic perspective.

PART II

Stated preference models

Choices are constantly made by both businesses and consumers, especially in a market context. Market choices are extensive and varied, such as what brand of detergent to buy, what flavor of ice cream to eat, what stock keeping unit (SKU) to purchase from a wholesaler, which product to sell, and, of course, what price to charge. And the list goes on. Some choices are complex, others are simple. In fact, there are so many choices that we are becoming more and more stymied by the number we have to make each day. There is now a *paradox of choice*: we have so many choices that we do not choose. This is well discussed by [63]. This paradox is comparable to the philosophical problem known as *Buridan's ass*.[1] There are many versions of this paradox, some of which go back to Aristotle, but a basic one is that the animal (a donkey) comes to a fork in a road, where it is confronted by what appears to be a simple binary choice: go left or go right. It could not make a decision in this simple situation – it was stymied by the choices – so it died. The donkey actually had a trinary choice: go left, go right, or choose neither and die. The poor animal had a *none* or *null* choice option and it is this *none* option that it chose. In modern discrete choice analysis, the *none* option is important and will be discussed in Chapter 5.

Regardless of the complexity of the choice, the choices ultimately affect price points and pricing strategies. Higher-level business managers, the ones who make the decisions about pricing, need information about the choices consumers make so they can make rational decisions (i.e., choices) about price points. To obtain this information, they call on market researchers to analyze market choices and make strategic recommendations. The researchers have a tool kit of methodologies for analyzing choices. This tool kit contains a family of choice models, each applicable to a different type of choice situation and data.

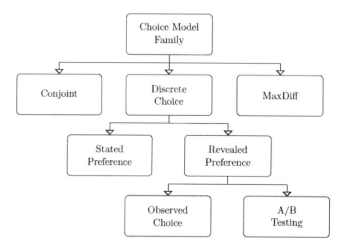

FIGURE II.1 The choice model family tree is extensive.
Source: Based on [57].

The choice model family tree, illustrated in Figure II.1, consists of the conjoint, discrete choice, and MaxDiff main branches. Conjoint was originally developed to study the trade-off among product features or *attributes*. This makes it perfect for product optimization – to answer the question "*What are the best features to build into a product?*" Conjoint relies on an experimental design and regression modeling to determine the importance of (weights for) different levels of the attributes. The weights are sometimes call *part-worths*. The sum of the weights is the utility of the product and the goal is to find that combination of attribute levels with the highest utility. Conjoint is discussed in Chapter 4.

Discrete choice is an extension of conjoint. In fact, and very unfortunately, many market researchers misuse the word "conjoint" by referring to a discrete choice study as a conjoint study. Sometimes they qualify the former as "choice-based conjoint." A conjoint analysis is an analysis of preference ratings on a single product configuration, while discrete choice analysis is an analysis of choice from among two or more product configurations in a *choice set*. It provides information to marketing and pricing managers on market share, or share of preference, or share of wallet. The discrete choice approach is often preferred over conjoint per se because it more realistically reflects market choices. Conjoint asks consumers to view a product in isolation so no other products are considered; this is very unrealistic. Discrete choice asks consumers to make selections from sets of two or more products, which is more realistic of market choices. Also, conjoint does not have an economic theory foundation, despite the fact that the estimated values are often called "utilities." Discrete choice, on the other hand, has a solid economic theory foundation. In this book, "conjoint" will refer to conjoint and "discrete choice" will refer to discrete choice, and, to paraphrase Kipling, never the twain shall meet. Discrete choice models and their economic foundations are discussed and developed in Chapter 5.

A feature of discrete choices consists of the levels of attributes of products. Price, for example, could have several price points; these are levels. MaxDiff, short for *maximum difference*, is a relatively new procedure introduced in the 1990s and is now very popular. It is ideal for determining preferences for messages or products without regard to product attributes. There are no ratings per se in MaxDiff, just selections from a choice set similar to the sets used in discrete choice. In MaxDiff, however, the consumer selects the most and least preferred alternatives in the choice set. From these selections, utilities are estimated for each alternative and the alternatives are then rank ordered. MaxDiff is discussed in Chapter 6.

Discrete choice analysis can be divided into two categories depending on how the data are collected. If observed choices are used, then the study is a revealed preference study. It is called "revealed preference" because consumers reveal their actual preferences in their market choices. The data could be collected by recording what shoppers take off a store shelf and put in their physical or virtual shopping cart, or the data could be collected by recording transactions such as with scanner data. These revealed preferences are observed without regard for experimental design principles. A/B testing is a variation that uses some (albeit very simple) design principles to observe what consumers actually select in controlled real-choice situations. This is usually done online when consumers make purchases from a website. A/B price testing is discussed in Chapter 7. Two other methodologies – van Westendorp and Gabor–Granger – are also discussed in Chapter 7. These two, however, have limited usefulness, especially the first one.

For revealed preference, the choices are for products that are actually available in the market. Stated preference, however, is artificial, based on experimental design principles. Choice sets consisting of different products that may not (and typically are not) available in the market are presented to consumers in sets. They are then asked to select their most preferred product from each set. This is now usually done online with sophisticated survey programs. The consumers do reveal their preferences, but they do so by stating them in response to a question as opposed to revealing them in the market, hence the name "stated preference."

Note

1 See http://en.wikipedia.org/wiki/Buridan%27s_ass.

4

CONJOINT ANALYSIS

The basic principles of conjoint analysis are developed in this chapter. In my opinion, conjoint has limited use in marketing choice studies because the situation it portrays is unrealistic. People make choices and evaluate products in context (i.e., against other products). Conjoint does not have this context. Nonetheless, it is widely used. It is developed here, in part because of its continued use, but also because it relies on concepts, definitions, terms, and principles used elsewhere in this book so they are best stated upfront.

This chapter is divided into 11 sections. Section 1 presents a Pricing Scenario as a choice situation. The scenario will be used throughout the chapter. Section 2 specifies the basic conjoint model as a linear regression model. Section 3 describes what a consumer will see in a conjoint study and how data are collected. Section 4 provides advice on how to specify the price variable. Section 5 lays the foundations for the experimental design concepts used in conjoint design and in later problems, while Section 6 discusses estimation methods. Section 7 illustrates utility calculations and Section 8 shows some standard utility analyses. Other approaches are discussed in Section 9. I briefly discuss software in Section 10 and summarize the chapter in Section 11.

4.1 Pricing Scenario

This section describes a Pricing Scenario used throughout this chapter. Terms, definitions, and concepts will be introduced and developed using this scenario.

4.1.1 The pricing problem

The owner of a home generator manufacturing company wants to develop and price a new natural gas-powered home generator. She can only market one product.

There are four *options, factors,* or *attributes* (all interchangeable terms) for the generator, each having different values or *levels.* Based on extensive focus groups from an initial qualitative phase of research that also included interviews with some subject matter experts (SMEs) and key opinion leaders (KOLs), she identified four attributes and some levels for each:

- Price: $2997, $3727, $4457;
- Watts: 11 kW, 16 kW, 20 kW;
- Response time (seconds): 10, 15, 30;
- Remote monitoring: yes, no.

The watts is the amount of power measured in kilowatts (kW) of electric power produced by the generator. The higher the kW, the more zones of a house that can be powered. A zone might be a bedroom or the main appliances in the kitchen. 20 kW would power an entire house. The response time is the delay in seconds from the instant power to the house is lost to when the generator activates. The remote monitoring refers to the ability of the homeowner to check the status of the generator while away using a special app on a smartphone or tablet.

4.1.2   Terminology

Attributes are discrete or continuous characteristics of a product or service. If an attribute is discrete, it has distinct, mutually exclusive, and completely exhaustive *levels* or values, although this may not always be the case. The attribute Remote Monitoring is discrete with two levels – Yes and No – which are all the possibilities. Watts and Response Time are also treated as discrete, with three levels each that cover all possibilities for this manufacturer. The manufacturer cannot have a response time of, say, 20.5 seconds. If the attribute is continuous, then it can have any set of values in R, but from a practical business perspective, a finite set of discrete values is usually selected. SMEs, KOLs, focus groups, and a knowledge of the business (i.e., gut instinct) are useful for identifying these discrete levels. For this example, the Price attribute is inherently continuous with values in R^+, but only three have practical market relevance, so there are only three discrete levels – the three price points.

An *alternative* is a combination of attributes defining a product. An alternative is referred to as a *treatment* in the design of experiments (DOE) literature. In this literature, each combination of levels, one level from each factor or attribute, is a treatment. If there is only one attribute with l levels, then there are l treatments. If there are two attributes, one with two levels and one with three levels, then there are six treatments. I tend to use "alternatives" and "treatments" interchangeably. For the Pricing Scenario, a 16-kW generator with remote monitoring and a 15-second response to a power outage priced at $2997 is one alternative or product, while a 20-kW generator without remote monitoring and a 10second response to a power outage priced at $4457 is another.

If there are k alternatives, then each one can be viewed as a *k-tuple*, which is an ordered set of k objects, elements, or components. For the generators, each possible generator alternative is a 4-tuple with components in the order Price, Watts, Response Time, and Remote Monitoring, with each component set at one of its levels.

The research question posed by the generator manufacturer is: *"What is the best generator to sell and at what price?"* As in all data-based questions, as for this problem, a study design and model are needed to answer this question. The *study design*, not to be confused with a *treatment design*, is how the choice situations will be presented to consumers. The treatment design is how the alternatives are defined by the levels of the factors. For this Pricing Scenario, the pricing analyst initially opted to present each consumer with all the generators in the treatment design, one generator at a time. For each generator shown, the consumer would be asked to provide a preference rating for it on a rating scale (a ten-point Likert scale is typical). The preference rating is a *response variable*. The set of all responses is a *response pattern*. Other options are to ask purchase intent (also usually on a ten-point scale) or to allocate a fixed, given number of "chips," points, dollars, or some other fixed sum to the product, the amount allocated representing the product's value or worth to the consumer. The generators would be shown without the context of other generators so consumers would have to judge each generator on its own merits (i.e., Price, Watts, Response Time, and Remote Monitoring). All the generators in a treatment design would be shown to a consumer. If the sample size is C, the treatment design is replicated C times.

The model for the responses is a *conjoint model*, the analysis is a *conjoint analysis*, and the study is a *conjoint study*. These terms tend to be used interchangeably. The next section describes the model typically used in a conjoint study.

4.2   Basic conjoint model

Consider an alternative defined by the 4-tuple (j, k, l, m) that has the jth level of the first attribute, the kth level of the second, the lth level of the third, and the mth level of the fourth. Clearly, there are $j \times k \times l \times m$ 4-tuples or alternatives. For the generators, there are $3 \times 3 \times 3 \times 2 = 54$ alternatives. To simplify notation, let τ be a k-tuple in the set T of all k-tuples so that $\tau \in T$. The number of tuples in T is N. For the generators, τ is a 4-tuple generator, T is the set of all generators, and $N = 54$. The 54 generators are clearly more than one consumer can handle, but for now just assume each consumer will see all 54 as the pricing analyst initially plans. This issue is discussed later. The following is based on [57].

The basic conjoint model for four attributes for the alternative defined by the 4-tuple $\tau = (j,k,l,m)$ for consumer r in a sample of size C is a linear regression or general linear model specified as

$$Y_\tau^r = \beta_0^r + \beta_{aj}^r + \beta_{bk}^r + \beta_{cl}^r + \beta_{dm}^r + \varepsilon_\tau^r \tag{64}$$

where

β_0^r = grand mean preference
β_{aj}^r = part-worth utility for level j, attribute a
β_{bk}^r = part-worth utility for level k, attribute b
β_{cl}^r = part-worth utility for level l, attribute c
β_{dm}^r = part-worth utility for level m, attribute d

and Y_τ^r is the total utility or *total worth* to consumer r of a product defined by τ. The coefficients, called *part-worths*, are the contributions to the total worth. For the generator problem, the part-worths are

β_{aj}^r = part-worth for Price at price point j
β_{bk}^r = part-worth for Watts at power level k
β_{cl}^r = part-worth for Response Time at seconds l
β_{dm}^r = part-worth for Remote Monitoring at level m, or Yes/No.

The ε_τ^r term is the usual regression disturbance term reflecting consumer heterogeneity. I will assume that it has the usual regression properties: normality, zero mean, constant variance, zero covariance with any other disturbance term, and zero covariance with any attribute.

When all N tuples in T are shown to each consumer r in a sample of C consumers, the rating task is said to be replicated C times as noted above. A task is *repeated* if each consumer is asked the same choice task several times, while it is replicated if different consumers are asked the same rating task. The distinction is important because repetition measures within consumer variation of responses so you can derive a within subject error variance, while replication measures between-consumer variation so you can derive a between-subject error variance. Since people should be consistent in their choices but differ from each other because of consumer heterogeneity, the within consumer error variance will be smaller than the between-consumer error variance (see [75]).

There is a part-worth for each level of each attribute for each consumer. The goal is to estimate these part-worth utilities so you could calculate overall utility or "preference." Since the model is linear, ordinary least squares (OLS) regression is usually used for estimation. With enough degrees of freedom for each consumer, estimation could be done at the individual level, hence the superscript for the part-worths, but then this would require another step – aggregation across consumers. The advantage of estimating at the individual level is that other analyses can be done. For example, consumers can be segmented based on their part-worth estimates.

Typically, however, a set of aggregate part-worths is estimated for all consumers, so the model is

$$Y_\tau^r = \beta_0 + \beta_{aj} + \beta_{bk} + \beta_{cl} + \beta_{dm} + \varepsilon_\tau^r. \tag{65}$$

Barring the research need for further analyses, I prefer one aggregate linear regression estimation using all consumers at once with the part-worths constant for all consumers. OLS can be used to estimate the parameters of (65). Another estimation approach, binary logit regression, is discussed later.

The only data actually collected are the preferences, the dependent or Y data. For simplicity, suppose you have two factors, each at two levels, and suppose you have one replication (one consumer). The high level of a factor will be designated by "1" and the low level by "−1". These are just symbols and any symbols could be used. For the generator problem, Price, for example, has three symbols: $2997, $3727, and $4457. If you identify the attributes by 2-tuples where the first symbol represents the first factor and the second symbol the second factor, then the set of tuples is $T = \{(1,1),(1,-1),(-1,1),(-1,-1)\}$ and $N = 4$. Using the pairs of symbols as subscripts on Y to identify which tuple the response is associated with, you have a 4×1 vector of responses $\mathbf{Y}' = \left[Y_{(1,1)}, Y_{(1,-1)}, Y_{(-1,1)}, Y_{(-1,-1)} \right]'$. This is a response pattern. The independent variables are the arrangements of the "1" and "−1" symbols that can be placed in a matrix

$$\mathbf{X} = \begin{bmatrix} 1 & 1 \\ 1 & -1 \\ -1 & 1 \\ -1 & -1 \end{bmatrix}$$

The $\mathbf{X}$ matrix is called the *design matrix* or the *treatment matrix*. I tend to use the terms interchangeably. For the generator problem, the matrix has size 54×4. Each row of $\mathbf{X}$ defines an alternative; each column defines settings for an attribute. The issue is the specification of the design matrix. Section 4.5 provides a background on the development and specification of this matrix.

The model in (65) has a constant term, β_0, which is not part of the design matrix $\mathbf{X}$, so you need to allow for it for estimation. You can augment the design with a column vector of 1s as

$$\mathbf{X}_A = \begin{bmatrix} 1 & 1 & 1 \\ 1 & 1 & -1 \\ 1 & -1 & 1 \\ 1 & -1 & -1 \end{bmatrix}$$

where the first column of all 1s is for the constant and the remaining columns are the design matrix, $\mathbf{X}$. The model in (65) is then written in matrix notation as

$$\mathbf{Y}' = \mathbf{X}_A \beta + \varepsilon' \tag{66}$$

where ε' is the disturbance term and $\beta' = \left[\beta_0, \beta_1, \beta_2 \right]'$ is the vector of part-worths plus the constant. This is a classical OLS regression model. Estimation issues are considered in Section 4.6.

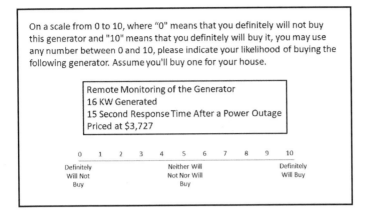

On a scale from 0 to 10, where "0" means that you definitely will not buy this generator and "10" means that you definitely will buy it, you may use any number between 0 and 10, please indicate your likelihood of buying the following generator. Assume you'll buy one for your house.

> Remote Monitoring of the Generator
> 16 KW Generated
> 15 Second Response Time After a Power Outage
> Priced at $3,727

0   1   2   3   4   5   6   7   8   9   10

Definitely
Will Not
Buy

Neither Will
Not Nor Will
Buy

Definitely
Will Buy

FIGURE 4.3.1 Example of a conjoint card for the Pricing Scenario. There will be as many cards similar to this one as there are rows in the design matrix. The consumer's response, some number from 0 to 10, is the Y value used in the model.

4.3   What the consumer sees

For the Pricing Scenario, the value Y_t^r for the 4-tuple (j,k,l,m) is a preference rating response by consumer $r \in C$ after seeing a *card* with these levels for the attributes drawn from a row of a design matrix. Before online survey systems, consumers were handed physical cards, each one describing a product with one product per card. Now consumers see virtual cards on a computer or tablet screen, but the intent is the same. The term "card" is still used today. A typical card might look like the one in Figure 4.3.1.

4.4   Specifying the Price attribute

Not all possible price points have to be tested since a statistical model will be estimated. The model can be specified so that the effect of any intermediate price that was not part of the study can be determined through interpolation. I recommend using evenly dispersed price points. Do not have, for example, $1, $3, $5, and $25. Interpolation involves finding linear segments between points and, without an even spread, interpolation complicates the problem. Interpolation is frequently done in a *simulator*, which allows you to test any price point. An effect of a price outside the range of those shown, however, cannot be determined.

In addition to not using all possible price points, ensure sufficient variation in what is used for the reasons discussed above for observational data. You are not hampered by actual market prices, so flexibility is gained in specifying price points. I do not recommend price points that are too close to one another or that increase by small increments. For example, avoid prices such as $1.10, $1.15, $1.20, and $1.25 because there is not much distinction between $1.10 and $1.15 or between $1.20 and $1.25 for many products. When consumers are asked to make comparisons, they could (and probably will) view the difference between $1.10 and $1.15 as too trivial to be important. Their focus would then be on other factors, minimizing the importance of price. As a result, price would become insignificant when in fact it should be highly significant.

Managers frequently say that prices for their product category will never fall below the current market minimum price (or rise above the current market maximum price), so why waste time using a lower price in the study, and similarly for higher prices? Then one month after the study is completed, a competitor announces a lower price, completely negating the study! The purpose of the conjoint approach is to evaluate what-if scenarios in a simulator, a programmed tool for analyzing different combinations or settings of the attribute levels. If it is really believed that a lower price is impossible in the market, then it should be ignored in the simulator. I typically recommend price points at least one step below the current market minimum price and at least one step above the current market maximum price.

4.5 Design matrix background

The design matrix, $\mathbf{X}$, is developed using concepts and principles from the DOE literature. DOE is the area of statistics that deals with the optimal arrangement of *treatments* in an experiment such that each treatment is represented equitably. This allows you to determine the effect of each treatment on the item measured, the dependent or response variable. Without an equitable representation of each treatment, you may not be able to adequately measure the treatment's effect.

In our context, the attribute levels form the treatments. A *treatment design* is the way attribute levels are arranged to create alternatives. A few treatment designs are:

- Orthogonal;
- Hadamard;
- Full factorial;
- Fractional factorial;
- Foldover;
- Balanced incomplete block.

See [59], [35], and [51] for discussions of treatment designs.

4.5.1 Orthogonal design

An orthogonal design has columns that are independent of each other. Mathematically, the pairs of columns are perpendicular, which means that the cosine of the angle between each pair is zero. If k is the number of columns, then there are $k \times (k-1)2$ pairs, all of which are perpendicular to each other. Another way to express this is to say that the k pair-wise correlations are all zero. For example, the design shown in Table 4.1a for three factors, each at two levels, is orthogonal. The 3×3 correlation matrix has zeros in the off-diagonal cells. Orthogonality can also be calculated by the inner product (also called the dot product) of each pair of factors. The

TABLE 4.1 Part (a) is an orthogonal design matrix for three factors (L, M, and H), each at two levels, usually at "Low" and "High." The "1" traditionally represents the High level of the factor and the "−1" the Low level. There are three pairs: L–M, L–H, and M–H. The correlation matrix in part (b) has zeros for each of the off-diagonal elements, indicating no correlation. In addition, the inner products (also called the *dot products*) are zero for each pair, as is easily verified. As an example, the first inner product for the L–M pair in part (a) is (1)(1) + (1)(1) + (1)(−1) + (1)(−1) + (−1)(1) + (−1)(1) + (−1)(−1) + (−1)(−1) = 4 − 4 = 0.

(a) Design matrix

L	M	H
1	1	1
1	1	−1
1	−1	1
1	−1	−1
−1	1	1
−1	1	−1
−1	−1	1
−1	−1	−1

(b) Correlation matrix

	L	M	H
L	1	0	0
M	0	1	0
H	0	0	1

inner product is the sum of the products of each pair of elements for factors j and k: $X_j \cdot X_k = \sum_{i=1}^{n} X_{ij} \times X_{ik}$. This will be zero for an orthogonal design. It is easy to verify that the three inner products for Table 4.1a are all zero. It can be shown that

$$cos(\theta) = \frac{\mathbf{X}_j \cdot \mathbf{X}_k}{\|\mathbf{X}_j\| \, \|\mathbf{X}_k\|} \tag{67}$$

where $\mathbf{X}_j$ is the length of the vector $\mathbf{X}_j$. If the two vectors are perpendicular, then $cos(\theta) = 0$, which implies that $X_j \cdot X_k = 0$.

More formally, an orthogonal design is an array or matrix characterized by the number of rows, N; the number of columns, k; the number of "symbols," s; and the "strength," which is a positive integer $t \leq k$. The typical notation for an orthogonal array is $OA(N,k,s,t)$. The symbols are objects such as letters or numbers arranged in an array with one symbol per cell. The "−1" and the "1" symbols used earlier represent an example. This number can vary $s_i, i = 1,\ldots,k$, but here I will use s as constant for all columns. The strength is the number of columns in a subset of the k columns, $t \leq k$, such that each of the s^t ordered rows of that subset appear the same number of times. For the previous paragraph, pairs were considered so $t = 2$. This means that for every pair of columns, such as the first and last in Table 4.1a, the rows for these two columns, with the elements of the rows in the order shown (that is, as 2-tuples), appear the same number of times. In Table 4.1a, each 2-tuple appears twice. If $t = 3$, then each 3-tuple appears the same number of times. In general, each t-tuple appears the same number of times. The replication is sometimes represented by λ, so $\lambda = 2$ for Table 4.1a. Note that $N = \lambda s^t$. For Table 4.1a, $s = 2$, $t = 2$, and $\lambda = 2$, so $n = 2 \times 2^2 = 8$: the design matrix has eight rows. See [55], from which this section draws heavily. Also see [26] for the authoritative and challenging work in this area.

The strength is important because it says what can be estimated in a linear model such as (64). The terms on the right-hand side of a linear model with two variables, X_1 and X_2, can be of the form X_1, X_2, and $X_1 \times X_2$. The two single-variable terms are *main effects*, while the product term is a *two-way interaction*. The main effect of a factor is the mean value of the response when that factor is at its high vs. low level averaged over all levels of the other factors. In short, the main effect of factor X_1 is the effect of changing X_1, but this change could be done at two levels of X_2. Figure 4.5.1 will help you understand this.

The main effect of X_1 is

$$\frac{1}{2} \times \left[\left(\overline{Y_{11}} - \overline{Y_{01}} \right) + \left(\overline{Y_{10}} - \overline{Y_{00}} \right) \right]$$

where $\overline{Y_{11}}$ is the mean response when X_1 is at its high level and X_2 is at its high level; similarly for the other terms. The subscripts are in the order "factor 1" followed by "factor 2," with "1" indicating high level and "0" indicating low level in this case. The main effect for factor X_2 is

$$\frac{1}{2} \times \left[\left(\overline{Y_{11}} - \overline{Y_{10}} \right) + \left(\overline{Y_{01}} - \overline{Y_{00}} \right) \right]$$

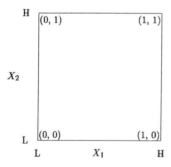

FIGURE 4.5.1 This is the factor square for a 2^2 problem consisting of X_1 and X_2 with each factor at a Low (0) and High (1) level. Since there are four 2-tuples, you can use them to define a square with each 2-tuple being a corner. The corners are labeled with the levels of the factors. So the corner labeled (0,1) has X_1 at its Low level and X_2 at its High level. It can be seen that X_1 has an effect on Y when X_2 is at its Low and High levels.

The interaction between the two factors is

$$\frac{1}{2} \times \left[\left(\bar{Y}_{11} - \bar{Y}_{01} \right) + \left(\bar{Y}_{10} - \bar{Y}_{00} \right) \right]$$

See [26] for more details.

With more than two variables, there will be more main effects, several two-way interactions, and higher-order interactions (three-way, etc.). With k design columns, there is a potential for $2^k - 1$ right-hand terms, which include main effects and two-way and higher interaction terms. For $k = 3$, you could have three main effect terms, three two-factor interactions, and one three-factor interaction, or seven terms in total ($= 2^3 - 1$). Most researchers look for main effects and some two-factor interactions; interactions between more than two factors are rarely used. An example of a two-factor interaction commonly used is one formed by a *Price* and *Brand* variable. The model would have a *Price* main effect, a *Brand* main effect, and a *Price* × *Brand* interaction. The interaction would capture a symbiotic relationship between *Price* and *Brand* so that a price elasticity could vary by brand.

If $t = 2$, then estimates of main effect coefficients are unbiased, but coefficients for two-way and above interactions cannot be estimated, as noted in [26]. If $t = 4$, then estimates of main effect coefficients and two-way interaction coefficients can be estimated. Other implications are noted in [26].

4.5.2 Hadamard design

A Hadamard design is a square matrix of size n, sometimes written as H_n. The central property is that $\mathbf{H}_n \mathbf{H}_n' = n \times \mathbf{I}_n$ where $\mathbf{I}_n$ is an identity matrix of size n. The matrix entries are -1 and $+1$ values with orthogonal columns (and orthogonal rows). If the rows and columns are permuted, the result is still Hadamard. If all entries are multiplied by -1, the result is still Hadamard (see [10] and [59]). Examples of Hadamard matrices from [26] are shown in (68).

$$H_1 = \begin{bmatrix} 1 \end{bmatrix}, \; H_2 = \begin{bmatrix} 1 & 1 \\ 1 & -1 \end{bmatrix}, \; H_4 = \begin{bmatrix} 1 & 1 & 1 & 1 \\ 1 & -1 & 1 & -1 \\ 1 & 1 & -1 & -1 \\ 1 & -1 & -1 & 1 \end{bmatrix}. \tag{68}$$

These matrices are difficult to use since a Hadamard matrix does not exist for all problems. A conjecture, the *Hadamard Conjecture*, states that "*If a Hadamard matrix* $\mathbf{H}_n$ *exists, then n is 1, 2 or a multiple of 4*" (see [26]). This conjecture is unproven.

Although the conjecture is unproven, these matrices are still important for the construction of orthogonal arrays of levels $s = 2$ and strength $t = 2$. A discussion of Hadamard matrices is beyond the scope of this book, but [26] has a challenging, detailed treatment.

4.5.3 Foldover designs

A foldover design is just an orthogonal design mirrored on itself (hence the "foldover").

4.5.4 Balanced incomplete block designs

A *balanced incomplete block design* (BIBD) is an important class of designs that apply when there are more factors or attributes than one consumer can evaluate at once. Subsets of the factors are combined into *blocks* or groups, but since each block has just a subset of all treatments, the blocks are *incomplete*. Not all subsets can or should be created. They have to meet a criterion: the factors are *balanced* across all blocks. BIBDs and their creation is a complex topic. BIBDs are discussed in Chapter 6.

4.5.5 Full factorial design

When all possible combinations of the factors are present in the design, the design is then called a *full factorial*. If there are two factors with the first at three levels and the second at two, and whichever level of the first is present in a design has no bearing on which level of the second is present, then by disjunctive counting (i.e., *Fundamental Principle of Counting*) there are $3 \times 2 = 6$ arrangements of the two factors. For the Pricing Scenario, there are four attributes, three at three levels each and one at two levels, so there are $3 \times 3 \times 3 \times 2 = 3^3 \times 2 = 54$ arrangements or 4-tuples of the four factors. The arrangements are called *cards* or *runs* or *profiles* or *alternatives*, all interchangeable terms.

4.5.6 Fractional factorial design

Sometimes the number of k-tuples is too numerous for consumers to handle. As noted by [57], they become a cognitive challenge. Consumers are unable to process too many cards before boredom or fatigue sets in, or they start to believe that every card is the same so they respond the same way. As a rule of thumb (ROT), I often recommend approximately 16 cards or less. For the Pricing Scenario, only a fraction of the full factorial is needed. The subset must satisfy conditions, but this is beyond the scope of this book. See [5] for an excellent discussion. A fractional factorial design is the most commonly used design in conjoint studies.

Table 4.2 shows the number of levels for the Pricing Scenario and the associated number of parameters required for estimation. Our model will have seven parameters for the treatments. You also need one parameter for the constant term, so eight parameters are needed overall. This means you need at least eight cards or runs for estimation. You cannot estimate a model less than eight.

A design with exactly the number of cards as parameters to estimate (including the constant) is called a *saturated design*. You would be able to estimate each parameter,

TABLE 4.2 Parameters needed for the generator Pricing Scenario. Although attributes such as Price, Watts, and Response Time each have three levels, only two parameters are needed for estimation. Remote Monitoring has only two levels, *Yes* and *No*, so only one parameter is needed. The rule for determining the number of parameters is to sum the number of levels across all attributes, subtract the number of attributes, and add 1 for the constant: $\# Parameters = \# Levels - \# Attributes + 1$, where $\# Levels = \sum_{i=1}^{A} l_i$, where A is the number of attributes and l_i is the number of levels of attribute i. See [57] for a discussion.

Attributes	Number of levels	Needed parameters
Price	3	2
Watts	3	2
Response Time	3	2
Remote Monitoring	2	1
Total	11	7

TABLE 4.3 Possible fractional designs for the generator Pricing Scenario. The one-third fraction at 18 cards or runs comes closest to the ROT of 16. The 27 and 18 runs are too much for consumers to handle without then becoming fatigued or bored. The six run is too small. Nine is doable, but there will be only one degree of freedom for the variance (see [57]).

Fraction	Number of cards
1/2	27
1/3	18
1/6	9
1/9	6

but you would be unable to estimate the variance. Because of this, the statistical validity and usefulness of the model would be questionable to say the least.

The main idea of a fractional factorial design is that not all effects, aside from the main effects, are important. The main effects obviously are important because they show what happens when the attributes, each alone and independent of the others, change. Two-way and higher interactions are often unnecessary or unimportant. Their effects can be so negligible that they can be safely ignored. As noted by [26], discussions with SMEs and KOLs may be needed to identify which interactions can be ignored. In general, however, three-way and higher interactions can be ignored, as well as most two-way interactions.

With 54 cards, you need a number less than (approximately) sixteen but more than eight. Possibilities are shown in Table 4.3. A one-sixth fraction of nine cards is passable, while a one-third fraction of eighteen cards may be too large. Some software recommends twelve runs based on a heuristic. The heuristic is basically the number of runs for a saturated design plus a few extra.[1] This number is doable by consumers so this is what was used for the generator problem.

4.5.7 Why use a design?

A question frequently asked, especially by SMEs, is: *Why use an experimental design*? Consider, for simplicity, a study, similar to the generator Pricing Scenario, but with only three factors at two levels each: Price, Watts, and Response Time, with levels of just Low and High. The Price factor, for example, could be at $2997 and $4457. [10] notes that you could interpret the low value as the current value or condition and the high value as the target expected to improve some business metric. The low price of $2997 would be the current market price and $4457 would be the value expected to improve revenue (hopefully accounting for an elasticity effect).

The full factorial for this example is shown in Table 4.4. A response column is included in the table showing how a hypothetical consumer may have rated each generator on these three factors. This design table can be represented as a cube with sides Price, Watts, and Response Time as shown in Figure 4.5.2.[2]

One-factor-at-a-time experiments

A naive way to conduct a study, often espoused by SMEs unaware of design principles, is to vary each factor, one at a time, measuring the response each time a factor is changed. This is called, of course, a *one-factor-at-a-time* (OFAT) approach. The first factor changed is typically the one considered most important, followed by the second most important, and so forth. What is important could be determined by the SMEs. Assume they believe price is most important. Then the pricing analyst would measure and compare consumer responses for the Low and High levels of Price, each with Watts and Response Time set at their Low levels. The responses from Table 4.4 at the Low and High levels of Price are 3 and 1, respectively, so the Low Price would be used as the value for Price in further

TABLE 4.4 A full 2^3 factorial for Price, Watts, and Response Time each at a Low (L) and High (H) level. A consumer was shown all eight treatment arrangements and was asked to provide a purchase intent rating, which is shown in the "Consumer response" column. The overall mean response is 5.25; the mean response at the Low price level is 5.00; the mean response at the High price level is 5.50.

Price	Watts	Response Time	Consumer Response
L	L	L	3
L	L	H	4
L	H	L	6
L	H	H	7
H	L	L	1
H	L	H	2
H	H	L	9
H	H	H	10

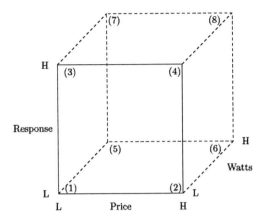

FIGURE 4.5.2 This is the factor cube for the 2^3 problem consisting of Price, Watts, and Response Time for generators with each factor at a Low (L) and High (H) level. There are eight arrangements, each of which is at a corner of the cube. The corners are labeled by the numbers in parentheses. Each factor has one of its levels at four corners. For example, the Price factor is at its Low level at the four corners: (1), (3), (5), and (7).

comparisons. The SMEs would say this was obvious and an experiment would not be needed to show it.

Now suppose the SMEs say Watts is the next most important factor. With Price set at its Low level and Response Time still at its Low level, a comparison is made between the Low and High levels of Watts: 3 and 6, respectively. So Watts is set at its High level.

With Price at its Low level and Watts at its High level, the responses for Response Time are now compared. The High level is best. Therefore, the best combination is Price Low, Watts High, and Response Time High. However, from Table 4.4 you see that the best combination in the sense of highest preference is Price High, Watts High, and Response Time High. This combination is never seen under the OFAT procedure so it is never rated. A possible reason for the high price is that consumers may view a low price as indicating poor quality. We know that quality, which is difficult to measure before actual purchase, is often judged by the price: low-quality items will sell at low prices, while high-quality items will sell at high prices. Price acts as a surrogate for quality (see [53] and [56]).

4.5.8 Generating a design

If an OFAT is inappropriate, how is a design actually generated so that all combinations are seen? For a simple three-factor problem with each factor at two levels, there are $2^3 = 8$ combinations as in the data cube. It is a simple task to write down these eight combinations. For a problem like the generator problem with 54 combinations, specialized software is needed. This is how I settled on the 12 runs mentioned above. Several software packages are discussed later in this chapter.

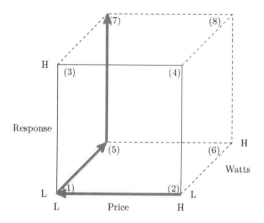

FIGURE 4.5.3 In this example, you first compare the response to Price at its Low and High levels with Watts and Response Time both set at their Low levels. Then you compare the response to Watts at its Low and High levels, but with Price set at its Low (best) level and Response Time still set at its Low level. Finally, you compare the response to Response Time at its Low and High levels with Price set at its Low (best) level and Watts set at its High (best) level. The arrow path shows the comparisons and the order shown to consumers. The overall best combination at corner (8) is never shown.

4.5.9 Creating the design

One could create the design by hand or using specialized software. For very simple problems, it is definitely possible to write down a design. For example, a full factorial for three factors each at two levels, a 2^3 factorial, is easy to write. Using effects coding, this would be the design shown in Table 4.5.

Although with only eight runs, suppose this design is too large for a consumer to handle. A one-half fraction of this design can be created. A one-half fraction of a 2^3 is written as $(1/2) \times 2^3 = 2^{-1} \times 2^3 = 2^{3-1}$. An example is shown in Table 4.6. The fractional design in Table 4.6 can be generated using the methods described in [5]. For more complex designs involving many factors with larger numbers of levels, software algorithms typically begin with a candidate design, which could be a full factorial design, but then successively try different combinations of rows of the candidate design in a smaller design. This raises the question of determining the final *optimal design matrix* from all the smaller designs tried.

For a linear model, the parameter estimates have a variance–covariance matrix represented as $\Omega = (X'X)^{-1}$, where X is the design matrix as a function of the data. The Gauss–Markov theorem proves that this variance–covariance matrix is the minimum for linear unbiased estimators. See [31] for the conditions for the theorem to hold. The estimates are said to be *efficient*. Since a design matrix for a treatment design is an arrangement of effects coded variables, the objective for an optimal experimental design is to find a design matrix X that minimizes the variance–covariance matrix Ω.

The inverse of the variance–covariance matrix is called the *Fisher Information Matrix*. The information referred to is what the design matrix contains about the

TABLE 4.5 An effects coded full factorial design for three factors, each at two levels coded as −1 and +1. The columns in this design matrix are orthogonal, as can be easily verified.

+1	+1	+1
+1	+1	−1
+1	−1	+1
+1	−1	−1
−1	+1	+1
−1	+1	−1
−1	−1	+1
−1	−1	−1

TABLE 4.6 An effects coded one-half fraction of the full factorial design in Table 4.5. The columns in this design matrix are orthogonal, as was the full factorial design.

+1	+1	+1
+1	−1	−1
−1	+1	−1
−1	−1	+1

unknown parameters. We want a treatment design that provides the maximum amount of information about the parameters. Since the information is the inverse of the variance–covariance matrix, maximizing the former is equivalent to minimizing the latter. The design matrix that maximizes the information has maximum efficiency.

The issue for an optimal design is determining when the information matrix has been maximized. A number of measures or criteria have been proposed, the most popular being the *D-optimality* criterion, which is based on the determinant of the information matrix (hence the "D"). The objective is to find a treatment design matrix that has the largest D-optimal measure. Other criteria are "*A-optimal*" and "*G-optimal.*" The *A-optimal* measure is based on the average of the trace of the design matrix, while the *G-optimal* measure is based on σ_M, "the maximum standard error for prediction over the candidate set."[3] These three are written as

$$D - optimal : 100 \times \frac{1}{N_D \times \left|(X'X)^{-1}\right|^{\frac{1}{p}}} \tag{69}$$

$$A - optimal : 100 \times \frac{P}{N_D \times tr(X'X)^{-1}} \tag{70}$$

$$G - optimal : 100 \times \frac{\sqrt{\frac{p}{N_D}}}{\sigma_M} \tag{71}$$

Design Diagnostics	
D Efficiency	95.84147
G Efficiency	80
A Efficiency	92.30769
Average Variance of Prediction	0.722222
Design Creation Time (seconds)	0

FIGURE 4.5.4 The three criterion measures for the generator example are shown here. The D-optimal measure, which is the most popular, shows that the design with 12 runs is 95.8% efficient.

where N_D is the number of rows in the design matrix and p is the number of design factors. The standard error is calculated as $x_{i'} (X'X)^{-1} x_i$, where x_i is the vector of values in the ith row of X.

As an example, consider a 2^3 problem; that is, three factors, each at two levels. This results in the full factorial design matrix in Table 4.1a. The columns of this matrix are orthogonal, as evidenced by the correlation matrix in Table 4.1b. The matrix product is a square matrix with 8 (the number of rows of the design matrix) on the main diagonal and 0 elsewhere. The matrix inverse then has 0.125 on the main diagonal and 0 elsewhere. The determinant of the inverse matrix is 0.001953125. The D-optimal measure is

$$D - Opt = 100 \times \frac{1}{N_D \left| (X'X)^{-1} \right|^{1/p}}$$

$$= 100 \times \frac{1}{8 \times 0.001953125^{1/3}}$$

$$= 100.$$

The efficiency measure is 100, so this design is 100% efficient. All perfectly orthogonal designs are 100% efficient. For simple problems, analysts strive for orthogonal designs, but perfect orthogonality is impossible for complex designs. A D-optimal design with the highest efficiency score is desirable.

The design with 12 runs has a D-optimal efficiency measure of 95.8%, so that it is very close to being perfectly efficient. The three measures are shown in Figure 4.5.4.

4.6 Estimation

There are several ways to estimate part-worth utilities:

- OLS regression;
- Binary logit;

- Hierarchical Bayes (HB);
- Polyhedral methods.

The advantage of OLS is that most pricing analysts are familiar with the basics of regression and all statistical software packages have it. Even spreadsheet packages have a simple regression function. The issue with OLS, however, is that a predicted preference rating could be outside the range of the preference scale. The typical scale is only bounded between, say, 1 and 10.

The advantage of the binary logit is that predictions will always be bounded, but the bounds are 0 and 1 since the logit is based on a probability scale. This means that the typical ten-point preference scale used in conjoint would have to be dummified into a binary variable by recoding. The usual recoding is to code the top three points of the scale as 1 and the remaining points as 0. This is called a "top three box" (T3B) recoding.[4] The idea is that a consumer who rates a product as T3B really likes it or is very likely to buy it; any rating below the T3B means the opposite. With a binary logit model, you model the likelihood of buying or the strength of preference. A disadvantage of the binary logit approach is that the estimated parameters are difficult to interpret. The interpretation, however, is not a major hindrance, since the estimated coefficients can be converted to odds ratios, which are easier to interpret and understand. The following two sections describe both methods applied to conjoint analysis, although they assume a basic knowledge of OLS and binary logit. For a background on OLS and binary logit regression modeling, see [20].

HB is a method used in a variety of fields, not just choice analysis. The name succinctly summarizes its two features: it is a hierarchical modeling method and it implements Bayesian statistical methods. Until the advent of HB methods, estimating Bayesian models was a challenge to say the least. Except for small models, the estimation task was nearly impossible. HB broke the barrier. I will discuss HB estimation in Chapter 6 when MaxDiff procedures are developed.

Polyhedral methods are also relatively new, although I suspect they have less use at present.

OLS will be the method used in this chapter.

4.6.1 Digression: Coding

Notice the design in Table 4.4. There are no numbers, just letters indicating the data points. For estimation, these letters have to be coded as numbers, since no estimation procedure will operate on letters. Even if numbers such as +1 and −1 are in the design matrix, they also must be coded for estimation if a software package interprets them as representing discrete levels. All discrete categorical variables must be coded for estimation. There are many coding schemes, but as mentioned above, the two most popular in pricing and market research are dummy and effects coding. These are discussed in the next two sections.

Dummy coding

Dummy coding, popular in econometrics, involves assigning 0 or 1 to the different levels of a qualitative factor. These values can be interpreted, respectively, as "absent" and "present," or "turned off" and "turned on," or "no" and "yes." For the generator problem, each of the four factors are qualitative with different numbers of levels. The coding scheme involves creating a new variable for each level of each factor with values 0 and 1. Each new variable is called a *dummy variable* because it is standing in for the actual values of the qualitative variable. For example, Price has three levels: $2997, $3727, and $4457. Three dummy variables could be created, one for each level. The first dummy variable, representing the $2997 level, would have a value of 0 whenever Price is not $2997 and a value of 1 whenever it is $2997. This coding is written as

$$D_{\$2997} = \begin{cases} 0 & \text{if } Price \neq \$2997 \\ 1 & \text{if } Price = \$2997. \end{cases} \tag{72}$$

A similar approach is taken for the other two levels to create three dummy variables.

A simpler, more compact form of (72) uses an *indicator function* to define the dummy variables, so the dummies are sometimes called *indicator variables*. The dummy variable is defined as

$$D_{\$2997} = I(Price = \$2997)$$

where $I(\cdot)$ is the indicator function that returns 1 if the argument evaluates as true and 0 otherwise. So $I(Price = \$2997)$ is 1 if Price equals $2997 and 0 if it does not. Similarly, $I(Yes) = 1$ if the argument evaluates to "Yes" and 0 otherwise.

You could treat price as a continuous variable rather than as categorical so that dummy coding is unnecessary. This could be done as you will see elsewhere below. If only three price points are considered, then treating them as categorical is appropriate since the price will be one of those three points and no others. The same holds for the Watts and Response Time factors. My ROT, although not infallible, is to treat a numeric variable as categorical if it has definite discrete levels that will not change. Statistical software generally allows you to specify a variable as Numeric or Character, and to further specify the former as Continuous, Ordinal, or Nominal. If it is Numeric/Ordinal or Numeric/Nominal, then the software will automatically treat it as categorical and code it for you.

For the Price factor, if all three dummy variables are used, the sum of the three is exactly 1, which happens to be the value for the constant term in a regression model. This is illustrated in Table 4.7. Hence, you would have perfect multicollinearity with the constant so you would fall into the dummy variable trap. The solution is to drop one of the dummy variables. The one dropped is called the *base* variable. See [20] for a discussion of the dummy variable trap.

The dummy variables represent parallel shifts in the regression line. To see this, consider the regression model (73) for a generator with just two out of three potential Price dummy variables: $D_{\$2997}$ and $D_{\$3727}$. The base is $4457.

$$Y = \beta_0 + \beta_1 D_{\$2997} + \beta_2 D_{\$3727} + \varepsilon. \tag{73}$$

This can be rewritten as

$$Y = \beta_0 + \beta_1 D_{\$2997} + \beta_2 D_{\$3727} + \varepsilon = \begin{cases} \beta_0 + \beta_1 + \varepsilon & \text{if } Price = \$2997 \\ \beta_0 + \beta_2 + \varepsilon & \text{if } Price = \$3727 \\ \beta_0 + \varepsilon & \text{if } Price = \$4457. \end{cases} \tag{74}$$

The constant term, β_0, is interpreted as the mean preference rating when the price is \$4457 since, from regression theory, $\overline{Y} = \beta_0$; $\beta_0 + \beta_1$ is the mean preference rating at \$4457, so β_1 is the *difference* in mean preference rating between the two price points; and similarly for $\beta_0 + \beta_2$. This is developed in the next section on the technical details of dummy coding.

The choice of a base is immaterial; you can choose any level as the base. All that happens is that the signs on the estimates change and the constant term is adjusted to reflect this. The interpretations just have to be modified. This is shown in the *Technical details* section below.

The general rules for creating the dummy codes are:

1. For a factor with L levels, $L - 1$ variables are created. The omitted L^{th} level is redundant. The Lth level is omitted to avoid the "dummy variable trap" of having perfect multicollinearity.
2. The base, or reference, level is assigned a value of 0. This level is arbitrary.
3. A level is set equal to 1 when that level is present, or equal to 0 otherwise.

Parameter Estimates: Model A

Term	Estimate	Std Error	t Ratio	Prob>|t|
Intercept	5	1.767767	2.83	0.0300*
Price Dummy (Low = Base)	0.5	2.5	0.20	0.8481

Parameter Estimates: Model B

Term	Estimate	Std Error	t Ratio	Prob>|t|
Intercept	5.5	1.767767	3.11	0.0208*
Price Dummy (High = Base)	-0.5	2.5	-0.20	0.8481

FIGURE 4.6.1 Two models estimated with a dummy variable for price at two levels just for illustration. In Model A, the base is the Low level of Price, and in Model B the base is the High level. Notice what happens to the two estimated coefficients. For Model A, the overall mean is 5.0 with Price at its Low level ($\beta_0 = 5$) and the effect of setting Price at its High level is 0.5, resulting in a mean of 5.5 (= $\beta_0 + \beta_1$). For Model B, the overall mean is 5.5 when Price is at its High level ($\beta_0 = 5.5$), in agreement with Model A, and the effect of setting Price at its Low level is -0.5, resulting in a mean of 5.0 ($\beta_0 - \beta_1$), again in agreement with Model A.

TABLE 4.7 This is a possible dummy variable design matrix for Price using three dummy variables, one for each of the three Price levels. The "Constant" column shows the values for the constant term, β_0. The last column shows the sum of the dummy variables. Notice that the sum in each row is 1.0, which corresponds to the constant term's values of 1.0. This is the basis for multicollinearity: the three dummy variables are linearly related to the constant term. The solution is to drop one of the dummy variables, the one selected as the base. Also note that one of the dummy columns is not needed; it is redundant. Consider the column labeled "$P_{\$4457}$." This is redundant given the other two columns. This is another reason to drop one dummy: it is not needed.

Price	Constant	$P_{\$2997}$	$P_{\$3727}$	$P_{\$4457}$	Sum of dummies
$2997	1	1	0	0	1
$3727	1	0	1	0	1
$4457	1	0	0	1	1

Technical details of dummy coding

There are two issues for dummy coding: multicollinearity and interpretation. This section addresses both.

For multicollinearity, consider the dummy variable coding of the three Price levels in Table 4.7. Notice that the sum of the dummy variables equals the constant term. This is the source of the collinearity: there is a perfect linear relationship between the three dummy variables and the constant term. As a result, all software will stop estimation.[5]

Now consider the interpretation issue. Using (74), sum the response values associated with the base Price of $4457, $Y_{\$4457}$. If $n_{Y_{\$4457}}$ is the sample size associated with these responses, then you have $\sum Y_{4457} = n_{\$4457} \times \beta_0$, or after rearranging $\beta_0 = \overline{Y_{\$4457}}$. So β_0 is the mean of the responses for the $4457 level. Now sum the response values for the $2997 level: $\sum Y_{\$2997} = n_{\$2997} \times \beta_0 + n_{\$2997} \times \beta_1$, or $\overline{Y_{\$2997}} = \beta_0 + \beta_1$. Therefore, $\beta_1 = \overline{Y_{\$2997}} - \beta_0 = \overline{Y_{\$2997}} - \overline{Y_{\$4457}}$. So β_1 is the difference between the two group means. This is called a *contrast*. We get a similar result for the $3727 Price level.

Suppose you define a dummy variable using indicator notation as

$$D = I(Yes).$$

Notice that the mean of the dummy variable is merely the sample proportion of *Yes* responses: $\overline{X_D} = p_{Yes}$ because you are summing 0 and 1 values and then dividing by the sample size, n.

Now reverse the coding to

$$DUM = I(No)$$

TABLE 4.8 An example of how to change a dummy variable's coding. Notice that each value of the new variable, DUM, is $1 - D$. As an example, $DUM = 1 - 0 = 1$ for the first row.

D	DUM
1	0
0	1
0	1
1	0

so that $\overline{X_{DUM}} = p_{No} = 1 - p_{Yes}$. What happens? First, observe that

$$DUM_i = 1 - D_i$$

An example is shown in Table 4.8.
Let the initial model be simply

$$Y_i = \beta_0 + \beta_1 D_i + \varepsilon_i.$$

Then,

$$\widehat{\beta_0} = \bar{Y} - \widehat{\beta_1} p_{Yes} \widehat{\beta_1}$$
$$= \frac{\sum (D_i - p_{Yes})(Y_i - \bar{Y})}{\sum (D_i - p_{Yes})^2}$$

where the formulas follow from least squares theory (see [20]). Now let the model with reversed coding be

$$Y_i = \beta_0^\star + \beta_1^\star DUM_i + \varepsilon_i.$$

With the reversed coding you have for $\hat{\beta}_1^\star$

$$\widehat{\beta_1^\star} = \frac{\sum (DUM_i - p_{No})(Y_i - \bar{Y})}{\sum (DUM_i - p_{No})^2}$$
$$= \frac{\sum (DUM_i - 1 + p_{Yes})(Y_i - \bar{Y})}{\sum (DUM_i - 1 + p_{Yes})^2}$$
$$= -\frac{\sum (D_i - p_{Yes})(Y_i - \bar{Y})}{\sum (D_i - p_{Yes})^2}$$
$$= -\widehat{\beta_1}$$

The sign is merely reversed.
What happens to the intercept, $\hat{\beta}_0$? It becomes $\hat{\beta}_0 = \hat{\beta}_0 - \hat{\beta}_1$ to reflect the mean of the new base. A little algebra will show this.

Effects coding

Another coding scheme, *effects coding*, is popular in market research and is usually used in conjoint and discrete choice analyses. Effects coding is similar to dummy coding in that a new variable is defined for each level of the qualitative factor with one of the levels selected as the base. But the coding is different. Instead of 0 and 1, −1, 0, and +1 are used. The −1 is used for the base, the +1 is used for the level under consideration, and the 0 is used for all other levels. Obviously for a two-level factor, only −1 and +1 are used. This is the coding used in Table 4.1a.

For the generator price at three levels with $4457 as the base, the first effects variable is defined as

$$E_{\$2997} = \begin{cases} 1 & \text{if } Price = \$2997 \\ 0 & \text{if } Price = \$3727 \\ -1 & \text{if } Price = \$4457. \end{cases} \tag{75}$$

The second effects variable is

$$E_{\$3727} = \begin{cases} 0 & \text{if } Price = \$2997 \\ 1 & \text{if } Price = \$3727 \\ -1 & \text{if } Price = \$4457. \end{cases} \tag{76}$$

The third one, which would not be used since it represents the base price of $4457, is

$$E_{\$4457} = \begin{cases} 0 & \text{if } Price = \$2997 \\ 0 & \text{if } Price = \$3727 \\ -1 & \text{if } Price = \$4457. \end{cases} \tag{77}$$

This is summarized in Table 4.9.

The interpretation of the effects coded variables is different from the dummy coded variables. With the dummy variables, the constant is the mean of the *base level* and the other parameters are the contrasts with the base level mean; they are contrasts between two levels. In effects coding, the constant is the grand, overall mean, not the base level mean, for a factor. The other parameters are the difference between the factor level's mean and the overall factor mean. So if $\overline{\overline{Y}}_f = \frac{1}{n} \sum_{l=1}^{L} \sum_{j=1}^{n_l} Y_{flj}$, $n = \sum_{l=1}^{L} n_l$ is the grand, overall mean over L levels of factor f, each level with n_l observations and n is the total sample size, then $\beta_{fl} = \overline{Y}_{fl} - \overline{\overline{Y}}_f$, where $\overline{Y}_{fl} = \frac{1}{n_l} \sum_{j=1}^{n_l} Y_{flj}$.

For the generator problem, you would code two effects variables for Price. With $4457 as the base, the two price effects variables are shown in Table 4.9.

TABLE 4.9 The variable E_1 represents the $2997 price level and the variable E_2 the $3727 level. The third effects variable, $E_{\$4457}$, is omitted. Notice that the two variables sum to 0. This is a feature of effects coding: the sum of the levels for each new variable sum to 0. This summation is horizontal and vertical so that the sum in each column is zero and the sum of the sum of each row is zero. That is, $\sum_{i=1}^{3} \sum_{j=1}^{2} E_{ij} = 0$, where i indexes the rows and j indexes the columns. So they are contrasts.

Price	$E_{\$2997}$	$E_{\$3727}$	$E_{\$2997} + E_{\$3727}$
$2997	1	0	1
$3727	0	1	1
$4457	−1	−1	−2
Sum	0	0	0

The general rules for creating the effects codes are:

1. For a factor with L levels, $L - 1$ variables are created. The omitted L^{th} level is redundant. The Lth level is omitted to avoid the "dummy variable trap" of having perfect multicollinearity. This omitted level, however, can be retrieved as shown below.
2. The base, or reference, level is assigned a value of −1. This level is arbitrary, just as for dummy coding.
3. A level is set equal to 1 when that level is present; equal to −1 if the base level is present; and equal to 0 otherwise. As a result, the coefficients sum to 0.0.

Although the base level is dropped in the coding, the coefficient for this level can be retrieved as the negative sum of the estimated coefficients. For Price, you have, with $4457 as the base level,

$$\beta_{\$4457} = (-1) \times \left(\beta_{\$2977} + \beta_{\$3727} \right)$$

You estimate only two parameters, but you can calculate (retrieve or "expand to") the third.

Technical details on effects coding

Since effects coding is typically used in conjoint and discrete choice modeling, I should spend a moment examining the technicalities of this coding scheme. That is the focus of this section.

Consider prices at three levels: *Low*, *Medium*, and *High*. Let *High* be the base or reference level. To avoid multicollinearity, I will create two effects dummies since there are three levels for price. The coding is shown in Table 4.10. The model is

$$Y = \beta_0 + \beta_1 P + \beta_2 P_2$$

TABLE 4.10 Hypothetical effects coding for the generator at Low, Medium, and High prices. Only two effects dummies are needed. If the High price is the base, then P_1 is for the Low price and P_2 is for the Medium price. Whenever price is High, the two effects dummies are coded as −1.

Price	P_1	P_2
Low	1	0
Medium	0	1
High	−1	−1

where Y is the preference rating for the generator. The subscripts are omitted to simplify notation. This is really three separate models, one for each of the three price levels, which is written as

$$\hat{Y}_L = \hat{\beta}_0 + \hat{\beta}_1 \times (1) + \hat{\beta}_2 \times (0) = \hat{\beta}_0 + \hat{\beta}_1 \tag{78}$$

$$\hat{Y}_M = \hat{\beta}_0 + \hat{\beta}_1 \times (0) + \hat{\beta}_2 \times (1) = \hat{\beta}_0 + \hat{\beta}_2 \tag{79}$$

$$\hat{Y}_H = \hat{\beta}_0 + \hat{\beta}_1 \times (-1) + \hat{\beta}_2 \times (-1) = \hat{\beta}_0 - \hat{\beta}_1 - \hat{\beta}_2 \tag{80}$$

Summing the three predicted Ys, you get $\sum \hat{Y} = 3 \times \hat{\beta}_0$, or $\overline{\overline{Y}} = \hat{\beta}_0$, where $\overline{\overline{Y}}$ is the overall, grand average since the $\hat{\beta}_1$s and $\hat{\beta}_2$s cancel. Therefore, the intercept is the overall average of the $\hat{Y}$s.

It is easy to show that the overall mean is the average of the group means. I will assume balanced data (i.e., an equal number of observations at each level), so $n_L = n_M = n_H = (1/3) \times n$. Then,

$$\begin{aligned}
\overline{Y} &= \frac{\sum Y}{n} \\
&= \frac{\sum Y_L + \sum Y_M + \sum Y_H}{n} \\
&= \frac{\sum Y_L + \sum Y_M + \sum Y_H}{3 \times n_L} \\
&= \frac{\overline{Y}_L + \overline{Y}_M + \overline{Y}_H}{3}
\end{aligned}$$

The concept is similar, but the result is a bit more complicated, for unbalanced data.

Now sum just the $\hat{Y}$ values associated with the *Low* price in (78). There are n_L values, so the sum is $\sum \hat{Y}_L = n_L \hat{\beta}_0 + n_L \hat{\beta}_1$. Dividing by n_L, the mean is

$$\begin{aligned}
\overline{Y}_L &= \hat{\beta}_0 + \hat{\beta}_1 \\
&= \overline{\overline{Y}} + \hat{\beta}_1
\end{aligned}$$

So $\widehat{\beta_1} = \overline{Y_L} - \overline{\overline{Y}}$ and is the deviation of the mean preference rating at the *Low* price from the overall mean preference rating. We say that it is the *contrast* between the mean preference rating at the *Low* price from the overall mean preference rating. If $\widehat{\beta_1} > 0$, then it is the amount by which the mean preference rating at the *Low* price is greater than the overall mean preference rating. We have a similar result for $\widehat{\beta_2}$ for the *Medium* price. For dummy coding, on the other hand, $\widehat{\beta_1}$ is the contrast between the mean rating at the *Low* price and the mean rating at the base price, which is a completely different contrast.

We can do a similar operation for the *High* price:

$$\overline{Y_L} = \widehat{\beta_0} - \widehat{\beta_1} - \widehat{\beta_2}$$
$$= \overline{\overline{Y}} - \widehat{\beta_1} - \widehat{\beta_2}.$$

Therefore, $\overline{Y_H} - \overline{\overline{Y}} = -\widehat{\beta_1} - \widehat{\beta_2} = \widehat{\beta_3}$. So you retrieve the omitted estimated coefficient as minus the sum of the other two coefficients. This coefficient, as for the other two, has the interpretation of a deviation of the overall, grand mean preference rating from the group mean. It should be clear that $\widehat{\beta_1} + \widehat{\beta_2} + \widehat{\beta_3} = \sum \overline{Y_j} - 3 \times \overline{\overline{Y}} = 0$, the sum of the estimated coefficients is 0.0.

Creating an effects coded design

Dummy and effects coding are related in that the effects codes can be derived from the dummy codes. This means, of course, that the dummy codes can be retrieved from the effects codes. To see this, consider the dummy coding for four variables in Table 4.11a. In this case, if the value of a categorical variable with four mutually exclusive and completely exhaustive levels is, say, 1, then D1 = 1, or 0 otherwise; similarly for the other three levels. If the last column of the dummy codes (D4) is the base and is subtracted from each column, including the last one itself, then the effects codes in Table 4.11b result. To retrieve the dummy codes from the effects codes, simply add the last or base dummy (D4) to each of the four effects coded variables.

4.6.2   OLS estimation for the Pricing Scenario

For the Pricing Scenario, you treat the preference rating as a continuous dependent variable and use the effects coded design matrix for the independent variables. The estimation results are shown in Figure 4.6.2. Notice that the base levels have been retrieved so the estimated coefficients for a factor sum to 0.0 as explained above.

For price, the main focus of this study, you see that the highest price, $4457, has the lowest part-worth value (−0.38), while the lowest price, $2997, has the highest part-worth value (0.58). The direction for the part-worths from low to high price

TABLE 4.11 Effects codes can be derived from dummy codes.

(a) Dummy variables

D1	D2	D3	D4
1	0	0	0
0	1	0	0
0	0	1	0
0	0	0	1

(b) Effects variables

E1	E2	E3	E4
1	0	0	0
0	1	0	0
0	0	1	0
−1	−1	−1	0

TABLE 4.12 An effects coded set of variables is created by subtracting the base dummy variable ($P_{\$4457}$ in this example) from the other two dummies. The last effects variable is dropped.

Price	$P_{\$2997}$	$P_{\$3727}$	$P_{\$4457}$	$E_{\$2997}$	$E_{\$3727}$	$E_{\$4457}$
$2997	1	0	0	1	0	0
$3727	0	1	0	0	1	0
$4457	0	0	1	−1	−1	1

agrees with the demand theory outlined in Chapter 2 (as well as agreeing with intuition). These part-worths are illustrated in Figure 4.6.3. The other part-worths' interpretations are obvious.

The conjoint model could be estimated with price as a continuous variable rather than a discrete variable. This would yield only one estimated part-worth for price. The estimation results for this model version are shown in Figure 4.6.4.

4.6.3 Logit estimation for the Pricing Scenario

Another estimation possibility, not explored here, is to recode the response variable to *T3B* using the indicator function

$$T3B = I(response \geq 8)$$

and then to estimate a binary logit model. Although this can be done, the most common estimation procedure is OLS.

Expanded Estimates

Nominal factors expanded to all levels

Term	Estimate	Std Error	t Ratio	Prob>|t|
Intercept	5.8712121	0.009964	589.23	<.0001*
Price[$2,997.00]	0.5795094	0.014854	39.01	<.0001*
Price[$3,727.00]	-0.199567	0.014854	-13.44	<.0001*
Price[$4,457.00]	-0.379942	0.014854	-25.58	<.0001*
Watts[11K]	-0.220635	0.014854	-14.85	<.0001*
Watts[16K]	-0.50101	0.014854	-33.73	<.0001*
Watts[20K]	0.721645	0.014854	48.58	<.0001*
Response.Time[10 Seconds]	-1.561616	0.014854	-105.13	<.0001*
Response.Time[15 Seconds]	1.858153	0.014854	125.10	<.0001*
Response.Time[30 Seconds]	-0.296537	0.014854	-19.96	<.0001*
Remote.Monitor[No]	-0.42619	0.009964	-42.77	<.0001*
Remote.Monitor[Yes]	0.4261905	0.009964	42.77	<.0001*

FIGURE 4.6.2 Conjoint estimation results with retrieved parameter estimates. The estimates for each factor sum to zero since effects coding was used. For example, the sum of the Price parameter estimates is $0.5795094 + (-0.199567) + (-0.379942) = 0$.

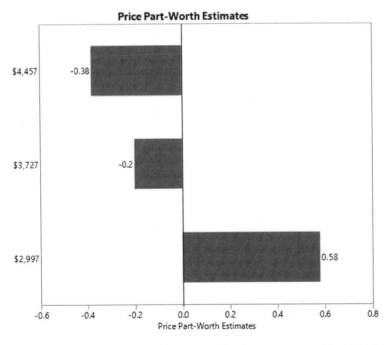

FIGURE 4.6.3 Price part–worth estimates for the generator problem. The best price is the lowest, as should be expected.

Expanded Estimates

Nominal factors expanded to all levels

Term	Estimate	Std Error	t Ratio	Prob>|t|
Intercept	8.3204425	0.067707	122.89	<.0001*
Price	-0.000657	0.000018	-36.59	<.0001*
Watts[11K]	-0.200678	0.015064	-13.32	<.0001*
Watts[16K]	-0.481053	0.015064	-31.93	<.0001*
Watts[20K]	0.6817316	0.014834	45.96	<.0001*
Response.Time[10 Seconds]	-1.541659	0.015064	-102.34	<.0001*
Response.Time[15 Seconds]	1.8781097	0.015064	124.67	<.0001*
Response.Time[30 Seconds]	-0.33645	0.014834	-22.68	<.0001*
Remote.Monitor[No]	-0.42619	0.010156	-41.96	<.0001*
Remote.Monitor[Yes]	0.4261905	0.010156	41.96	<.0001*

FIGURE 4.6.4 Conjoint estimation results with a continuous price. Price has the expected sign, while the estimates for the other factors sum to 0.0 as before.

4.7   Utility calculations

We can calculate total utility using the part-worth estimates. The highest total utility is the combination of attribute part-worths that are the "best" or highest. The highest part-worths for each attribute are shown in Table 4.13. The highest total utility is

$$Utility = 5.87 + 0.57 + 0.72 + 1.86 + 0.43$$
$$= 9.45.$$

The lowest total utility is similarly found as $5.87 - 0.38 - 0.50 - 1.56 - 0.43 = 3.00$.

The utilities, incidentally, can be found using the factor cube previously shown in Figure 4.5.2. That cube had three factors, whereas the generator problem has four, so one cube is drawn for each level of the remote monitoring factor, which are just *Yes* and *No*. Figure 4.7.1 shows cubes for the estimated total utilities for each combination of attribute levels of the generator design.

4.8   Analysis

Some typical or standard analyses are done using the estimated part-worth utilities. These are discussed in this section.

4.8.1   Part-worth summary plots

The part-worths are typically plotted either as line or bar charts. An example is shown in Figure 4.6.3. Another display shows the part-worth utilities for each level of each attribute as in Figure 4.8.1.

TABLE 4.13 Estimated part-worths for the generator problem. These are the highest values from Figure 4.6.2.

Attribute	Level	Best part-worth
Price	$2997	0.57
Watts	20 kW	0.72
Response Time	15 seconds	1.86
Remote Monitoring	Yes	0.43

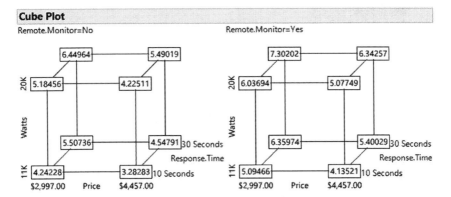

FIGURE 4.7.1 The estimated total utilities are shown for each combination of attribute levels. Notice that intermediate levels of some attributes are not shown.

4.8.2 Attribute importances

You may want to know the variability of total utility. One measure of variability is the range, which is simply the maximum total utility minus the minimum total utility: $9.45 - 3.00 = 6.45$. This alone is not very informative. What contributes to this range? The contributions can be found by extending the simple range calculation to include the part-worths on the right-hand side. This is illustrated as

$$9.45 = 5.87 + 0.57 + 0.72 + 1.86 + 0.43$$
$$-3.00 = 5.87 - 0.38 - 0.50 - 1.56 - 0.43$$
$$6.45 = 0.00 + 0.95 + 1.22 + 3.42 + 0.86.$$

Be careful how the negative signs are handled.

Clearly, the range for the total utility is the sum of the ranges for the factors, with the constant term dropping out. Dividing by the total utility range gives the contribution of each factor to the total range and these contributions sum to 1.0. Each contribution is sometimes called an *attribute importance* and are usually expressed as percentages. Figure 4.8.2 is a typical graph of the importances for the Pricing Scenario. Response Time is clearly the most important factor, followed by Watts. These two make sense because, in an emergency, the power should be restored

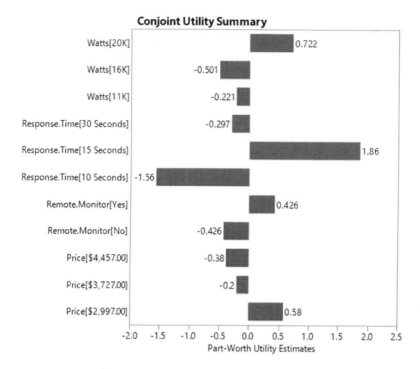

FIGURE 4.8.1 The estimated part-worth utilities can be displayed for each level of each attribute.

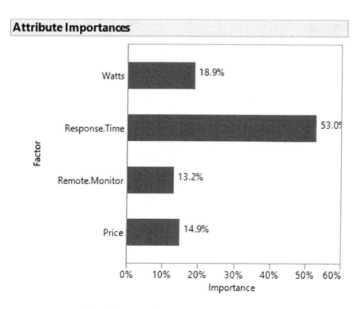

FIGURE 4.8.2 Conjoint attribute importances are the percentage contributions of each attribute to the range of the total utility estimates. Notice that Response Time is the most important contributor to the utility range.

Effect Summary

Source	LogWorth		PValue
Response.Time	1595.139		0.00000
Watts	430.816		0.00000
Remote.Monitor	336.244		0.00000
Price	293.620		0.00000

Effect Tests

Source	Nparm	DF	Sum of Squares	F Ratio	Prob > F
Price	2	2	720.7398	785.6324	<.0001*
Watts	2	2	1137.1609	1239.546	<.0001*
Response.Time	2	2	8287.3258	9033.484	<.0001*
Remote.Monitor	1	1	839.1690	1829.449	<.0001*

FIGURE 4.8.3 The conjoint attributes or effects are tested for statistical significance. The bar chart is the p-value for each attribute plotted on a log to the base 10 scale (and negated), called a logWorth. The bars are in descending order of importance. The vertical blue line shows $-log_{10}(0.01) = 2$, so any bar that exceeds 2 on the logWorth scale is significant at the 0.01 level.

quickly and enough power should be generated to handle the whole house. Price is third.

Another way to assess the importance of the attributes is to test the statistical significance of each effect (i.e., attribute) in the model. This is an F-test of significance. The results are shown in Figure 4.8.3. The F-test p-values are all very small, which makes them difficult to use to rank the attributes, but they can be transformed to make them more usable. One transformation is to a logWorth scale, which is $-log_{10}(p-value)$. Log_{10} is used because it was found through experimentation to give the best rendering. The negative sign merely converts the log_{10} value to a positive number, since the log_{10} of a number between 0 and 1 is negative. The logWorths are shown in the report along with a bar chart of the values. The vertical line plotted at a logWorth of 2.0 is for a 0.01 level of significance since $2 = -log_{10}(0.01)$. This is a very strict criterion for most market research studies, which typically use 0.05. In this case, the vertical line would be drawn further to the left at 1.3 $(= -log_{10}(0.05))$. The vertical line as shown is still a good benchmark for judging significance. From this perspective, you can see that Response Time and Watts are the most important features, agreeing with the attribute importances chart in Figure 4.8.2.

4.8.3 Elasticities

Elasticity calculations differ depending on the specification of the price variable. If it is discrete, then some extra calculations are necessary. The reason is that different combinations of prices and other attribute settings must be tried to gauge the effects on the response variable, the elasticities being calculated based on how much the response changes. If the price is treated as continuous, then a separate

TABLE 4.14 Total utilities for the generator problem at its three price points. These are the highest values with the other three attributes set at their best levels as determined by their highest part-worth values. The calculations include the intercept since total utility is calculated.

Price point	Total utility
$2297	9.45
$3727	8.68
$4457	8.50

regression model is recommended that produces the elasticity automatically. The two approaches are shown in the following two subsections.

In either case, a *base case* scenario is needed. The base case is the one to which all others will be compared. It is sometimes called the *most likely view*, or the *status quo*, or the *current market situation*. Suppose the base case for the Pricing Scenario is the best combination of attribute levels, which you know has a total utility of 9.45.

Discrete price case

For the Pricing Scenario, assume that the base case is the best combination of attribute levels based on the part-worths. The only thing that will change is the price. The total utility values at the three price points are shown in Table 4.14.

The elasticity is calculated using the arc elasticity formula in (81). Notice that the price part is $P_L - P_H$, so that the price points are consistent with the utility points.

$$\eta = \frac{\dfrac{U_H - U_L}{(U_H + U_L)/2}}{\dfrac{P_L - P_H}{(P_L + P_H)/2}}. \tag{81}$$

Substituting the relevant numbers from Table 4.14, you get

$$\eta = \frac{\dfrac{9.45 - 8.50}{(9.45 + 8.50)/2}}{\dfrac{2297 - 4457}{(2297 + 4457)/2}}$$

$$= -\frac{0.1058}{0.6396}$$

$$= -0.1655.$$

This generator combination is inelastic. The revenue elasticity from Chapter 2 is $1 + \eta = 1 + (-0.1655) = 0.8345$.

Another approach to calculating the elasticity is to run a simple regression on the three sets of data points in Table 4.14. The best model form to use is (82).

$$U = \beta_0 P^{\beta_1}. \tag{82}$$

This is a *constant elasticity model*. To see where this comes from, consider that you want to have an elasticity such that $\eta_P^U = c$, where η_P^U is the elasticity of U with respect to the price and c is a constant. Given the definition of an elasticity from Chapter 2, you want

$$\frac{dU}{U} = c \times \frac{dP}{P}. \tag{83}$$

Define $c = \beta_1$. A solution to (83) is

$$\ln(U) = c \times \ln(P) + \gamma$$

where γ is a new constant that could be defined as $\gamma = \ln(\beta_0)$.[6] Exponentiating both sides of this solution and using the definition of γ yields

$$U = e^{\ln(\beta_0)} \times P^{\beta_1} = \beta_0 \times P^{\beta_1}$$

using the fact that $e^{\ln(X)} = X$.[7] Reverting back to log form, you have

$$\ln(U) = \beta_0 + \beta_1 \times \ln(P). \tag{84}$$

This is the log-log regression model.

It is easy to show that β_1 is the elasticity. Differentiating both sides of (84), you get

$$\frac{1}{U} = \beta_1 \times \frac{1}{P} \times dP.$$

Solving for β_1, you get

$$\beta_1 = \frac{P}{U} \times \frac{dU}{dP}.$$

In other words, $\eta_P^U = \beta_1$. Taking the natural logs of the total utilities and price points and regressing the log of utility on the log of price, you get an estimated elasticity of -0.163, which is very close to the arc elasticity value. The regression results are shown in Figure 4.8.4.

Continuous price case

For the continuous case, the elasticity is given by (85).

$$\eta = \frac{\bar{P}}{\bar{U}} \times \beta_{Price} \tag{85}$$

Response Log[Utility]

Whole Model

Summary of Fit

RSquare	0.994236
RSquare Adj	0.988472
Root Mean Square Error	0.006024
Mean of Response	2.182367
Observations (or Sum Wgts)	3

Analysis of Variance

Source	DF	Sum of Squares	Mean Square	F Ratio
Model	1	0.00625973	0.006260	172.4852
Error	1	0.00003629	0.000036	**Prob > F**
C. Total	2	0.00629602		0.0484*

Parameter Estimates

Term	Estimate	Std Error	t Ratio	Prob>|t|
Intercept	3.5072826	0.100942	34.75	0.0183*
Log[Price]	-0.163134	0.012421	-13.13	0.0484*

FIGURE 4.8.4 The data in Table 4.14 were modeled using the natural log of utility and price. The estimated parameter is the elasticity estimate: −0.163.

where β_{Price} is the estimated price coefficient. From Figure 4.6.4, this is −0.0006. The mean price is simply \$3727 for this problem. The mean utility is the mean across all possible utility values. This requires that all possible combinations of the attribute levels, including the price points, be developed and then the average of the resulting total utilities can be found. There are 54 combinations. It is simple to write a program to determine this mean. The mean utility is 5.87, so the elasticity is−\$37275.87 × (−0.0006) = −0.38.

4.9   Other conjoint approaches

This chapter focused on using a preference scale for rating each alternative displayed on a card. If a consumer is shown 12 cards, then he/she is shown 12 alternatives and there are 12 preference ratings. These preference ratings are viewed as being continuous measures, hence the use of OLS for estimation. Other approaches are:

1. *Ranking*: A consumer sees all alternatives at once and is asked to place them in sorted (i.e., ranked) order. These data are analyzed by an estimation method

called *exploded logit*, which will not be discussed here (see [7]). Ranking may be difficult for consumers if there are many alternatives, so that the ranking task becomes a challenge.

2. *Constant sum*: A consumer sees all alternatives at once and is asked to allocate a fixed sum (points, chips, dollars), usually 100, to each alternative based on the strength of their preference for each alternative. Like the ranking task, if there are too many alternatives, allocation of a constant sum can become more than the consumers can handle. Nonetheless, the data could be analyzed by OLS. Better yet, the allocations can be converted to proportions (obviously by dividing each allocation by the constant sum, which is, again, usually 100) and using a beta regression approach. See [15] for a discussion of beta regression models.

3. *Self-explicated*: A consumer sees each level of all attributes and is asked to rate the desirability of each level; they also see each attribute and are asked to rate the importance of each attribute. The two measures, desirability and importance, are multiplied to yield an estimate of the part-worth for each level of each attribute. In essence, the desirabilities are weighted by the importances. This is sometimes done when the number of attributes and levels is very large (see [19], [48], and [101]).

4. There are also other designs that are succinctly described in [101].

4.10   Software

There are two parts or phases to a conjoint study: the treatment design and the estimation. For the treatment design, R, SAS, SPSS, and JMP can easily create the needed designs. R has a package called AlgDesign. For estimation, if OLS is used, then any statistical package can be used. For a beta regression, R has the package betareg.

4.11   Summary

This chapter highlighted the principles for a conjoint study. In particular, the ideas behind an experimental design and effects coding were emphasized. These concepts will be used in the next chapter on discrete choice analysis. There will be some modifications, however, because the discrete choice problem has a different focus and set of equations. As you will see, the discrete choice problem is concerned with estimating a choice probability, while the conjoint problem is concerned with estimating a rating (or something similar).

Notes

1 JMP, for instance, uses the number of runs for the saturated design plus 4, hence the 12 noted in the text.
2 This example is modeled after [10].
3 See [41].

4 When surveys were done with paper questionnaires, respondents indicated choices by checking boxes. Modern online surveys still have boxes.
5 Some software will drop one of the variables for you and then proceed with estimation. In effect, the software chooses the base. However, this may not be the base you want, even though technically any base can be selected. So, it is best to be aware of the problem and select your own base.
6 This solution results from integrating both sides of the equation: $\int_{\mathbf{R}^+} dL/L = c \times \int_{\mathbf{R}^+} dP/P$. The integrations are for the positive set of real numbers, $\mathbf{R}^+ = \{x \in \mathbb{R} : x \geq 0\}$, since neither price nor quantity can be negative. They could, of course, be zero. The γ is the integration constant.
7 Let $Y = e^{\ln(X)}$. Then $\ln(Y) = \ln(X)$. Exponentiating both sides yields $Y = X$.

5

DISCRETE CHOICE MODELS

In this chapter, I introduce the next member of the choice model family: discrete choice models. These models have gained in popularity in the past few years because they have two nice properties, although one is a theoretical concern. First, discrete choice models mimic real-world competitive markets because they ask consumers to make choices (hence the name), rather than just provide a preference rating as in conjoint. Consumers make choices from among two or more products on a store shelf every day, so the discrete choice framework is perfect for studying what consumers always do. The store shelf metaphor can be viewed as a set of products – a *choice set* – from which the consumer must select. Conjoint is a bit unrealistic because choices per se from a choice set are not involved; in fact, there is no choice set.

Second, discrete choice is based on well-accepted utility maximization concepts in economic theory; conjoint, despite the use of the word "utility," is not – it is just a regression model. This is of concern to academics, not practitioners, but nonetheless it does say something about the foundations of the approach. See [47] for a discussion of this point.

This chapter is divided into ten sections. Section 1 first presents a Pricing Scenario as a choice situation for pricing strategies. The scenario will be used throughout the chapter. Section 2 discusses terminology. Section 3 lays the foundations for the experimental design used with this type of problem. Section 4 discusses estimation and interpretation. Sections 5–7 discuss estimation and design issues, while Section 8 emphasizes analysis using the estimated take rates. Section 9 discusses software that can be used to design and estimate the models introduced in the previous sections. Section 10 is the summary.

5.1 Pricing Scenario

This section describes a Pricing Scenario used throughout this chapter. Terms, definitions, and concepts will be introduced and developed using this scenario.

5.1.1 The pricing problem

Drones, more formerly called *small unmanned aerial systems* (sUASs), are becoming more popular and widespread in a variety of areas. Examples include hobbyists, military, agricultural and livestock management (e.g., for surveying crops and cattle), industry (e.g., for examining industrial plants), and utilities (e.g., for examining power lines). There are many issues associated with sUASs, such as privacy, mid-air collisions with commercial and military aircraft, and terrorist and criminal uses, to mention just a few.

A small manufacturer of sUASs, FlyDrone, Inc., targets hobbyists. The company has several products that are considered second tier by most hobbyists in a market with two other major drone manufacturers. The FlyDrone, Inc., marketing team plans to produce and sell a new drone model that has six attributes or characteristics that the team believes are important to the hobbyist space and will thus move the company to the market leader position. The six attributes and their levels, plus the dominant brands in the market, are:

- Price: $79.99, $99.99, $119.99;
- Maximum Flight Time (in minutes): 5, 7, 9;
- Integrated GPS: Yes, No;
- Integrated Camera: Yes, No;
- Video Resolution: 640 × 480, 720 × 576, 1280 × 720;
- Brand: FlyDrone, Inc., Birdie, Inc., SkyFly, Inc.

The team, under the advisement of the marketing research manager plus an outside consultant hired to develop the marketing and pricing strategy, decided to use a discrete choice model framework to determine the best price and feature settings to offer. A study was commissioned to survey hobbyists about their preferences for sUASs and the best price to charge. The hobbyists' willingness to pay for each feature was critically important to the team.

5.2 Types of choice models

There are two types of discrete choice studies: *stated preference* and *revealed preference*. In a stated preference study, consumers are presented with alternative products that are artificially created, meaning that the products do not necessarily exist in the market, although some configurations may eventually be introduced. The products are presented to consumers in sets called *choice sets* with several sets in a study. The products comprising the sets are called *alternatives*. The presentation is part of a survey in which consumers are asked to state which alternative in each choice set they prefer the most (i.e., which one they would buy). So they state their preference.

Revealed preference studies also have choice sets, but these are not artificial. They are, if you wish, the actual store shelves. Consumers are not asked to select one item from the set during a survey – they actually make a selection in the market. The selection could be recorded using scanner technology or by direct observation using an ethnographic approach. So consumers reveal their preferences by their actions.

You could have a labeled or unlabeled study design. A labeled study has descriptive, meaningful labels or names for the alternatives such as car, bus, and train for a commuter mode study or specific brand names for a consumer product study. An unlabeled study uses nondescript labels such as "Option 1" and "Option 2." For a labeled study, the labels convey meaning, while they do not in an unlabeled design; clearly, "Option 1" has no meaning other than the fact that this alternative is the first one. In an unlabeled study, items such as commuter mode and brand name would be treated as attributes no different than price, form, flavor, and so forth.

The Pricing Scenario is a stated preference, unlabeled study.

5.3 The choice model – Utility maximization

Chapter 2 summarized neoclassical consumer demand theory. This postulates that a consumer chooses a combination of goods that maximizes his or her utility when he or she is faced with a budget constraint. A major assumption is that the goods are infinitely divisible. The solution to the constrained optimization problem yields an optimal rate of consumption. The emphasis is on the word "rate," since the goods are consumed each period (e.g., weekly) so that consumption is viewed as continuous. This is acceptable for many goods and services consumers purchase, but not all. There are many cases for which the goods are purchased in discrete units – in the simplest case, only one is purchased. Consumers then make discrete choices, not continuous ones. The theory from Chapter 2 has to be modified.

In discrete choice situations, a consumer again chooses a product that maximizes his or her utility. This chapter will develop the foundations of discrete choice models from this concept of utility maximization. The nature of utility will be explored with an emphasis on the stochastic properties of utility. The stochastic aspect reflects a distinction between group and individual variation (i.e., consumer homogeneity and heterogeneity). In a sense, this distinction between homogeneous and heterogeneous sets the stage for the price discrimination methods discussed in Chapter 8.

5.3.1 Consumer homogeneity

Homogeneous market groups are defined as groups of individuals who face the same values for some observed independent variables. For instance, if price, income, and age are three observed independent variables, then a homogeneous group is defined such that all its members face the same price for the alternatives, have the same income, and are the same age. Clearly, such groups may be costly to develop empirically. They are, however, convenient theoretically since they allow you to introduce random variation among the members of the groups.

The use of homogeneous groups is not uncommon in economics, marketing, market research, and pricing. Market segmentation and price segmentation (i.e., price discrimination) are widely used because of this. In these schemes, consumers are assigned to homogeneous groups, but each group is different from the next in order to reflect heterogeneity among consumers. Price segmentation will be discussed in Chapter 8, so this notion of groups will be further developed.

Suppose the market is divided into S groups or segments so that consumers are homogeneous within a segment but heterogeneous among the segments. The collection of all segments is $\mathcal{S} = 1, 2, \ldots, S$. The number of segments (i.e., the size or cardinality of $\mathcal{S}$) is $|\mathcal{S}|$. Each segment $s \in \mathcal{S}$ has a size n_s. If the total market size is N consumers, then

$$\sum_{s=1}^{|S|} n_s = N.$$

If $|S| = 1$, then there is only one segment, which is the entire market, so $n_s = N$. If $|S| = 2$, then there are two segments. This case would correspond to the market organization for the third-degree price discrimination discussed in Chapter 3.

5.3.2 Utility specification

Neoclassical consumer demand theory is based on the concept of utility, an index of the "satisfaction" that the individual receives from consuming various combinations of goods. It is a function of the goods that can be purchased, although it can be written as a function of price and income so that utility is then indirect utility. Demand functions can then be found by applying Roy's Identity to the inverse function, thus avoiding any optimization problems.

For discrete choice models, individuals are assumed to possess an indirect utility function for the various alternatives they face. This is a matter of convenience because the budget constraint and, hence, the problem of constrained optimization do not have to be explicitly considered. This indirect utility function for discrete alternatives is a function of prices, income, and, as noted in Chapter 2, other items that may affect choice.

The mean utility for a group $s \in \mathcal{S}$ for alternative or product j is the expected value of the distribution of utilities for product j of the members of the segment. Let V_{sj} be this expected value. It is represented as a linear function of the attributes of the alternatives

$$V_{sj} = X_{sj}\beta_s \tag{86}$$

where X_{sj} is a vector of attributes of the good (e.g., price, color, size) and characteristics of the group (e.g., income). The β_s weight is a vector of part-worths assumed to be constant within the segment, but varies from one segment to the next. Mean utility is conditioned on this constant part-worths vector. This is important because only one set of parameters has to be estimated for a segment. If $|S| = 1$, then $\beta_s = \beta$ and there is only one set of parameters for the market. This will be changed in a later chapter. The mean utility for a group is sometimes called *systematic utility* and, as a mean, it is the utility of the representative consumer of the segment. I will use this terminology going forward.

Although all the members of a segment face the same values of the independent variables, they will not all choose the same alternative. The systematic utility only represents the average behavior. An individual consumer's choice depends not only on the observed variables of systematic utility, but also on unobserved variables. The latter may be attributed to the idiosyncrasies of the consumer, unobserved attributes of the consumer, or unobserved characteristics of the alternatives as perceived by the consumer. These unobserved variables can be combined into a single function. Since this function influences choice, it is also part of the utility function.

Assume that a consumer's total utility function is separable into the systematic utility and a part representing unobserved characteristics. Since the function is separable, I will assume that arguments of the systematic utility are independent of those of the unobserved part. This unobserved part varies over the members of the group and can take on any value depending on the individual chosen; the unobserved part is a random variable. Any consumer's utility can be represented as the sum of systematic utility and this random variable, so total utility is also a random variable. Total utility is then written as

$$U_{i(s)j} = V_{sj} + \varepsilon_{i(s)j} \tag{87}$$

where $\varepsilon_{i(s)j}$ is the random part of utility for consumer i, who is a member of or is nested in group s, for alternative j.

This formulation of total utility is the same form as any model in statistics. A basic regression model is $Y_i = \beta_0 + \beta_1 X_i + \varepsilon_i$ where $E(Y_i) = \mu = \beta_0 + \beta_1 X_i$ based on the usual assumptions that $\varepsilon_i \sim (0, \sigma^2)$ and $COV(\varepsilon_i, \varepsilon_{i'}) = 0$. Therefore, you can write $Y_i = \mu + \varepsilon_i$. The same holds for analysis of variance models, although these models are just special cases of regression models. Fundamentally, any linear model is a decomposition of data into a mean, or signal, plus noise, where the signal is the linear combination of the explanatory variables. There is a *link* or *link function* between the mean of Y and the linear combination of the explanatory variables. There are many link functions. For the linear regression model, the link is the identity function (see [78]). The goal for any statistical model is to find the signal by minimizing the noise.

Since all members of a group have the same mean utility but the unobserved part varies over individuals, only one member of the group needs to be observed in order to determine the choice probabilities for that group. This follows from the stochastic nature of the unobserved part of utility. In what follows, only a representative from each group will be considered; "individual" and "representative individual" will be synonymous.

It should be noted that this specification of "individual" economizes on data collection. Data are not needed on a sample of members of each group, just on one individual from each group. Variation across all others in the group, variation that can affect choice, is taken care of by the probability distribution on the unobserved part of utility. The purpose of the homogeneous group was to allow the specification of systematic utility and a random part of utility, which are later used to derive choice probabilities.

If there is only one group, which is the entire market, then the average is the average for the population and the individual consumer will deviate from the average by a random factor. In this case, the subscript s is not needed, so that V_j is the mean and $U_{ij} = V_j + \varepsilon_{ij}$. This is reflected in the constancy of β for the market.

5.3.3 Utility maximization

Let $j = 1,\ldots,J$ be discrete alternatives arranged in choice sets presented to each consumer in the market. Let $i = 1,\ldots,C$ be representative consumers. Also, let U_{ij} be the indirect utility function of individual i for alternative j in a choice set. Then individual i will choose alternative j over another alternative k in the same set if

$$U_{ij} > U_{ik} \tag{88}$$

which is the appropriate choice calculus mentioned previously.

5.4 Choice probabilities

Since the utility is a random variable, you can describe the probability that j will be chosen by i if (88) holds. Probability is the appropriate concept because of the random variation due to the ε_{ij}. The utilities U_{ij} and U_{ik} are random variables, so there is a probability distribution associated with the rule in (88). That is,

$$Pr_i(j) = Pr(U_{ij} > U_{ik}) \tag{89}$$

where $Pr_i(j)$ is the probability that individual i will choose alternative j. Since each utility is the sum of the systematic utility and a random component, you can write (89) as

$$\begin{aligned} Pr_i(j) &= Pr(V_{ij} + \varepsilon_{ij} > V_{ik} + \varepsilon_{ik}) \\ &= Pr(\varepsilon_{ij} - \varepsilon_{ik} < V_{ik} - V_{ij}) \end{aligned} \tag{90}$$

$$= Pr(\varepsilon_{ij} - \varepsilon_{ik} < V_{ik} - V_{ij}). \tag{91}$$

It is clear that this choice probability is a cumulative probability distribution function that depends on the specification of a distribution function for the unknown random part of utility, ε. In OLS regression, normality is assumed so that $\varepsilon \sim \mathcal{N}(0, \sigma^2)$ with the additional assumption that $COV(\varepsilon, \varepsilon') = 0$; that is, any two disturbance terms are unrelated. As noted by [23], this covariance assumption may not hold for two products if the two are in close proximity on a preference scale; that is, if they are close substitutes. The implication of this will be explored below.

Three distribution functions have been proposed implying different choice probability formulations:

- Linear;
- Normal;
- Extreme value type I (*Gumbel*).

See [114] for a discussion of these plus others. The linear distribution results in a linear probability model, which is just an OLS model with a discrete dependent variable. If the dependent variable, Y, is binary with values 0 and 1 and you assume $Pr(Y = 1) = p$ so $Pr(Y = 0) = 1 - p$, then the expected value of this dependent variable is p. As an OLS model, you have $Y = \beta_0 + \beta_1 X + \varepsilon$ and $E(Y) = \beta_0 + \beta_1 X = p$ with an identity link, hence the name *linear probability model*. This model has several well-known problems, not the least of which is that it can predict a value for Y outside the 0–1 interval, which is certainly unacceptable.

The normal distribution results in a model called the *probit*. This is a very important model for many reasons, but it has a major drawback. It is computationally challenging even with modern software and computers because it requires numeric integration to estimate the unknown parameters. This is doable for small problems, but a challenge for larger ones.

The *extreme value type I* (EVI) or *Gumbel* distribution is a mathematical convenience in the sense that it is easier to work with. More importantly, however, it results in a closed-form solution called the *logit model* that is tractable and easy to explain. In addition, it has been shown that if the unknown parts of utility are independently and identically distributed EVI, then a "logit" expression for the choice probabilities results, while a normal distribution produces a "probit" expression. I will only focus on the logit expression since this is the most commonly used in pricing research. The specification of a distribution function distinguishes one choice probability model from another. Up to this specification, however, the models are all identical in the sense that they all come from the same underlying utility maximization assumption in (88) (see [145] for discussions).

5.4.1   Digression: The EVI distribution

There is actually a family of extreme value distributions so the family is called the *generalized extreme value distribution* (GEV) family. The cumulative distribution function is given by

$$F(x; \mu, \sigma, \xi) = exp\left\{-\left[1 + \xi\left(\frac{x - \mu}{\sigma}\right)\right]^{-\frac{1}{\xi}}\right\}$$

where μ is a location parameter, σ is a scale parameter, and ξ is a shape parameter. The probability density function is given by[1]

$$ f(x;\mu,\sigma,\xi) = \frac{1}{\sigma} exp\left[-\left(\frac{x-\mu}{\sigma}\right)\right] exp\left\{-exp\left[-\left(\frac{x-\mu}{\sigma}\right)\right]\right\}. $$

For differently shaped parameter settings, three special cases result that are most used in practice, albeit for different applications. In particular, if $\xi = 0$, then the EVI or *Gumbel distribution* results. In this case, the cumulative distribution function is

$$ F(x;\mu,\sigma) = e^{-e^{-\left(\frac{x-\mu}{\sigma}\right)}}. $$

Conventionally in choice modeling, $\mu = 0$ and $\sigma = 1$ so the standard cumulative distribution function is

$$ F(x) = e^{-e^{-x}} \tag{92} $$

and the probability density function is

$$ f(x) = e^{-x}e^{-e^{-x}}. \tag{93} $$

5.4.2 The conditional logit choice probability

It was shown in [145] that the probability statement shown in (90) in conjunction with the distribution function (92) can be written as

$$ Pr_i(j) = \frac{e^{V_{ij}}}{\sum_{k=1}^{J} e^{V_{ik}}}. \tag{94} $$

This is the *choice probability* for a discrete choice and is a function solely of the systematic utilities. It is the probability that any individual selected at random, possessing certain characteristics and facing a set of alternatives with certain attributes, will select alternative j over any other. Since (94) is a probability that the individual consumer will choose alternative j, $\sum_{j=1}^{J} Pr_i(j) = 1$ for each individual. This probability is a *take rate*, or *acceptance rate*, or *share of preference*. I use these terms interchangeably. See [166] for another derivation of this choice probability.

The systematic utility is a linear function of the attributes. In this formulation, the part-worths are constants for all consumers as noted above. This means that the weight placed on an attribute is the same no matter which consumer is studied. The systematic utility is said to be conditioned on the constant parameter.

The overall model is called a *logistic model* or *multinomial logit model* (MNL) or *conditional logit model* (Clogit). Although the name "multinomial logit" is often used, it should be avoided because there is another econometric model form with the same name that does not have constant parameters. The one I am considering does. I prefer the last name – conditional logit – because it emphasizes the conditionality of the parameters – they are constant – and avoids confusion.

The formal problem of estimating the unknown parameters and hence actually calculating the choice probabilities relies on maximum likelihood procedures. I will assume that the estimated parameters are known and thus turn my attention to the use of the choice probabilities given by (94). In particular, I will consider how demand and elasticities are calculated and the potential drawbacks of using (94).

5.4.3   Choice probability properties

The choice probability for the logit model is a function of observed variables via the systematic utility function. Since the individual's utility function is an indirect utility function, the systematic utility is also indirect. It is, therefore, a function of prices, income, and other variables that may affect choice. These other variables are called *attributes* or *features* of the products. This section will consider what variables enter the systematic utility function and how.

The systematic utilities are functions of observed variables associated with alternative j. Since $Pr_i(j)$ is a function of all the systematic utilities, then it is a function of variables that vary over all alternatives. The first requirement for a variable, therefore, is its variability over alternatives. The reason will be clear shortly. The second requirement for estimation purposes is that the variable varies over individuals.

The two most important variables affecting consumer choice are price and income. Since the alternatives are distinct, their associated prices are distinct. Prices certainly vary over alternatives. For a given problem, prices may not vary across individuals. This may be rectified by interacting price with another variable that does vary across individuals; they are case-invariant. For instance, in a revealed preference transportation study for a metropolitan area, light rail transit fares would be the same for all commuters in a sample, but differ from bus fares. Fares could be divided by commute time for each member of the sample, giving the time cost of a transit ride. Since commute time would vary across individuals, time cost would also vary.

Equivalent differences property

Income varies over individuals but not over alternatives. To see the effect of this, let P_{ij} be the price consumer i sees for alternative j and let Y_i be the consumer's income. Clearly Y_i does not vary by alternatives. The systematic utility can be written as a linear function of these two variables: $V_{ij} = \beta_1 P_{ij} + \beta_2 Y_i$, where β_1 and β_2 are the respective constant part-worths. Then, from (94), you have

$$Pr_i(J) = \frac{e^{\beta_1 P_{ij} + \beta_2 Y_i}}{\sum e^{\beta_1 P_{ik} + \beta_2 Y_i}} \qquad (95)$$

$$= \frac{e^{\beta_2 P_{ij}} \times e^{\beta_1 Y_i}}{e^{\beta_1 Y_i} \times \sum e^{\beta_2 P_{ij}}} \qquad (96)$$

$$= \frac{e^{\beta_1 P_{ij}}}{\sum e^{\beta_1 P_{ik}}}. \qquad (97)$$

This property of a conditional logit model is sometimes called the *Equivalent Differences Property* (see [57] and [40]). Basically, it means that if a constant is added to each systematic utility, that constant will cancel from the probability formula. This is important because it says that any variable that does not vary with the attributes – in other words, that it is constant with respect to the attributes – has no effect on the take rate. A good example is income, as just shown. The same holds for age, gender, ethnicity, and so forth. It also holds for a constant or intercept term, which is why the systematic utility shown above does not have one.

The way to correct the problem is to interact income with another variable that does vary by alternative. This second variable may be an alternative specific dummy variable (called an *Alternative Specific Constant* or ASC) that is 1 for one alternative and 0 for the others. This variable is important in its own right, as will be explained shortly. By multiplying an ASC and income, a new variable is created that takes the value of income for one alternative and is 0 for the others. Of course, several ASCs can be defined so that a new variable takes the value of income for more than one alternative and is 0 for the others. At least one alternative must have a 0 value or else an indeterminate problem results. The definition of the ASC is up to the analyst. Theory or experimentation can act as guides.

The ASC can be used on its own. The unobserved part of utility is supposed to represent all the unobserved characteristics of the alternative or individual that may affect choice. It may be felt that some of these characteristics are too important to be ignored. Since they cannot be observed, a way is needed to reflect them. The ASCs serve the purpose of reflecting unobserved characteristics. For J alternatives, there are at most $J - 1$ ASC dummies.

In summary, variables can enter the systematic utility function if they:

1. Vary over individuals;
2. Vary over alternatives;
3. Reflect characteristics of alternatives or individuals.

The Independence of Irrelevant Alternatives property

To motivate a second important property, consider the ratio of two take rates – one for alternative j and one for alternative k. Since the denominator for both take rates is the same, the denominators cancel in the ratio. Only the numerators remain, which can be written as the exponentiated value of the difference in the systematic utilities as shown in (98).

$$\frac{Pr_i(j)}{Pr_i(k)} = e^{V_{ij}-V_{ik}}. \tag{98}$$

This shows that the ratio does not depend on any other alternative, just the two involved in the ratio. The ratio is the odds of selecting alternative j over alternative k. If alternative k is interpreted as a base product – maybe a base case, leading product, or existing product – then the ratio is the odds of taking product j relative to the base case. The odds are a function solely of the attributes of the two products, nothing else.

This result is called the *Independence of Irrelevant Alternatives* or simply IIA. In choosing between two products, where one could be interpreted as a base case, only the features of these two count; features of other products do not.[2] This actually makes intuitive sense. If a consumer takes his or her standard product off a store shelf but then suddenly picks up another to compare the two, only the features of the two products – their relative size, color, fragrance, and of course price – matter. A third or fourth product is not part of this comparison. They are irrelevant.

The IIA property can be useful, and an issue. It is useful because the choice set does not have to be large. Because of the constancy of the part-worths, other products could always be added to an analysis post-data collection and estimation. Basically, you can always forecast the take rates for new products. It can be a problem, however, as illustrated by a famous example known as the *red bus–blue bus* problem. This section draws heavily from [57], [72], and [40].

Consider a classic example of a travel mode choice between a red bus and a car. There are no other alternatives. The choice probabilities are shown in Table 5.1. The odds of car to red bus is 2.333:

$$\frac{Pr(Car)}{Pr(Red\ Bus)} = \frac{0.70}{0.30}$$
$$= 2.333.$$

TABLE 5.1 These are the base probabilities for taking or selecting a car vs. a red bus.

Mode	Probability
Car	0.70
Red bus	0.30

TABLE 5.2 These are the probabilities suggested by intuition for taking or selecting a car vs. a red or blue bus. Notice that the car probability should be unchanged.

Mode	Probability
Car	0.70
Red bus	0.15
Blue bus	0.15

Consumers are more than twice as likely to select a car than a red bus.

Suppose a new bus is introduced exactly like the red one, except that it is blue. Pure intuition suggests that the take rate for the car should not change. If a consumer chose a bus before, why should he or she suddenly change his mode of transportation? The take rate for the red bus should be split 50–50 with the blue bus because the red bus riders now have a second bus choice. The color of the bus should not matter – except for those who really love blue and hate red or a car, an oddity you will not worry about. The new take rates should be those shown in Table 5.2.

This is where the IIA property becomes an issue because it states that the odds of 2.333 must still hold for the car to the red bus. This implies that the take rates must change for all three modes, not just two. Before the blue bus is introduced, you have

$$Pr^2_{Car} = 0.70 = \text{Share of Car with 2 modes}$$
$$Pr^2_{Red\ Bus} = 0.30 = \text{Share of Red Bus with 2 modes}$$
$$\text{Odds of Car to Red Bus} = 2.333$$

where the exponent "2" just refers to the two modes.[3]

After the blue bus is introduced, you now have a new statement for it. The symbols have been adjusted for this case by changing the exponent to "3" to reflect three modes. The odds are still the same at 2.333.

$$Pr^3_{Car} = \text{Share of Car with 3 modes}$$
$$Pr^3_{Red\ Bus} = \text{Share of Red Bus with 3 modes}$$
$$Pr^3_{Blue\ Bus} = \text{Share of Blue Bus with 3 modes}$$
$$\text{Odds of Car to Red Bus} = 2.333.$$

It is clear that with three modes you have the following set of equations:

$$Pr^3_{Car} + Pr^3_{Red\ Bus} + Pr^3_{BlueBus} = 1$$
$$Pr^3_{Red\ Bus} = Pr^3_{Blue\ Bus}$$
$$Pr^3_{Car} = 2.333 \times Pr^3_{Red\ Bus}.$$

In summary:

1. The sum of the three probabilities for the three-mode case must be 1.
2. The take rate for the two buses must be the same as suggested by intuition. Why would you expect otherwise?

3. Finally, since the odds for the car to the red bus must be fixed at 2.333, then the take rate for car must be 2.333 times the new take rate for the red bus.

These are three equations in three unknowns, the three takes rates, so they can be solved simultaneously for the take rates. A simple solution is found using

$$\begin{bmatrix} 1 & 1 & 1 \\ 0 & 1 & -1 \\ 1 & -2.333 & 0 \end{bmatrix} \times \begin{bmatrix} Pr^3_{Car} \\ Pr^3_{RedBus} \\ Pr^3_{BlueBus} \end{bmatrix} = \begin{bmatrix} 1 \\ 0 \\ 0 \end{bmatrix}.$$

The solution is

$$Pr^3_{Car} = 0.538$$
$$Pr^3_{Red\,Bus} = 0.231$$
$$Pr^3_{Blue\,Bus} = 0.231.$$

Notice that (1) the new take rates sum to 1, (2) the take rates for the two buses are the same, and (3) the odds of car to red bus are still 2.333 (at least within rounding for here). Incidentally, the odds for the red to blue bus are 1, indicating that these two are the same (i.e., there is no difference between the two buses, as suggested by intuition).

Table 5.3 shows that there is an estimation error if the Clogit model is used and the IIA property is ignored. This is potentially serious.

The IIA problem stems from the fact that the two buses are the same, except for color. They are perfect substitutes, which is what led to an intuitive notion that the car take rate should not change. This is the basis for the [23] observation about alternative products in close proximity on a preference scale. In this situation, you need to use another formulation of the model such as a *nested logit model*. In this formulation, products that are very similar would be nested together so that separate nests would have products that have different natures. For another classic example involving restaurants, there could be two major groupings: fast-food and fine dining. Wendy's, McDonald's, and Burger King would be nested together in the fast-food group, while any group of five-star

TABLE 5.3 Summary of the effect of introducing the blue bus and using the Clogit model and IIA as a restriction. Based on [57].

Mode	Without blue bus	With blue bus (intuitive)	With blue bus (Clogit)	Estimation error
Car	0.700	0.700	0.538	Under
Red bus	0.300	0.150	0.231	Over
Blue bus	NA	0.150	0.231	Over
Sum	1.000	1.000	1.000	

restaurants in midtown Manhattan would be in another nest. The consumer's decision problem is which type of restaurant to select and, given that type, which specific restaurant to visit. For most stated preference discrete choice studies, such nesting is not an issue.

5.4.4 The none option

In most real-life choice situations, consumers have the option to refrain from buying. They could continue to shop, stay with an old brand, or just wait to make a purchase. This is generically a *none* option, which should be included in the choice sets.

Since a *none* option, by definition, does not have any of the attributes used for the other alternatives, it cannot be included in the treatment design, but it can be included on choice cards that would be presented to consumers. Therefore, it should be clear that the *none* option does not have a systematic utility since it does not have any attributes. The systematic utility for a *none* alternative is zero.

The take rates have to be modified slightly to handle a *none* alternative. This is done by adding a "1" to the denominator of the take formula. This is equivalent to adding a systematic utility component that is zero since $e^0 = 1$. Basically, another choice option is added to the denominator sum so that

$$Pr_i(j) = \frac{e^{V_{ij}}}{e^0 + \sum_{k=1}^{J} e^{V_{ik}}}$$

$$= \frac{e^{V_{ij}}}{1 + \sum_{k=1}^{J} e^{V_{ik}}}.$$

The *none* take rate is this adjusted denominator divided into 1. The 1 in the numerator follows because it is supposed to be $e^{V_{ij}}$, but $V_{ij} = 0$ for the *none* option, so again you have $e^0 = 1$.

The take rates including a *none* alternative are then

$$Pr_i(j) = \begin{cases} \dfrac{e^{V_{ij}}}{1 + \sum_{k=1}^{J} e^{V_{ik}}} & j \neq None \\ \dfrac{1}{1 + \sum_{k=1}^{J} e^{V_{ik}}} & j = None \end{cases} \tag{99}$$

The sum of these adjusted take rates is still 1, as is easily verified. If a *none* option is included, then a constant can be added since it will not cancel. This constant is an ASC.

5.5 Estimation – Introduction

To estimate a choice model, you need to form the odds like the odds described above. If a *none* option is included, this is usually the base or denominator of the odds. Since the *none* does not have a systematic utility, the odds are just the exponentiated systematic utility for the numerator of the take rate.

The odds are a function of the linear combination of the attributes. So if you take the natural log of the odds, you get that linear combination. The log of the odds, called the *log odds* or *logit* for short (hence the name for the model), is the dependent variable in a regression model. The independent variables are the linear combinations of attributes. Regression per se is not used since more efficient methods are available. Generally, maximum likelihood methods are used, but it is not important to delve into the complexity of this method. Suffice it to say that some member of the regression family is used for estimation.

The attributes I just mentioned that are used in estimation are actually from the treatment design. So the design matrix is again an issue.

5.6 Treatment design: A Bayesian perspective

For a conjoint study, creating the design matrix was straightforward because it relied on what are called *linear design* concepts. This is the case because the conjoint model is linear; it is the OLS model. Unfortunately, the model for the discrete choice take rates is not linear; it is highly nonlinear. This means that the design principles I discussed earlier cannot be used.

At a very high level, the linear design method used for conjoint relies on the *variance–covariance matrix* of the part-worths. This matrix is used in the calculation of a D-optimality value. The variance–covariance matrix is independent of the part-worths, being just a function of the data that are the effects codes. The calculation of the D-optimal value is easy. Given the data, you can calculate it and then find the design matrix to give you the best part-worth estimates. This was what I did in the conjoint chapter.

This breaks down for the logit model because of the nonlinearity of the take rates as well as the fact that proportions (i.e., probabilities) are involved. This was not the case for conjoint. You now need the part-worth estimates to calculate the criterion measure to find the best design, but you need the criterion measure to find the part-worths. A circular problem is involved. This circularity is broken by using a Bayesian approach for developing the choice designs.

The Bayesian approach relies on prior means and variance–covariances. These priors are used to find the D-optimality value, which yields a design matrix for finding the part-worths. In a sense, you get the linear process that is easy to work with. Using the Bayesian approach, however, is a challenge. It involves randomly selecting values from a distribution, each time updating what is needed for finding the best or optimal design matrix. Needless to say, software easily handles this problem.

Design						
Choice Set	Price	Flight Time (Minutes)	Integrated GPS	Integrated Camera	Video Resolution	Brand
1	99.99	7	No	Yes	720x576	SkyFly Inc
1	79.99	5	Yes	No	640x480	Birdie Inc
2	79.99	9	No	Yes	720x576	Birdie Inc
2	99.99	5	Yes	No	1280x720	FlyDrone Inc
3	119.99	9	Yes	No	720x576	Birdie Inc
3	79.99	7	No	No	1280x720	FlyDrone Inc
4	119.99	7	Yes	Yes	720x576	Birdie Inc
4	99.99	9	No	No	1280x720	FlyDrone Inc
5	99.99	7	Yes	No	1280x720	Birdie Inc
5	79.99	5	No	Yes	640x480	FlyDrone Inc
6	119.99	9	No	No	1280x720	SkyFly Inc
6	99.99	5	No	No	720x576	FlyDrone Inc
7	99.99	5	No	Yes	1280x720	Birdie Inc
7	119.99	7	Yes	Yes	640x480	FlyDrone Inc
8	99.99	9	No	No	720x576	FlyDrone Inc
8	119.99	5	Yes	Yes	1280x720	SkyFly Inc
9	119.99	5	Yes	Yes	720x576	FlyDrone Inc
9	79.99	7	No	Yes	640x480	Birdie Inc
10	79.99	7	No	No	1280x720	FlyDrone Inc
10	99.99	9	Yes	Yes	640x480	SkyFly Inc
11	99.99	5	No	Yes	1280x720	Birdie Inc
11	119.99	7	Yes	No	640x480	FlyDrone Inc
12	79.99	9	Yes	No	720x576	SkyFly Inc
12	119.99	9	No	Yes	1280x720	Birdie Inc

FIGURE 5.6.1 This is the design matrix used for the Pricing Scenario. There are 12 choice sets, each with 12 alternatives. A *none* option is not part of the design matrix since, by definition, a *none* has no features. The *none*, however, would be included on the cards shown to consumers.

The priors depend on prior information. If you have this prior information, then use it. This begs another question: *What prior information and where does it come from?* Intuition, economic theory, past studies, as well as subject matter experts and key opinion leaders, are examples of sources of prior information. Some other examples are:

- Low prices are preferred to high prices;
- More bedrooms are (typically) preferred to fewer bedrooms;
- Fast computer speeds are preferred to slow speeds; etc.

For the Pricing Scenario, several priors were set based on economic theory and experience:

- A lower price is preferred;
- More flight time is preferred;

Please review the following two drones and indicate the one you would most likely buy. You could select *Neither Drone* if neither appeals to you.

Drone 1		Drone 2	
Flight Time	7 Minutes	Flight Time	5 Minutes
Integrated CPS	No	Integrated GPS	Yes
Integrated Camera	Yes	Integrated Camera	No
Video Resolution	720x576	Video Resolution	640x480
Brand	SkyFly, Inc.	Brand	Birdie, Inc.
Price	$99.99	Price	$79.99

☐ Drone 1   ☐ Drone 2   ☐ Neither Done

FIGURE 5.6.2 This is an example of what a choice card might look like. This is one choice set with two alternatives. The first two rows of the design matrix shown in Figure 5.6.1 are the components for the card. A *neither* option is available.

- Integrated GPS and camera are preferred;
- High-resolution video is preferred.

A prior was also set for brand, with the client's brand being most preferred. This was based on the aggressive advertising and sales campaign they were planning. The design matrix is shown in Figure 5.6.1. It has 12 choice sets, each with two alternatives.

What if there is no prior information? Then you can use a utility-neutral design that basically sets all the part-worths to zero before the random draws begin for the Bayesian approach. Use this if you do not have any priors.

The choice sets could now be arranged on cards, which might look like the one in Figure 5.6.2. Notice the *none* or *neither* option.

5.7 Estimation – Continued

Each consumer in the study selected one of the drones or *neither*. The choice was recorded as 1, 2, or 3 for the alternatives in the order on the card. This was done for each choice set for each consumer. The responses were merged with the design matrix and the part-worths were estimated. Effects coding was used for the categorical variables as was done for the conjoint estimation. The results are shown in Figure 5.7.1. This report has three sections, but the contents will vary by software product.[4] The *effect summary* report shows the importance of each attribute as determined by the p-values, which are for the likelihood ratio chi-square tests of significance shown in the *Likelihood Ratio Tests* report. The logWorth values and bar chart show that all effects are significant at the 0.01 level of significance.

Effect Summary

Source	LogWorth		PValue
Video Resolution	55.482		0.00000
Integrated Camera	46.942		0.00000
No Choice Indicator	36.239		0.00000
Integrated GPS	35.629		0.00000
Price	25.222		0.00000
Flight Time (Minutes)	21.119		0.00000
Brand	5.418		0.00000

Parameter Estimates

Term	Estimate	Std Error
Price	-0.05090454	0.0051592189
Flight Time (Minutes)[5]	-1.11415911	0.1285009088
Flight Time (Minutes)[7]	0.13891592	0.0766376900
Integrated GPS[Yes]	1.06142007	0.0916396206
Integrated Camera[Yes]	1.22255157	0.0925140280
Video Resolution[640x480]	-1.72095168	0.1294706137
Video Resolution[720x576]	0.41894545	0.0742235560
Brand[FlyDrone Inc]	-0.24770588	0.0933161082
Brand[Birdie Inc]	0.31218766	0.0675689877
No Choice Indicator	-6.31453342	0.5457496889

AICc	1521.7666
BIC	1572.4823
-2*LogLikelihood	1501.5816
-2*Firth LogLikelihood	1443.023

Converged in Gradient
Firth Bias-Adjusted Estimates

Likelihood Ratio Tests

Source	L-R ChiSquare	DF	Prob>ChiSq	
Video Resolution	255.506	2	<.0001*	
Integrated Camera	210.364	1	<.0001*	
No Choice Indicator	161.338	1	<.0001*	
Integrated GPS	158.546	1	<.0001*	
Price	110.971	1	<.0001*	
Flight Time (Minutes)	97.256	2	<.0001*	
Brand	24.951	2	<.0001*	

FIGURE 5.7.1 The estimation results are shown here. Effects coding was used so the base level for each attribute can be easily retrieved.

The *Parameter Estimates* section of the report shows the usual parameter estimates and standard errors. Effects coding was used for the discrete variables with the last level in alphanumeric order as the base. The label in square brackets is the non-base level of the attribute. The base can be retrieved as explained in the conjoint chapter. These base levels are shown in the *Effects Marginals* report along with the estimated parameters (see Figure 5.7.2).[5] A perusal of the marginal utilities shows an expected pattern: high-resolution videos are preferred to low-resolution videos; longer flight time is preferred to shorter flight time; and so forth.

The *Parameter Estimates* report also shows some fit statistics. The AICc is the corrected Akaike Information Criterion (AIC), which is interpreted as a measure

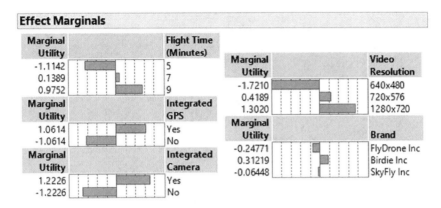

FIGURE 5.7.2 The estimated marginal effects are shown here. These are the estimated part-worths.

of badness of fit, as opposed to the R^2 in OLS, which is a goodness-of-fit measure. As a measure of badness of fit, a lower value for AICc is preferred since it shows the least "badness." The BIC is the Bayesian Information Criterion, the Bayesian counterpart to the AICc. Both are functions of $-2 \times$ logLikelihood, which is also reported. Unlike the R^2 in OLS, which lies between 0 and 1, the AICc and BIC are unbounded. Extremely large and negative numbers are not unusual. The AICc and BIC are both useful in comparing models in a portfolio of models, not for assessing just one model in isolation. The *Firth logLikelihood Adjustment* corrects for estimation bias due to small samples. See [57] for a review of the reports. Also see [120] and [129] for background on the Firth adjustment. Finally, see Chapter 9 for a detailed discussion of information criteria.

The *Likelihood Ratio Tests* report shows the likelihood ratio chi-square test of significance for each attribute. The attributes are sorted by the chi-square values. The p-values are the same ones shown in the *Effects Summary* report.

5.8   Analysis

Once the part-worths are estimated, the results can be analyzed in a manner similar to the conjoint results. Attribute importances, elasticities, and willingness to pay can be calculated and profilers or simulators can be used to determine impacts of changing attribute settings.

5.8.1   Attribute importances

Attribute importances can be calculated using the method described in the conjoint chapter. This was done for the Pricing Scenario. The importances are shown in Figure 5.8.1. An alternative way to display the attribute importances is to use the plot of the logWorths. The conjoint-style and logWorth-style importances are based on two different methods so it should not be surprising that the results differ.

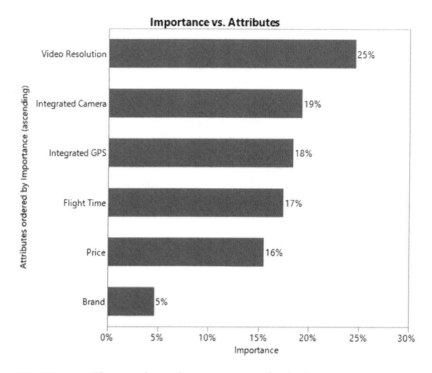

FIGURE 5.8.1 These are the attribute importances for the Pricing Scenario calculated using the method described in the conjoint chapter.

Source	LogWorth		PValue
Integrated Camera	47.030		0.00000
Video Resolution	45.250		0.00000
Integrated GPS	36.423		0.00000
No Choice Indicator	30.783		0.00000
Price	28.307		0.00000
Flight Time (Minutes)	24.098		0.00000
Brand	5.410		0.00000

FIGURE 5.8.2 These are the attribute effects for the Pricing Scenario based on the logWorths. Notice that the ordering of the attributes is similar to the ordering in Figure 5.8.1.

Nonetheless, they are approximately the same. The top two attributes are the video resolution and the integrated camera, indicating that consumers value images. Price is not high in the ranking, which is reasonable for hobbyists.

5.8.2 Demand and choice elasticities

The demand for an alternative is the sum of the choices of numerous individuals making independent decisions. Aggregate demand for an alternative is obtained by averaging the choice probabilities for the population so that

$$D_j = \frac{1}{N} \times \sum_{i=1}^{N} Pr_i(j)$$

where N is the population size. This amounts to completely enumerating the values of the independent variables, plugging these values into the take rate formula and then adding the choice probabilities for each member of the population. This is a consistent aggregation procedure because it is exactly the definition of aggregate demand. The procedure, however, is obviously costly to implement because it requires knowing the population size. Most marketing departments, however, have estimates of what I refer to as the *addressable market*. This is the size of their customer base. Other market research or just knowledge of the business will help with this number. An approximation to aggregate demand or aggregate unit sales is then

$$D_j = M \times Pr(j)$$

where M is the size of this addressable market and $Pr(j)$ is the average take rate in the market for alternative j. Once the total unit sales are estimated, you can calculate expected revenue as unit sales times price. Finally, if average cost is known, the contribution and contribution margin can also be calculated.

5.8.3 Elasticity analysis

Elasticities for the discrete choice model are more complex. Their derivation involves taking the derivatives of the take formulas, (94), with respect to the attributes. The results for price depend on how price is treated in the model: continuous or discrete (see [46] for a discussion).

For an unlabeled choice design, elasticities do not make sense to calculate, although they can be calculated since calculations are just mechanical operations. Elasticities do not make sense because the choices are for nondescript alternatives arbitrarily called "Option," "Alternative," or "Object," which have no inherent meaning. How do you interpret an own-price elasticity for "Option 1"? A labeled design is different, however, since the labels have meanings such as "Car," "Bus," and "Train."

Continuous price variable

If price is treated as a continuous variable in estimation, then there is only one part-worth utility for price: β^P. The own-price elasticity for alternative j seen by consumer i is then

$$\eta_{P_{ij}}^{Pr_i(j)} = \beta^P \times P_{ij} \times [1 - Pr_i(j)] \tag{100}$$

and the cross-price elasticity is

$$\eta_{P_{ik}}^{Pr_i(J)} = -\beta^P \times P_{ik} \times Pr_i(j) \tag{101}$$

TABLE 5.4 These are the take elasticities for the first consumer for the first alternative when the price is treated as a continuous variable. All attributes were set at the same levels for the first and second alternatives. The base price was $119.99 for both alternatives. For the own-price elasticity, only the own-price for the first alternative was lowered to $99.99. For the cross-price elasticity, only the cross-price for the second alternative was lowered to $99.99. Notice that the own-price elasticity indicates unit elasticity, while the cross-price elasticity is positive, indicating that the two alternatives are substitutes as should be expected.

Own-price elasticity	Cross-price elasticity
−1.02	3.25

for prices P_{ij} and P_{ik}. These are the *instantaneous* or *point price elasticities* for consumer i for alternative j. For the Pricing Scenario, the elasticities are shown in Table 5.4 for the first consumer. There are separate own- and cross-elasticities for each consumer that are impractical to use, except perhaps in a first-degree price discrimination situation. It is better to aggregate the elasticities. Aggregation is discussed below.

It was noted by [46] that there is actually a single elasticity formula if an indicator function is introduced. Let $I(j, k)$ be an indicator function defined as

$$I(j, k) = \begin{cases} 1 & j = k\,(\text{Own} - \text{Price}) \\ 0 & j \neq k\,(\text{Cross} - \text{Price}) \end{cases} \tag{102}$$

Then the elasticity formula is simply

$$\eta_{P_{ik}}^{Pr_i(j)} \beta^P \times P_{ik} \times [I(j,k) - Pr_i(j)].$$

Discrete price variable

If price is discrete, there is a different part-worth for each level of price, so it would seem that only the part-worths in (100) and (101) have to be modified. This is incorrect because of the discreteness of the variable. When the percentage changes are actually calculated, they would be too large and would thus give a distorted impression of the price responsiveness. This is usually corrected by using *arc elasticities*. The own-price arc elasticity is

$$\eta_{P_{ij}}^{Pr_i(j)} = \frac{\dfrac{Pr_i^1(j) - Pr_i^0(j)}{P_{ij}^1 - P_{ij}^0}}{\dfrac{Pr_i^1(j) + Pr_i^0(j)}{P_{ij}^1 + P_{ij}^0}} \tag{103}$$

and the cross-price elasticity is

TABLE 5.5 These are the take elasticities for the first consumer for the first alternative when the price is treated as a discrete variable. All attributes were set at the same levels for the first and second alternatives. The base price was $119.99 for both alternatives. For the own-price elasticity, the own-price was lowered to $99.99. For the cross-price elasticity, only the cross-price for the second alternative was lowered to $99.99. Notice that the cross-price elasticity is positive, indicating that the two alternatives are substitutes.

Own-price elasticity	Cross-price elasticity
−3.37	4.57

$$\eta_{P_{ik}}^{Pr_i(j)} = \frac{\dfrac{Pr_i^1(j) - Pr_i^0(j)}{P_{ik}^1 - P_{ik}^0}}{\dfrac{Pr_i^1(j) + Pr_i^0(j)}{P_{ik}^1 + P_{ik}^0}} \tag{104}$$

for $j \neq k$. For the Pricing Scenario, the elasticities are shown in Table 5.5 for the first consumer. See [46] and [28] for discussions of elasticities.

Aggregation

Since there is a pair of elasticities for each consumer, there should be an aggregation of the elasticities over all consumers, otherwise there are too many elasticities to be useful. The issue is the aggregation method. Several have been proposed and are implemented in software.

1. *Simple average elasticity*: Calculate the arithmetic average of the elasticities for all respondents:

$$\eta_{P_{ik}}^{Pr_i(j)} = \frac{1}{C} \times \sum_{i=1}^{C} \eta_{P_{ik}}^{Pr_i(j)},$$

    $j, k = 1, \ldots, J$. The problem with this approach is that each consumer has the same weight in the calculation disregarding any differences in the magnitude of their take rates. Those with a low take rate (e.g., close to zero) would have the same weight as those with a very high take rate (e.g., close to 1.0).
2. *Weighted average elasticity*: Calculate the weighted average of the elasticities where the weights are based on the take rates:

$$^{w}\eta_{P_{ik}}^{Pr_i(j)} = \sum_{i=1}^{C} w_i \times \eta_{P_{ij}}^{Pr_i(j)}$$

    where $w_i = \dfrac{Pr_i(j)}{\displaystyle\sum_{i=1}^{C} Pr_i(j)}$ with $\displaystyle\sum_{i=1}^{C} w_i = 1$ and C is the number of consumers in the study. [46] refers to this as the *method of sample enumeration*.

5.8.4 Willingness-to-pay analysis

A fundamental economic (welfare) question is: *How much does someone have to pay or be compensated for a change in their environment so as to be no better off or worse off after the change as before?* The environment for the problem is an attribute and the situation you want unchanged is their utility.[6] This concept can be applied to choice analysis to determine the amount a consumer would be willing to pay for a change in the level of an attribute so as to maintain the same level of utility.

For the Pricing Scenario, the economic question is framed as: *How much would a consumer be willing to pay to have an integrated camera?* The situation before a change is "No Camera" and after the change it is "Have Camera." Intuitively, getting a camera would make a consumer better off, so utility would be higher. Paying an extra amount for it, however, would reduce utility. How much does this payment have to be so that utility is the same as before the change? Anything more would make the consumer worse off; anything less would make the consumer better off. The amount of price increase is the willingness to pay (WTP). This is a dollar amount added to or subtracted from a base price so that utility remains constant.

For simplicity, let the initial systematic utility, as a function of price and the jth attribute X for consumer i, be $V_{ij}^0 = \beta_1 P_{ij}^0 + \beta_2 X_{ij}^0$, where the exponents merely symbolize the initial value. Now let the level of the attribute change. The new systematic utility is $V_{ij}^1 = \beta_1 (P_{ij}^0 + \Delta P) + \beta_2 X_{ij}^1$, where a factor, ΔP, was added to the price to compensate for the attribute change. The ΔP factor is the WTP. The two utilities are required to be equal, with ΔP being the equilibrating factor, so that

$$\beta_1 P_{ij}^0 + \beta_2 X_{ij}^0 = \beta_1 (P_{ij}^0 + \Delta P) + \beta_2 X_{ij}^1.$$

Solving for the WTP, ΔP, you get

$$WTP = \Delta P$$

$$= -\frac{\beta_2}{\beta_1} \times (X_{ij}^1 - X_{ij}^0).$$

The WTP is the ratio of the part-worth utility for the attribute over the part-worth utility for the price times the difference in the two levels of the attribute. For the Pricing Scenario, a logical setting for the levels is $X_{ij}^0 = No$ and $X_{ij}^1 = Yes$. Since the levels are qualitative, they must be coded as discussed in the conjoint chapter. If dummy coding is used with "No" as the base, then $X_{i,Camera}^1 - X_{i,Camera}^0 = 1 - 0 = 1$, so

$$WTP = -\frac{\beta_2}{\beta_1}.$$

If $\beta_2 > 0$ and $\beta_1 > 0$ (as it should be for price), then $WTP > 0$, so a consumer would be willing to pay more for an integrated camera. The WTP is the extra amount they would pay. If effects coding is used with "No" again as the base code as -1, then $X^1_{i,Camera} - X^0_{i,Camera} = 1-(-1) = 2$ so

$$WTP = -\frac{2 \times \beta_2}{\beta_1}.$$

If the attribute has more than two levels, such as the video resolution attribute, then the WTP expression is more complicated and it is best to leave the computation to software.

WTP was calculated for the Pricing Scenario with all attributes set at their lowest level as the bases. The results are shown in Figure 5.8.3. WTP uses a baseline set of values (i.e., a "before situation"). These are shown in the first part of the report. The baseline price is $79.99. The other baseline values are reflected in the seven-column report at the bottom of Figure 5.8.3 as having zero values; these are the starting points. If that attribute is "moved" from its baseline value, the price will change as shown in the column labeled "Price Change"; this is the WTP. When integrated GPS is moved from not being present to being present in a drone, the WTP is $41.70: consumers will pay $41.70 over and above the baseline price of $79.99 for the GPS. This makes the new price $121.69 as shown in the last column.

Willingness to Pay

Factor	Baseline Value
Price	79.99
Flight Time (Minutes)	5
Integrated GPS	No
Integrated Camera	No
Video Resolution	640x480
Brand	FlyDrone Inc

Baseline Utility
-9.4386

Factor	Feature Setting	Price Change	Std Error	Lower 95%	Upper 95%	New Price
Flight Time (Minutes)	5	$0.00	.	.	.	$79.99
Flight Time (Minutes)	7	$24.62	3.21487	$18.32	$30.92	$104.61
Flight Time (Minutes)	9	$41.05	3.67542	$33.84	$48.25	$121.04
Integrated GPS	Yes	$41.70	2.88593	$36.05	$47.36	$121.69
Integrated GPS	No	$0.00	2.88593	($5.66)	$5.66	$79.99
Integrated Camera	Yes	$48.03	3.2594	$41.64	$54.42	$128.02
Integrated Camera	No	$0.00	3.2594	($6.39)	$6.39	$79.99
Video Resolution	640x480	$0.00	3.2594	($6.39)	$6.39	$79.99
Video Resolution	720x576	$42.04	3.92523	$34.34	$49.73	$122.03
Video Resolution	1280x720	$59.38	4.43677	$50.69	$68.08	$139.37
Brand	FlyDrone Inc	$0.00	4.43677	($8.70)	$8.70	$79.99
Brand	Birdie Inc	$11.00	3.0672	$4.99	$17.01	$90.99
Brand	SkyFly Inc	$3.60	3.80256	($3.85)	$11.05	$83.59

Standard deviations for Price Change calculated by Delta method.

FIGURE 5.8.3 The WTP was calculated for each attribute for the Pricing Scenario.

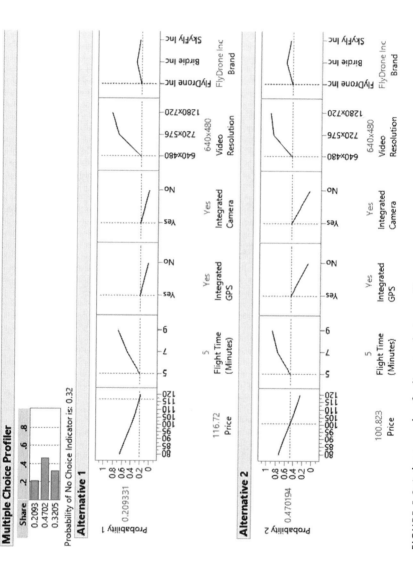

FIGURE 5.8.4 An example of a discrete choice profiler.

The maker of this drone (FlyDrone, Inc.) could charge \$121.69 if an integrated GPS is included while all other attributes are at their base level.

5.8.5 Profilers and simulators

Profilers and simulators were described in the conjoint chapter. Figure 5.8.4 illustrates one for the discrete choice Pricing Scenario.

5.9 Software

JMP, SAS, Stata, and Limdep, all commercial products, will easily handle the discrete choice issues discussed in this chapter. JMP has platforms for designing, estimating, graphing, and reporting the types of models I considered in this chapter. This also holds for SAS. Stata and Limdep will handle estimation. R will also handle them but, although free, it requires additional programming that may deter most analysts from using it and thus has a hidden cost that must be accounted for. Limdep and R are at the forefront of estimation methodologies, which were only briefly touched upon here. JMP was used for the design and analysis, including the profiler, of the Pricing Scenario in this chapter.

5.10 Summary

This was a technical chapter that, like the previous chapter on conjoint analysis, is more theoretically detailed. This is necessary in order for you to understand the strengths and weaknesses of discrete choice analysis for pricing. This approach is more realistic than conjoint analysis and should be used whenever possible. The issues with it have to be understood so that incorrect designs and analyses are avoided.

Notes

1 This notation follows closely the notation in https://en.wikipedia.org/w/index.php?title=Generalized_extreme_value_distribution oldid=758211774.
2 [23] take issue with this name. They would prefer to call it "independence among alternatives." I agree, since the assumption is that the alternatives are far enough part in attribute preference space that that they are not good substitutes for each other. The IIA name, however, is the one used in the literature.
3 The notation was used by [72].
4 The estimation and report shown here were produced using JMP.
5 These are in the column labeled "Marginal Utility." These are the part-worth utilities.
6 If you are familiar with microeconomic theory and indifference curve analysis, then you should recognize this as the amount of income a consumer must be given or have taken away after a price change in order to maintain the same level of utility.

6
MAXDIFF MODELS

This chapter introduces the third member of the choice family, MaxDiff. This member is most useful for strategy development, although this claim will be modified in Section 6.5. The chapter is divided into seven sections. Section 1 presents a Pricing Scenario as a choice situation for pricing strategies. Section 2 discusses design matrix creation and terminology. Section 3 discusses estimation and interpretation, while Section 4 focuses on analysis, including *total unduplicated reach and frequency* (TURF) analysis of individual-level utilities. Section 5 introduces a second Pricing Scenario that describes a common pricing situation involving add-on options that can be handled with MaxDiff models. Section 6 discusses software. Section 7 is a summary.

6.1 A Pricing Scenario: Casino pricing strategies

This section describes a Pricing Scenario for pricing strategies. Terms, definitions, and concepts will be introduced and developed using this scenario. Another Pricing Scenario for product add-on options will be introduced in Section 6.5.

6.1.1 The Pricing Scenario

A major revenue source for casinos, in addition to gambling, is beverage purchases. See [76] for an interesting overview of issues surrounding pricing strategies for beverages at Las Vegas casino bars. A casino's management team identified ten pricing strategies based on focus groups to enhance revenue:

1. Higher prices during peak hours;
2. Lower prices during off-peak hours (midnight–6 a.m.);
3. Product incentives (up-sell);

4. Product specials (e.g., free beverages);
5. Happy Hours;
6. Buy one piece, get another of lesser value at 50% off;
7. Early Bird specials;
8. Frequent gamer (high-roller) discounts;
9. Ladies' Night;
10. European Bottle Service.

The team can implement several of these, but it would like to know consumers' ranking of them in order to introduce and promote the best ones. A team member argued that casino patrons could simply be asked to rate their preferences for each strategy on a ten-point Likert scale. They would then use the mean ratings to rank the ten strategies. Another team member noted that this approach is monadic: each strategy is rated in isolation as in a conjoint study. Alternatively, she argued, the patrons could be asked to rank the ten strategies or select their favorite. The problem with this approach is that the rankings are ordinal, which implies that the distance between the rankings of two strategies is unknown. You can only say that one is ranked, say, first and another is ranked second, but you cannot say how much the first differs from the second.

A consultant advocated for a MaxDiff approach that avoids these problems by asking the patrons to compare strategies in choice sets. Take rates are calculated for each strategy and then ranked based on the take rates. Since take rates are ratio scaled, the difference in ranking between any two strategies is easily determined. The management team could then develop financial analyses for each strategy to determine their revenue gains and contribution margins by applying the take rates to the average number of patrons. The management asked for more details on the MaxDiff procedure before agreeing to its use.

6.1.2 The MaxDiff procedure

In a MaxDiff approach, consumers are shown sets (called *choice sets* as in a discrete choice study) of pricing strategies and for each set they are asked to select the most and least preferred strategy:

Most preferred: The pricing strategy that is the most attractive and thus most likely to incentivize them to buy more beverages.
Least preferred: The pricing strategy that is the least attractive and thus least likely to incentivize them to buy beverages.

The advantage of this two-fold question (most/least preferred), in addition to a comparison of two (or more) strategies at once (the number in the choice set), is that scale is not an issue. With a Likert scale, respondents may not use the whole scale, so you really do not know if they are evaluating the strategies similarly. You do know, however, the range of their preferences, which is a maximum difference, hence the name *MaxDiff*, short for *Maximum Difference Scaling*. This allows you to deduce most of the relationships of the options without actually asking about them all. To see this, assume you have a four-item choice set: A, B, C, D. With four items, there are $\binom{4}{2} = 6$ comparisons. Suppose a consumer states that A is most preferred and D is least preferred. You immediately know that $A \succeq B, A \succeq C, A \succeq D, B \succeq D$, and $C \succeq D$, where "$\succeq$" means "is preferred to or is the same as." The only unknown relationship is B vs. C. From two answers you get five out of six comparisons. This is not possible with a simple preference rating on a Likert scale. It is possible with a ranking approach, but the number of ranking tasks is still an issue. This example is based on [158].

6.1.3   MaxDiff vs. discrete choice

MaxDiff models are closely akin to discrete choice models. In a discrete choice framework, consumers are asked to select one alternative from a choice set (or *none*). This is obviously their most preferred option. In a MaxDiff approach, they make the same choice in addition to the opposite one (i.e., their least preferred option). Since the two selections are diametrically opposed, the discrete choice data setup and estimation procedures can be used after the data for the "least" selection is correctly coded. Fortunately, software handles this, so it, along with the mechanical estimation, will not be discussed here, although a later section will discuss other estimation issues.

Although MaxDiff and discrete choice are akin, they are still not the same in three regards. First, discrete choice attributes have levels that are combined into alternatives. There is a step prior to specifying the alternatives. In MaxDiff, there are just attributes with no levels, so there are just alternatives. A perusal of the Pricing Scenario's options will confirm this where the strategies are the attributes.

The lack of levels has an implication for the design matrix, the second difference from a discrete choice model. In discrete choice, a design matrix is developed by arranging the levels into nondescript alternatives allocated to choice sets. In MaxDiff, it is developed by arranging the alternatives directly into choice sets. How this is done is discussed in the next section.

Finally, the discrete choice part-worths are estimated for each attribute level. Utilities are calculated, which are then used to calculate take rates. For MaxDiff, there are no part-worths, but there are utilities that are transformed into take rates for a more intuitive interpretation. In discrete choice, the take rates are the primary result; in MaxDiff take rates are a convenient aid for interpretation.

6.2   Design matrix development

You need a design matrix for the treatments (pricing strategies in this case) so you can show consumers the strategies in an optimal manner. There are several criteria for this design matrix, which makes it different from the others discussed in the previous two chapters. In particular, the rows of the design matrix, which represent choice sets, cannot contain all the strategies (i.e., alternatives). If all strategies were in one choice set, there would be only one set (the set of everything), but more importantly, this would be overwhelming for a consumer, to say the least. Consider showing just pairs of strategies, which is the minimum number to present on a card. With ten strategies, there are $\binom{10}{2} = 45$ pairs requiring 45 cards, which is too much for any consumer to handle. You had the same issue with the conjoint design. If you have four strategies on a card, you need $\binom{10}{4} = 210$ pairs or 210 cards, which is definitely more than any consumer can handle.

A solution is to show subsets of the strategies in choice sets, but optimally arranged over all choice sets. There are some conventionally accepted, almost intuitive, criteria to satisfy for developing the design matrix so that a consumer is not overburdened. You want to

- Show all strategies;
- Have each one viewed the same number of times for balance (i.e., equity);
- Have each *pair* of strategies seen the same number of times (also for balance).

The "pair" criterion does not mean that only a single pair is in a choice set. The minimum size of a set is two, so it is possible to have just one pair. Nonetheless, a set could contain more than two alternatives on a card, so there would be more than one pair on that card. Suppose, for illustration, that a single choice set has three pricing strategies: A, B, and C. There are three pairs in the one set: AB, AC, and BC, which is $\binom{3}{2}$. To satisfy the pairs criterion, the pair AC must appear the same number of times across *all* choice sets as the pair AB and the pair BC.

The design matrix satisfying these criteria is called a *balanced incomplete block design* or a *BIBD*. For terminology, a card in this problem is also called a *block*. To be consistent with the design literature, I will frequently use the word *treatment* interchangeably with *option, object, item, attribute, strategy*, or *message*.

There are several conditions for a BIBD, but two important ones are:

1. Each object must occur the same number of times.
2. Each pair of objects must occur the same number of times.

These two conditions satisfy the conditions listed above. The complete set of conditions will be discussed shortly.

A BIBD does not exist for all problems; you may have to come "close." Coming "close" means using a partially balanced incomplete block design (PBIBD). As an example of a design that is not a BIBD, consider a problem with five treatments on four cards (or blocks) with only three treatments per block. Table 6.1a is an

TABLE 6.1 Part (a) is not a BIBD because one pair of elements, 2 and 5, appears three times, while all other pairs appear once. In addition, each number does not appear the same number of times: 2 and 5 appear three times each, while the others appear twice each. Part (b) is a BIBD because it meets the two conditions stated in the text.

(a) Example of a non-BIBD design

Block or card	Treatment arrangements		
1	1	3	4
2	2	4	5
3	2	3	5
4	1	2	5

(b) Example of a BIBD design

Block or card	Treatment arrangements		
1	1	2	3
2	1	4	5
3	1	6	7
4	2	4	6
5	2	5	7
6	3	4	7
7	3	5	6

example arrangement where the treatments are represented by the digits 1–5. This is not a BIBD because it does not meet the two criteria listed above. Now consider the design in Table 6.1b. This is for seven treatments in seven blocks with three treatments per block. It is a BIBD because each number appears three times and each pair (there are $\binom{7}{2} = 21$ pairs) appears once.

6.2.1 Conventional BIBD notation

Some concepts are needed to better understand the structure of a BIBD such as the one in Table 6.1b. A BIBD involves an assignment of treatments into blocks, but not all of them are assigned to a block. Let t be the number of treatments and b the number of blocks or rows of the matrix. The treatments are assigned to k slots or positions in each block with $k < t$. The total number of treatments assigned to all k positions in all blocks is n where $n = b \times k$. For Table 6.1b, $b = 7$ and $k = 3$, so $n = 21 = 7 \times 3$.

Across the entire design matrix of b rows and k columns, the treatments are replicated (i.e., repeated), which should be clear for the example in Table 6.1b since there are only seven treatments but 21 slots filled by these treatments. In general, the replication could be different for each treatment. Let r_i be the number of replications for treatment i, $i = 1, \ldots, t$. Clearly, $\sum_i r_i = n = b \times k$. Having many different replications is, however, difficult to use, so a simplification is $r_i = r, \forall i$. This is an *equi-replication* assumption. In this case, $\sum_i r = r \times t$. Therefore, an important property of a BIBD design is

$$n = b \times k = r \times t.$$

This obviously holds for Table 6.1b.

Another issue deals with pairs of treatments that appear across all blocks. The number of pairs, called the *concurrence*, of two treatments i and j, $i \neq j$ and $i < j$, is denoted by λ_{ij}. Only one pair can appear in a block, so λ_{ij} is the number of blocks containing the pair of treatments i and j. In Table 6.1a, λ_{ij} varies: $\lambda_{ij} = 1$ for all pairs except the pair $\{2, 5\}$, where $\lambda_{ij} = 3$. It should be clear that $\sum_i \sum_{j, i \neq j} \lambda_{ij} = n = b \times k$. If λ_{ij} is a constant, then the BIBD is simplified so that all pairs of treatments appear the same number of times. In Table 6.1b, $\lambda = 1$ so each pair of treatments appears only once. The property that the number of pairs of treatments is a constant is the *constant concurrence property*. See [88] and Chapter 11 for discussions on concurrence and incomplete block designs.

With t treatments, there are $\binom{t}{2}$ possible treatment pairs, but by the constant concurrence property there are $\lambda \binom{t}{2}$ treatment pairs in the design matrix. For Table 6.1b, $\binom{t}{2} = 21$, and with $\lambda = 1$ there are 21 pairs altogether. Also, in each block there are $\binom{k}{2}$ pairs of treatments and $b \binom{k}{2}$ pairs in the entire design matrix since there are b blocks. You have the important result that

$$\lambda \times \binom{t}{2} = b \times \binom{k}{2}. \tag{105}$$

The number of blocks is then

$$b = \frac{\lambda \times \binom{t}{2}}{\binom{k}{2}}.$$

Using the previous result that $bk = rt$ and substituting the expression for b, a more general important result is

$$\lambda \times (t - 1) = r \times (k - 1).$$

This is the classic way to express the BIBD condition with constant concurrence, λ, and equi-replication, r.

There is one more condition. You can show that $t \leq b$. The proof, provided in [36], involves a $t \times b$ matrix called the *incidence matrix*, **N**, with elements that are the counts of the number of times each treatment occurs in each block. Using some results from linear algebra, it can be shown that $r(\mathbf{N}) \leq \min(b,t)$, where $r(\mathbf{N})$ is the rank of **N**. That is, the rank of **N** is less than or equal to the minimum of b or t. [36] shows that the rank of **N** is t, so $t \leq b$.

To summarize, there are three important relationships for a BIBD:

1. $n = b \times k = r \times t$;
2. $\lambda \times (t - 1) = r \times (k - 1)$;
3. $t \leq b$.

These are important because they place restrictions on defining a BIBD. For example, for Table 6.1b with $n = 21$, $t = 7$, $k = 3$, $r = 3$, $b = 7$, and $\lambda = 1$, the three conditions are met. However, a BIBD is not possible with $t = 5$ as in Table 6.1a and the other settings remaining the same. With $t = 5$ treatments, you need

$$b = \frac{\binom{5}{2}}{\binom{3}{2}}$$
$$= \frac{5 \times 4}{3 \times 2}$$
$$= \frac{20}{6}$$
$$= 3.33$$

blocks, which is not possible; you cannot have a fraction of a block (i.e., a row of the matrix). Also, the number of blocks is less than the number of treatments, which also is not possible. An important conclusion follows: a BIBD does not exist for all problems, as noted above.

Since these five parameters define the existence of a BIBD, a BIBD is usually denoted as $BIBD(t,b,r,k;\lambda)$.

6.2.2 Generating a BIBD

Generating a BIBD is not a trivial task because of the three conditions. One method given by [38] involves listing the main effects and all interactions for a 2^n factorial system and then marking the arrangements that contain like symbols. One of the 2^n arrangements, however, is the null arrangement, so there are really $2^n - 1$ useful arrangements. These are interpreted as the treatments. As an example, following [38], consider the problem of creating a BIBD design for seven treatments in seven blocks with three treatments per block: $t = 7, b = 7, k = 3$. You can use a 2^3 factorial with factors A, B, C. There are 8 ($=2^3$) possible combinations, one of

TABLE 6.2 The 2^3 factorial with interactions can be recoded to indicate all interactions. Notice that Part (a) is a BIBD because it meets the two conditions stated in the text. Each digit in Part (b) occurs three times; each pair occurs once. So this is a $BIBD(t = 7, b = 7, r = 3, k = 3; \lambda = 1)$. Part (b) is also the one shown in Table 6.1b.

(a) Example of a $2^3 - 1$ design generator

A	B	AB	C	AC	BC	ABC
1	2	3	4	5	6	7
X	X	X				
X			X	X		
X					X	X
	X		X		X	
	X			X		X
		X	X			X
		X		X	X	

(b) The BIBD design matrix

1	2	3
1	4	5
1	6	7
2	4	6
2	5	7
3	4	7
3	5	6

which is the null combination with none of the factors, so there are $2^3 - 1 = 7$ useful combinations or treatments. These are A, B, C, AB, AC, BC, ABC. These are displayed in Table 6.2a with the numbers 1–7 assigned to each letter combination. Each number (or check mark in the table) occurs once and each pair occurs once. The blocks are then the arrangement shown in Table 6.2b.

There are catalogs of designs that can be used for simple problems, which is certainly easier. The best is found in [8]. Many software packages have these tables programmed with simple look-up features. Software packages are discussed in Section 6.6.

6.2.3 Pricing Scenario BIBD

For the Pricing Scenario with ten strategies, it was determined that 15 choice sets of size four each are possible for consumers to handle. This number was based on the consultant's experience so there is little scientific reason for it. Therefore, $t = 10$, $b = 15$, $k = 4$. To make this a BIBD, the other two parameters were set as $r = 6$ and $\lambda = 2$ for a $BIBD(t = 10, b = 15, r = 6, k = 4, \lambda = 2)$ design. It is easy to see that the three conditions are satisfied. Each consumer would see 15 choice sets or cards, each set containing four strategies. These are shown in Table 6.3. Fifteen sets may seem like a lot for any consumer, but this size is not unusual; consumers actually can easily

TABLE 6.3 Each number corresponds to a pricing strategy. Regarding the three conditions for a BIBD, you can see that they are all met. This design matrix was generated using a SAS macro (see [140]).

10	1	3	9
4	8	2	10
4	5	1	8
3	6	1	4
9	1	8	7
9	4	10	6
2	3	4	7
3	6	7	8
8	3	10	5
7	9	4	5
2	5	9	3
6	8	2	9
1	10	7	2
5	2	6	1
10	7	5	6

handle this number. Four choice alternatives in each set, sometimes called a *quad*, is typical. Sets of size two, three, and five are also common. Experience shows that sets of size six and greater are too much for consumers to handle. [158] recommends that the set sizes be at most half the number of treatments. Therefore, as a rough rule of thumb (ROT), you should have $2 \le k \le \left\lfloor \frac{t}{2} \right\rfloor$, where $\lfloor x \rfloor$ indicates the largest integer less than or equal to x.

6.2.4 An alternative design approach: Split-plots

An alternative way to develop a design matrix is to use a *split-plot design*. This is a more complicated approach that allows for blocking and choice sets within a block. See [37] for a good discussion of split-plot designs. For advanced treatments, see [54], [32], and [29].

Split-plot designs originated in the agricultural area where treatments (e.g., fertilizers) had to be applied to segments or *plots* of land. The treatments are certainly experimental factors, but so are the plots of land. The treatments can be easily varied or randomized, but it is difficult to change or randomize the plots since they are fixed by nature. Designs were developed to accommodate this situation in which some factors are easy to change and others are hard to change.

The basic rationale for using a split-plot design in general is that at least one factor is hard to change, but not always impossible. Consequently, changing this factor throughout an experiment involves a cost. This cost increases each time the factor is changed: the more changes, the higher the cost of the experiment. The advantage of a split-plot design is that it is more cost effective: the hard-to-change factor is varied only a few times. See [37] for a discussion and an example involving an industrial experiment.

A second reason for using a split-plot design is that estimations are more valid (see [37] for a discussion).

As noted by [37], "a split-plot experiment is a blocked experiment, where the blocks themselves serve as experimental units for a subset of the factors. Thus, there are two levels of experimental units. The blocks are referred to as whole plots, while the experimental units within blocks are called split plots, split units, or subplots." In terms of a MaxDiff design, the whole plots are groups of choice sets and each split plot is a choice set within a group. The treatments are the alternatives within a choice set. The groups are treated as very hard to change, the choice sets as hard to change, and the alternatives as easy to change.[1]

How does this help? A design could be created that has groups of choice sets. A consumer (the experimental unit) would be randomly assigned to a group. Within that assigned group, the consumer would be shown each choice set one at a time (perhaps in random order) and they would then select the best and worst option within each choice set.

6.2.5   Pricing Scenario final design

To make the design simple, the consultant for the Pricing Scenario decided that it would be better if they used four groups of choice sets. Assuming 30 respondents per group, the required sample size would be 120 people. Each consumer would be randomly assigned to one of these four groups. The four groups would be divided into eight choice sets each so there would be two choice sets per group. It was decided that each choice set would have four alternatives so there have to be 32 (= 8 sets ×4 alternatives per set) runs in the design matrix. In general, the number of runs is

$$\# Runs = \# Groups \times \# Sets.$$

The final design matrix for this study is shown in Figure 6.2.1.

6.3   Estimation

As noted above, the take rates for a MaxDiff model are transformed utilities that can be estimated at an aggregate or disaggregate (i.e., individual) level. These estimations are discussed in the following sections after a brief discussion of how the data should be arranged.

6.3.1   Data arrangement

Regardless of the level of estimation, the responses have to be organized for estimation. There are several ways the data could be organized, but these depend on

Whole Plots (Groups)	Subplots (Choice Sets)		Alternatives
	1	1	Ladies Night
	1	1	Early Bird specials
	1	1	Lower prices during off-peak hours (midnight -- 6 AM)
First	1	1	Product specials (e.g., free beverages)
Group	1 Two Choice Sets	2	Buy 1 piece, get another of lesser value at 50% off
	1	2	Frequent gamer (high-roller) discounts
	1	2	Higher prices during peak hours
	1	2	Happy Hours
	2	3	Happy Hours
	2	3	Frequent gamer (high-roller) discounts
	2	3	Lower prices during off-peak hours (midnight -- 6 AM)
	2	3	European Bottle service
	2	4	Ladies Night
	2	4	Buy 1 piece, get another of lesser value at 50% off
	2	4	Early Bird specials
	2	4	Product incentives (up-sell)
	3	5	Higher prices during peak hours
	3	5	Early Bird specials
	3	5	European Bottle service
	3	5	Buy 1 piece, get another of lesser value at 50% off
	3	6	Product specials (e.g., free beverages)
	3	6	Lower prices during off-peak hours (midnight -- 6 AM)
	3	6	Frequent gamer (high-roller) discounts
	3	6	Product incentives (up-sell)
	4	7	Buy 1 piece, get another of lesser value at 50% off
	4	7	Product incentives (up-sell)
	4	7	Happy Hours
	4	7	Product specials (e.g., free beverages)
	4	8	Ladies Night
	4	8	Lower prices during off-peak hours (midnight -- 6 AM)
	4	8	Higher prices during peak hours
	4	8	European Bottle service

FIGURE 6.2.1 The split-plot design for the casino Pricing Scenario.

the software. One way is to have each respondent in a row of a data table, one respondent per row. The first column should be a respondent ID.[2] The second column should be the group number the respondent was randomly assigned to if groups were used in a split-plot design. Finally, the remaining columns or fields should be in the order *best–worst* for as many alternatives as there are per choice set. If there are three alternatives per set, then there are six pairs or selections. The *best–worst* pairs should be in the order shown in Table 6.4. Another layout is shown in Figure 6.3.1.

The entries for the *best–worst* pairs should be the number identifying the alternative in the design.

6.3.2 Aggregate-level estimation

The model estimation framework for an aggregate-level analysis is the same as the discrete choice framework described in the previous chapter. The exact way to specify the data depends on the software; however, estimation is usually facilitated

TABLE 6.4 The layout varies depending on the software. A common layout is shown here for a design with three alternatives in a choice set. The subscripts refer to the alternative, so $Best_1$ is the best choice for alternative 1 and $Worst_1$ is the corresponding worst choice. The ID is the respondent ID and Block# is the number of the block to which the consumer was randomly assigned.

ID	Block#	$Best_1$	$Worst_1$	$Best_2$	$Worst_2$	$Best_3$	$Worst_3$

by creating two data sets and then vertically concatenating them into a single data set for estimation.[3] The first data set represents the best choice and the second the worst choice. For the best choice data set, dummy variables indicate which strategies were included in the choice sets seen by the respondents and a separate dummy variable indicates which strategy was selected as best. The second data set represents the worst choice and is almost a mirror image of the best data set. The difference is that the dummies indicating the strategies included in the choice sets are all −1 rather than +1. The dummy indicating which strategy was selected as the worst is, of course, different in this data set. The two data sets are vertically concatenated and sorted on a respondent ID, choice set ID, and alternative ID. A typical data layout is illustrated in Figure 6.3.1. With this data layout, a discrete choice model is then estimated.

Estimation is done at once over the entire data set without regard to the individual respondent per se. Only one set of parameter estimates results. This is illustrated below.

6.3.3 Disaggregate-level estimation

The only benefit of doing individual level estimation is that you would have partworths for each respondent, allowing you to do further analyses such as segmentation or study response patterns by well-defined subgroups. For the casino example, you could segment the customer base to identify segments for further marketing promotions. If you know *a priori* beverage buying segments based on experience or management judgement as discussed in Chapter 1, then analyses could be done for those segments assuming they are represented in the data. Individual-level estimation is typically done with a *Hierarchical Bayes* (HB) procedure. This is reviewed in the next section.

Digression: HB

In classical statistics and econometrics, a parametric model is specified with constant parameters. As a result, only one model statement is made. As an example, a simple linear regression model for a consumer study is

$$Y_i = \beta_0 + \beta_1 X_i + \varepsilon_i$$

Record	ID	Block	Set	Best	Worst	Best Strategy	Worst Strategy
1	1	1	1	4	10	Product specials (e.g. free beverages)	European Bottle Service
2	1	1	2	6	3	Buy 1 piece, get another of lesser value at 50% off	Product incentives (up-sell)
3	1	1	3	3	9	Product incentives (up-sell)	Ladies Night
4	1	1	4	1	2	Higher prices during peak hours	Lower prices during off-peak hours (midnight -- 6 AM)
5	1	1	5	9	10	Ladies Night	European Bottle Service
6	1	1	6	10	4	European Bottle Service	Product specials (e.g. free beverages)
7	1	1	7	7	8	Early Bird specials	Frequent gamer (high-roller) discounts
8	1	1	8	5	3	Happy Hours	Product incentives (up-sell)
9	1	1	9	6	5	Buy 1 piece, get another of lesser value at 50% off	Happy Hours
10	1	1	10	2	10	Lower prices during off-peak hours (midnight -- 6 AM)	European Bottle Service
11	1	1	11	10	3	European Bottle Service	Product incentives (up-sell)
12	1	1	12	9	6	Ladies Night	Buy 1 piece, get another of lesser value at 50% off
13	2	1	1	9	8	Ladies Night	Frequent gamer (high-roller) discounts
14	2	1	2	7	6	Early Bird specials	Buy 1 piece, get another of lesser value at 50% off
15	2	1	3	4	9	Product specials (e.g. free beverages)	Ladies Night
16	2	1	4	3	7	Product incentives (up-sell)	Early Bird specials
17	2	1	5	7	9	Early Bird specials	Ladies Night
18	2	1	6	10	4	European Bottle Service	Product specials (e.g. free beverages)
19	2	1	7	2	4	Lower prices during off-peak hours (midnight -- 6 AM)	Product specials (e.g. free beverages)
20	2	1	8	3	1	Product incentives (up-sell)	Higher prices during peak hours
21	2	1	9	9	7	Ladies Night	Early Bird specials
22	2	1	10	2	10	Lower prices during off-peak hours (midnight -- 6 AM)	European Bottle Service
23	2	1	11	10	3	European Bottle Service	Product incentives (up-sell)
24	2	1	12	9	8	Ladies Night	Frequent gamer (high-roller) discounts

FIGURE 6.3.1 This layout is used by some programs for estimation. In this version, the strategy numbers are shown in the columns labeled "Best" and "Worst." The corresponding descriptions were joined with this table and are shown in the columns labeled "Best Strategy" and "Worst Strategy."

where Y_i is consumption by consumer i and X_i is the price point. It is assumed that $\varepsilon_i \sim \mathcal{N}(0, \sigma^2), \forall i$. You can see that $E(Y_i) = \beta_0 + \beta_1 X_i = \mu_i$ and $V(Y_i) = \sigma^2$, since ε_i is assumed to be normally distributed. Then $Y_i \sim \mathcal{N}(\mu_i, \sigma^2)$.

The problem with this model is that β_0 and β_1 are constant across all consumers. The implication is that they place the same weight on X no matter the value of X; they are homogeneous regarding preferences. This is unrealistic because consumers are different, with different preferences and therefore weights. They are heterogeneous. People in a market for a product, even though they may seek to buy the same product, have different reasons for buying it, not to mention having different capabilities (e.g., income) to buy it and different price sensitivities. They place different weights on the attributes determined by their personal proclivities and economic situations. In short, consumers are heterogeneous. The aggregate model ignores this. Heterogeneity will be explored further in Chapter 8 on price segmentation.

In addition, because weights vary in the population, there is uncertainty regarding their values. Constancy says there is no uncertainty (except for the fact that the weights are technically unknown). Only one set of constant parameters is estimated.

Another approach views the parameters in the parametric model as random variables that reflect either uncertainty or heterogeneity in the population. Such a model specifies two parts or components in the model statement. The first is the model as stated above. The second specifies the probability distribution for the parameters. This new distribution is the one the parameters are randomly drawn from and itself has a mean and variance. There is thus a hierarchy of models written as

$$Y_i \sim \mathcal{N}(\mu_i, \sigma^2) \tag{106}$$

$$\mu_i = \beta_0 + \beta_1 X_i \tag{107}$$

$$\beta_0, \beta_1 \sim \mathcal{N}(0, V) \tag{108}$$

$$\sigma^2 \sim \text{Inverse Gamma.} \tag{109}$$

The inverse gamma is, as the name suggests, the inverse of a random variable that has a gamma distribution. This is a common distributional assumption for the variance of a normal distribution.[4] The parts for the hierarchical model are therefore:

1. A statistical model for Y_i with unknown parameters that define the mean and variance of Y_i. This is a model for the data given the two parameters, μ_i and σ^2.
2. Distributions for the unknown parameters, which are independent of the data.

This model specification is hierarchical with a top-level model, the statistical model, and a sub-model or series of sub-models (the distribution models), hence the first part of the name for the structure: Hierarchical Bayes. The second part will be discussed next.

Notice in (106) that Y_i has a distribution dependent on the parameters. You can write this as $p(y \mid \theta)$, where θ represents the vector of parameters. For the model above, θ is a vector $(\beta_0, \beta_1, \sigma^2)$.[5] The parameters themselves have a distribution, but this is independent of the Y_i (i.e., it is independent of the data). You can write this second distribution as $p(\theta)$.

The distribution for a parameter is called a *prior distribution*, while the one for the data given the parameters is a *likelihood function*. The information in the data is reflected in the likelihood function, while each parameter is a random draw from its prior. The likelihood can be combined with the prior to form a new distribution called the *posterior distribution* for the parameters as a function of the data written as $p(\theta \mid y)$, where θ is the parameter of interest. *Bayes Theorem* is used to connect the two distributions, $p(y \mid \theta)$ and $p(\theta)$, to give the posterior distribution. Bayes Theorem follows from a basic conditional probability statement:

$$p(y \mid \theta) = \frac{p(y, \theta)}{p(\theta)}$$

so

$$p(y, \theta) = p(y \mid \theta) \times p(\theta).$$

Clearly, you could also write $p(y, \theta) = p(\theta \mid y) \times p(y)$. Therefore,

$$p(y \mid \theta) \times p(\theta) = p(\theta \mid y) \times p(y) \text{ or}$$

$$p(\theta \mid y) = \frac{p(y \mid \theta) \times p(\theta)}{p(y)}.$$

The denominator is just a scaling factor and can be ignored. Consequently, you can write

$$p(\theta \mid y) \propto p(y \mid \theta) \times p(\theta).$$

The term $p(\theta \mid y)$ is the posterior distribution for the parameter θ given the data y, and is proportional to the likelihood for y given the parameter times the prior for the parameter. The likelihood function contains all the information about the data (i.e., the statistical model). The prior embodies our "prior" information or beliefs about the parameters, while the likelihood function is our basic statistical model. The prior beliefs could be based on past studies, management experience, and subject matter expert and key opinion leader understandings of the markets. The prior updates the likelihood function with this information to yield the posterior distribution.

The prior distribution can be either *uninformative* or *informative*. If you do not know enough to specify a distribution for the prior (e.g., not enough past experience), then the prior is uninformative, yet you need one to implement the posterior. A uniform distribution can be used so that each possible value for a parameter is equally likely. As the prior distribution deviates from the uniform, say by becoming "spiked," then it becomes informative because it says which value is more likely to occur. A distribution spiked at a single value (i.e., a degenerate distribution) is perfectly informative, but this is just the classical assumption of non-Bayesian statistical theory – the parameter is a constant.

Each parameter in the statistical model or the likelihood function has a prior distribution. These distributions in turn have parameters called *hyper-parameters*. In (106)–(109), the hyper-parameters are V and those of the inverse gamma. You can have distributions for them as well with their own parameters, but this leads to a proliferation of parameters, which only complicates an already complicated problem. Usually, only one set of hyper-parameters is specified as in (106)–(109).

How does this help? If prior distributions have to be introduced and posterior distributions determined, then this suggests a more complex model structure than just a plain and simple ordinary least squares (OLS) model that could be easily estimated even with a spreadsheet package. A simple OLS model would be an aggregate model like the one discussed in the conjoint chapter.

Estimating a disaggregate OLS model has a potential estimation issue if the data to estimate a model for each consumer are insufficient. Quite often, because of the nature of the treatment design and the number of parameters to estimate, there are insufficient observations relative to the number of parameters to estimate at the individual level so that $n < p$.[6] This may sound like a reason to estimate an aggregate model, but it is not.

Estimation at the level of one consumer can still be done if information can be "borrowed" from the data for other consumers. This borrowing is called *exchangeability* and occurs because the equations for the parameter estimators have a component reflecting the data in the whole data set. For the ith consumer, the expected value for a parameter (which is a random variable) can be written as

$$E\left(\beta_i \mid Y\right) = E\left[W\hat{\beta}_i + \left(I - W\right)Z\right] \tag{110}$$

where $\hat{\beta}_i$ is the OLS estimator for β_i for the ith consumer, I is the identity matrix, and W is the weight as a function of the ith consumer's data and is the covariance matrix for the parameters. The covariance matrix reflects all consumers. The Z term represents the posterior mean of the parameters and also reflects all consumers. In essence, the estimators are weighted averages of the data for a single consumer and the entire data set. If the weights are skewed in favor of the consumer (i.e., $W = I$), then the OLS estimator $\hat{\beta}_i$ results. The weights would be skewed to a consumer if there are sufficient data to estimate a model for each consumer; otherwise, information from the entire data set would be included. This is the essence by which information is borrowed or exchanged from the whole data set (see [143] and [141]).

The idea behind (110) is that borrowing shrinks a consumer's estimator to be in line with those for all other consumers. This is the basis for the distributional assumption for the parameters. They are random draws from a distribution that reflects the heterogeneity in the market, but the distribution nonetheless has a constant mean and variance, suggesting some commonality. Each consumer is "shrunk" back to that commonality in the market (see [141] and [152]).

Until recently, implementing this Bayesian approach was a challenge for mathematical reasons. All but the simplest problems were mathematically difficult enough (to say the least) to prohibit using this approach. With the advent of an algorithm called Markov Chain Monte Carlo (MCMC) implementation of the Bayesian approach became easier, but computationally intensive nonetheless. This works by successively sampling parameters from the posterior distribution, each time using a previous draw's parameter value as a given in the draw for the next parameter. This is done a very large number of times (e.g., 20,000 times). Sampling for each parameter one after another is the Markov Chain part and the random draws from the posterior distribution is the Monte Carlo part. There are a number of sampling methods, with Gibbs Sampling and Metropolis–Hastings being the most dominant.

6.4 Analysis

There are three ways to analyze MaxDiff data:

1. Counting analysis;
2. Aggregate utility analysis;
3. Disaggregate utility analysis.

6.4.1 Counting analysis

Counting the number of times each alternative was selected *best* and *worst* is the simplest form of analysis. The results can be displayed as a simple table as in Figure 6.4.1, with perhaps an accompanying bar chart of the counts as in Figure 6.4.2. This is too simplistic and ignores statistical variations and interactions, so it is rarely used.

| | Best or Worst | | | | | |
| | Best Strategy | | | Worst Strategy | | |
Strategy	N	Column %	Row %	N	Column %	Row %
Buy 1 piece, get another of lesser value at 50% off	126	10.50%	48.28%	135	11.25%	51.72%
Early Bird specials	117	9.75%	48.95%	122	10.17%	51.05%
European Bottle Service	141	11.75%	51.09%	135	11.25%	48.91%
Frequent gamer (high-roller) discounts	107	8.92%	46.32%	124	10.33%	53.68%
Happy Hours	106	8.83%	45.89%	125	10.42%	54.11%
Higher prices during peak hours	96	8.00%	48.73%	101	8.42%	51.27%
Ladies Night	107	8.92%	46.12%	125	10.42%	53.88%
Lower prices during off-peak hours (midnight -- 6 AM)	92	7.67%	48.42%	98	8.17%	51.58%
Product incentives (up-sell)	195	16.25%	64.36%	108	9.00%	35.64%
Product specials (e.g., free beverages)	113	9.42%	47.08%	127	10.58%	52.92%

FIGURE 6.4.1 This table illustrates the counts of the number of times a strategy was selected *best* and *worst* for the casino Pricing Scenario.

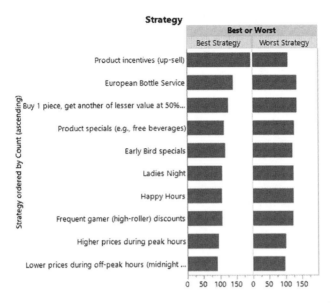

FIGURE 6.4.2 This bar graph illustrates a plot of the counts of the number of times a strategy was selected *best* and *worst* for the casino Pricing Scenario. These counts correspond to the ones shown in Figure 6.4.1.

6.4.2 Aggregate-level analysis

The result of an aggregate-level estimation is a set of parameters interpreted as utilities. These are difficult to explain in their raw form so they are usually transformed to a more meaningful scale. Several transformations are possible:

- Center the utilities for each respondent so that the sum of the utilities is zero.
- Transform the utilities for a respondent to be the probability that the respondent would select each option. The logit transformation is used:

$$Pr_i(\text{option j}) = \frac{e^{u_{ij}}}{\sum_{k=i}^{n} e^{u}_{ik}}$$

where u_{ij} is consumer i's estimated part-worth utility for option j.
- Use the logit probability scaling but adjust for the number of items.

$$Pr_i(\text{option j}) = \frac{e^{u_{ij}}}{\sum_{k=i}^{n}(e^{u}_{ik} + k - 1)}$$

- where k is the number of items.

The last is recommended by [158]. Also see [140], p. 1123 for discussion of transformations or rescalings.

Pricing Scenario: Aggregate estimation

For the Pricing Scenario, the part-worth utilities were estimated and transformed to a logit scale. These are shown in Figure 6.4.3. Notice that only nine strategies are shown in the estimation table while there are ten strategies in the study. One had to be dropped for estimation because effects coding was used. The dropped strategy was the *European Bottle Service*. For the logit transformation, the missing part-worth was set to zero so the exponentiated value was 1.0. The sum of the ten exponentiated values was divided into each individual exponentiated value to give the probability for that strategy. These probabilities are shown in the top portion of Figure 6.4.3. Product incentives (up-sell) is the best strategy.

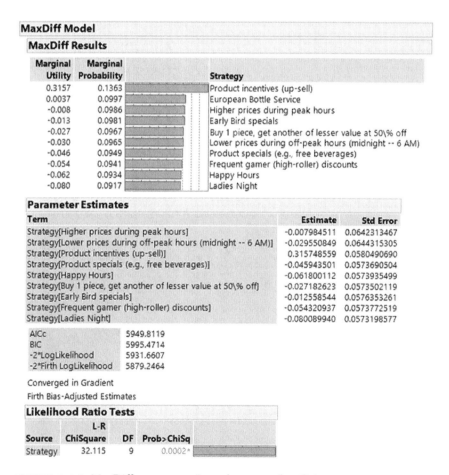

FIGURE 6.4.3 MaxDiff aggregate estimated part-worth utilities.

6.4.3 Disaggregate-level analysis

When disaggregate- or individual-level estimation is done, you have several options for analyzing the results. You could simply average the utilities, transform them as described above, and report the take rates as if an aggregate estimation was done. This, however, defeats the purpose of the disaggregate estimation. The individual-level part-worth utilities can be used in further analyses such as a *total unduplicated reach and frequency* (TURF) analysis or segmentation. TURF is explained below. Segmentation is discussed in Chapter 8.

Pricing Scenario: Disaggregate estimation

The MaxDiff HB estimates are shown in Figure 6.4.4. Notice that the results are close to those obtained for the aggregate estimation. The individual part-worths can be saved for further analysis. The posterior mean is just the mean of the individual part-worths as shown in Figure 6.4.5 for the strategy *higher prices during peak hours*.

A brief introduction to TURF analysis following MaxDiff

TURF originated in advertising, where the goal was to advertise in magazines that reach (i.e., touch or are seen by) the largest number of readers, but without reaching

MaxDiff Model

MaxDiff Results

Marginal Utility	Marginal Probability		Strategy
0.3324	0.1384		Product incentives (up-sell)
0.0039	0.0997		European Bottle Service
-0.003	0.0990		Early Bird specials
-0.006	0.0987		Higher prices during peak hours
-0.027	0.0967		Buy 1 piece, get another of lesser value at 50\% off
-0.028	0.0966		Lower prices during off-peak hours (midnight -- 6 AM)
-0.054	0.0941		Product specials (e.g., free beverages)
-0.059	0.0936		Frequent gamer (high-roller) discounts
-0.072	0.0924		Happy Hours
-0.087	0.0910		Ladies Night

Bayesian Parameter Estimates

Term	Posterior Mean	Posterior Std Dev	Subject Std Dev
Strategy[Higher prices during peak hours]	-0.006381906	0.0555231274	0.1122701819
Strategy[Lower prices during off-peak hours (midnight -- 6 AM)]	-0.027889039	0.0647530507	0.1091064883
Strategy[Product incentives (up-sell)]	0.332446610	0.0535383850	0.1385268644
Strategy[Product specials (e.g., free beverages)]	-0.053828564	0.0561192163	0.0985388760
Strategy[Happy Hours]	-0.071833522	0.0493529499	0.1180055884
Strategy[Buy 1 piece, get another of lesser value at 50\% off]	-0.026706854	0.0584011497	0.1083636441
Strategy[Early Bird specials]	-0.003201620	0.0576474008	0.1029564135
Strategy[Frequent gamer (high-roller) discounts]	-0.059403337	0.0569629089	0.1130672607
Strategy[Ladies Night]	-0.087063356	0.0564707755	0.1181379650

Total Iterations	5,000
Burn-In Iterations	2,500
Number of Respondents	100
Avg Log Likelihood After Burn-In	-2920.004

FIGURE 6.4.4 MaxDiff disaggregate estimated part-worth utilities.

Distributions

Strategy[Higher prices during peak hours]

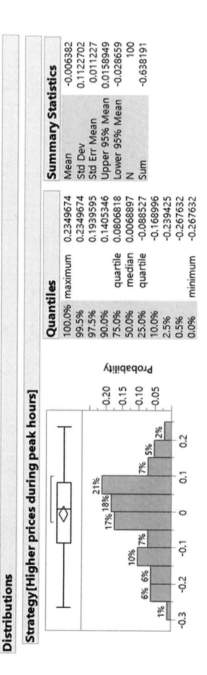

Quantiles

100.0%	maximum	0.2349674
99.5%		0.2349674
97.5%		0.1939595
90.0%		0.1405346
75.0%	quartile	0.0806818
50.0%	median	0.0068897
25.0%	quartile	-0.088527
10.0%		-0.168996
2.5%		-0.239425
0.5%		-0.267632
0.0%	minimum	-0.267632

Summary Statistics

Mean	-0.006382
Std Dev	0.1122702
Std Err Mean	0.011227
Upper 95% Mean	0.0158949
Lower 95% Mean	-0.028659
N	100
Sum	-0.638191

FIGURE 6.4.5 MaxDiff disaggregate estimated part-worth utilities distribution of *Higher Prices During Peak Hours*.

the same reader twice (or more times). Many people read several magazines, so advertising in all the ones they read would reach the same person several times; this is not cost efficient for the advertiser. TURF analysis was designed to answer the question: *What is the best combination of magazines that reach as many readers as possible without duplicating who is reached?* It is now used in a variety of applications beyond magazine readership. These applications include product line extension, direct marketing to customers without duplicating mailings, identifying the best combination of new products to offer or stock, and identifying optimal pricing strategies, to name just a few.

To understand how TURF works, first consider the traditional example of magazine readership. Consumers could be surveyed and asked to indicate the magazines they read. This would be a *check all that apply* (CATA) question. The data would be recorded as 0/1 with 0 = "*no*" and 1 = "*yes.*" Consumers could alternatively be asked their preference for each magazine measured on a ten-point Likert scale. This could be recoded as 1 = T3B and 0 otherwise.[7] In both cases, the data are recorded as 0/1. This is the scale needed for a TURF analysis.

Assume there are 385 consumers and three magazines: *A*, *B*, and *C*. The ads can only be placed in two because of budget constraints, so the research question is: *Which two of the three would provide the best advertising exposure (i.e., reach)?* Each consumer was asked to indicate which magazine they read, so this is a CATA question. The choices were recorded as 0/1. The frequency counts or readerships are: *A*: 253, *B*: 227, and *C*: 143. There are three pairs of magazines $\binom{3}{2}$, with total readership as shown in Table 6.5.

Intuition and the data suggest advertising in *A* and *B* since they have the largest joint readership: 480. Is this correct? Obviously it is not since, there were only 385 consumers in the study. Some must be double counted, and similarly for *A* and *C*. The double counting must be removed to have an accurate view of the market. Many researchers look at the relative frequencies or proportions rather than the absolute frequencies to select the two best magazines. The relative frequencies are shown in Table 6.6. Again, magazines *A* and *B* would be selected.

TABLE 6.5 Total readership for three combinations of size two for three magazines.

	A&B	*A&C*	*B&C*
Total frequency	480	396	370

TABLE 6.6 Relative frequencies for each magazine. The proportions have a base of $n = 385$.

	A	*B*	*C*
Frequency	253	227	143
Proportion	0.657	0.590	0.371

Consider the following scenario:

- 167 of the 253 A readers also read B;
- 64 of the 143 C readers also read A;
- 49 of the 227 B readers also read C.

Since 167 A readers also read B, this implies there are 86 unique A readers for the pair $A\&B$, while there are 60 unique B readers. The total for $A\&B$ is 86 + 167 + 60 = 333 out of 385 readers. This is shown in Table 6.7, along with the $A\&C$ and $B\&C$ pairs.

The 167 people for the pair $A\&B$ are listed as "unduplicated" because they read both A *and* B, so they are in both categories A and B; they are duplicated or counted twice. As unduplicated, they are counted only once for the pair, as they should be. It should be recognized that this is just a Venn Diagram analysis where you want to know the number of people who read A or B. This is the number who read A plus the number who read B less the number who read both. If you consider a Venn Diagram for all pairs, you get the diagram shown in Figure 6.4.6.[8]

Reach in TURF analysis is the number of unduplicated consumers who are touched or reached by a claim, message, offer, or strategy. This is sometimes expressed as a percentage of the total number of consumers in the relevant market. As a percentage, reach can be interpreted as the probability that someone would select at least one of the items. For the magazines, there are 385 readers, so the reach numbers are: $A\&B$ = 81.4%; $A\&C$ = 86.4%; $B\&C$ = 83.6%. The probability of touching a reader is highest with $A\&C$.

Frequency in TURF analysis is the number of times someone is touched or reached. If someone buys two magazines, they are reached once, but they have two counts or frequencies of events. Typically, a threshold of 1 is used to determine reach: if they have a frequency of 1 or more, then reach is counted as 1; otherwise, it is counted as 0.

The TURF algorithm uses an exhaustive search through all combinations of items (three magazines in our example; ten pricing strategies for the first case study). The number of combinations could be very large. For example, for the ten pricing

TABLE 6.7 Readership for three combinations of size two for three magazines for the scenario.

$A\&B$		$A\&C$		$B\&C$	
Read A only	86	Read A only	189	Read B only	179
Unduplicated	167	Unduplicated	64	Unduplicated	49
Read B only	60	Read C only	79	Read C only	95
Total unduplicated	313	Total unduplicated	333	Total unduplicated	322

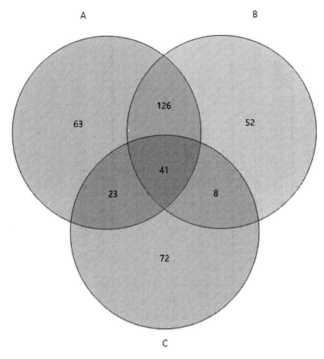

FIGURE 6.4.6 A Venn Diagram illustration of the TURF analysis.

strategies with combinations of size two, there are $45 \left[= \begin{pmatrix} 10 \\ 2 \end{pmatrix} \right]$ combinations. If management instead wanted the best combination of four strategies, there would be $210 \left[= \begin{pmatrix} 10 \\ 4 \end{pmatrix} \right]$ combinations to examine. Clearly, TURF can become computationally intensive. Some have proposed a binary linear programming solution (see [161] for an example).

A TURF analysis can be done using the MaxDiff utilities, preferably after they have been rescaled to take rates that sum to 1.0 for each consumer. These take rates must be dummified since TURF operates on 0/1 values, as noted above. There are several possibilities for recoding the take rates:

- Take rates greater than an arbitrarily specified value (e.g., 0.50) are recoded as 1, 0 otherwise.
- Take rates greater than a specified quantile (e.g., 0.50, 0.75) of all take rates are recoded as 1, 0 otherwise.
- Take rates greater than the mean take rate plus 1, 2, or 3 standard deviations are recoded as 1, 0 otherwise.

Whichever method is used, it must result in a matrix of 0/1 values. The TURF algorithm uses these 0/1 values and calculates all possible combinations of the variables. Depending on the size of the problem (i.e., the number of messages), all combinations of messages are created, and for each combination, reach counts and proportions of the total sample are calculated. These combinations are then rank ordered, allowing one to determine the best combination in terms of reach.

Pricing Scenario: TURF analysis

For the casino Pricing Scenario, management wanted to know the best strategies out of the ten proposed in combinations of one to three. The size one bundles are, of course, just the proportion for each strategy. The numbers of combinations are: ten for size one at a time; 45 for size two at a time; and 120 for size three at a time. The total number of combinations to be examined is thus 175. The MaxDiff utilities were estimated at the individual level using a HB procedure. They were then recoded to take rates for each individual using the logit transformation. The take rates were dummified using the mean for all take rates plus 3 standard deviations. Results are shown in Figure 6.4.7. Although Strategy #10: *European Bottle Service* is the second highest ranked individual item, it is not included in the top 2-tuple or 3-tuple bundles. This illustrates why a TURF analysis should be done rather than just relying on individual rankings.

6.5   Pricing product add-on options

Quite often, consumers are presented with options they could buy to enhance a basic purchase. A common example is a car purchase. A consumer can add features to the basic car such as a moon roof, leather seats, and heated seats, to name just a few. Other examples of add-on options are:

- Excursions, or side trips, offered by tour companies to enhance the basic trip experience;
- Special meetings, lunches, or events at professional conferences that are additions to the basic conference meetings;
- Special packages offered by house cleaning services (e.g., window cleaning, floor waxing, carpet shampooing);
- Extended warranties offered when major household appliances are purchased;
- Restaurant menus with a basic entree and optional side dishes;
- Airlines with seat upgrades;
- Different insurance coverages for new appliances.

The issue is which options appeal the most to consumers and at what price points. MaxDiff can be used for this situation. See [105] for a discussion, which is the basis for this section. Options have been studied in the economics literature. See [118] for a good discussion with examples.

Turf Analysis Summary

Housekeeping Data

Client	Project	Report Date and Time
Casino XX	Casino Beverage TURF	02Dec2016:11:05:35

Data Sources

Data: casino turf
Items: 092916_1 Casino Profiles

Parameters

Parameters	Values
Number of Items	10
Number of Bundles to Show	3
Bundle Size	1 to 3
Threshold	1
Max Possible Frequency	1000

Number of Combinations Examined

Bundles of Size:	Number of Combinations
1	10
2	45
3	120

Item Definitions

Item Number	Description
1	Higher prices during peak hours
2	Lower prices during off-peak hours (midnight – 6 AM)
3	Product incentives (up-sell)
4	Product specials (e.g., free beverages)
5	Happy Hours
6	Buy 1 piece, get another of lesser value at 50% off
7	Early Bird specials
8	Frequent gamer (high-roller) discounts
9	Ladies Night
10	European Bottle Service

TURF Details

Top 3 Bundles

Run	Bundle Composition	Reach Count	Reach Percent	Frequency	Frequency Percent of Max
1,1	Col3	100	1	100	0.1
1,2	Col10	68	0.68	68	0.068
1,3	Col1	59	0.59	59	0.059
2,1	Col1/Col3	100	1	159	0.159
2,2	Col2/Col3	100	1	140	0.14
2,3	Col3/Col4	100	1	137	0.137
3,1	Col1/Col2/Col3	100	1	199	0.199
3,2	Col1/Col3/Col4	100	1	196	0.196
3,3	Col1/Col3/Col5	100	1	190	0.19

Items Summary

Size 1

Items in Top Bundle		Items in Second Top Bundle	
Item Identifier	Description	Item Identifier	Description
Col3	Product incentives (up-sell)	Col10	European Bottle Service

Size 2

Items in Top Bundle		Items in Second Top Bundle	
Item Identifier	Description	Item Identifier	Description
Col1	Higher prices during peak hours	Col2	Lower prices during off-peak hours (midnight – 6 AM)
Col3	Product incentives (up-sell)	Col3	Product incentives (up-sell)

Size 3

Items in Top Bundle		Items in Second Top Bundle	
Item Identifier	Description	Item Identifier	Description
Col1	Higher prices during peak hours	Col1	Higher prices during peak hours
Col2	Lower prices during off-peak hours (midnight – 6 AM)	Col3	Product incentives (up-sell)
Col3	Product incentives (up-sell)	Col4	Product specials (e.g., free beverages)

FIGURE 6.4.7 This is a summary of the TURF analysis for the casino Pricing Scenario.

6.5.1 Pricing Scenario: Wedding caterer options

A wedding caterer has a basic wedding package that has proven successful for many weddings. Due to heavy competition, however, she would like to offer options over and above the basic wedding catering package to differentiate itself from the competition. She developed nine options by studying what other caterers offer. These are:

1. Choice of Eleven Hors d'oeuvres;
2. Imported and Domestic Cheese Display;
3. Fresh Fruit Display;

4. Vegetable Display;
5. Antipasto Display;
6. Choice of Three Hot Appetizers;
7. Choice of Two Culinary Displays;
8. Choice of Two Chef-Attended Stations;
9. Raw Oyster Bar.

The caterer also decided on three price points each, which, for simplicity in this example, are merely labeled *Low/Medium/High* for each option. The problem is to find the option and the price point that is the best pair to offer.

6.5.2 Treatment design

Two steps are involved in creating a design for an option problem with prices. The first step is to create a BIBD for the options. This ensures that the options are distributed "equitably." Then, randomly assign price points to the options. Do not assign price points to the options and then create a design because it is possible that one option could appear several times in one block with different prices. The lowest-priced version will always win. You want different options at different price points in each block. Creating the option design first ensures this.

A treatment design of the options was first created for this problem. This had ten blocks of choice sets, with each block consisting of five sets and each set having four options. This resulted in a data table of 200 rows. Prices were then randomly assigned to each row of the table. A section of the design matrix is shown in Table 6.8.

6.5.3 Estimation

Estimation was first done at the aggregate level. The results are shown in Figure 6.5.1. The interpretation is same as before. The take rates (i.e., marginal probabilities)

TABLE 6.8 This is a small section of the design matrix for the wedding caterer Pricing Scenario. Only two choice sets of the first of ten blocks are shown.

Block	Set	Alternative	Option	Price
1	1	1	Choice of Three Hot Appetizers	High
1	1	2	Choice of Two Chef-Attended Stations	High
1	1	3	Antipasto Display	Medium
1	1	4	Raw Oyster Bar	Medium
1	2	1	Choice of Three Hot Appetizers	High
1	2	2	Fresh Fruit Display	Low
1	2	3	Raw Oyster Bar	Medium
1	2	4	Antipasto Display	Medium

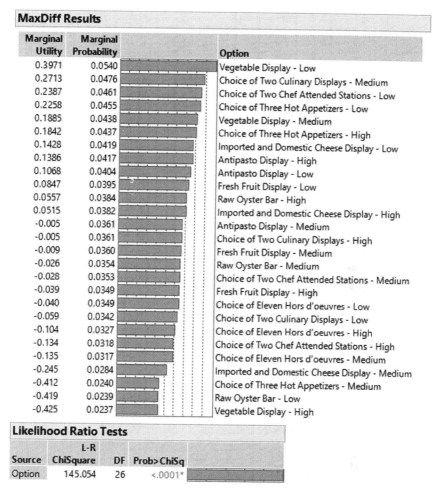

MaxDiff Results

Marginal Utility	Marginal Probability		Option
0.3971	0.0540		Vegetable Display - Low
0.2713	0.0476		Choice of Two Culinary Displays - Medium
0.2387	0.0461		Choice of Two Chef Attended Stations - Low
0.2258	0.0455		Choice of Three Hot Appetizers - Low
0.1885	0.0438		Vegetable Display - Medium
0.1842	0.0437		Choice of Three Hot Appetizers - High
0.1428	0.0419		Imported and Domestic Cheese Display - Low
0.1386	0.0417		Antipasto Display - High
0.1068	0.0404		Antipasto Display - Low
0.0847	0.0395		Fresh Fruit Display - Low
0.0557	0.0384		Raw Oyster Bar - High
0.0515	0.0382		Imported and Domestic Cheese Display - High
-0.005	0.0361		Antipasto Display - Medium
-0.005	0.0361		Choice of Two Culinary Displays - High
-0.009	0.0360		Fresh Fruit Display - Medium
-0.026	0.0354		Raw Oyster Bar - Medium
-0.028	0.0353		Choice of Two Chef Attended Stations - Medium
-0.039	0.0349		Fresh Fruit Display - High
-0.040	0.0349		Choice of Eleven Hors d'oeuvres - Low
-0.059	0.0342		Choice of Two Culinary Displays - Low
-0.104	0.0327		Choice of Eleven Hors d'oeuvres - High
-0.134	0.0318		Choice of Two Chef Attended Stations - High
-0.135	0.0317		Choice of Eleven Hors d'oeuvres - Medium
-0.245	0.0284		Imported and Domestic Cheese Display - Medium
-0.412	0.0240		Choice of Three Hot Appetizers - Medium
-0.419	0.0239		Raw Oyster Bar - Low
-0.425	0.0237		Vegetable Display - High

Likelihood Ratio Tests

Source	L-R ChiSquare	DF	Prob>ChiSq
Option	145.054	26	<.0001*

FIGURE 6.5.1 These are the take rate estimates for the wedding caterer options Pricing Scenario.

were saved along with the attribute/price labels. A heat map, shown in Figure 6.5.2, was created.

6.6   Software

Software to design and estimate MaxDiff models includes the products from Sawtooth Software and JMP's MaxDiff functions. R, the open-source program, also has packages for designing BIBDs and estimating HB models. SAS has a series of macros for determining feasible designs and then creating them. SAS was used to create the design for the casino case study. For TURF analysis, an

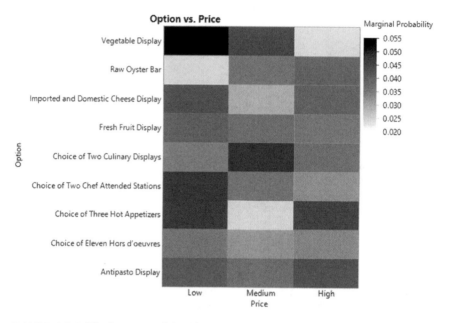

FIGURE 6.5.2 The heat map of the take rate estimates for the wedding caterer options Pricing Scenario shows the relationships between the options and prices.

add-in package is available for JMP that estimates reach. Figure 6.4.7 was developed using this add-in.

6.7 Summary

In this chapter, I extended the choice family to include the MaxDiff methodology. This approach to choice analysis is most useful for understanding strategy options rather than to determine an optimal price point. However, when prices are coupled with options in a somewhat simple fashion, the method can be insightful for determining the best option and price point.

Notes

1 As a programming analogy, consider a series of three do-loops with the groups as the outermost loop, the choice sets as the next innermost loop, followed by the alternatives as the last innermost loop. The groups would vary slowly, followed by the choice sets, followed by the alternatives, which would vary quickly.
2 I always like to have a respondent ID to ensure that I can match against other data sets if needed.
3 JMP uses the data layout shown in Figure 6.3.1.
4 See https://en.wikipedia.org/wiki/Inverse-gamma_distribution.

5 For a linear regression model, the likelihood function $p(y \mid \theta)$ is the product of the individual normal densities because the sample of size n is a random sample. Or,

$$p(y \mid \theta) = \prod_{i=1}^{n} \frac{1}{\sigma\sqrt{2\pi}} e^{-(Y_i - \beta_0 - \beta_1 X_i)^2 / 2\sigma^2}$$

6 The data matrix would be less than full rank.

7 "T3B" is the top three box rating on the ten-point Likert scale.

8 The cardinality or size of the union is the sum of the cardinalities of two strategies less the cardinality of the intersection. In set notation, $n(A \cup B) = n(A) + n(B) - n(A \cap B)$, where the size or count (i.e., the cardinality) is represented by $n(\cdot)$.

7

OTHER STATED PREFERENCE METHODS

The previous three chapters were concerned with survey methodologies that are now staples in pricing analysis. There are, however, three others that often appear and are worthy of some attention. These are the van Westendorp Price Sensitivity Meter, Gabor–Granger pricing methodology, and A/B price testing. I describe these in the following three sections. Each section has its own Pricing Scenario. Software is mentioned in Section 4, while Section 5 is a summary.

7.1 van Westendorp Price Sensitivity Meter

There is no "best" price for planning purposes and early business case development before the launch of a new product. There are too many unknowns at the early stage, especially for a completely new-to-the-world product, for a definitive price point to be determined. A range of prices is preferable for planning purposes, but this begs a new question: *What is the best range*? This differs from the previous main pricing question – *What is the best price*? – by focusing on a range as opposed to a point.

The *van Westendorp Price Sensitivity Meter* is a method for determining the optimal range of prices for a product. Developed in 1976 by the Dutch economist Peter van Westendorp, it is a method to elicit consumers' subjective valuations based on a series of simple questions designed to reveal a range of prices acceptable to consumers. It provides a *range* of prices, not an "optimal" price, although one price determined by the method is sometimes viewed as the "optimal" one. Nonetheless, this range is useful for new product pricing. See [147] for an application that emphasizes ranges. Also see [169] for the original paper.

The questions are designed to elicit perceptions of "cheapness" and "expensiveness" of a product from consumers. It is assumed they have these perceptions based on illustrations or descriptions or prior use of similar products or simple notions of what is "right" or "fair." These perceptions are subjective and have to be revealed through surveys. Economists tell us that market prices reveal these subjective valuations, but barring a market for a new product, you must use survey methods to make consumers state them.

7.1.1 Pricing Scenario

A software developer is seeking venture capital to help finance the development and marketing of a new product targeted to small businesses struggling to manage invoices. The product makes it easier to record, categorize, and cross-reference invoices. The vendor believes the price should be in the range of $100–$550. A more realistic price range is needed for the business plan to be submitted to potential backers.

A pricing consultant recommended the van Westendorp method for determining a range of prices for a business case analysis. A crucial first step is determining candidate price points to use in the study, so the consultant conducted focus groups and interviewed key opinion leaders and subject matter experts to determine these proposed prices. The consultant believed four or more are required. Fewer than four is not informative enough since the respondents will be asked to use the prices to answer four questions giving one price per question. The client wondered why price points are needed since the goal is to determine price points, so this seemed circular to him. *Why not just ask the consumers for the prices?* he wondered. The consultant explained that prices should be provided; they should not be supplied by consumers in terms of how much they would be willing to pay, since many unrealistic prices (especially zero) would be mentioned. The consultant described a shampoo study she worked on the previous year in which consumers were asked the prices rather than being given options to select from. Many stated $0 and $75 and higher just for shampoo! These were unrealistic and therefore of no value to the study, resulting in the client paying for useless data. The client also explained that, for a new product, consumers also do not have an anchor point to use as a reference to formulate their responses, so they need guides.

Ten price points were settled on that ranged from $100 to $550 in $50 increments. The respondents would be asked to select one of the ten for each of the four questions. The analysis would use responses to each question to provide the client with the needed price range.

7.1.2 The four questions

The fours questions are:

1. A "too expensive" question:
    *   At what price is the product so expensive you would not buy it?
2. An "expensive" question:
    *   At what price is the product becoming expensive so you would have to think about buying it?

3.   An "inexpensive" or "bargain" question:
    • At what price is the product a bargain, great value for the money?
4.   A "too inexpensive" or "cheap" question:
    • At what price is the product so inexpensive you would feel the quality is questionable?

The exact wording of each question varies depending on the product or services, but the essence of each must be maintained.

7.1.3 Analysis

Responses to the four questions are used to calculate a cumulative frequency distribution for each question. The four distributions are plotted as price points vs. cumulative percentage of respondents. Traditionally, the two inexpensive curves are plotted with negative slopes. Figure 7.1.1 shows an example. The intersections of the curves can be interpreted. Four intersections are generally discussed, although there are no uniform definitions for them.[1] Referring to Figure 7.1.2, the intersections are:

> *Optimal Price Point (OPP):* The price at which the number of consumers who rated the product too expensive equals the number rating it cheap: Too Expensive = Cheap. It is the equilibrium price between not buying the product and doubting its quality.
>
> *Indifferent Price Point (IPP):* The price at which the number of consumers who rated the product as expensive equals the number rating it a bargain: Expensive = Bargain.[2]
>
> *Point of Marginal Cheapness (PMC):* The lower bound of a range of acceptable prices where consumers are on the edge or "margin" of questioning the product's quality: Expensive = Cheap.

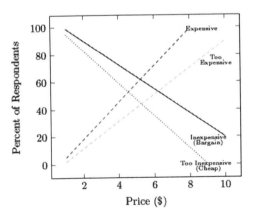

FIGURE 7.1.1 Illustrative van Westendorp price plot of the four key curves. The vertical axis is the cumulative percentage of respondents.

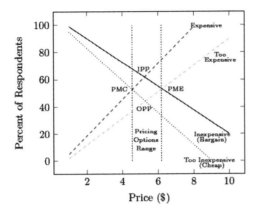

FIGURE 7.1.2 Illustrative van Westendorp price plot with pricing ranges.

Point of Marginal Expensiveness (PME): The upper bound of a range of acceptable prices where consumers are on the edge or "margin" of viewing the product as outside their means: Too Expensive = Bargain.

There are two other values sometimes calculated that help define the optimal price range: a *Stress Range* and a *Pricing Options Range*. These are:

Stress Range: The OPP to IPP range: the range of prices for which the optimal is less than the indifference price.
Pricing Options Range: The PMC to PME range: the optimal range of prices. This is the range the marketing manager should focus on.

The OPP is sometimes interpreted as an optimal price (obviously because of the name), but this is incorrect. It is not really the *single* optimal price, since the basic questions strive to determine ranges. Also, the method relies on consumers having some understanding of prices in the market, the anchor price mentioned earlier. If a consumer has not purchased or shopped within the recent past, their knowledge of prices will be very limited and this method will have limited use. This points out the need for a screener question on frequency and recency of purchase.

To interpret the intersections of the classical van Westendorp diagram, you need to understand the relationship between price, quality, and value. There is a large literature, and certainly much casual evidence, that price is an indicator of quality. Sometimes quality can be assessed by merely looking at a product. Other times, however, quality is difficult to judge, and it is especially difficult to judge the quality of a new product. Quality is perceived by the consumer, and each consumer has a different perception. Monetary price, which is objectively determined by the market, plays the role (among many) of indicating the quality. In general, the higher the price, the higher or better the perceived quality; the lower the price, the lower the perceived quality. If there are two products sitting on a store shelf in the same product category (e.g., two shampoos) and one is priced high and the other low, the low-priced one will be deemed to have lower quality. The low-quality product has a low price because the demand is lower. The product will be viewed as "cheap" and not worth a high price. Because of this relationship between price and quality, product managers can use price to position a product as a high- or low-quality item – the price sends a signal to the market.

Value is subjective and more difficult to define. In fact, there is a huge economics literature that is centuries old that deals with value. Basically, it is the utility someone receives from a product. It is the worth to a consumer. To quote an example from Wikipedia[3]:

> The real value of a book sold to a student who pays $50.00 at the cash register for the text and who earns no additional income from reading the book is essentially zero. However; the real value of the same text purchased in a thrift shop at a price of $0.25 and provides the reader with an insight that allows him or her to earn $100,000.00 in additional income is $100,000.00 or the extended lifetime value earned by the consumer. This is value calculated by actual measurements of [return on investment] instead of production input and or demand vs. supply. No single unit has a fixed value.

So, value has a relationship to price. Value clearly goes beyond the monetary aspect of the product. Basically, if consumers see a high-quality product at a reasonable monetary price, they will perceive the product as having a high value. Perceived quality, perceived value, and monetary price are highly correlated. The van Westendorp methodology considers this relationship and tries to capture the value–quality–price nexus with the four questions. Intuitively, between some limits or bounds, the monetary price may act as an indicator of quality, but not a barrier or hindrance to purchasing, because the product still has value. However, outside these limits, the price may hinder purchase. Above the limits, quality may be judged too high and exceed the consumer's perception of value; below the limits, the product is judged to have poor quality and little value.

Consumers can be viewed as resisting paying an unacceptable price for a product. They have a perceived value in mind based on their perceived quality assessment, which is signaled by the monetary price. The issue is – where is purchase resistance highest and lowest?

The point where the cheap and too expensive curves intersect (OPP) is the point where purchase resistance is the lowest. Any lower price means the quality is poor; any higher price means that it is getting out of reach for their fixed income and the perceived quality, so it has low value to them. This is sometimes interpreted as the price consumers would like to pay. Any lower price would not be tolerated because of the poor quality signal.

The outer, or most extreme, points for pricing are given by the marginal values. Marginal in economics means "on the edge" of doing one thing or another. At the PMC and PME, the consumers are on the edge of buying or not buying. This is a range some analysts prefer to use.

The point where the bargain and expensive curves intersect (IPP) is that point where there is value in the product and price is not a hindrance. The quality is judged to be good or fair so it is worth the money. The product is not cheap. This can be looked at as the point of highest price resistance. Any higher monetary price would not be tolerated because of the resulting low value signal – it is not worth the cost.

The cumulative percentages on the vertical axis of the van Westendorp chart can help with interpretation of the IPP. If the intersection occurs at a high percentage of consumers (the vertical axis), it indicates consumers believe that, even though expensive, it is a bargain – high value. The consumers will have low price consciousness because they are not aware of how high the price actually is. On the other hand, if the intersection occurs at a low percentage of consumers, it indicates that consumers are questioning value – it is not expensive, but not a bargain. The consumers are more price conscious because they see the value more than the consumers at a high intersection point.

The *stress* is the pressure in the market to lower the price. Basically, the price consumers would like to pay (OPP) is less than the price at which they view the product as a bargain (IPP), so they are "stressed" as to what to do, and this "stress" is reflected in the market as a downward pressure on price. The closer the IPP and OPP, the less stress in the market, since the highest and lowest resistances are equal – quality and value match at a single monetary price.

7.1.4   The Pricing Scenario – Analysis

A survey was conducted with $n = 385$ consumers. They were each given a description of the new product concept and then they were told the proposed price points and then asked the four questions.

Once all the data were collected, a quality check was done to make sure that the selected price points of each consumer were logically consistent. This means that the order should be *Too Expensive* ≥ *Expensive* ≥ *Bargain* ≥ *Cheap*. If for any consumer this relationship does not hold, then that consumer must be deleted. The distribution of the valid and invalid responses for the Pricing Scenario is shown in Figure 7.1.3. The effective sample size is $n = 312$.

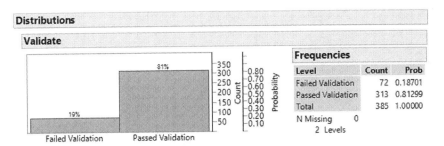

FIGURE 7.1.3 This shows a distribution of a validation check of van Westendorp data. The sample size is 385 consumers, but 72 had inconsistent data so they had to be deleted.

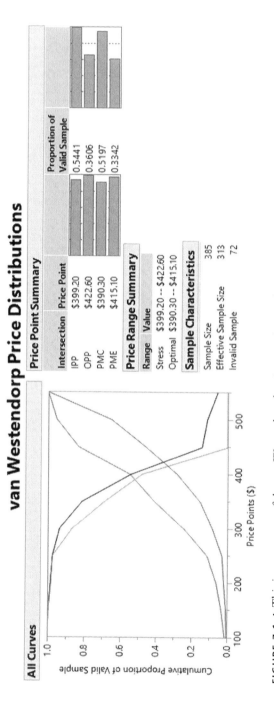

FIGURE 7.1.4 This is a summary of the van Westendorp key intersections and ranges.

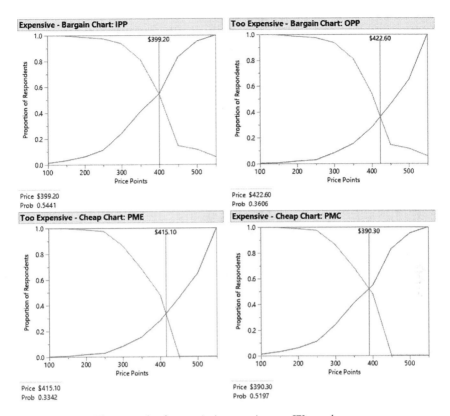

FIGURE 7.1.5 These are the four main intersecting van Westendorp curves.

A summary of the van Westendorp chart and price points is shown in Figure 7.1.4. Notice that the intersection points are all quite close to each other, which makes it difficult to graphically label the intersections. More detailed plots are shown in Figure 7.1.5 and Figure 7.1.6. The optimal range is $390.30–$415.10. This is the range the pricing consultant recommended for the business case.

7.2 Gabor–Granger

The *Gabor–Granger* pricing methodology is an old method for determining a demand curve for a product. The economists Clive Granger[4] and André Gabor developed the methodology in the 1960s. Since then, more sophisticated techniques have been developed, especially discrete choice analysis. The Gabor–Granger methodology is still occasionally used because of its intuitive appeal, but it is outdated and not the best (see [123] and [53]).

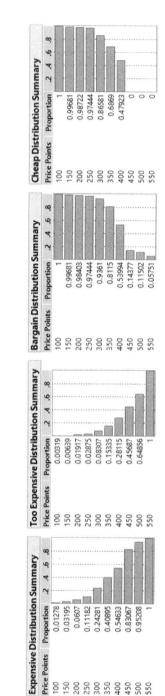

Expensive Distribution Summary	
Price Points	Proportion
100	0.01278
150	0.03195
200	0.0607
250	0.11182
300	0.24281
350	0.40895
400	0.54633
450	0.83067
500	0.95208
550	1

Too Expensive Distribution Summary	
Price Points	Proportion
100	0.00319
150	0.00639
200	0.01917
250	0.02875
300	0.08307
350	0.15335
400	0.28115
450	0.45687
500	0.64856
550	1

Bargain Distribution Summary	
Price Points	Proportion
100	1
150	0.99681
200	0.98403
250	0.97444
300	0.9361
350	0.8115
400	0.53994
450	0.14577
500	0.11502
550	0.05751

Cheap Distribution Summary	
Price Points	Proportion
100	1
150	0.99681
200	0.98722
250	0.97444
300	0.86581
350	0.6869
400	0.47923
450	0
500	0
550	0

FIGURE 7.1.6 These distributions are of the van Westendorp responses.

7.2.1   Methodology

For pricing analytics, consumers are asked their willingness to buy a product at different price points. It is assumed that this querying will reveal the price point at which the consumer will no longer be interested in buying the product. Consumers respond with a "buy–not buy" response to each price so the method is sometimes called the "buy-response method." The constant querying enables you to trace out a demand curve. Once the demand curve is derived, a revenue curve can be overlaid to help determine the optimal price, which is where the revenue curve is a maximum. A price elasticity can then be derived. Figure 7.2.1 illustrates the price–revenue curve and its maximization. Notice that the revenue curve first rises as price increases, but then declines as price continues to rise. The point where revenue is at its maximum is the optimal price point. This was described in Chapter 2.

The approach involves asking a series of questions that are similar in spirt to the van Westendorp questions in the sense that they are of the form "*At what price...?*" In this approach, a consumer is presented with a price for a product. The first price point sets a standard for comparing other prices, so this point is often set at random or based on an "expected" price level. Most studies start at a predetermined price point. The consumer is then asked if he/she would buy the

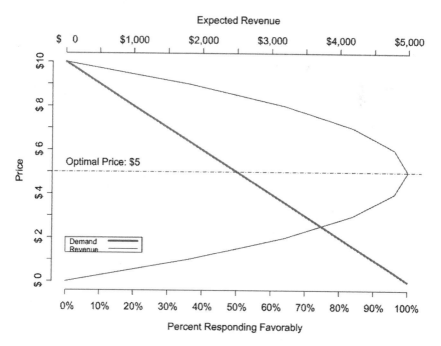

FIGURE 7.2.1 The Gabor–Granger price and revenue curves are basically the ones described in Chapter 2.

product at that price point. There is no standard way to ask this question. Some possibilities are:

- "Would you buy the product at this price?"
- "How likely are you to buy this product at this price?"
- "Would you be willing to pay Y for this product?"

The consumer is then shown another price and the question is repeated. There are several ways to determine the next price to ask:

- Purely random selection;
- Increase or decrease the price dependent on whether the respondent said they would or would not buy, respectively;
- Increase or decrease at random.

7.2.2 Analysis

Across all consumers, you calculate the proportion responding favorably at each price point and then plot the proportions of consumers vs. price points. You can calculate the expected revenue per 100 people at each price point as

$$Revenue = (\text{Percent Responding Favorably}) \times Price.$$

Then plot revenue versus the price points. The optimal price is where the revenue curve is a maximum. Elasticities can also be calculated several ways:

- Calculate the mean percentage change in responses per percentage change in price.
- Estimate a simple linear (or linearized) model with responses as the dependent variable and prices as the independent variable.

$$Response = \beta_0 + \beta_1 Price + \varepsilon.$$

- The elasticity is

$$\eta = \widehat{\beta_1} \times \frac{\overline{Price}}{\overline{Response}}$$

- where $\overline{X}$ is the average.
- A better analytical approach is to recognize that the response from each consumer is binary: buy or not buy. These responses are better analyzed using a logistic regression model to model the probability of a randomly selected consumer responding "buy" to a particular price. The model is

$$Pr(Buy) = \frac{e^Z}{1 + e^Z}$$

- where $Z = \beta_0 + \beta_1 Price$. The elasticity is then

$$\eta = \widehat{\beta_1} \times \text{Price} \times [1 - Pr(Buy)].$$

- Revenue is estimated as

  Revenue = Addressable Market $\times Pr(Buy) \times Price$

- where the *addressable market* is the number of consumers. You can build a simulator so you can vary the price to gauge the effect on units sold (= Addressable Market $\times Pr(Buy)$) and revenue.

7.2.3 Pricing Scenario

A cafe owner has several restaurant locations in a major metropolitan area. He has a new children's sandwich (with chips and a soft drink) he wants to add to his menu, but he is not sure what price to charge. An outside food consultant helping to prepare the menu was asked to conduct a survey of parents to determine the optimal price point (and other features of a children's menu). The consultant decided that a Gabor–Granger approach would suffice for this problem since the sandwich's attributes (e.g., bread, condiment, etc.) were already set. Prior to the study, the consultant predicted that the take rate for the sandwich would be very elastic because there are many other sandwiches on the menu, plus cafes are very competitive and plentiful in the metropolitan area, especially with children's menus.

The cafe owner believed the price points to test should range from $3.95 to $7.95 in increments of $1.00. The consultant used a sample size of $n = 385$. Each parent was asked a series of questions that began with *"Assuming your child would eat this sandwich, would you pay ____ for it?"* with the blank randomly filled with one of five price points: $3.95, $4.95, $5.95, $6.95, $7.95. Each respondent saw each price point in random order until he/she answered *"No."* At that point, any higher price should also be a *"No,"* assuming the consumer is consistent and so would not be asked. The responses were coded as 1 for *Yes* or 0 for *No* and each respondent had five such values. A nominal logistic regression model was fit with the dependent variable being the binary indicator and the independent variable the price points.

Estimation results are shown in Figure 7.2.2. The estimated price coefficient is highly significant. The price elasticity is calculated using the average price point and the take rate is calculated at that average price. For this Pricing Scenario, the average price is $5.95 and the take rate calculated at that average is 0.617. This can be seen in the profiler in Figure 7.2.3. The elasticity is then −1.5 and the revenue elasticity is −0.5. The take rate is elastic as expected. In an elastic environment, raising the price 1% will lower revenue 0.5% because more patrons will go elsewhere or choose something else on the menu.

Lack Of Fit

Source	DF	-LogLikelihood	ChiSquare
Lack Of Fit	3	1.1288	2.257625
Saturated	4	1128.2953	**Prob>ChiSq**
Fitted	1	1129.4241	0.5207

Parameter Estimates

Term	Estimate	Std Error	ChiSquare	Prob>ChiSq
Intercept	4.381383	0.2465908	315.70	<.0001*
Price	-0.6563815	0.0389825	283.51	<.0001*

For log odds of Buy/Not Buy

Effect Likelihood Ratio Tests

Source	Nparm	DF	L-R ChiSquare	Prob>ChiSq
Price	1	1	336.247367	<.0001*

FIGURE 7.2.2 Gabor–Granger parameter estimates based on a logit model. The logit is the log odds of buying to not buying the product.

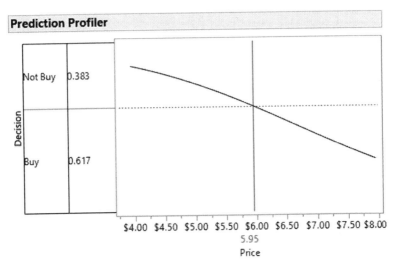

FIGURE 7.2.3 At the price point of $5.95, the take rate is 0.617. The vertical line indicates where the price is set; $5.95 in this case. The take rate is automatically calculated and displayed. The vertical line can be dynamically moved to any price point and the take rate will be updated automatically.

7.2.4 Problems with the methodology

The Gabor–Granger pricing method has several major problems. These include:

- It does not ask the consumer to trade off price for other product attributes, a normal consumer decision. The preferred pricing research methods allow trade-offs. Conjoint is good when a price structure has already been developed and the optimal price in that structure needs to be identified. Discrete choice is good when competitive products are available and, as with conjoint, a proposed pricing structure is already available.
- Consumers may understate the price they will pay. Therefore, the phrasing of the "Will you buy?" question is very important.
- Consumers are not given a reference frame for answering the questions. Research shows they need a consistent reference frame.
- Most consumers do not consider buying a product at a single price – a make-or-break price point – but instead are willing to buy within a range of prices, and Gabor–Granger does not allow for a range.

I recommend using either conjoint or discrete choice because of these problems, although I prefer discrete choice.

7.3 A/B price testing

This is a method used in an online environment to test different website landing pages, advertising and email messages, promotional offers, calls to action, as well as price points. The aim is to determine the impact on a key business metric, usually sales (click rates are also possible).

7.3.1 Pricing scenario

A software as a service company wants to determine the best pricing for its product sold through its online store. The marketing and tech teams proposed the following price points to the Chief Marketing Officer (CMO): marketing: $19.95; tech: $29.95. Which one should the CMO implement? The company can offer each price point on its website and track conversions (i.e., take). The data automatically go to the marketing department and are available for analysis. The questions are:

- How does the marketing department conduct a test?
- How does the marketing team analyze the data?
- Which price point should be used and what would its revenue impact be?

7.3.2   *Methodology*

In its simplest form, there are two steps:

1.   Randomly assign each online store visitor to one of the two prices. Record the visitor's action. They either made a purchase (i.e., converted) or they did not make a purchase.
2.   Arrange the data in a 2×2 table and conduct a statistical test to determine if there is a difference in sales between the two prices. Such a table is shown in Table 7.1.

The study period was two weeks and the total hits were 16,188. A summary of the results in a 2×2 contingency table is shown in Figure 7.3.1, where not only are the responses "*Yes*" and "*No*" qualitative, but so are the two prices in this context. The conversion rate is the percentage of respondents who saw each price point and who then bought the product. You can see that 234 people saw $19.95 and bought the product. This is 3.1% of the sample who saw the product, so this is the conversion rate.

You can test if the conversion rates are statistically the same across the two price points. In other words, the null hypothesis is

$$H_O : p_{\$19.95} = p_{\$29.95} = p$$

against the alternative that the proportions differ. If the proportions are the same, it does not matter which one the CMO selects; the conversion rate will be the same regardless of price. This implies that the demand is price inelastic. Obviously, the higher price should be selected in such a case. If there is a statistical difference, however, then the lower price should be selected. The test is a chi-square goodness-of-fit test. There are two possibilities: Pearson chi-square and likelihood-ratio chi-square. For the Pearson chi-square test, the test statistic is

$$X^2 = \sum_{i=1}^{L} \frac{(O_i - E_i)^2}{E_i}$$

where O_i is the observed frequency and E_i is the expected frequency if the null hypothesis is true. This test statistic follows an asymptotic chi-square distribution

TABLE 7.1 This is a standard 2×2 table layout for an A/B test. Chi-square tests can be done using this layout.

Price	Buy	Not buy
$19.95	n_{11}	n_{12}
$29.95	n_{21}	n_{22}

Contingency Table

Count Total % Col % Row %	Buy		
	Yes	No	Total
$19.95	234 1.45 31.71 3.11	7284 45.00 47.15 96.89	7518 46.44
$29.95	504 3.11 68.29 5.81	8166 50.44 52.85 94.19	8670 53.56
Total	738 4.56	15450 95.44	16188

FIGURE 7.3.1 This contingency table shows the raw sample counts for an A/B Pricing Scenario.

with $L - 1$ degrees of freedom. The p-value tells you the significance. As a ROT, a p-value < 0.05 indicates a significant difference between the two conversion rates. The p-value is for the upper tail of the chi-square distribution since only large values contradict the null hypothesis.

The likelihood-ratio chi-square test is based on the log of the ratio of the observed to expected frequencies, weighted by the observed frequencies

$$G^2 = 2 \times \sum_{i=1}^{L} \left(O_i \times \ln \frac{O_i}{E_i} \right).$$

This also follows an asymptotic chi-square distribution with $L - 1$ degrees of freedom. See [1] for a discussion of the tests.

The two test results are shown in Figure 7.3.2. Notice that both the Pearson and the Likelihood Ratio chi-square tests give similar answers: there is a statistical difference between the conversion rates for the two price points.

You can extend the analysis by calculating the odds of buying at $19.95 relative to the odds of buying at $29.95. The odds are defined as

$$Odds = \frac{Pr(Success)}{Pr(Failure)}.$$

For this problem, "Success" is a conversion while "Failure" is a non-conversion. Odds can be easily calculated for each row of a 2×2 table. Figure 7.3.3 shows the

Tests

N	DF	-LogLike	RSquare (U)
16188	1	34.719852	0.0116

Test	ChiSquare	Prob>ChiSq
Likelihood Ratio	69.440	<.0001*
Pearson	67.493	<.0001*

Fisher's Exact Test	Prob	Alternative Hypothesis
Left	<.0001*	Prob(Buy=No) is greater for Price=$19.95 than $29.95
Right	1.0000	Prob(Buy=No) is greater for Price=$29.95 than $19.95
2-Tail	<.0001*	Prob(Buy=No) is different across Price

FIGURE 7.3.2 This is a summary of two chi-square tests of significance for an A/B test. The two chi-square test statistics, the Pearson and Likelihood Ratio statistics, have similar values and are highly significant.

results of a nominal logistic fit of *Buy* using price as the independent variable, but treating it as a qualitative factor. Effects coding was used for price with $29.95 as the base. The odds calculation at the bottom of the report shows that at a price of $29.95, the odds of a consumer buying are almost twice as high than at a price of $19.95. The odds are 1.9 times higher, or 190% of the odds at $19.95 or they are 90% higher – all are comparable interpretations. This indicates that the higher price is preferable, which may seem odd at first, but considering that hobbyists are the target market, this may make sense. Hobbyists are more inclined to want the "latest" and "greatest" and so may be willing to pay more; except for an extremely high price, for these people price may not be a factor.

Digression on odds calculation

The odds reported in Figure 7.3.3 are actually odds ratios. Notice that they are listed as "Level 1/Level 2," a ratio, or "$29.95 to $19.95" and then the reverse. The $29.95 price is Level 1 and $19.95 is Level 2 on the first line. The odds ratio is the ratio of two odds, the numerator odds conditioned on $29.95 and the denominator odds conditioned on $19.95. The second line is just the inverse. The odds themselves are calculated as I described earlier. The ratio is calculated by writing the ratio using the definitions of the probabilities, appropriately conditioned, for the numerator and denominator. Defining *OR* as the odds ratio, then

$$OR = \frac{Odds_{\$19.95}}{Odds_{\$29.95}}$$

Nominal Logistic Fit for Buy

Converged in Gradient, 6 iterations

Whole Model Test

Model	-LogLikelihood	DF	ChiSquare	Prob>ChiSq
Difference	34.7199	1	69.4397	<.0001*
Full	2965.2003			
Reduced	2999.9202			

RSquare (U)	0.0116
AICc	5934.4
BIC	5949.78
Observations (or Sum Wgts)	16188

Parameter Estimates

Term	Estimate	Std Error	ChiSquare	Prob>ChiSq
Intercept	-3.1116363	0.0403651	5942.4	<.0001*
Price[$19.95]	-0.3264781	0.0403651	65.42	<.0001*

For log odds of Yes/No

Effect Likelihood Ratio Tests

Source	Nparm	DF	L-R ChiSquare	Prob>ChiSq
Price	1	1	69.4397033	<.0001*

Odds Ratios

For Buy odds of Yes versus No

Odds Ratios for Price

Level1	/Level2	Odds Ratio	Prob>Chisq	Lower 95%	Upper 95%
$29.95	$19.95	1.9212118	<.0001*	1.6400516	2.2505723
$19.95	$29.95	0.5205048	<.0001*	0.4443314	0.6097369

Normal approximations used for ratio confidence limits effects:
Price
Tests and confidence intervals on odds ratios are Wald based.

FIGURE 7.3.3 Logit-estimated parameters for an A/B test. The logit is the log odds of "*Yes*" to "*No.*"

Indicator Function Parameterization

Term	Estimate	Std Error	ChiSquare	Prob>|t|
Intercept	-2.785158	0.045898	3682.3	<.0001*
Price[$19.95]	-0.652956	0.08073	65.42	<.0001*

FIGURE 7.3.4 This is an estimation report equivalent to the one in Figure 7.3.3, but based on dummy variable coding.

where the odds of $29.95 is in the denominator because the effects coding used $29.95 as the base, as can be seen in the Parameter Estimates section of Figure 7.3.3. Then you can write

$$OR = \frac{\dfrac{Pr(Buy\,|\,\$19.95)}{Pr(Not\,Buy\,|\,\$19.95)}}{\dfrac{Pr(Buy\,|\,\$19.95)}{Pr(Not\,Buy\,|\,\$19.95)}}.$$

Substituting the logit formulations and simplifying, you will find that $OR = e^{\beta_1 \times (\$19.95 - \$29.95)}$. You know, however, from Chapter 4 that qualitative factors have to be coded using either dummy or effects coding. Effects coding was used here with $29.95 as the base so it is assigned a value of -1; $19.95 is assigned a value of 1. Therefore,

$$\begin{aligned}OR &= e^{\beta_1 \times [-1-(+1)]} \\ &= e^{-0.326478059 \times (-2)} \\ &= 1.92\end{aligned}$$

as shown in Figure 7.3.3. This is the odds of buying at $29.95 to the odds at $19.95. The inverse odds ratio of $19.95 to $29.95 is just 1/1.92 or 0.52, as also shown in Figure 7.3.3. It is easy to show that $0.52 = e^{-0.326478059 \times 2}$. Incidentally, if dummy coding is used, the odds ratio is simply $OR = e^{-0.326478059}$ because the base is coded as 0. In other words, simply exponentiate the coefficient if dummy coding is used. You can verify that this odds ratio is correct using the dummy variable version of the parameter estimates shown in Figure 7.3.4.

7.4 Software

Estimations and analyses for the three methodologies described in this chapter can be done with most statistical packages such as JMP, R, SAS, and Stata. A JMP add-in script was used for the van Westendorp analysis.

7.5 Summary

This short chapter presented three methodologies that are often used despite the fact that other methods, especially discrete choice, are available. The van Westendorp approach is likely the most useful in the early business case development stage for a new product in order to identify a price range. Discrete choice can then be used in the later stages to identify a price point.

Notes

1 See www.ipsos-ideas.com/article.cfm?id=2166 for some discussion of these definitions.
2 Some refer to this as the "normal" price in the market.
3 See https://en.wikipedia.org/wiki/Value_(economics).
4 The 2003 Nobel Memorial Prize in Economic Sciences.

PART III
Price segmentation

In the second part of this book, I presented survey-based methods for determining an optimal price point for a product or service. A nuance of this presentation is that the price point is applicable to the entire market for the single product. The prices are uniform in the market, so they are known as *uniform prices*. It may be that different price points can be used for different parts of the market, the parts being *segments* in marketing parlance. Determining the price and the associated segment are two important activities, but they are not separate activities; they should be done simultaneously. Unfortunately, this is often not the case. This third part of this book is devoted to price segmentation, the simultaneous determination of price and segments. Prices will still be uniform, but now within each segment rather than in the market as a whole.

There are two chapters in the part. Chapter 8 focuses on "traditional" methods for segmenting a market, but it adds the twist of estimating price elasticities at the same time. The methods presented here are basic and rely on a tandem approach to price segmentation: first find the segments and then find the elasticities for those segments. In Chapter 9, I present more advanced methods, primarily latent class regression analysis, for simultaneously determining segments and their elasticities. The latent class approach is recommended for reasons I will discuss later.

8

PRICE SEGMENTATION: BASIC MODELS

This chapter is the first of two on price segmentation, which is the same as the price discrimination I discussed in Chapter 3. I use the phrase "price segmentation" to be consistent with marketing terminology, but also to highlight that it is a combination of pricing and market segmentation. Each is a difficult problem on its own; the combination more than doubles the pricing challenges because they are not separate activities, but are "joined at the hip," forming the *price segmentation nexus* illustrated in Figure 8.0.1. Price segmentation is a two-fold process: (1) identify segments and (2) estimate a price elasticity for each segment. Once elasticities are developed, optimal price points can be developed for those segments using the price elasticity relationships developed in Chapter 3.

I identify two sets of price segmentation methodologies:

1. Traditional or basic;
2. Advanced.

The first is based on classical regression analysis, perhaps used in tandem with clustering methods, but not always. The regression analysis can be ordinary least square (OLS), logistic regression, or any other member of the regression family. The family is *Generalized Linear Models* with each member identified by a *link function* that relates the mean of the dependent variable to a linear function of the independent variables. The link function for OLS is the identify function and the link function for logistic regression is the logit.

The clustering can be hierarchical (any one of an infinite variety), k-means, decision trees and its varieties, self-organizing maps, or by intuition and experience. These are usually two-step tandem methods because segments are identified first and then elasticities are estimated for those segments, in that order. The second set

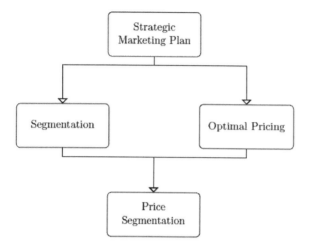

FIGURE 8.0.1 Pricing and segmentation are joined together in a nexus, as illustrated here. Segmentation is the first step of the *strategic marketing process*, while the optimal pricing is part of the marketing mix.

of methods simultaneously finds the segments and estimates price elasticities. Latent class regression (sometimes called latent profile analysis), latent class discrete choice, and multilevel models are in this set.

I recommend the advanced methods because they make more efficient use of the data and the segments and elasticities are consistent with one another since they come from the same model. In addition, they are model based, so there are statistical tests you can apply to the results to assess one solution versus another. This cannot be done for any in the first set except separately and not in unison. Nonetheless, both sets of methods will be discussed and illustrated in this and the next chapter. This chapter focuses on the basic methods; the next will develop the advanced ones.

This chapter is divided into nine sections. Section 1 define price segmentation, while Section 2 discusses the importance of segmentation in the marketing mix while also emphasizing the importance of price segmentation as an iterative process. Section 3 discusses segmentation and consumer heterogeneity that is actually an expansion of the discussion introduced in Chapter 5 about discrete choice models. This notion of heterogeneity permeates all pricing models. This section is meant to be a high-level overview since the literature on segmentation is too vast to adequately summarize here, as well as being outside the scope of this book. Good references are [57] for a brief discussion and [73] for a thorough exposition. Section 4 discusses ways to develop price segments. Section 5 introduces a Pricing Scenario. Sections 6 and 7 focus on two classes of methods for developing segments and price elasticities, each using the Pricing Scenario as a base. Finally, Section 8 discusses software that can be used for segmentation and elasticity estimation, while Section 9 summarizes the major points of the chapter.

Some background material for this and the next chapter can be found in [57].

8.1   What is price segmentation?

Market segmentation is about increasing profitability by providing more latitude for manipulating the marketing mix components. For example, a business could develop promotional messages for different segments and then use a MaxDiff choice study to determine the optimal ranking of the messages that most motivate customers in those segments to buy its product. Alternatively, it could use the pricing component of the marketing mix in conjunction with segmentation to develop differentiated pricing by segments. Price segmentation is the offering of different price points to different homogeneous groups of customers, reflecting their different willingness to pay (WTP).

It is important to clarify what price segmentation is and is not. It is market-driven segmentation, not "deal"-driven segmentation. This means it is based on market conditions, primarily differentiated elasticities. It is the offering of different price points to different groups of customers in the market based on economic conditions. Price segmentation is not about making a deal from a price schedule or within allowable limits (i.e., with discounts) just to make a sale.

8.2   Why price segment the market?

Recall that the marketing mix, consisting of the *Five Ps of Marketing*, is the cornerstone of marketing strategy. There is some controversy about the number (if it is four, seven, or more) and its usefulness. Nonetheless, marketers are trained in it and probably most follow it, more or less.[1] The development of a marketing strategy is a linear process that includes four steps, with mix development as the last. The first three steps are segmentation, targeting, and positioning. This is a linear process because once the market has been segmented, specific targets can be identified and positioning statements written for those targeted segments. An appropriate mix is then developed for the position the marketing team wants to command within the targeted segment. The whole process is sometimes called the *Strategic Marketing Process*. See [57] for more discussion. Also see [151], [149], and [136].

The identification of segments followed by the research and development of prices for them is also treated as a linear process, but it should not be. Segmentation is iterative, with initial segments identified and then reworked based on input from subject matter experts (SMEs), key opinion leaders (KOLs), management, consultants, and marketing personnel. Since it is iterative, why should pricing be separate, to be added on almost as a second thought, since the pricing would be based on the segments? Pricing should be part of the iterative cycling so that it is developed at the same time as the segments. Methodological approaches for this simultaneous process are developed in Chapter 9. This chapter keeps them separate as a linear process since this is what is most often used, based on my experience.

8.3   Segmentation and heterogeneity

Segmenting the market is natural because you tend to think of people as heterogeneous, not homogeneous. However, it was not always this way (see [57] for a brief discussion). The notion of heterogeneity is the basis for the discrete choice models in Chapter 5 where a random, unobserved component was added to a systematic utility shared by everyone in a market group (i.e., segment). The systematic utility represented the commonality (i.e., homogeneity) among the members of a group, while the random component introduced a heterogeneity part for that group. It may seem odd that, on the one hand, the members of a group are homogeneous (represented by the systematic utility), yet, on the other hand, heterogeneous (represented by the random component of utility); however, it is not because people in a group are never exactly the same. They can be the same on some measured attributes (e.g., age, income, location), but be different based on other, albeit unobserved, attributes (e.g., religion; cultural tastes, values, and preferences; political philosophy). In the discrete choice development, the systematic utility varied because of variations in product attributes, while variations in consumer attributes such as income and gender were ignored because of the *equivalent differences property*, although they could be introduced through *Alternative Specific Constants* (ASCs) or more advanced modeling techniques. The discrete choice framework is broad enough to handle these heterogeneity-inducing factors. The observed or observable consumer attributes define the groups and, because they are observed, they can be included in a model.

Unknown and unknowable attributes representing another form of heterogeneity cannot be included in a model, except by the introduction of a random component. This is what gives rise to different distributions (a.k.a., segments). What you observe in the market is a mixture of segments defined by two types of heterogeneity:

Observed: Inter-group differences measured by predictor or regressor or driver or independent variables in a model context. A "model" has to be defined.

Unobserved: All other differences that are attributed to individual idiosyncrasies, impossible-to-measure attributes (e.g., tastes), and socio-demographic factors that are not generally revealed in the market (e.g., cultural tastes).

See [86] for discussions of these types of heterogeneity in the context of price discrimination.

There are two potential views of the market: a total market view and a segmented view. As an example, consider an online retailer with a large database of customers. For each customer, the retailer knows when that customer buys, especially when the last purchase was made, how often the customer buys, and how much that customer typically spends. Using this information, the retailer can calculate the lifetime value (CLV) of each customer. A smooth density curve of a histogram of the CLV shows the general pattern of the distribution of all customers.

An example of a density curve is shown in Figure 8.3.1a. This curve is bimodal because there is not one class or group of customers, but two (or more) underlying densities commingled or mixed together when the one density curve was fitted to the data. Density curves illustrating two classes are shown in Figure 8.3.1b. The weighted sum of the two is the market density in Figure 8.3.1a. The bimodality of the one view is seen to be the result of the single modality of two distributions for two groups or segments, each with a different distribution for preferences. This is the basis for segmentation.

The two distributions reflect inter-group or *between-group heterogeneity*, while the variance of each reflects the intra-group or *within-group heterogeneity*. Observed attributes of consumers (e.g., gender) can be used to characterize or profile the two groups, and thus rationalize their relative positioning, while the unobserved attributes will account for their spread. Both sets of factors work in conjunction to yield the market distribution in Figure 8.3.1a. This is the relevant market distribution for uniform pricing (i.e., one price point to serve the entire market), but this clearly is inappropriate (i.e., suboptimal) because the bimodality suggests that some other structure exists in the market that a uniform price is not exploiting. Figure 8.3.1b, on the other hand, suggests that price discrimination can be used.[2] A comparable set of graphs is shown in [124], but the marketing and economic implications are not explored.

There is an econometric implication of consumer heterogeneity. The basic OLS framework is founded on controlled experiments, where it is reasonably assumed that all model parameters are constant for all experimental units. Unfortunately, market data "come from the very complicated process of everyday life."[3] The implication is that the basic OLS model may not be appropriate because the parameters may not be constant for all subsets of the data. There may be *parameter heterogeneity*. [132] cites two cases:

1. Varying intercepts;
2. Varying intercepts and slopes.

Ignoring the heterogeneity and fitting a constant parameter model is a model misspecification with parameter estimates that mislead and are meaningless. In either case, the wrong pricing decisions could and would be made. An example of a model ignoring parameter heterogeneity is a *completely pooled model*, while one that accounts for the heterogeneity is *partially pooled*. A completely pooled model uses all the data without regard for separate model specifications; basically, all the data are put into one big "pot" and one model is estimated. A partially pooled model consists of a separate regression model for each group. These are sometimes called *multilevel models*. If there is a time series component to the data structure in addition to a cross-sectional component, then the models are *panel data models*, although the name "multilevel" can apply here. Ignoring a segmentation possibility is equivalent to estimating a completely pooled model. Acknowledging segments, a multilevel

The Market

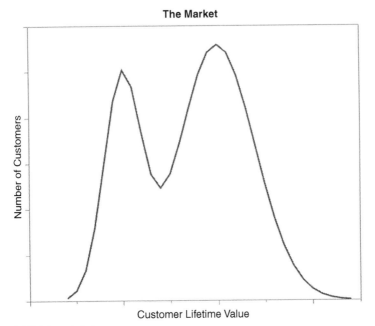

(a) Total market view

The Market with Two Classes of Customers

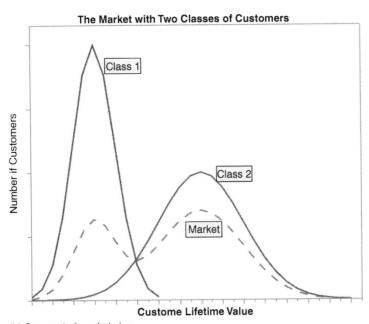

(b) Segmented market view

FIGURE 8.3.1 The smooth density curve in part (a) is fitted over a histogram of the number of customers by CLV bins and is clearly bimodal. This reflects the heterogeneity in the market. The two density curves in part (b) show the underlying distributions for two classes or segments. This reflects the market heterogeneity.

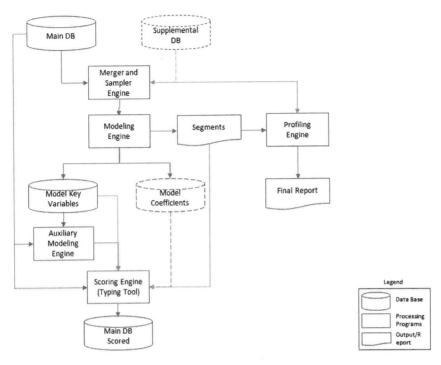

FIGURE 8.4.1 The process for developing segments and pricing together is more complex than considering them separately. This is reflected in this diagram.

model could be estimated. The econometric issues associated with a multilevel model are discussed in Chapters 9 and 11.

8.4 Developing pricing segments

The practical complexity of combining two tasks (i.e., segmentation and pricing) into one is reflected in the overall data modeling schema in Figure 8.4.1. The process consists of using a database of transactions, perhaps supplemented with outside information (e.g., demographics). The two databases would be merged. Typically, this merged database is large, so sampling may be needed to produce a more workable one. This is a typical first step in most data-mining procedures. For example, The SAS Institute advocates a series of steps for data mining that it calls SEMMA, which is an acronym for five steps: *Sample, Explore, Modify, Model,* and *Assess.*[4] Once the data have been sampled, they can be submitted to a *modeling engine* responsible for producing the segments and elasticities. After the segments are identified, they have to be profiled based on their dominant features. These could be demographics, lifestyles, and buying behaviors, to mention just a few. The segments are usually given names that succinctly characterize them. In addition

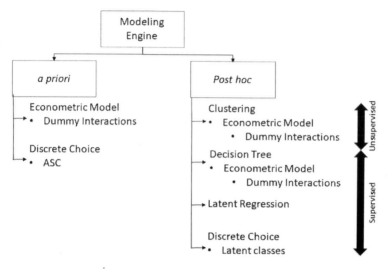

FIGURE 8.4.2 The modeling engine consists of two main groups of methods: *a priori* and *post hoc* methods. Each is illustrated here along with their components. Based on [57].

to this profiling, the model results may be passed to other subordinate engines for further analysis and use, such as scoring the larger database for target marketing. In the linear two-step tandem methods discussed in this chapter, the *modeling engine* consists of two parts: one for segment development and one for elasticity estimation. For the advanced methods discussed in Chapter 9, the *modeling engine* is just one model.

Survey data could be used instead of transactions data from a data warehouse with no change in the modeling scheme. In fact, many segmentation studies rely on survey data. The survey data set, being much smaller than a data warehouse, can nonetheless be viewed as a database. The order of magnitude is immaterial.

The root word "model" in "*modeling engine*" should not be taken literally for segmentation because a statistical model per se may not be used. It is best to think of this engine as a means for identifying and extracting meaningful and actionable segments from the data. There are many ways to do this, but they can all be subsumed under two major headings: *a priori* and *post hoc*. These two headings and their components are illustrated in Figure 8.4.2. The following sections discuss the methods.

8.4.1 Modeling engine: A priori *methods*

The *a priori* segmentation methods are based on the specification of the type and number of segments before data are collected, so they are not data driven. Basically, the segments are known from prior experience, judgement, or input from SMEs and KOLs. Econometric and statistical models are applied to these predefined segments to develop price elasticities.

8.4.2 Modeling engine: Post hoc methods

The *post hoc* segmentation methods are based on data, but they may not be based on econometric or statistical models. There are two approaches: *unsupervised* and *supervised*. When statisticians talk about using a methodology to analyze data, they talk about that method learning from the data; the method is taught by the data. This teaching can be supervised by a dependent variable that directs what the data can reveal, or the teaching can be unsupervised without a dependent variable guiding what the data can reveal.

You are used to thinking of a supervised method as an econometric or statistical model, such as a regression model or a member of the regression modeling family, which has a dependent variable, a set of independent variables, and a functional form, usually linear. This class of models is said to supervise how the data are manipulated to extract estimated parameters in order to best explain or account for the dependent variable's variance. The model learns from the data and the estimated parameters are the learnings.

There are other statistical methods, however, that extract learnings from the data, but they are not in a model form: there is no dependent variable to guide the learning, no set of independent variables, and no functional form. So these methods are unsupervised. Cluster analysis is the primary example of this class of unsupervised learning techniques.

Regardless of the learning mechanism for identifying segments, econometric and statistical models must still be used to estimate elasticities. These are supervised models because they have a dependent variable (i.e., some measure of quantity) and independent variables: price and some indicators of the segments. The indicators will be discussed later and again in Chapter 9. These supervised learning models, of course, are also used with the *a priori* methods. So each segmentation approach under the *post hoc* classification still requires that a learning method be coupled with it.

8.5 Pricing Scenario

A *learning management system* (LMS) is a software system for managing and delivering course content to a wide variety of learners (previously called "students"). The systems have grade books for instructors to record and learners to review grades; resource folders where lecture notes, videos, assignments, and so forth are posted; chat rooms where learners exchange information and questions with other learners and the instructor; class rosters; and many more features. These systems are used by colleges and universities as well as companies that offer instruction in business-related topics or in-house training for professional development. The courses can be online, in a traditional classroom format, or a hybrid of the two; the software usually supports all three approaches.

Several pricing strategies are used by LMS providers: pay-per-learner (PPL), pay-per-use, limited licensing, and perpetual licensing.[5] This Pricing Scenario LMS provider offers a PPL pricing model.

8.5.1 The business problem

A LMS company markets to hospitals that offer professional development opportunities to their doctors, nurses, technicians, and staff to enhance their skills and maintain their professional credentials. In addition, new hires have to be indoctrinated into the operations of a hospital, as well as the benefits offered to employees. The LMS company's service is cloud based so learners can access the system anywhere and at any time via an Internet connection. This is the best, most cost-effective way for hospitals to offer development opportunities, especially to the physician and nursing staffs.

The company's sales force targets both urban and rural hospitals, which has earned the company a 20% market share in the urban market and a 10% share in the rural market. The American Hospital Association reports that in 2015 there were 4862 hospitals in the USA.[6] This consisted of 3033 urban hospitals and 1829 rural hospitals. In general, rural hospitals are in serious trouble in the USA, with many closing for financial reasons. Urban hospitals also have issues, but these are not as serious as those in rural hospitals.

Although the marketing team manages pricing, the sales force really determines the price points needed to close a deal. They believe they could make an offer based on their knowledge of the customers and the offer is the right one for winning a bid. The price points, however, are often close to costs, so profit margins are low and sometimes negative. Upper management, believing too much money is left on the table, wants to improve profitability by instituting a new pricing system managed by a new pricing department.

A management consulting company engaged to help with this effort quickly decided that a pricing strategy had to be devised at the same time a pricing system was being created because it knew that a strategy consists of both a structure and a level within that structure. The structure in this case is either a single uniform price or multiple prices in a segmented market. The sales force would then be required to adhere to these prices with little variation. The structure also consists of a plan such as the PPL, pay-per-use, limited licensing, and perpetual licensing mentioned above. The consultants recommended a MaxDiff study to determine the best plan, but the management team wanted to stay with its current plan. It reasoned that current customers know this plan and would become confused with a new one, potentially driving them to the competition. The management team did not want to take this risk. The management consultants had to devise a structure and set of price points within this plan constraint.

The consultants decided to segment the market and develop a different uniform price point for each. They reasoned that third-degree price discrimination can be used to enhance profitability because the hospitals could not practice arbitrage.

Although upper management agreed with this, it already decided that there were just two segments: its traditional rural and urban markets. The team is open to suggestions, but the first effort must be on these two *a priori* segments. So the consultants had an additional constraint.

8.5.2   Likely elasticities

Price responses will differ among hospitals depending on the *a priori* segment each hospital belongs to. The consultants expected rural hospitals to be more price elastic than urban hospitals because rural hospitals have more difficulty passing their training costs onto patients or insurers for many reasons, such as[7]:

- Rural hospitals are mostly in smaller geographic areas with older and poorer patients who are more likely to have chronic diseases than those in urban areas.
- Rural hospitals have a higher percentage of care in outpatient settings and are more likely to offer home health, skilled nursing, and assisted living, all of which have lower Medicare margins than inpatient care.
- Rural hospitals may rely more heavily on reimbursement from public programs whose payments fall short of costs.

8.5.3   Company data

The company maintains an in-house database of the number of monthly learners accessing the LMS at each hospital as well as the monthly fee per learner charged at each hospital. There are two years of data that will be used for price segmentation. The price variable has sufficient price variation from the discounts offered by the sales force. Recall that this monthly fee will differ from one hospital to the next because the sales force tends to make price "deals." The annual number of learners is also maintained since this information is used to invoice the hospitals.

8.5.4   Simulated data

Data for this problem were simulated for 1500 hospitals. Variables include Inpatient: Number of Discharges; Inpatient: Number of Discharge Days; Beds Licensed or Certified; Admissions; Licensed MDs; Full-time Physicians; Full-time Interns and Residents; Full-time registered nurses (RNs); Full-time Staff; Month and Year of Invoicing; and State Where the Hospitals Are Located. The price per learner negotiated by the LMS sales force and the annual average number of learners are included.

In addition, since the LMS classifies hospitals as rural or urban, the hospital type is included as a dummy variable defined below. Figure 8.5.1 shows the distribution of the hospitals based on the LMS definition of type.

Since the number of learners a hospital will allow through a training program is a function of the price per learner, the consultants expected to see a negative relationship between price and learners. Figure 8.5.2 confirms this expectation.

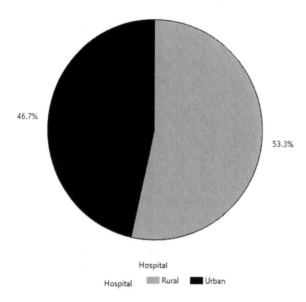

46.7%

53.3%

Hospital

Hospital   ▨ Rural ■ Urban

FIGURE 8.5.1 The distribution clearly leans toward rural hospitals.

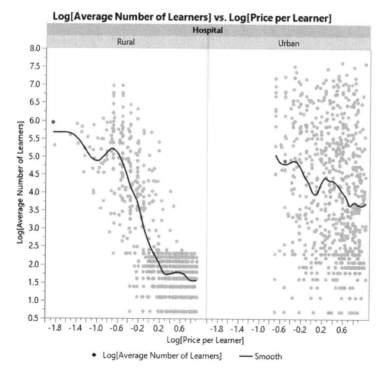

FIGURE 8.5.2 This scatterplot shows the expected negative relationship between the price and number of learners by type of hospital. Both variables are on a natural log scale. The curvy line in the plots is a "smooth" that shows the general trend of the data. It is clear that there is a negative relationship between price and learners for both types, which agrees with economic theory, intuition, and experience.

8.5.5 Digression: Multilevel effects

A hospital can be viewed as embedded or nested within a geographical area such as a state. In this situation, the data are hierarchical or *multilevel*. Since the states have varying economic and cultural differences, this multilevel feature may be important for elasticity estimation. The same holds for the month and year indicators because there may be seasonal or trend effects that may be important. Multilevel models are more complex and so a discussion of them is postponed until Chapters 9 and 11. For now, a geographic effect is ignored.

8.6 A priori modeling

An econometric model was specified for elasticity estimation for the segments initially predefined by management. The dependent variable is the number of learners. Although a hospital needs to train its personnel, it still has to be aware of the cost of the training (i.e., the price per learner). As should be expected, the higher the price, the fewer the number of learners it will admit to training. Therefore, if L_i is the number of learners for hospital i, then $L_i = f(P_i)$ with $dL_i dP_i < 0$ is a demand function for hospital i. The following subsections develop this demand function.

8.6.1 Model specification

Define a dummy variable to categorize the hospitals as

$$hospital = \begin{cases} 1 & \text{if hospital } i \text{ is urban} \\ 0 & \text{if hospital } i \text{ is rural.} \end{cases}$$

The hospital segment should have an effect on both the price response and the placement of the demand curve in the price–quantity plane. That is, the segment represented by the dummy variable would affect both the intercept and slope of the demand curve.

A constant elasticity demand curve was specified. Recall from Chapter 4 that this means you want to have an elasticity such that $\eta_P^L = c$, where η_P^L is the elasticity of learners with respect to the per learner price and c is a constant. In this case, $c = \beta_1 + \beta_2 \times hospital$, so that $c = \beta_1$ for rural hospitals and $c = \beta_1 + \beta_2$ for urban hospitals. Notice that c is a constant in both cases. A solution to the elasticity statement is $\ln L = c \times \ln P + \gamma$, where γ is a constant defined as $\gamma = \beta_0 + \beta_3 \times hospital$. This leads to

$$L = e^{\beta_0 + \beta_3 \times hospital} \times P^{\beta_1 + \beta_2 \times hospital},$$

or reverting back to log form

$$\ln(L) = \beta_0 + \beta_3 \times hospital + (\beta_1 + \beta_2 \times hospital) \times \ln P. \tag{111}$$

The demand function is

$$\ln(L) = \begin{cases} (\beta_0 + \beta_3) + (\beta_1 + \beta_2) \times \ln(P) & \text{if hospital } i \text{ is urban} \\ \beta_0 + \beta_1 \times \ln(P) & \text{if hospital } i \text{ is rural.} \end{cases} \quad (112)$$

The elasticities are simply

$$\eta_P^L = \begin{cases} \beta_1 + \beta_2 & \text{if hospital } i \text{ is urban} \\ \beta_1 & \text{if hospital } i \text{ is rural} \end{cases} \quad (113)$$

so the parameter β_2 shows the effect on the elasticity as you change from a rural to an urban hospital. The demand equation can be expanded for other factors affecting demand by expanding the definition of the γ function.

You could also determine the effect on the number of learners as you move from a rural to an urban hospital. That is, you can determine ΔL, or better yet the percentage change $\%\Delta L = \Delta L / L$. To do this, note that using (112), you can write

$$\Delta L = e^{\beta_0 + \beta_3} e^{(\beta_1 + \beta_2) \times \ln(P)} - e^{\beta_0} e^{\beta_1 \times \ln(P)}$$
$$= e^{\beta_0} e^{\beta_1 \times \ln(P)} \times [e^{\beta_3} e^{\beta_2 \times \ln(P)} - 1].$$

The percentage change, $\%\Delta L = \Delta L / L$, is

$$\frac{\Delta L}{L} = \frac{e^{\beta_0} e^{\beta_1 \times \ln(P)} \times [e^{\beta_3} e^{\beta_2 \times \ln(P)} - 1]}{e^{\beta_0} e^{\beta_1 \times \ln(P)}}$$
$$= e^{\beta_3} e^{\beta_2 \times \ln(P)} - 1.$$

8.6.2 Model estimation

A simple regression model (OLS) was estimated for the natural log of the average number of learners as a function of the natural log Price per learner, the type as a dummy variable, and the interaction of type and log Price. It could be argued that the number of learners is a discrete count and not a continuous variable, so a Poisson regression model is more appropriate. This will be ignored for this problem because the goal is just to illustrate general methods; the procedure is the same regardless of the regression model (i.e., the link function).

The regression results are shown in Figure 8.6.1. Although they are mediocre, with an adjusted $R^2 = 0.43$, you can still determine elasticities, which are just the estimated parameters. These are all highly significant. For rural hospitals, $hospital = 0$, so the elasticity is directly the estimated log Price parameter; for urban hospitals, it is the sum of the log Price estimated parameter and the type dummy–log Price interaction estimated parameter. These are shown in Table 8.1. The classification of the elasticities meets intuition: rural hospitals are price elastic, while urban hospitals are price inelastic.

Response logLearners

Summary of Fit

RSquare	0.434776
RSquare Adj	0.433643
Root Mean Square Error	1.361943
Mean of Response	3.291942
Observations (or Sum Wgts)	1500

Analysis of Variance

Source	DF	Sum of Squares	Mean Square	F Ratio
Model	3	2134.4960	711.499	383.5800
Error	1496	2774.9150	1.855	Prob > F
C. Total	1499	4909.4110		<.0001*

Parameter Estimates

Term	Estimate	Std Error	t Ratio	Prob>|t|
Intercept	3.7293901	0.042452	87.85	<.0001*
l_Price	-1.513094	0.073888	-20.48	<.0001*
Hospital[Rural]	-0.702665	0.042452	-16.55	<.0001*
Hospital[Rural]*l_Price	-0.698181	0.073888	-9.45	<.0001*

Effect Tests

Source	Nparm	DF	Sum of Squares	F Ratio	Prob > F
l_Price	1	1	777.85671	419.3547	<.0001*
Hospital	1	1	508.18284	273.9693	<.0001*
Hospital*l_Price	1	1	165.61655	89.2865	<.0001*

Expanded Estimates

Nominal factors expanded to all levels

Term	Estimate	Std Error	t Ratio	Prob>|t|
Intercept	3.7293901	0.042452	87.85	<.0001*
l_Price	-1.513094	0.073888	-20.48	<.0001*
Hospital[Rural]	-0.702665	0.042452	-16.55	<.0001*
Hospital[Urban]	0.7026648	0.042452	16.55	<.0001*
Hospital[Rural]*l_Price	-0.698181	0.073888	-9.45	<.0001*
Hospital[Urban]*l_Price	0.6981809	0.073888	9.45	<.0001*

Indicator Function Parameterization

Term	Estimate	Std Error	t Ratio	Prob>|t|
Intercept	4.432055	0.067277	65.88	<.0001*
l_Price	-0.814913	0.117244	-6.95	<.0001*
Hospital[Rural]	-1.40533	0.084904	-16.55	<.0001*
Hospital[Rural]*l_Price	-1.396362	0.147776	-9.45	<.0001*

FIGURE 8.6.1 The regression results based on an *a priori* segmentation of the hospital market show that all variables are highly significant. The R^2 is mediocre at best, indicating that other factors are important for determining the number of learners. The parameter estimates are shown under the heading "Indicator Function Parameterization" for the dummy coding. The price elasticities are -0.815 for urban hospitals and -2.211 ($= -0.815 - 1.396$ where the -1.396 is the estimated coefficient for rural hospitals interacted with log price) for rural hospitals. The estimated coefficient for rural hospitals alone (-1.405) shifts the intercept and is not part of the elasticity calculation.

TABLE 8.1 The elasticities are determined directly from the estimated parameters.

Hospital type	Elasticity	Classification
Rural	−2.211	Elastic
Urban	−0.815	Inelastic

8.7 *Post hoc* modeling

Post hoc modeling uses data to develop the segments. There are two subordinate classes of methods available: unsupervised and supervised learning methods. These are discussed in the next subsections.

8.7.1 *Unsupervised learning methods*

Recall that unsupervised learning refers to procedures that do not rely on a statistical model per se. This is the form most people think about for segmenting markets other than using *a priori* segmentation. There are two popular forms of unsupervised learning: *hierarchical cluster analysis* and *K-means cluster analysis*. Hierarchical clustering seeks groups or clusters or segments of objects (e.g., people) based on a collection of variables using a "distance" measure. The measure finds objects that are close based on a metric that is a function of the variables. Objects are merged based on a function of these measures, with the most popular being Ward's method. Other methods will yield different cluster solutions so the end result of hierarchical clustering is subjective, since it comes down to which method and solution you like. The result of the clustering is presented in a *dendrogram* or tree. Dendrograms are the reason for the method's popularity since they are (sometimes) easy to interpret. The number of segments is determined by cutting the dendrogram at some arbitrary level.

The other popular clustering method, K-means clustering, also finds the distance between variables, but the distances are based on means of the variables (hence the method's name). Both approaches require that you specify the number of segments separately: hierarchical clustering by locating a good cut-point on the dendrogram; K-means by specifying the number of clusters before the algorithm determines distances. An interesting difference between the two approaches is in the nature of the variables used for segmentation. Table 8.2 highlights the differences.

The K-means approach is often preferred because the output includes the means for each segment, which facilitates profiling the segments. Hierarchical clustering requires an additional step to profile the segments, so this approach is itself virtually a tandem procedure: cluster and then profile. See [57] for some details about hierarchical and K-means clustering. Also see [13], [34], and any multivariate statistics text.

For either method, a second step is still needed to estimate elasticities. This step is really no different from that used in the *a priori* approach, except that the segments are not defined *a priori*.

TABLE 8.2 The variable types differ for the two clustering approaches. The K-means algorithm requires numeric continuous data because means are calculated.

Method	Variable type
Hierarchical	Character or numeric (nominal/ordinal/continuous)
K-means	Numeric/continuous only

Pricing Scenario: Hierarchical clustering

A hierarchical clustering with Ward's method was used to segment the hospitals. The variables were all the numeric/continuous variables in the database: Inpatient: Number of Discharges; Inpatient: Number of Discharge Days; Beds Licensed or Certified; Admissions; Licensed MDs; Full-time Physicians; Full-time Interns and Residents; Full-time RNs; Full-time Staff; as well as the *hospital* dummy variable, which is nominal. A problem with hierarchical clustering is that the results are impacted by the scales and skewness of the data. Consequently, it is recommended that all variables be appropriately standardized to remove the scale issue. The standardization could be done robustly to correct for outliers (i.e., the skewness). Both were done here.

The resulting dendrogram is shown in Figure 8.7.1. Five clusters are shown. See [57] for a discussion of ways to determine the number of clusters. Five were selected here just for illustration. Each hospital was assigned to one of the five. The color coding suggests the relative sizes of the segments, but Figure 8.7.2 and Figure 8.7.3 better show the distribution.

Elasticity estimation could be done two ways. The first is to use a separate regression for each segment where each regression model is defined only with a log Price variable. A more efficient, but slightly more cumbersome way is to define a dummy variable for each segment and include an interaction between price and segment in one model. To avoid the dummy variable trap, one segment has to be defined as a base for all comparisons and that base variable would not have a dummy defined for it. There is controversy about which approach is better. I prefer the single-model approach because it makes more efficient use of the data. See [20] on the dummy variable trap and [165], [130], and [159] on approaches.

The results for a single model are shown in Figure 8.7.4. Elasticity estimates are shown in Table 8.3. Segments 1 and 2 are predominately rural hospitals and happen to be very price elastic, especially segment 1. Segment 3 is slightly more urban, but the elasticity is also slightly above unit elastic. This can be tested, but that will not be pursued here. Segments 4 and 5 are definitely urban and also inelastic.

A more complex version of the model would have the hospital type also interact with the segments and the log Price variable. This is not shown here because the setup and analysis are similar to the above.

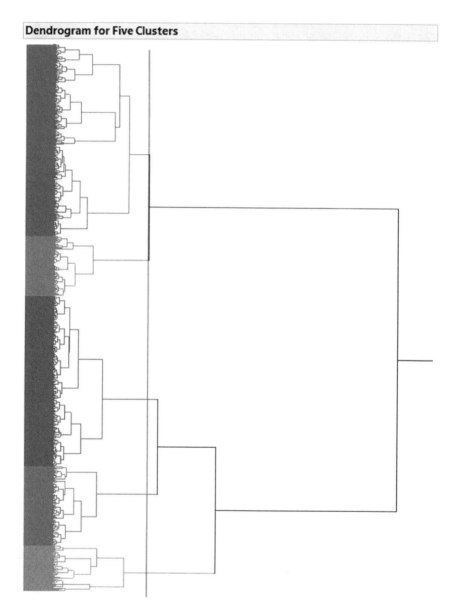

FIGURE 8.7.1 A hierarchical clustering with Ward's method was used with corrections for scale and outliers. The vertical line demarcates five clusters.

Once the segments are developed, they are usually profiled in the sense that their major characteristics or features are identified. This leads naturally to naming the segments by looking for dominant patterns in the features. The profiling is part art and part science since some statistical and definitely graphical tools can be used

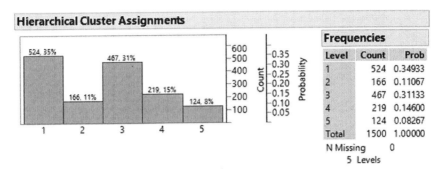

Hierarchical Cluster Assignments

Frequencies

Level	Count	Prob
1	524	0.34933
2	166	0.11067
3	467	0.31133
4	219	0.14600
5	124	0.08267
Total	1500	1.00000

N Missing   0

5 Levels

FIGURE 8.7.2 Each hospital was assigned to one and only one segment. The distribution of the five segments is shown here.

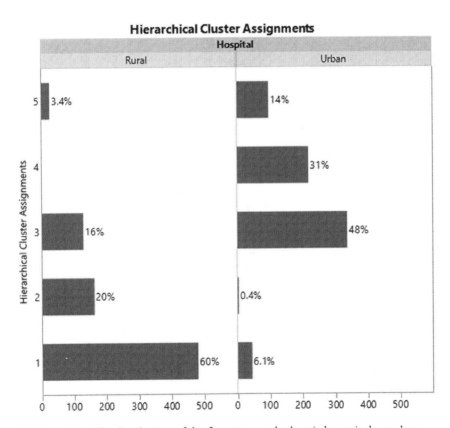

FIGURE 8.7.3 The distribution of the five segments by hospital type is shown here.

Response Log[Average Number of Learners]

Summary of Fit

RSquare	0.426659
RSquare Adj	0.422808
Root Mean Square Error	1.374909
Mean of Response	3.291942
Observations (or Sum Wgts)	1500

Analysis of Variance

Source	DF	Sum of Squares	Mean Square	F Ratio
Model	10	2094.6423	209.464	110.8056
Error	1489	2814.7687	1.890	Prob > F
C. Total	1499	4909.4110		<.0001*

Parameter Estimates

Term	Estimate	Std Error	t Ratio	Prob>|t|
Intercept	3.7418533	0.052188	71.70	<.0001*
Log[Price per Learner]	-1.475552	0.088816	-16.61	<.0001*
Hospital[0]	-0.942232	0.055056	-17.11	<.0001*
Hierarchical Cluster Assignments[1]	0.1510463	0.087163	1.73	0.0833
Hierarchical Cluster Assignments[2]	0.3584824	0.113984	3.15	0.0017*
Hierarchical Cluster Assignments[3]	-0.054247	0.083095	-0.65	0.5140
Hierarchical Cluster Assignments[4]	-0.367127	0.120721	-3.04	0.0024*
Hierarchical Cluster Assignments[1]*Log[Price per Learner]	-0.600772	0.12314	-4.88	<.0001*
Hierarchical Cluster Assignments[2]*Log[Price per Learner]	-0.893882	0.170934	-5.23	<.0001*
Hierarchical Cluster Assignments[3]*Log[Price per Learner]	0.2481828	0.143007	1.74	0.0829
Hierarchical Cluster Assignments[4]*Log[Price per Learner]	0.5883841	0.189627	3.10	0.0020*

Indicator Function Parameterization

Term	Estimate	Std Error	t Ratio	Prob>|t|
Intercept	4.5959313	0.176034	26.11	<.0001*
Log[Price per Learner]	-0.817464	0.285687	-2.86	0.0043*
Hospital[0]	-1.884464	0.110111	-17.11	<.0001*
Hierarchical Cluster Assignments[1]	0.2392005	0.20182	1.19	0.2361
Hierarchical Cluster Assignments[2]	0.4466366	0.222855	2.00	0.0452*
Hierarchical Cluster Assignments[3]	0.033907	0.191887	0.18	0.8598
Hierarchical Cluster Assignments[4]	-0.278973	0.214374	-1.30	0.1933
Hierarchical Cluster Assignments[1]*Log[Price per Learner]	-1.258859	0.306229	-4.11	<.0001*
Hierarchical Cluster Assignments[2]*Log[Price per Learner]	-1.55197	0.342311	-4.53	<.0001*
Hierarchical Cluster Assignments[3]*Log[Price per Learner]	-0.409904	0.320302	-1.28	0.2008
Hierarchical Cluster Assignments[4]*Log[Price per Learner]	-0.069703	0.358331	-0.19	0.8458

Expanded Estimates

Nominal factors expanded to all levels

Term	Estimate	Std Error	t Ratio	Prob>|t|
Intercept	3.7418533	0.052188	71.70	<.0001*
Log[Price per Learner]	-1.475552	0.088816	-16.61	<.0001*
Hospital[0]	-0.942232	0.055056	-17.11	<.0001*
Hospital[1]	0.9422321	0.055056	17.11	<.0001*
Hierarchical Cluster Assignments[1]	0.1510463	0.087163	1.73	0.0833
Hierarchical Cluster Assignments[2]	0.3584824	0.113984	3.15	0.0017*
Hierarchical Cluster Assignments[3]	-0.054247	0.083095	-0.65	0.5140
Hierarchical Cluster Assignments[4]	-0.367127	0.120721	-3.04	0.0024*
Hierarchical Cluster Assignments[5]	-0.088154	0.14782	-0.60	0.5510
Hierarchical Cluster Assignments[1]*Log[Price per Learner]	-0.600772	0.12314	-4.88	<.0001*
Hierarchical Cluster Assignments[2]*Log[Price per Learner]	-0.893882	0.170934	-5.23	<.0001*
Hierarchical Cluster Assignments[3]*Log[Price per Learner]	0.2481828	0.143007	1.74	0.0829
Hierarchical Cluster Assignments[4]*Log[Price per Learner]	0.5883841	0.189627	3.10	0.0020*
Hierarchical Cluster Assignments[5]*Log[Price per Learner]	0.6580873	0.238452	2.76	0.0059*

FIGURE 8.7.4 The regression results show that some terms are significant, while others are not. The R^2 is, as before, mediocre at best at 0.42, indicating once more that other factors are important for determining the number of learners.

ned by adding the relevant estimated parameters assegment 5 is just the log price coefficient, since segment 5 was the
base for the segment dummies.

Segment	Add	Elasticity	Classification
Segment 1	$\beta_1 + \beta_7$	$-0.81 + (-1.26) = -2.07$	Elastic
Segment 2	$\beta_1 + \beta_8$	$-0.81 + (-1.55) = -2.36$	Elastic
Segment 3	$\beta_1 + \beta_9$	$-0.81 + (-0.41) = -1.22$	Elastic
Segment 4	$\beta_1 + \beta_{10}$	$-0.81 + (-0.07) = -0.88$	Inelastic
Segment 5	β_1	-0.81	Inelastic

TABLE 8.4 The CCC was calculated for each of the four K-means solutions. The best solution is the one with the maximum CCC value, segment size 4.

Segment size (k)	CCC	Best
2	11.9413	
3	9.5676	
4	12.2472	Optimal CCC
5	9.9234	

to discern the features. Boxplots, histograms, multiway tables, and correspondence analysis are usually employed at this stage. Naming the segments, on the other hand, is all art. This is usually the joint effort of the researcher, consultants, marketing personnel, SMEs, and KOLs.

Pricing Scenario: K-means clustering

K-means clustering was also done on the hospital data. Since numeric/continuous data are needed, the same variables used for the hierarchical clustering except for the nominal dummy variables were used here. The number of segments (the "K") must be specified, so a range of two to five was selected. The *Cubic Clustering Criterion* (CCC) was used to determine a good or optimal segment size. The segment solution with the maximum CCC is the optimal solution. Table 8.4 shows the CCC values for the different segment sizes. Size 4 is the best one. See [57] for a discussion of the CCC.

There are several problems associated with using the K-means algorithm. The first, as already noted, is that all the variables must be numeric/continuous, since means are calculated. This may not be viewed as a serious issue, but if there are variables that are numeric/nominal that may be influential for determining segments, then the inability to use them could bias results. Second, the K-means algorithm works by first specifying a starting or seed set of k values, one for each segment. These form the initial segments centered at these values. Other values are "added" to these to create new means based on how far the new values are from the initial mean. The distances are Euclidean distances. The new means are new centers to which new values are added again based on Euclidean distances. This process is continued until a stopping rule is met. The initial seed values, however, play a major role in determining the final cluster solution. Several proposals are implemented in software, including just a random selection for the initial seed values. A final issue with the K-means approach is the effect of outliers. Since means are calculated, outliers, which distort means, will also distort the K-means solution. Standardization of all values is usually done because of this.

Once the segments have been identified, they can be profiled and named using the means of the variables for each segment. Elasticities can then be estimated as described for the hierarchical clustering solution above. Figure 8.7.5 shows the means by segment that can be used for profiling the segments.

Digression on coding and elasticities

Recall that there was a lengthy discussion about coding qualitative or categorical factors using effects coding in Chapter 4. As a brief summary of that discussion, effects coding is used to show the effect on the estimated dependent variable of changing a qualitative factor from a base level to another level. The effect is the change in means, so a contrast in means is determined. The coding involves assigning a 1 to the level of the factor in question, a −1 to the base level, and a 0 to all other levels.

Dummy coding, popular in econometrics, was mentioned as an alternative. It is popular because it shows or measures the change from a base level as with the effects coding, but it does not measure the contrast in means; it measures shifts relative to a base, usually the intercept in a regression model. Dummy coding was used in this Pricing Scenario.

You should expect the two coding schemes to give the same elasticity estimates since there should be only one set of elasticities; the elasticities should not change simply because the coding is changed, so they should be invariant with respect to the coding. This is, in fact, the case. To see this, recall how an elasticity is calculated. Using dummy coding as described above, the price elasticity for each segment is the sum of the estimated coefficients for the (log) price term and the estimated coefficient for the interaction term for that segment. The comparable calculations are done using effects coding. These are shown in Figure 8.7.6. The implication is that it does not matter which coding scheme is used: the elasticities, properly calculated, will be the same.

8.7.2 Supervised learning

The previous section discussed unsupervised learning, which is not model based; supervised learning is model based. There is a dependent variable that "directs" the model learning process in the sense that the model has to reproduce as best

K Means NCluster=4

Columns Scaled Individually

Cluster Means

Cluster	Inpatient: Number of Discharges	Inpatient: Number of Discharge Days	Beds Licensed or Certified	Admissions	Licensed MDs	Full-time Physicians	Full-time Interns and Residents	Full-time RNs	Full-time Staff
1	3819.86486	33672.9257	149.125	3909.37162	76.5574324	10.5777027	65.4662162	147.172297	744.560811
2	882.285714	11335.165	54.0812808	909.283251	67.135468	21.6921182	41.9458128	98.4359606	539.775862
3	10453.6781	52732.2747	241.965665	10502.3605	331.18454	38.111588	169.785408	433.042918	2134.86695
4	10564.8159	52808.223	244.943363	10539.0478	292.378761	26.1044248	46.619469	350.950442	1411.99469

FIGURE 8.7.5 The four-segment K-means cluster solution is shown here. The means enable you to profile the segments.

Dummy Coding

Term	Estimate
Intercept	4.596
Log[Price per Learner]	-0.817
Hospital[0]	-1.884
Hierarchical Cluster Assignments[1]	0.239
Hierarchical Cluster Assignments[2]	0.447
Hierarchical Cluster Assignments[3]	0.034
Hierarchical Cluster Assignments[4]	-0.279
Hierarchical Cluster Assignments[1]*Log[Price per Learner]	-1.259
Hierarchical Cluster Assignments[2]*Log[Price per Learner]	-1.552
Hierarchical Cluster Assignments[3]*Log[Price per Learner]	-0.410
Hierarchical Cluster Assignments[4]*Log[Price per Learner]	-0.070

Effects Coding (Expanded)

Term	Estimate
Intercept	3.742
Log[Price per Learner]	-1.476
Hospital[0]	-0.942
Hospital[1]	0.942
Hierarchical Cluster Assignments[1]	0.151
Hierarchical Cluster Assignments[2]	0.358
Hierarchical Cluster Assignments[3]	-0.054
Hierarchical Cluster Assignments[4]	-0.367
Hierarchical Cluster Assignments[5]	-0.088
Hierarchical Cluster Assignments[1]*Log[Price per Learner]	-0.601
Hierarchical Cluster Assignments[2]*Log[Price per Learner]	-0.894
Hierarchical Cluster Assignments[3]*Log[Price per Learner]	0.248
Hierarchical Cluster Assignments[4]*Log[Price per Learner]	0.588
Hierarchical Cluster Assignments[5]*Log[Price per Learner]	0.658

Elasticities

Segment 1	-2.076
Segment 2	-2.369
Segment 3	-1.227
Segment 4	-0.887
Segment 5	-0.817

Elasticities

Segment 1	-2.076
Segment 2	-2.369
Segment 3	-1.227
Segment 4	-0.887
Segment 5	-0.817

FIGURE 8.7.6 This reconciles the elasticities calculated using dummy and effects coding in Figure 8.7.4. In both cases, the elasticities are the sum of the (log) price coefficient and the appropriate interaction term. For instance, using dummy coding, the elasticity for segment 1 is $-0.817 + (-1.259) = -2.076$. The comparable sum for effects coding yields the same elasticity: $-1.476 + (-0.601) = -2.077$ within rounding. For the base segment, which is segment 5 for both codings, there is no estimated interaction coefficient for the dummy coding, so the elasticity is simply -0.817 for dummy coding, but for the effects coding, there is a coefficient that is retrieved as described in Chapter 4. The elasticity using effects coding is $-1.476 + 0.658 = -0.817$ within rounding.

as possible the features (i.e., trend, patterns, variance) of the dependent variable without overfitting the data. Overfitting means fitting every single data point, which amounts to fitting the random noise. This accomplishes nothing and so should be avoided. In unsupervised learning, there is no dependent variable, so there is nothing to direct learning in this sense (see [22] for discussions).

Decision trees

In this section, I will discuss one approach to supervised learning sometimes used in segmentation: *decision trees*. The name fully describes the essence of the methodology in the sense that a tree display of subsets of the sample is developed. By following different branches of the tree, where each branch is defined as a bifurcation of a variable, one can decide the composition or features of the segments. This supervised learning method differs from the unsupervised methods in that the segments are profiled at the same time they are developed. The profiling is not extensive, however, since all the variables or factors available in a study are not used to develop a decision tree. Nonetheless, enough are used to develop a good picture of the segments. See [57] for a discussion of decision trees in survey analysis. Also see [98] for the definitive work on trees. Finally, see [92] for an interesting perspective on decision trees and regression analysis.

The advantage of a decision tree is that a tree can be grown regardless of the nature of the scale of the independent variables. The variables can be any type of numeric or character variable. In addition, skewness is not an issue since measures such as means or distances are not used to determine the bifurcations or importances (i.e., the order of the variables in the bifurcations). This provides more opportunities for exploring key drivers for segments. Some software also provides capabilities that allow you to determine which variables should be used at each stage of the tree growing rather than having the algorithm make those decisions. A drawback to decision trees, however, is that they tend to overfit the data. Ensembles of trees (i.e., forests) are then grown if this is an issue for the analyst. Ensembles are briefly discussed below.

The development of a decision tree involves the specification of a dependent variable and a set of independent variables much like in a regression model. The dependent variable can be either categorical or continuous. If the former, then the model is similar to a logit model and is called a *classification tree*; if the latter, then it is similar to an OLS model and is called a *Regression Tree*. Because of the possibility of either type of dependent variable being used in one approach, decision trees were originally called *Classification and Regression Trees*.

Once the variables are specified, a tree is "grown" – but upside down. The root is at the top of the display[8] with branches emanating downward from the root. Nodes or "leaves" are at the end points of the branches. The tree is grown by finding the best variable at each step or branch of the tree that accounts for the most variation in the dependent variable. The tree is then split into two branches at this juncture with nodes or leaves on the new branch. This splitting into two new branches is a feature of decision trees. All splits are bifurcations of a prior branch.

Splitting continues until a stopping rule (usually a minimum number of observations remaining in a terminal node) is reached. A tree can quickly become very large when there are many variables, so it may have to be pruned back to a more manageable and interpretable size. Once the final tree is developed, the objects (e.g., consumers) can be assigned to each terminal node on the tree based on the feature of the variables defining the path from the root to the terminal node. See [176] for the technicalities of growing trees. Also see [98]. Finally, see [57] for growing and interpreting trees.

Pricing Scenario: Decision tree

A decision tree was developed for the LMS problem using the average number of learners as the dependent variable and the characteristics of the hospitals as the independent variables. For illustrative purposes, a small tree was grown and is shown in Figure 8.7.7. Each node is split into two subordinate nodes, the split determined by the best possible variable to explain the dependent variable. Starting at the root node with all 1500 hospitals, the best variable to account for the number of learners is the size of the full-time staff. The full-time staff data are themselves examined to find the level appropriate for splitting the staff into two parts. The tree algorithm determined that this level is 1194. Hospitals with full-time staff of less than 1194 people were assigned to the left split, and the others to the right. Of the 1500 hospitals, 792 were assigned to the left node and 708 to the right. The mean number of learners in the left node was 54.2 per hospital and 219.2 per hospital on the right.

The next best variable to explain the dependent variable and also to split the first-level variable is the number of admissions. It happens in this case that the number of admissions splits both the left and right nodes, but this does not have to be the case.

I arbitrarily stopped or pruned the tree at four terminal nodes. The bifurcation could have continued until a stopping rule was reached. There could be several rules, but one rule was based on the sample size in a node. Nodes two and four had small sample sizes so they would not be split any further. The sum of the hospitals in the four terminal nodes was 1500, the total sample size.

The four terminal nodes from left to right define four segments. A path from the root to a terminal node provides a profile of that node or what can now be called a segment. So Segment 1 in Figure 8.7.7 consists of hospitals with less than 1194 full-time staff and fewer than 11,051 admissions per year. The decision methodology results in segmentation and profiling simultaneously.

Once segments are identified, segment labels (the numbers 1–4 in out example) can be assigned to the main data table just the way they were for hierarchical clustering. Regression models can be developed as before for estimating price elasticities as previously described.

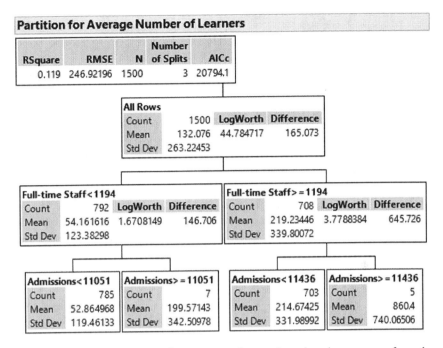

Partition for Average Number of Learners

RSquare	RMSE	N	Number of Splits	AICc
0.119	246.92196	1500	3	20794.1

All Rows

		LogWorth	Difference
Count	1500	44.784717	165.073
Mean	132.076		
Std Dev	263.22453		

Full-time Staff < 1194

		LogWorth	Difference
Count	792	1.6708149	146.706
Mean	54.161616		
Std Dev	123.38298		

Full-time Staff > = 1194

		LogWorth	Difference
Count	708	3.7788384	645.726
Mean	219.23446		
Std Dev	339.80072		

Admissions < 11051

Count	785
Mean	52.864968
Std Dev	119.46133

Admissions > = 11051

Count	7
Mean	199.57143
Std Dev	342.50978

Admissions < 11436

Count	703
Mean	214.67425
Std Dev	331.98992

Admissions > = 11436

Count	5
Mean	860.4
Std Dev	740.06506

FIGURE 8.7.7 A decision tree has a root at the top, branches that emanate from the root, and leaves or nodes at the ends of the branches. This tree was purposely grown to be small with only two branches and two terminal leaves or nodes on each branch for a total of four terminal nodes. These four nodes are the segments, each defined by the path from the root to the terminal node.

Ensembles of trees

A drawback of a the decision tree approach is that they tend to overfit the data, as I noted above. One way to handle this is to grow a number of trees – a forest – and then average them. Since there is only one data set for growing trees, growing a forest can be problematic. One way to handle this is to randomly select data from the one data set and then grow a tree for that random selection. This is then followed by another random selection with another tree grown, and so on. The issue is the random selection.

You could use a resampling or bootstrap method to randomly select data for growing a tree. Bootstrapping in general is the iterative random selection of observations from a data set. If there are n observations, then a random sample of size n is drawn with replacement. This implies that some observations could be in the sample multiple times. Each sample of size n is followed by a calculation (growing a tree in this case). The process of sample–calculate is repeated N times where N is the desired size of the forest. For growing a random forest, there would be N trees in the forest. This process has proven to be very useful and powerful for a wide range of problems in statistics, so its application is widespread and not restricted to growing a random forest. See [125], [111], and [104] for discussions about bootstrap methods in statistics.

The major use of a random forest is to identify important variables for other analyses. A by-product of a forest is an importance measure similar to the importances calculated for conjoint attributes as discussed in Chapter 4. The random forest importances similarly lie between 0 and 1 and sum to 1.0. Although a random forest is useful in this regard, it actually has limited use in segmentation because there is not one tree, but a multitude of them (after all, it is a forest!), which means that there is not one final set of terminal nodes. So which of the trees in the forest identifies segments? Consequently, I do not recommend ensembles for this purpose.

8.8   Software

All the major statistical software packages have functions for cluster analysis. SAS, JMP, and Stata are prime examples, with SAS probably having the most extensive set of functions, each with many options. Also, they all can handle regression analysis in all its flavors. JMP is very good for decision trees and was used for this chapter.

8.9   Summary

Two traditional approaches for developing segments and associated price elasticities were presented in this chapter. Each has a common feature: they are tandem approaches. This means that segments are first defined, followed by elasticity estimation for the segments. This is different from a simultaneous approach – the focus of the next chapter – in which segments and elasticities are developed at the same time using a model-based approach. I recommend this latter approach.

Notes

1 See the Wikipedia article https://en.wikipedia.org/wiki/Marketing_mix.
2 Assuming that the conditions for discrimination, primarily no arbitrage, are satisfied.
3 [132], p. 5
4 See the Wikipedia article on SEMMA at https://en.wikipedia.org/wiki/SEMMA. Also see [50].
5 See https://elearningindustry.com/learning-management-systems-pricing-models-insiders-guide for a discussion.
6 See www.aha.org/research/rc/stat-studies/fast-facts.shtml#community.
7 The following list is based on www.ruralhealthinfo.org/topics/hospitals for rural and urban hospitals.
8 Some software gives you the option to grow a tree to the side, but the typical direction is downward.

9

PRICE SEGMENTATION: ADVANCED MODELS

This chapter introduces advanced approaches for price segmentation based on latent regression models and multilevel regression models. Econometric models were used in the previous chapter, but as a second step following an initial segmentation. For the *a priori* approach, the initial segmentation was, of course, a mere stating of the segments, while the other methods involved using a multivariate statistical approach for identifying segments. The econometric models were then applied to the segments to estimate price elasticities. This amounted to a two-step tandem process. In this chapter, segments and elasticities are estimated simultaneously using a single-step model-based approach rather than a two-step tandem approach. This single-step approach makes more efficient use of the data and allows for a statistical analysis of the segments and elasticities.

This chapter is divided into five sections. The first section introduces latent variable models and their variants. The second introduces Gaussian mixture models as a variation on a theme of latent variable modeling. In Section 3, multilevel models are introduced in terms of when they can be used, their complexities, and their relationship with the dummy variable model of the previous chapter. In each section, the learning management system (LMS) pricing scenario from the last chapter will be used. Multilevel models are further developed in Chapter 11. Section 4 summarizes software, while Section 5 summarizes the chapter.

9.1 Latent variable modeling

Most, if not all, statistics and certainly all econometric textbooks develop the fundamentals of regression analysis using a set of known independent variables. See [20], [127], and [65] for classic developments. This is reasonable for textbooks, but a bit unrealistic for most real-world problems because the full set is never known completely. Advanced econometric textbooks discuss this issue in the context of omitted variable bias (OVB). To understand this bias, consider a simple regression model with one explanatory variable:

$$Y_i = \beta_0 + \beta_1 X_{1i} + \varepsilon_i.$$

Suppose Y_i is really determined by two variables, X_{1i} and X_{2i}, but X_{2i} is unknown and thus omitted from the model. The true model is given by

$$Y_i = \beta_0 + \beta_1 X_{1i} + \beta_2 X_{2i} + \varepsilon_i$$

which is not estimated. As a result of omitting X_{2i}, the ordinary least squared (OLS) estimator for β_1 is biased depending on the correlation between X_{1i} and X_{2i} and the sign of β_2. This omission results from either not being able to measure the variable or not fully understanding that the variable is needed or required. This is standard discussion in most econometric textbooks (see the references above plus [84] and [83]).

There may be variables that are unobserved or unobservable that influence the dependent variable not directly as implied by the OVB issue, but indirectly by influencing or determining the known and included independent variables. These other variables are *latent* or hidden, so that you cannot measure them as you can measure the variables that are included in the model, yet you know they have an influence and should be accounted for by some means. An example could be a household's socioeconomic status, level of confidence in the future, and expectations of future employment prospects, to mention a few.[1] While there may be several latent variables, I will assume just one for simplicity.

There are many ways to interpret a latent variable. The interpretation I espouse is that a latent variable is an abstract concept that may have theoretical meaning but no real-world counterpart that can be measured, observed directly, or captured in any meaningful sense. Yet you know and understand its influence and importance, so you can talk about it as if it is real. It is also a variable that is frequently difficult to define, with many "experts" providing different perspectives. The very notion of a latent variable is itself an example. Other examples of abstract concepts you just assume are real are intelligence (from psychology), understanding (from education), and permanent income (from economics), to mention just a few. Market segmentation is also an example, since you cannot directly observe or measure segments, but only infer from data (i.e., indicators that point to them). You define the concept of segments, which is the basis for saying they are abstract. Consumers do not define their own segments and then behave based on these self-defined segments. You act as if segments are real and "out there" by developing marketing mixes for them, but they are not real. You just behave and operate as if they are. This is one reason why it is so difficult to identify segments, so that segmentation is more art than science. The tools outlined in the previous chapter and that are continued here make it seem that it is science, but this science part is only a small piece of the whole process of segmentation. See [138] and [95] for some discussions about interpreting latent variables, and especially the latter on the abstract view of latent variables. [138] (p. 74) is also important because he notes that latent variables are different from proxy variables, which are surrogates for a variable that has no measurements at all, while the former are "well understood but rarely rigorously defined" and have no measurable counterparts.

As an abstract concept, you can view segments as levels or classes or groups (all interchangeable words) of a single latent discrete variable. Since the discrete variable is latent, so are its levels (i.e., segments). The latent segments are "fuzzy" in the sense that it is not always clear to which segment a consumer belongs since you do not know the segments. This can be seen in Figure 9.1.1, where the points could be consumers and the areas above and below the line are latent segments. The line is unknown so you cannot definitively state where a consumer should be assigned. The best you can do is state the probability that a consumer belongs to one segment versus another. In Figure 9.1.1, there are many data points that clearly belong to one group or the other, so their probability of belonging to a group is 1.0. The data points close to the boundary, however, could go either way, so their probability of belonging to one segment is less than 1.0. There is thus a probability distribution over the segments.

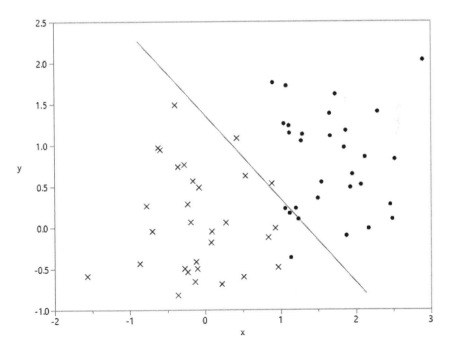

FIGURE 9.1.1 These are simulated data. The boundary line separates two groups of data: those marked with a dot and those marketed with an X. There are some data points, however, that could fall into either group, so that the boundary is fuzzy.

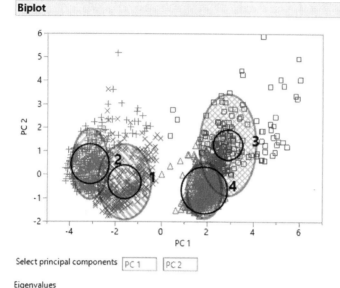

FIGURE 9.1.2 This is a biplot of the first two principal components of the data. The circles are drawn at the centers of the clusters with their sizes proportional to the number of data points in the cluster. The shaded ellipsoids are the 90% confidence intervals.

Figure 9.1.2 shows a biplot of the first two principal components for the four-segment K-means solution from Chapter 8 for the LMS case study. The circles show the centroids of the segments based on the initial seeds; the centers of the circles are the means. The circles are also proportional to the number of data points in the cluster. The colored or shaded areas are 90% confidence ellipsoids around the means. The graph clearly shows that many data points could fall within more than one segment.

If the latent variable is discrete, then the probability distribution is discrete. The discrete probabilities are interpreted as weights for assigning consumers to each segment. In the content of Figure 8.3.1a, there are *mixture weights* that combine the segments into a total market view. The mixture weights are the probabilities a consumer belongs to each segment. The goal of all latent variable modeling is to identify these mixture weights. Consequently, latent variable modeling is also in the class of *mixture models*. Since, at least theoretically, there could be an infinite number of mixture weights, which is impractical to work with, mixture problems are often limited to a finite number of weights or probabilities. Hence, the class of models is referred to as *finite mixture models*. See [119] for a comprehensive presentation on finite mixture distributions. Also see [57] for a summary of the weights.

A latent variable's influence may be suggested or manifested by a correlation between the included explanatory variables that are measured. It is common in econometric analysis for a correlation to exist between two explanatory variables.

This is multicollinearity, a common topic in most econometric textbooks. The cause of the correlation is never discussed except for the sole case of perfect correlation, but even then the explanation is that you mistakenly introduced a perfect linear relationship. The dummy variable trap is the usual example (see [20]). The correlation, however, could be due to the latent variable affecting both explanatory variables.

The observed explanatory variables are sometimes called *manifest* or *indicator* variables in the context of latent variable analysis, although the "indicator" label may be confusing because dummy variables are sometimes also called indicator variables. The context dictates the meaning. For latent variable analysis, the explanatory variables point to or indicate the latent variable and are used to estimate the probability distribution (i.e., the mixture weights) for the latent variable.

9.1.1 Types of latent variable models

There is a bewildering array of models involving latent variables that all hinge on the nature of the dependent and latent variables. The explanatory variables in a regression model can be either continuous or discrete; so can the dependent variable. The type of dependent variable defines the type of regression model: OLS for a continuous dependent variable, logit for a discrete (0/1 coded) dependent variable, and Poisson for a count (discrete) dependent variable. The latent variable can also be continuous or discrete. With two possible types for the dependent variable and two for the latent variable, there are four possible model types as shown in Table 9.1 (see [57] and [9]).

Factor analysis is probably the better known of the four models and is often used in market research, although usually incorrectly because both the indicator and latent variables are supposed to be continuous. This may be acceptable for the latent variable (although this is most often not acknowledged or justified), but is often unacceptable for the indicator variable(s). The indicators are frequently a series of Likert-scaled responses. There is controversy regarding how to properly interpret such a Likert variable. Some treat it as representing a continuous measure, which justifies calculating means and conducting various tests of means. Others view it

TABLE 9.1 The type of latent variable model depends on the type of latent and indicator variables. This classification is one popular scheme often used in textbooks. It is obviously limited since the indicator variables could be combinations of continuous and discrete variables (see [57] and [9]).

		Latent variables	
		Continuous	Discrete
Indicators	Continuous	Factor analysis	Latent profile
	Discrete	Latent trait	Latent class

as an ordinal variable, while others simply view it as discrete to avoid the issue. The problem with treating a Likert variable as ratio is that it does not have a fixed zero point. You could add a constant to a Likert variable and the meaning of the variable would not change. You cannot do this with a true ratio variable such as price: adding \$100 to a product priced at \$1 changes the whole nature and perception of the product. Interval measures imply that the distances between values has meaning and is the same. So the distance between 1 and 3 is the same as the distance between 3 and 5 on a five-point scale. There is no basis for this, however, because you do not know that respondents place the same meaning on a gap of two between 1 and 3 as between 3 and 5; you just know the size of the gap. Nominal is also inappropriate because the points on the scale are given definite labels and meanings. Ordinal is the best; however, the calculation of means is not appropriate for ordinal data. I am in the camp that says the Likert variable is discrete and ordinal, which makes factor analysis inappropriate as frequently used in market research. See [144] for details about Likert variables.

Latent trait analysis is sometimes called *item response analysis*, which is popular in educational research. *Latent class analysis* involves both discrete latent and indicator variables and is often used to model or analyze contingency tables. See [57] for a discussion and examples. Also see [9].

Latent profile analysis is sometimes referred to as a modeling of means for continuous random variables. This can be confused with a regression model where the dependent variable is also continuous. I will refer to a regression model in all its flavors as a *latent regression analysis* (LRA) and keep latent profile analysis, which I will not discuss any further, for just means analysis. In LRA, the goal is to identify discrete levels of a latent variable that are associated with the regression model. See [154] for details on latent profile analysis.

9.1.2 What is latent variable modeling?

Latent variable modeling is based on the supposition that there exists a latent or hidden (from the analyst) discrete variable, L, with S levels. Each object (i.e., consumer, business, and so forth) has a probability of belonging to one of the S segments. The response exhibited by the object to stimuli, the object's *response pattern*, is based on the object's latent segment. The response pattern could be a dependent variable in a regression model context or membership in a cell of a contingency table. So, for example, the pattern could be the amount of purchases of a product or the responses to two categorical survey questions. The particular response pattern, however, is a random variable. This is clear in the classic regression model where the dependent variable, Y_i, is a random variable. This variable is the ith object's response to a stimulus such as price. It may be a single response or multiple responses. Regardless, there is a pattern, and this response pattern has a probability distribution. This is a conditional probability distribution, conditioned on the segment for the object. For a regression context with Y_i as a continuous response, then the conditional distribution is $Pr(Y_i \mid s)$, where $s = 1, \ldots, S$ is a segment. The joint probability of the response and the segment is written as $\Pr(Y_i \cap s) = \Pr(Y_i \mid s) \times \Pr(s)$. The marginal probability, $\Pr(s)$, is the mixture weight showing the probability of any object belonging to segment s.

9.1.3 Latent regression analysis

LRA is a finite mixture model in which regression models are mixed with a finite number of discrete mixture weights. An LRA, therefore, has two components:

1. A specification of a regression model given a segment;
2. A specification of a probability distribution for the mixture weights.

Model components

This section explains the latent model components. First, however, a digression on notation is needed because notation will differ from the usual regression notation, a slight change that will help to explain the overall model.

Digression on notation

Textbooks (e.g., [20]) write a regression model as

$$Y_i = \beta_0 + \beta_1 X_{1i} + \beta_2 X_{2i} + \ldots + \beta_p X_{pi} + \varepsilon_i$$

where ε_i is the disturbance term assumed to be normally distributed with mean 0 and variance σ^2 for case i. Based on this normality assumption and the linearity of the model, the Y_i are also normally distributed by the reproductive property of normals. See [115] for details on the reproductive property. The mean is $E(Y_i) = \beta_0 + \beta_1 X_{1i} + \beta_2 X_{2i} + \ldots + \beta_p X_{pi}$, so the link function is the identity function, and the variance is $V(Y_i) = \sigma^2$. So Y_i is compactly written as

$$Y_i \sim \mathcal{N}(E[Y_i], \sigma^2).$$

This is standard notation. Because of the distributional property, you could use an alternative notation $f(Y_i \mid X_i, \theta)$ where $f(\cdot)$ is the normal density conditioned on the vector of independent variables, X_i for case i, and the vector of parameters θ, which includes all the βs and the σ^2.

The regression family is quite large, as previously noted, with the typical textbook model as a special case. The family consists of:

- Linear regression for a continuous Y;
- Binomial regression for a discrete Y with two values (0/1);
- Multinomial logistic regression for a categorical Y with more than two levels;
- Poisson regression for counts.

These are the most popular for applied work. The corresponding distributions are normal, logistic, multinomial, and Poisson, respectively, so the definition of $f(\cdot)$ depends on the problem. I will focus on the normal distribution for a linear regression for a continuous Y_i.

Latent regression model

The latent regression model framework assumes that a single latent variable, L, exists that is nominally scaled with $1 \leq s \leq S$ *levels* or *components* or *classes* or *groups* or *segments*, all terms that are used interchangeably. The regression model is assumed to hold for each segment, but with a different parameter vector, β_s, for each. The X_{is} data vector for segment s determines the response Y_{is} in s. There could also be another data vector, Z_s, which determines the segment, but not the responses within the segment. These are sometimes called *covariates*, which are observable characteristics of consumers that account for their heterogeneity. Demographic variables such as age, gender, income, and education are just a few examples. For the LMS case study, the numbers of beds, admissions, and full-time staff at the hospitals are other examples. So a difference from a standard regression model is the presence of two types of right-hand side variables: independent variables that determine responses within a segment and covariates that determine the segments.

The regression model is written as

$$f(Y_i \mid X_i, Z_i, \theta) = \sum_{s=1}^{S} g(Y_i \mid X_i, \beta_s, \sigma_s^2) \times Pr(s \mid Z_s, \gamma_s) \tag{114}$$

where θ is a vector of all parameters, γ_s is the vector of parameters for the segments, β_s and σ_s^2 are the regression parameters specific to segment s, and $Pr(\cdot)$ is the probability a case belongs to segment s. The $Pr(\cdot)$ are the mixture weights. As probabilities or weights, the two conditions

$$Pr(s \mid Z_s, \gamma_s) \geq 0$$
$$\sum_{s=1}^{S} Pr(s \mid Z_s, \gamma_s) = 1$$

must hold. You can view (114) as a weighted average of regression functions, so it has an intuitive basis. It can also be viewed as the result of marginalizing over one element in a joint distribution conditioned on a third variable.

Estimation – The expectation maximization algorithm

Estimation of the parameters of a latent regression model (114) involves estimating the mixture weights for the segments (and maybe parameters for the weights if covariates are used) and the parameters of the conditional probabilities for each segment. For the mixture weights, the latent variable L is assumed to be drawn from a multinomial distribution, which could be a function of covariates if they are specified. The expected value of the conditional probabilities is a linear function of the independent variables. This is just a linear regression model.

The *Expectation Maximization* (EM) algorithm is usually used for the estimation. Discussion of the algorithm is beyond the scope of this book. In essence, however, the EM algorithm is an iterative procedure that estimates the parameters of each component of the model by randomly drawing values from an assumed distribution, updating the parameter values, and then redrawing values and updating the parameters again. The iterations continue until there is either a small change in the parameter values or a maximum number of iterations is reached. In either case, the resulting parameter values will be the true parameters. See [103] and [112] for descriptions of the algorithm. Also see [97] for details on convergence. Finally, see [100] for a discussion in the context of other optimization procedures.

Selecting the number of segments

A major advantage of latent class modeling is the availability of statistical diagnostics. These are not available for traditional multivariate clustering methods such as hierarchical clustering and K-means, although the Cubic Clustering Criterion can be used as described in Chapter 8. Typical latent variable modeling diagnostics are based on information criteria. The basic notion is that all data sets contain information that has to be extracted for decision making. The goal is to extract as much information as possible, so a measure of the amount extracted, or, conversely, the amount left in the data, is needed. The various information criteria used in empirical work measure the amount of information left in the data. Since the goal is to leave as little information as possible, the minimum for any information criteria is sought. The information criteria are sometimes referred to as measures of "badness of fit," in contrast to an OLS R^2, which is a measure of goodness of fit. Unlike R^2, which lies in the interval $(0, 1)$, the information criteria are unbounded and can be negative, but like R^2, they are unitless (see [99] for details). The basic information criterion is due to [80] and was extended to a Bayesian context by [160]. The former is known as the *Akaike Information Criterion* (AIC) and the latter is sometimes known as the *Bayesian Information Criterion* (BIC). The formulas, plus variants of AIC, are shown in Table 9.2.

Information criteria (IC) measures are functions of the likelihood function (actually, the log likelihood), which itself is a function of the model parameters, in particular σ^2. If σ^2 is large, the likelihood function is flat and spread out so that the maximum value is low. In contrast, if σ^2 is small, the likelihood function is peaked with a large maximum value. The maximum value, therefore, could be greater than or less than 1.0; there is no reason it must be less than 1.0 since it does not measure probability. Figure 9.1.3 illustrates these points.

TABLE 9.2 The formulas for the information criteria (IC) based on the (natural) log-likelihood are shown here: n is the sample size; p is the number of estimable parameters; L is the maximum likelihood. See [82] and [113] on AIC3 and latent variable models.

Measure	Formula	Comments
AIC	$2 \times p - 2 \times ln(L)$	Fundamental IC measure
BIC	$ln(n) \times p - 2 \times ln(L)$	BIC
AIC3	$3 \times p - 2 \times ln(L)$	May be better than AIC or BIC for latent variable models
CAIC	$[ln(n) + 1] \times p - 2 \times ln(L)$	Consistent AIC

If the density is less than 1.0 because σ^2 is small, then the (natural) log of this maximum value is negative; if it is greater than 1.0, then the (natural) log value is positive. If the maximum log likelihood value is positive, then AIC < 0 is possible depending on the number of parameters, p. The actual value of the AIC for one model is not important; just the order is important relative to the AIC for other models. The smallest AIC indicates that the associated model leaves the least amount of information in the data. So for two models, one with AIC $= -20$ and the other with AIC $= -10$, the one with the -20 "wins."

See [173] and [121] for discussions about IC. In particular, see the latter for applications for latent class models. Also see [99] for details on information theory as the background for AIC and the derivation and analysis of the AIC.

Pricing Scenario: Latent regression model

A latent regression model was estimated for the LMS Pricing Scenario.[2] The dependent variable was the natural log of the number of learners as before and the independent variable was the natural log of the price per learner. The hospital measures were the covariates. The key information criterion measures are shown in Table 9.3. Based on the BIC, the $k = 3$ solution is the best. A price elasticity is the coefficient for the log price as before, but now there is one elasticity for each segment. The elasticities for the $k = 3$ solution are in Table 9.4, while the mixture weights are in Table 9.5.

There are parameters that can be used to predict the probability of belonging to a segment for each respondent. These are *posterior probabilities* that sum to 1.0 for each respondent. This distribution reflects the fuzziness of class membership. A typical rule for assigning each respondent to a single segment is to use the highest or modal posterior probability.

9.1.4 Choice latent class models

The latent class modeling framework can be extended to include the conjoint and discrete choice models discussed in previous chapters. These extensions will be briefly summarized here.

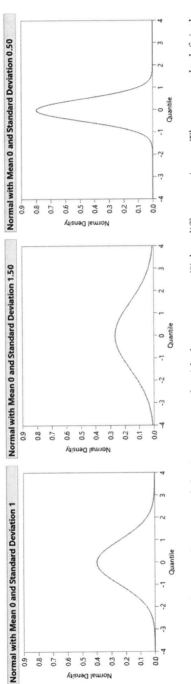

FIGURE 9.1.3 These are three normal density curves, each with the same mean (0) but different variances. The one on the left is the standard normal. The middle one has a smaller variance and is flatter than the standard normal. The one on the right has a larger variance is more peaked than the standard normal.

TABLE 9.3 The key information criterion measures for four solutions are shown here. Each can be calculated using the number of parameters and the log-likelihood value. For example, using $AIC = 2 \times NPAR - 2 \times LL$ for $k = 2$, you get $AIC = 2 \times 17 + 2 \times 2453.4161 = 4949.8321$, as shown in the table. Using the BIC measure, the best segmentation size is $k = 3$.

Statistic	$k = 2$	$k = 3$	$k = 4$	$k = 5$
Number of parameters (NPAR)	17	31	45	59
Log-likelihood (LL)	−2453.4161	−2351.6812	−2305.0568	−2276.4561
Log-prior	−5.5389	−6.9252	−7.4855	−8.0848
Log-posterior	−2458.9550	−2358.6064	−2312.5423	−2284.5409
BIC (based on LL)	5031.1569	4930.0723	4939.2084	4984.3922
AIC (based on LL)	4940.8321	4765.3625	4700.1135	4670.9122
AIC3 (based on LL)	4957.8321	4796.3625	4745.1135	4729.9122
CAIC (based on LL)	5048.1569	4961.0723	4984.2084	5043.3922

TABLE 9.4 The elasticities are determined as before for a log-log model, but in this case they are determined simultaneously for each segment. The number of segments is $k = 3$. Segments 1 and 3 are inelastic, while segment 2 is highly elastic.

Segment	Elasticity
1	−0.9016
2	−2.4762
3	0.0804

TABLE 9.5 The mixture weights are all greater than 0 and sum to 1.0.

Segment	Weight
1	0.3993
2	0.3556
3	0.2451

Conjoint latent class models

Extending the basic conjoint model to include latent segments is a natural step, especially since an early application of conjoint analysis was segmentation. In that early framework, segmentation was based on a two-step tandem approach:

1. Estimate conjoint part-worths for each individual for each attribute and level;
2. Cluster the part-worths.

This requires a design matrix with enough observations (i.e., runs) per respondent to provide sufficient degrees of freedom for estimating at the individual level. Calculating price elasticities then required a third step.

A latent class conjoint model is basically the latent regression model where the dependent variable is the preference rating and the independent variables are represented by the design matrix. The dependent and price variables would have to be treated as continuous variables so that (natural) logs could be used. The latent approach would produce the segments, part-worths, and elasticities in one step as opposed to three for the older approach. See [101] for a discussion of a latent class conjoint, although this paper does not have a pricing focus.

Discrete choice latent class models

A major assumption of the discrete choice model is that the preferences, represented by the part-worth utilities or coefficients of the systematic utilities, are identical for all consumers. This is a strong assumption that should be dispelled by the above discussion about heterogeneity. The discrete choice framework, however, does not have to be abandoned any more than does the conjoint framework. The adjustment involves modifying the systematic utility.

Recall that the systematic utility is the linear measure of the attributes comprising a choice set. This is written as $V(X_{ij} \mid \beta)$ for respondent i for choice j. Allowing for latent segments, the systematic utility is now written as $V(X_{ij} \mid \beta_s)$, where the part-worths are conditioned on the latent segment, s. The total utility is the sum of the systematic utility and the random disturbance term as before. The choice probability is now

$$\Pr_i(j \mid s) = \frac{e^{V_{ij} \mid \beta_s}}{\sum_{k=1}^{J} e^{V_{ik} \mid s}}. \tag{115}$$

See [148] and [128] for further developments. As a trivial observation, note that the take rate in Chapter 5 results when $S = 1$.

9.2 Gaussian mixture modeling

Several clustering methods were described in the previous chapter. They all have their strengths and weaknesses, but a major, albeit subtle, one is that each object is assigned to one and only one segment. Basically, the probability of assignment is 1.0, a certainty. In most applications, however, objects could be assigned to multiple segments, perhaps some more likely than others, but nonetheless they cannot be assigned to just one. The reason is that the segments are unknown, a concept that is further discussed in the next section, so you cannot be certain where the object actually belongs. There is a probability of assignment to a segment, with the probability being less than 1.0.

Determining the probability of assignment requires a model, the model either being a statistical model, such as one of the members of the regression family, or a probability model. The latter is based on a combination of distribution mixture weights. You can assume that the data are drawn from normal (Gaussian) distributions, each with some mean and variance. A mixture of these normal distributions can be found that summarizes the distribution of the observed data. The distributions are the segments. The number of segments is unknown, so they have to be pre-specified as for the K-means and latent class clustering.

For the Pricing Scenario, a three-segment mixture solution was estimated using the hospital attributes: Average Number of Learners; Inpatient: Number of Discharges; Inpatient: Number of Discharge Days; Beds Licensed or Certified; Admissions; Licensed Doctors; Full-time Physicians; Full-time Interns and Residents; Full-time RNs; and Full-time Staff. These are all numeric/continuous variables, which is appropriate for normal distributions. A report is shown in Figure 9.2.1. The top report labeled "Cluster Comparison" shows fit statistics for comparing this solution to ones with more or fewer segments. The BIC and AIC values are shown. Since only one solution is provided in this example, these two values are meaningless; they are useful when there are several solutions to compare. The report labeled "Cluster Summary" shows the count and proportion of hospitals in each segment. The proportions are estimates of the mixture weights. The cluster means are also shown and have the same interpretation as those for a K-means clustering.

Once clusters are determined using a Gaussian mixture approach, the probability of each object belonging to each of the segments is calculated. An object is assigned to one segment using the modal probability as for latent regression segmentation.

9.3 Multilevel models

If there is a hierarchical structure to the data, then you would most likely have parameter heterogeneity. The data are hierarchically structured if the units observed and measured are contained in or *nested* in other units that could be observed or measured. A traditional example from education that clearly illustrates a hierarchical structure is students in a school district. Students in the district could be measured on a standardized test. The students, however, attend a school, and a set of schools make up the district. It may be – but it is not necessarily so – that the students within a school are somewhat homogeneous because they come from the same neighborhood so they share the same socioeconomic status (SES) or racial or ethnic background, while students in different schools in the district would be somewhat heterogeneous, reflecting different neighborhoods. This would especially be the case in a large metropolitan area such as, for example, New York City. In this classic example, students are nested within a school and the schools are nested within a district so the district is at the top of a hierarchy and students are at the bottom. This hierarchical structure thus has three levels: students, schools, and district. The measurements (i.e., test scores) are at the student level.

Model Based Clustering

Cluster Comparison

Method	NCluster	BIC	AICc	Best
Normal Mixtures	3	185198	184211	Smallest BIC Smallest AICc

Normal Mixtures NCluster=3

Cluster Summary

Cluster	Count	Proportion
1	684	0.45600
2	326	0.21957
3	490	0.32443

Cluster Means

Cluster	Average Number of Learners	Inpatient: Number of Discharges	Inpatient: Number of Discharge Days	Beds Licensed or Certified	Admissions	Licensed MDs	Full-time Physicians	Full-time Interns and Residents	Full-time RNs	Full-time Staff
1	190.443967	10644.8433	53353.8602	247.974074	10628.9115	292.470706	22.754363	79.6411542	366.519815	1563.6121
2	190.115596	4654.90747	35034.5847	148.553057	4704.97252	172.837984	37.7339049	77.8662764	231.693598	1155.80152
3	10.756382	2218.40937	17794.9358	86.980988	2277.27493	72.5455694	15.565647	45.5933405	114.469628	584.744993

-LogLikelihood	BIC	AICc
91878.658	18519802	18421123

FIGURE 9.2.1 This is a Gaussian mixture solution for three segments. The mixture weights are in the "Cluster Summary" report.

For pricing with the country divided into marketing regions, perhaps based on an *a priori* view of the buying population, consumers in one geographic area would be somewhat homogeneous, having the same price elasticity, while consumers in different regions would have different elasticities. The heterogeneous elasticities would reflect a regional effect perhaps due to different SES levels, regional economic characteristics (e.g., unemployment, industry composition, population density), and so forth. Consumers would be nested within a region, so the hierarchical structure is simple with only two levels: consumers and region. It would be possible to consider the regions nested in the country if a country effect is needed. The measurements (e.g., purchases, price paid) are at the consumer level.

The hierarchical structure exists in many data sets used in pricing (and marketing analysis). Since such structures have levels, the models are called *multilevel models*. See [124] for a thorough introduction and exposition of multilevel models. Also see [139] and [163].

Multilevel models are discussed more thoroughly in Chapter 11, where it is emphasized that they make more efficient use of the hierarchical data structure. But more importantly, they provide unbiased estimates of parameters. Ignoring this structure is tantamount to running one grand (i.e., pooled) regression model. This is a serious misspecification. These issues are discussed in Chapter 11.

9.4   Software

JMP and Latent Class Gold are commercial software packages for estimating latent variable models. JMP only handles latent class models, while Latent Class Gold handles a wide array of models. The latent regression estimation in this chapter was done using Latent Class Gold 4.5. SAS will also do latent variable estimation using an add-in proc available at The Methodology Center of the Penn State College of Health and Human Development (https://methodology.psu.edu/downloads/proclcalta). There is a version available for R and Stata. There are R functions (such as *lmer()*) and BUGS. See [124] for discussions about these functions as well as many examples of their application.

9.5   Summary

A more advanced method for price segmentation was introduced in this chapter. The method is model based, which is my preferred way to price segment the market. Models are superior because there are test statistics that can be used to judge the model results and to compare one model to another. These are not available for the tandem approaches of Chapter 8.

Notes

1 See https://en.wikipedia.org/wiki/Latent_variable.
2 Latent Class Gold 4.5 was used.

PART IV

Big Data and econometric models

In this fourth and last part of the book, I switch gears and discuss pricing using Big Data. Part II focused on stated preference analysis, which is survey based, being the only way that preferences can be "stated," while Part III focused on data that could be either from surveys or databases. This part is strictly databases – very large databases. Chapter 10 defines Big Data and then dwells on the nature of and problems with using Big Data in *analytical* work. Some recommendations are made for working with Big Data in order to extract the most information and insight from it. Data visualization is emphasized at the end of this chapter. Chapter 11 is focused on using Big Data in econometric models. The nature of Big Data as panel data is used to define a class of econometric models. The nature of this class and the problems and issues associated with it for pricing are discussed. Chapter 12 focuses the content of the two previous chapters on to a discussion of nonlinear pricing. The pricing throughout this book until this chapter has been uniform or linear pricing. Many cases in the real world – quantity discounts, bundling, product-line pricing – are nonlinear. These are more complex problems, and some recommendations are made for handling them with econometric models. Big Data is the backdrop, but I have to admit that survey data could be used for some problems.

.

10

WORKING WITH BIG DATA

In this chapter, I will introduce the final approach to price modeling: econometric models. These models were used before in Parts II and III. This chapter, and in fact this whole part of the book, deviates from them by focusing on Big Data, whereas those parts looked mostly at survey data.

This chapter is divided into seven sections. In Section 1, I define Big Data. Sections 2–4 highlight issues associated with working with Big Data. All too often, the problems posed by Big Data are ignored, while only the "benefits" are highlighted. Knowing the problems is just as important as knowing the benefits. Section 5 presents some data visualization methods for examining Big Data and prices maintained in data warehouses and data marts. Finally, Section 6 discusses software and Section 7 is a summary.

10.1 A motivation for using Big Data

Recall from Chapter 3 that price discrimination is a widely used practice for optimizing revenue. Three forms of discrimination were discussed, with the third being the focus of Chapters 8 and 9. The first, simply called first-degree price discrimination, is based on a separate price schedule for each consumer, which amounts to individualized pricing. The marketing literature sometimes refers to this as "customer addressability": you know the address of each customer and so you can market directly to that person (see [102]). Until recently, economists believed that this form of discrimination was impossible, or at a minimum difficult and costly, to implement on a wide scale because the amount of information needed to identify the reservation price and willingness to pay (WTP) for each unit of the good for each consumer was too great and too costly to collect. With modern data collection, storage, and processing technologies, however, firms may be able to dynamically charge each consumer according to first-degree price discrimination, and current pricing strategies, which are predominately discriminatory, can morph into first-degree price discrimination (see [64]).

Obtaining and storing information for effective first-degree price discrimination can be viewed by consumers as an invasion of privacy. They have to willingly and accurately provide the information necessary for this discrimination to work. They may, for example, falsely identify themselves as low-value buyers in order to get a better deal, or they may refuse to provide any information. Some information, such as name, street address, email address, frequency of purchase, and amounts spent on each purchase, could still be obtained when a transaction is completed by requiring identification in order to qualify for rewards, discounts, or rebates, the identification being a government- or business-issued ID. Actually, this type of information has been collected this way for a long time through what is now considered normal transaction data collection. Scanner data on everything purchased at the grocery store is the prime example and, when accompanied by scanned store-provided check cashing, rewards, or membership cards, this provides a rich data set on customers. These scanner data are stored in massive databases (i.e., *data warehouses*). This is the basis for *Big Data*.

A major overlooked characteristic of these data is that they are all for past transactions: what the consumers *did* purchase, not *will* purchase, especially at different price points. The only way to know their willingness to purchase or purchase intent is by the methods in Part II.

If you know that a consumer bought a particular brand and type of shampoo on the past ten purchase occasions, you could send him or her a coupon or special offer for the next purchase. The price paid, however, does not tell you the *maximum* amount he or she is willing to pay for different attributes of a product. WTP, as described in Chapter 5, is not revealed in the market. If consumers are somewhat consistent in their behaviors and the products are stable in the market, then the transaction data coupled with econometric models can be used to estimate elasticities. One way to do this is with revealed preference discrete choice models, which look at the actual choices made as recorded in the transactions database. Chapter 5 focused on stated preference discrete choice models, but the same methodology can be applied to Big Data, so it will not be further discussed. Another way is with the econometric models I will discuss in Chapter 11. This chapter discusses the Big Data for these models.

10.2 Big Data: Definition and issues

What is "Big Data?" It is unfortunately ill-defined, meaning different things to different people. Some typical descriptors are:

- Huge quantities of data;
- Social media;
- Next-generation data management;
- Real-time data.

Although ill defined, you still can characterize it in terms of the *three Vs of Big Data*:

1. Volume;
2. Velocity;
3. Variety.

A fourth *V* sometimes mentioned is "Veracity" for data reliability and accuracy.[1]

Volume

We still view data by size – size always matters. We moved past "Small Data" to "Big Data" a long time ago, but this is all relative to our time and technology. The progression, shown in Figure 10.2.1, has an implication: we are drowning in data, but starving for information. This may be the case, for example, if you are analyzing market data from a data warehouse. Information remains hidden inside the data either because you do not use all of it (there is so much) or you try to use it all, which is just as bad. In either case, you confront *the curse of too much data*: relationships, trends, patterns, and anomalies in the data are hidden by the sheer volume. Volume can be managed; it always has been. Since we have always developed new technologies (i.e., storage) to manage volume, I tend to discount this as an issue.

Velocity

The velocity with which data arrive into data warehouses has people more anxious than the volume. So much is now coming so quickly that analysts are under pressure to analyze it all – and to do it now! The world is changing so quickly and markets evolving so rapidly, in part because of this data phenomenon, that some believe they cannot waste time. The stress level rises and the quality of analysis suffers because they simply cannot analyze it all at the rate it is received.

Variety

Variety has added a dimension that did not exist before. Not long ago, there was a limited variety of data that nicely matched simple structures. For example,

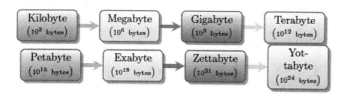

FIGURE 10.2.1 The top row shows storage progression on PCs and Macs to the present, while the bottom row shows where storage is heading (and quite rapidly). The sizes in this row are huge to say the least.

transactions databases contained data only on purchases, pricing, and dates. Now, in addition to these traditional types of data, there are emails, tweets, blogs, videos, and the list goes on. This adds to the volume and makes it all seem important, no matter the source. If you do not do something with all of these different data types, someone else (your competitors) will. You will overlook something important. Hence, an element of stress exists that is comparable to the velocity stress.

Veracity

Veracity is overplayed. I discount this as a new issue because accuracy has always been important. The old saying "garbage in = garbage out" still holds. The velocity and variety issues just mean that veracity is more difficult and challenging, just as volume is more challenging, but neither is overwhelming nor a cause for great concern.

10.2.1 Aspects of Big Data

Like all processes evolving through time, data started "small" and became "big."[2] Data have evolved regarding:

- Structure;
- Storage;
- Processing requirements.

They have now changed again with regard to their nature or features.

Structure for small data used to be important. It was not the size of "small" data that counted – it was how the data were organized. Simple rectangular arrays of rows and columns handled the data perfectly. Numbers and well-organized text (e.g., names and addresses) were easily stored in these arrays. Also, the small data sets were characterized by uniformity of data elements with well-defined and predefined features such as dates, sales volumes, stock keeping units (SKUs), and prices. The structure was often a *panel data set*, a combination of cross-sectional and time series data. Cross-sectional data are collected at one point in time for a series of units, while time series data are collected in time for one unit. These rectangular arrays would have, for example, Q variables such as SKUs, measured on N marketing items such as stores or customers, repeated for each of T time periods or purchase occasions such as days, weeks, or months. I will interchangeably refer to these N items as *cases, objects, observations*, and *instances*. A very large data panel would have Q in the hundreds, N in the thousands, and T in the thousands (for several years by day), making the total data set potentially very large. This is a traditional transaction database of size $(N \times T) \times Q$ (see [126]). Notation is based on this article.

Panel data are bi-dimensional with a spatial dimension (the cross-section of N items) and a temporal dimension (the time series of T items). They are sometimes called *longitudinal* because they track objects (e.g., customers) through time. A panel data set could contain different types of variables:

- Mixed measurement scales (e.g., nominal, ordinal, continuous);
- Numerous product features (e.g., SKU ID, SKU description, prices, sales);
- Disparate environmental features (e.g., region, customer, sales rep);
- Detailed time dimensions (e.g., day, month, year of transaction);
- Other variables available through technology advances (e.g., terms searched by someone who purchased online, which could be in the thousands, making Q very large).

There are advantages and disadvantages to using panel data. Among the advantages are:

- A larger number of data points are available so the degrees of freedom increase, thus enhancing statistical validity;
- A larger number of interesting business questions can be addressed;
- A better allowance for and analysis of the effects of consumer heterogeneity;
- Increased variability for estimations[3];
- Enhanced variability between units and within units over time;
- Enhanced ability to study time dynamics.

The disadvantages include:

- Data collection problems;
- Storage issues;
- Sampling problems.

These advantages and disadvantages are drawn in part from [132] and [90]. For a complex advanced treatment of panel data, see [171].

10.2.2 Pricing Scenario

Furn, Inc., is a leading, family-owned household furniture manufacturer in New Jersey. It sells furniture strictly wholesale to locally owned, boutique furniture retailers throughout the USA, which it has divided into four marketing regions consistent with US Census regions. The markets in each state are highly competitive, primarily because of a growing presence of foreign merchandise. Not only must Furn, Inc., compete on the quality of its furniture, but it must also meet very high price pressures from retailers.

The company carries approximately 43 SKUs divided into six product lines consistent with the major rooms in a house: Den, Dining Room, Kids' Room, Kitchen, Living Room, and Master Bedroom. Each product line is divided into a product class, which is a furniture category such as Chairs, Tables, and Baker's Racks for the

TABLE 10.1 The size of the database is $(N \times T) \times Q = (1,174,154) \times Q$.

Dimension	Description	Feature
N	SKUs	Product
T	Daily for three years	Time
Q	SKU description; prices; discounts; region; customer ID; sales rep	Environment

TABLE 10.2 Small snippet of the furniture data set for the furniture Pricing Scenario. The pocket price is explained in the text.

Product line	Product class	SKU	Transaction date	Pocket price
Den	Computer table	DNCTB	01/10/2005	$53.90
Den	Desk chair	DNDSC	01/10/2005	$31.94
Den	Desk chair	DNDSC	01/11/2005	$29.44
Den	Desk chair	DNDSC	01/12/2005	$28.75
Den	Desk	DNDSK	01/11/2005	$57.50
Den	Desk	DNDSK	01/12/2005	$60.23

Kitchen. Each class is further divided into product styles such as White Table – Oval, White Table – Square, Colonial Maple – Distressed for the Table class in the Kitchen product line. The product styles are the base units that have a SKU, a nine alphanumeric code representing the line, class, and style in that hierarchical order.

Sales are direct to a store location. Every sale is recorded in a transaction database which, for this Pricing Scenario, has 1,174,154 records for all SKUs. Each record has a date indicator for the day/month/year of the transaction for three years. Also, customer (a store) ID, region (4), and sales rep are recorded. The data are summarized in Table 10.1. A sample of the data is shown in Table 10.2.

10.2.3   Data warehouses and data marts

Storage became an issue for Big Data as small panels evolved into larger ones. Data are now kept in a *data warehouse*, which are enterprise-wide data collections on all aspects of the business. The data warehouses became more sophisticated and complex over time, frequently leading to smaller subsets or data marts. A *data mart* is a specialized subset of a data warehouse for a specific business department or function such as marketing, finance, engineering, and pricing, to mention a few. This allows for faster decisions in tightly defined functional areas (see Figure 10.2.2 and Table 10.3). For example, a marketing department would maintain a data mart of all the customers, marketing campaigns to them, and response or success rates, thus making the data readily available and easily accessible for market analysis.

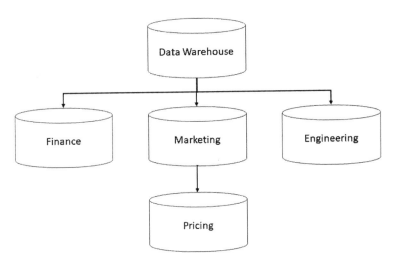

FIGURE 10.2.2 Data marts are functional area subsets of a data warehouse. Because they are subsets of a larger warehouse, they are more manageable and more accessible by functional area managers and analysts.

TABLE 10.3 Comparisons of a data warehouse and a data mart.

Category	Data warehouse	Data mart
Scope	Corporate	Line of business
Subject	Multiple	Single subject
Sources	Many	Few
Size (typical)	100 GB to TB+	<100 GB
Implementation time	Months to years	Months

Source: http://docs.oracle.com/html/E10312_01/dm_concepts.htm

A data mart, and also the data warehouse, usually has several *data tables*, each representing a different aspect of a case. The data tables are linked by common identifiers such as product ID, customer ID, order number, and so forth. The smaller tables have specialized, narrowly defined and highly focused data on customers (e.g., name, address, demographics), product descriptions, and orders. Different data tables efficiently organize the data by reducing duplication of some information, which leads to lower storage costs (even with modern computers!) and enhanced data integrity. This is known as *normalization*. For example, a data mart could consist of three tables containing customer information, order details, and product specifications so each has a specialized set of data.

Analysts naturally want to ask questions of (i.e., query) the data, so data query systems developed. The *Structured Query Language* (SQL) is the most popular, although it has many dialects. The "structured" part of the language name refers to the use of human-like or natural language sentences. So a typical command would be something like:

Select Sum(Sales) as totalSales
from CUST
where SKU = 10015

This is interpreted or read as "*Select* the variable Sales *from* the CUST data table *where* the SKU is 10015, then *sum* the sales and call the sum totalSales." This human-like language mimicked the nature of the databases – structured relational forms. Well-organized tables could logically be connected (i.e., joined) with standard operations applied (e.g., *Sum*).

As the demands for operating on tables (let alone analyzing data) increased, so did computing speeds. Moore's Law states that the number of transistors doubles about every two years, although some have extended it to every three years; others believe it is doomed by economics.[4]

These developments have implications for pricing. Predictive models could be built on extensive panel data and markets could be segmented for third-degree price discrimination.

10.3   Big Data and pricing

To put Big Data and its importance for pricing into perspective, it is best to first think about the distinction between data per se and information. The two words "data" and "information" are often used interchangeably and treated as synonyms. This is too simplistic. Data are raw, unfiltered, disorganized pieces of material (i.e., "stuff"). "Stuff" is collected and stored in closets. Modern-day data closets are computer files/folders, data marts, and data warehouses (and data lakes!).[5] Data are more usefully viewed as clay that is moldable and malleable and can be assembled in infinite ways, reflecting our creativity and questions. Information is what is extracted from data after molding it in different ways (i.e., viewing it and modeling it).

Information is not a binary concept, meaning you either have or do not have it. It is a continuum ranging from poor to rich information. This continuum is shown in Figure 10.3.1. Data per se are *poor information* that cannot tell you much about your consumers, especially their preferences. This is the mistake people make about Big Data stored in data warehouses. Big Data may hold the secrets about what consumers want, but the data themselves do not tell you directly what they want or need or their WTP for different features. *Rich information*, on the other hand, is extracted from data and directly tells you about consumers: their preferences and WTP are revealed through statistical and econometric methods. The *Analytical Bridge* in Figure 10.3.1 consists of the methods that take you from raw data, or poor information, to rich information. I focus on some tools in the Analytical Bridge in Chapter 11, while in this chapter I focus on issues associated with Big Data itself

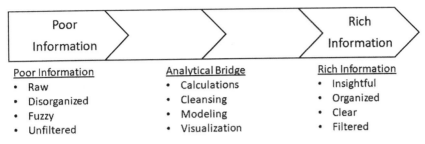

Poor Information	Analytical Bridge	Rich Information
• Raw	• Calculations	• Insightful
• Disorganized	• Cleansing	• Organized
• Fuzzy	• Modeling	• Clear
• Unfiltered	• Visualization	• Filtered

FIGURE 10.3.1 *Poor information* is best represented as raw data. This is what is in data warehouses and data marts. The goal is to extract the *rich information* for pricing. The *analytical bridge* consists of the steps to extract the *rich information*. Based on [175].

that must be considered before the methods are applied and cross the bridge. This chapter, therefore, is the backdrop to the next.

You can certainly ask if all these data, the poor information, are useful for pricing. The answer is probably no. Many of them are in the form of emails, tweets, and videos, the things that increase the volume of Big Data. They may be useful for marketing messages, customer relationship management, and new product development (e.g., designing and building individual products to satisfy every need), but I have reservations about their usefulness for pricing. Here, I restrict my discussion to data relevant for pricing analytics. These pricing-relevant data are maintained in a *pricing data mart* (PDM), a subset of, perhaps, a marketing data mart. The data in the PDM are a consolidation of transactions data. The variables may be prices (list and invoiced), unit sales, discounts, SKUs and their descriptions, time and date stamps of the transactions, sales locations, sales reps, bids, wins and losses, and competitor prices and information.

A PDM has two dominant uses in pricing: operations and predictive modeling. The operations part is used for tracking business outcomes. Dashboards are popular summary mechanisms for this so the PDM can act as input into a price monitoring system, informing managers of sales at different price points, current discount offerings (and leakages due to discounts), as well as competitive prices and general market price trends. The predictive modeling aspect is concerned with new product developments, segmentation, estimating elasticities, and calculating WTP. This is my focus. See [117] for some discussions of these uses.

A PDM, while simplifying data volume from a data warehouse to a marketing data mart to the pricing function, still has problems for pricing and predictive modeling. When you have millions of records and fewer columns in a data table (i.e., when $N \times T$ is large and Q is small with $N \times T \gg Q$, which is called *low-dimensional data*), statistical significance becomes an issue. When Q is large and $N \times T$ is small with $Q \gg N \times T$, which is *high-dimensional data*, then overfitting and multiple comparisons become issues. In both situations, there are statistical testing issues, which are discussed next. See [126], from which the notion of high- and low-dimensional data is drawn.

10.3.1 $N \times T \gg Q$: Significance testing issue

There is a subtlety in using a PDM for price modeling: everything will be highly significant when $N \times T \gg Q$. Statisticians have driven home the lesson of significance so that we live in a "cult of statistical significance" (see [177]). A quantitative result or finding of interest could be due to chance alone, "the luck of the draw." You need to determine whether or not the quantitative finding is a true finding or just a random error. A statistical test resulting in a p-value is usually conducted. The p-value shows the probability of getting a specific test result or something bigger purely by chance. Consequently, the goal is to have a small p-value, smaller than a predefined, arbitrarily selected value, α. Usually for market research and price analytic studies, $\alpha = 0.05$ is used, so a p-value less than 0.05 indicates statistical significance. There is a lot of controversy regarding the use of the p-value (see [167] and [146], as well as the comments included with the latter).

Unfortunately, the p-value will tend to zero, and thus be less than α, when the number of observations becomes large. The test statistic giving rise to the p-value is a function of the standard error of the estimator. The standard error is inversely related to the number of observations so that as the number of observations increases, the standard error decreases. The value of the test statistic then increases. For instance, the standard error for a sample mean $\overline{X}$ is $s/\sqrt{n}$, where s is the sample standard deviation and n is the sample size. A test statistic for the sample mean is $\overline{X} / \left(s/\sqrt{n} \right)$, so this test statistic becomes larger as n becomes larger. A test statistic and a p-value have an inverse relationship. Large test statistics or small p-values imply statistical significance. With very large data sets, all effects are statistically significant simply because of the n. The implication of small p-values is that every null hypothesis will be rejected. You will have so many important relationships that you cannot handle them all, but unfortunately most will be spurious. Important pricing decisions will be made on bad information, so in the context of the poor to rich information continuum, you would be back to poor information.

10.3.2 $Q \gg N \times T$: Multiple comparisons issue

Many traditional statistical and econometric analysis and modeling procedures were designed for low-dimensional data with $N \times T \gg Q$. High-dimensional data, with $Q \gg N \times T$, is now the norm because of the technology and other progressions mentioned above. In this situation, some analysts try to compare all variables to look for significant effects, sometimes any effects, because they believe each variable represents a different aspect of a customer or sale. The belief is that there must be a relationship between two or more of these variables and that relationship must be found before the competition finds it. Unfortunately, testing all possible relationships is not practical because of the *multiple comparisons problem*. There are multiple comparison test procedures that are widely known, but not frequently used by pricing analysts. More formally, in a multiple comparison situation, the significance level is inflated. The general formula for the inflation is

$$Pr(\text{Falsely Rejecting } H_0) = 1 - (1 - \alpha)^k$$

where k is the number of tests and α is the probability of falsely rejecting the null hypothesis on a single test. Considering three hypotheses with $\alpha = 0.05$, then $k = 3$ and $Pr(\text{Falsely Rejecting } H_0) = 1 - (1 - 0.05)^3 = 0.1426$ on multiple tests, which is much greater than 0.05 for a single test. The $\alpha = 0.05$ is sometimes called a comparison-wise error and the 0.1426 is a family-wise error rate. Researchers with a large number of variables try to test every pattern they can think of, but because of the multiple comparisons issue, some unimportant "fluke results" will be discovered. But these could very well be meaningless. The implication is that major pricing decisions could be made on false results. See [57] for a discussion. See [94] and [170] for a more extensive treatment of the multiple comparison problem.

10.4   A role for sampling

As I mentioned above, there is a belief that all the data have to be studied; to do otherwise would indicate a wasting of data, inefficiency, or "cheating." The massive amounts of data lead you to believe that you have the population and that all you need to do is study that population (i.e., the entire database). Practically speaking, however, this is not always possible or desirable. There are advantages and disadvantages associated with using all the data in a PDM. A major advantage is the wealth of rich information that could be extracted. A major disadvantage is computational feasibility.

Even with modern hardware and software, you are restricted by the number of operations that can be performed using the data, a concept known as *algorithmic complexity*, which can overcome the hardware processing power. The complexity of a statistical operation is measured by the order of magnitude of the algorithm, referred to as *The Big O*. This is an indicator of the time it takes for an algorithm to complete its operation as a function of the size of the input data set. The larger the data set (the larger is n), the longer the algorithm will take (i.e., the slower the algorithm). There is a direct cost implication of this slowness.

The Big O notation is $O(\cdot)$, short-hand for "On the order of" or "Is proportional to." An algorithm that is $O(1)$ will take a constant amount of time to complete regardless of the data set size; one that is $O(n)$ will have a completion time proportional to the size of the data set; one that is $O(n^2)$ will have a processing time proportional to the square of the data set size. For these three examples, $O(1) < O(n) < O(n^2)$.

As an example from [168], consider calculating the simple sample average: $\bar{X} = \sum X_i / n$. Its computation, although seemingly simple, is actually somewhat complex because it requires $n - 1$ additions and one division. These are the operations. The one division is clear since the sum is divided only once by n. To see the number of additions, consider adding just two numbers so $n = 2$: there is only one addition. If $n = 3$, there are two additions: adding the first two numbers producing a sum and then adding the third number to the first sum to produce the final sum. With $n - 1$ additions and one division, the order of magnitude of the operations to calculate the sample average is n, which is expressed as $O(n)$. The implication of $O(n)$ is that each data point is operated on only once so that with one million observations to average, the order of complexity is one million: there are one million operations. The larger the PDM, the larger the order of complexity and the higher the cost of processing all that data.

Different operations have different algorithmic complexities. Table 10.4 shows the orders of complexities for various "routine" statistical operations. Table 10.5 shows the time required for differently sized data sets. Time is now a factor to complete simple operations when n is large.

Sampling can reduce the magnitude of this issue by allowing you to work with a smaller scientifically selected subset of the PDM. There are several traditional sampling schemes you can use.

TABLE 10.4 Orders of magnitude for statistical operations. Some operations are on matrices such that $n = r \times c$. Note that for $n = 100$, a relatively small data set, $n^{1/2} = 10$; $n \times ln(n) = 460$; $n^{3/2} = 1,000$; and $n^2 = 10,000$. Based on [168].

Statistical operation	Order of complexity
Plot a scatterplot	$O(n^{1/2})$
Calculate means, variances, kernel density estimates	$O(n)$
Calculate fast Fourier transforms	$O(n \times ln(n))$
Solve a multiple linear regression	$O(n \times c)$
Solve a clustering algorithm with $r \propto n$ (low-dimensional data)	$O(n \times r)$ or $O(n^{3/2})$
Solve a clustering algorithm with c fixed and small so that $r \propto n$	$O(n^2)$

TABLE 10.5 These results assume a 4.2 gigaflop computer. The processing speeds would be faster with early twenty-first-century computers and multiple parallel processors, but nonetheless the time required would be high for some problems. This would especially be true on desktop or laptop computers, assuming they could even hold the data in memory for processing. Time is definitely now an issue.

Descriptor	$n^{1/2}$	n	$n \times ln(n)$	$n^{3/2}$	n^2
Tiny	2.4×10^{-9} seconds	2.4×10^{-8} seconds	4.8×10^{-8} seconds	2.4×10^{-7} seconds	2.4×10^{-6} seconds
Small	2.4×10^{-8} seconds	2.4×10^{-6} seconds	9.5×10^{-6} seconds	2.4×10^{-4} seconds	0.024 seconds
Medium	2.4×10^{-7} seconds	2.4×10^{-4} seconds	0.0014 seconds	0.24 seconds	4.0 minutes
Large	2.4×10^{-6} seconds	0.024 seconds	0.19 seconds	4.0 minutes	27.8 days
Huge	2.4×10^{-5} seconds	2.4 seconds	24 seconds	66.7 hours	761 years

Source: [168].

1. *Simple random sampling (SRS)*: Every object (i.e., record, person, event) has the same chance of being selected as every other object or, put another way, a sample of size *n* has the same chance of being selected as every other sample of size *n*. See [142] for a proof. Unfortunately, this is not easy to implement for large data sets and so it is not costless. The sampled elements must be stored and checked that they are, in fact, random. Most popular sampling algorithms do this using a reservoir. An initial set of records is added to the reservoir and succeeding records are added while others are deleted. The reservoir can be quite large, which adds to the complexity and cost. For a large PDM, many records may have to be processed so very efficient sampling algorithms are needed. Sophisticated software optimized for large enterprise databases have this capability, although the research and development of better algorithms continues.

2. *Systematic random sampling*: Every k^{th} record after a random start is selected.

3. *Stratified random sampling*: Sampling from homogeneous groups or strata is conducted. Sometimes weights are used to get the sample back into propor-tion to the entire database. Stratified random sampling is a general case of SRS since SRS assumes just one strata, so the cost issue for SRS also holds here.

4. *Cluster sampling*: Groups (i.e., clusters) are randomly selected and then all the objects in the selected groups are used. A variant is two-stage cluster sampling in which a random sample of clusters is selected and then a random sample of objects is drawn from each of the selected clusters. Under this sampling scheme, the randomly selected clusters are *primary sampling units* (PSUs) and the randomly selected objects within each PSU are *secondary sampling units* (SSUs). Cost is again an issue either if all the elements of a cluster are sampled or a random sample is selected from each cluster.

If there is a time series in the PDM, then you cannot randomly sample because the pattern of the time series will be broken simply because some time periods will not be selected. A time series must be complete in the sense that, for example, one calendar day or month must follow the previous calendar period.[6] Rather than randomly sampling across all records in the PDM when a time series is involved, you should instead randomly sample on the cross-sectional units. For example, if a PDM, as for the Pricing Scenario, has store locations for the cross-sectional units and monthly sales for the time series component with a month and year date indicator, then randomly sample stores and maintain the complete time series for each store.

Stratified random sampling is the most likely method to be used. Stratification allows you to select records to represent specific aspects of the data relevant for pricing. Some possible strata are region, sales rep or team, customers, classes/groups/segments of customers, product lines, and product classes. Recall that the panel notation is Q variables, N objects, and T periods. The strata would be the N objects. Do not stratify on time as I discussed above because time shows dynamics.

TABLE 10.6 Some possible sample sizes for several values of α and assuming the same parameter settings as in the text. Based on [96].

α	Sample size
0.0001	77,300
0.001	55,322
0.01	33,939
0.05	19,692
0.1	13,899

Sample size is always an issue. One suggestion for calculating sample size for estimating a regression model with a PDM is

$$n = 2 \times \left[\frac{Z_{\alpha/2}}{\ln(\gamma)} \right]^2 + p \tag{116}$$

where

p = number of independent or predictor variables
γ = percent range around the true value
$Z_{\alpha/2}$ = value from standard normal distribution
α = the desired significance level.

For the furniture manufacturer, the database has 1,174,154 records. You want to estimate a regression model with 100 independent variables, so p = 100. The prediction error is to be no more than 2%, so γ = 1.02. For α = 0.0001, Z = 3.89. Then the sample size is

$$n = 2 \times \left[\frac{3.89}{\ln(1.02)} \right]^2 + 100$$
$$= 77,300 \text{ cases.}$$

Some sample sizes for various values of α are shown in Table 10.6. See [96] (p. 74) for the sample size formula.

10.5 Data visualization

We are visual creatures. We have a difficult time identifying complex patterns, let alone trends and anomalies, in tables of numbers, so we cannot discern the information in them except in the simplest cases such as a 2 × 2 table. This is not to say that tables are not useful, but their ability to convey rich information quickly becomes limited. Yet we love large tables of numbers because they convey a false sense of authority: numbers matter and are data, and there are the numbers in nice tables just waiting for interpretation. Tables are, unfortunately, of limited analytical use.

Due to our visual orientation, analytical graphs are superior to tables for conveying rich information. Unfortunately, not all graphs, or visual displays, are useful. Pie and bar charts drawn in 3D, for example, are notorious for hiding key information because we have depth perception problems; 2D charts are better. Also, multiple colors are a problem because we tend to have color issues either physiologically or due to colors blending together in hues, making it challenging to discern the boundaries where one shade of color ends and another begins. These types of graphs are used in presentations (as in infographics), but are of limited use in analytical work.

The available tools for creating displays are not created equal. Some, like those typically found in spreadsheet packages and script-oriented languages such as ggplot2 in R and matplotlib and seaborn in Python, are static or non-interactive. You have to start all over again, either by rewriting programming code as in R or by reclicking through a series of menus as in a spreadsheet package, to have a slightly different view of the same data, perhaps to use lines rather than bars or to swap a series on one axis with a series on another. In addition, if you create, say, a histogram and then want to identify the data behind a single bar of the histogram, to drill-down on a bar, you have to use other means to identify those data points; the data and the graphs are not linked. The same issue applies to tables (i.e., cross-tabs) and the data – they are not linked.

A dynamic tool, on the other hand, allows you to interactively manipulate displays: you can drag and drop data onto a canvas to quickly create new views or simply click a button to change the graph type without starting over again. Also, you can link the visual display, such as bars in a histogram or a cell in a table, with the underlying data table or even another graph or table making drill-down easier and faster.

There are four things to look for in a graph:

1. Relationships;
2. Trends;
3. Patterns;
4. Anomalies.

Relationships are correlations or causality statements between two or more variables. Key driver analyses for purchase intent or customer satisfaction are examples. Trends are developments or changes over time (e.g., a tracking study). Patterns are groupings of objects as in market segments. Anomalies are outliers or unexpected values.

There are many ways to visualize data. The literature is huge and growing exponentially, especially as new dynamic software becomes available (e.g., see [174]; also see any of the books by Edward Tufte, such as [68] on best practices). I illustrate possibilities relevant for pricing data analysis in the following subsections.

10.5.1 Displaying leakages

Each SKU has a price stored in a PDB along with all the other data. First, however, the price may have to be calculated because frequently only the transaction revenue and quantity sold are recorded in a PDM; the final invoice price is frequently not included. Since *revenue = price × quantity*, the price for a transaction can be calculated as *reveune / quantity*. Sometimes the list price and discounts are recorded, but not the revenue. The basic price is the *list price* with discounts and adjustments, such as rebates and allowances, applied to this price. There is thus a difference between the list price and the final price that is called a *pocket* or *transaction* price. The numerical difference between list and pocket is attributed to *leakages*, amounts frequently given away just to win a sale.

When there is only one discount, the pocket price is easy to calculate. If d_1 is the discount factor (e.g., $d_1 = 0.10$ for a 10% discount), P_P is the pocket price, and P_L is the list price, then $P_P = P_L \times (1 - d_1)$. The dollar discount or *leakage* is $P_L \times d_1$ and the percentage discount is $(P_L \times d_1) / P_L = d_1$ or just the discount. If there are two discounts, then the pocket price results from chaining the discounts so that

$$P_P = P_L \times (1 - d_1) \times (1 - d_2) \tag{117}$$

$$= P_L \times (1 - d_1 - d_2 + d_1 \times d_2) \tag{118}$$

$$= P_L - P_L \times (d_1 + d_2 - d_1 \times d_2). \tag{119}$$

The leakage due to the first discount is $P_L \times d_1$; similarly for the second. These leakages, however, are adjusted by $P_L \times d_1 \times d_2$, reflecting the joint impact of the two discounts. The dollar discount or total leakage is $P_L \times (d_1 + d_2 - d_1 \times d_2)$ and the percentage discount is $(d_1 + d_2 - d_1 \times d_2)$.

In general, for n discounts, the pocket price is

$$P_P = P_L \times \prod_{i=1}^{n} (1 - d_i) \tag{120}$$

$$\approx P_L \times (1 - \sum_{i=1}^{n} d_i). \tag{121}$$

and $\sum_{i=1}^{n} d_i$ is usually used for the total percentage discount.

If there is a time dimension, which is usually the case, then either calculation would be done for each time period, resulting in a time series for each SKU. The pocket price is typically calculated with the approximation (120).

Knowing what generates a pocket price can enable you to advise management to effectively raise prices without actually doing anything to list prices by reducing leakages. A simple graphical display of leakages for the Pricing Scenario, sometimes called a *price waterfall*, is shown in Figure 10.5.1.

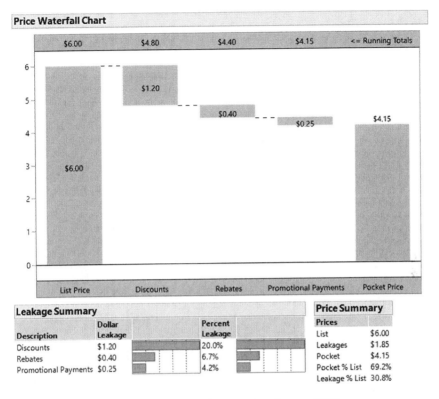

FIGURE 10.5.1 Price waterfall for the furniture data for one SKU.

Other graphs are possible to study leakages. The type you use depends on the continuity of the data; in other words, whether the data are discrete (nominal or ordinal; i.e., categorical) or continuous (interval or ratio). Discrete data are effectively displayed and analyzed with histograms for single variables and mosaic plots for several (typically two and, perhaps, three). For continuous data, boxplots and scatterplots (including scatterplot matrices) are effective. For scatterplots, a "smooth" such as a LOWESS curve can be added to show a general trend.[7] With some dynamic graphing tools, the plot points can be removed so that just the smooth trend line is visible. In addition, some of these tools have a control for the amount of smoothness of the curve with an upper bound on smoothness being just an OLS straight line. Also, some tools allow you to dynamically filter the entire data set and brush segments of a graph to drill down and explain specific subsets of data.

As an example of a distribution analysis, the furniture company pricing analyst used a dynamic data visualization tool's aggregation and sampling features to create a data set of discounts. The furniture company has three types of discounts: Dealer, Order Size, and Competitive Pricing. She stacked the three

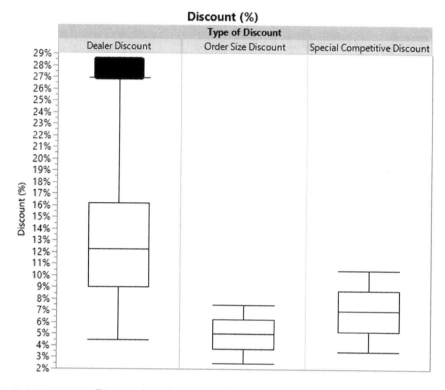

FIGURE 10.5.2 Discount boxplots for the furniture data for one SKU.

discounts so she could create one chart with three side-by-side boxplots. This is shown in Figure 10.5.2. It is clear from this chart that Dealer Discounts are the largest. They also have a number of outliers (very large discounts) that need further investigation. The black mass at the top of the Dealer Discount boxplot is this set of outliers. A single point is an outlier; here there are a large number of outliers indicating that many large discounts are offered to make a sale. Also notice that the Order Size Discount boxplot is compact and low on the scale. This indicates that this form of discount is almost all the same and is generally small compared to the Dealer Discount. Similarly for the Special Competitive Discount.

An example of a scatterplot with a superimposed smooth is shown in Figure 10.5.3 for a single SKU. This SKU is selected using a local data filter that allows you to focus on specific subsets of your data. If another SKU is selected using the filter (which is not shown here), the entire graph would automatically adjust to reflect the new selection. A second version of this graph is shown in Figure 10.5.4 so that price elasticities by region for this SKU can be determined.

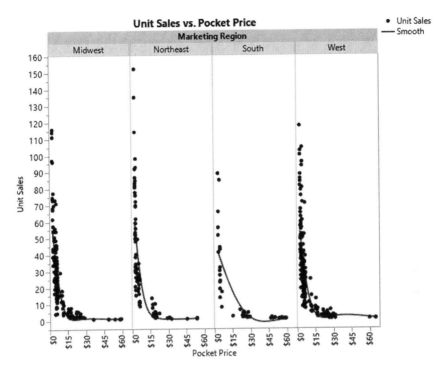

FIGURE 10.5.3 Scatterplot of unit sales by price for four marketing regions. The expected negative relationship between price and units is clear, but so is the nature of the relationship; it is a negative exponential. The curved lines are LOWESS smooths that highlight the negative exponential nature of the data.

One more chart is a *price dispersion chart* that is like Figure 10.5.4, but has the price difference (= *List − Pocket*) as a percentage of the list price versus the (log) unit sales. An example is shown in Figure 10.5.5.

Maps are also a very effective way to visualize geographic data. Many dynamic visualization tools have mapping capabilities. As an example, the furniture PDM has a state indicator for the customer locations. The pricing analyst calculated the total leakage as the difference between the list price and the pocket price of each SKU. A map was created with the states shaded by the size of the leakage. This is shown in Figure 10.5.6. A data filter was added to the visual to filter on the product lines. Figure 10.5.7 shows a map filtered on dining room furniture.

10.5.2   Trends

Unlike the economics textbook firm, a real-world business exists and operates in time. It sells products every day (hopefully). So after a year, the company has amassed a lot of time series data on each SKU. This can reveal the dynamic behavior of prices and leakages. Suppose the list prices have not changed, but salespeople have

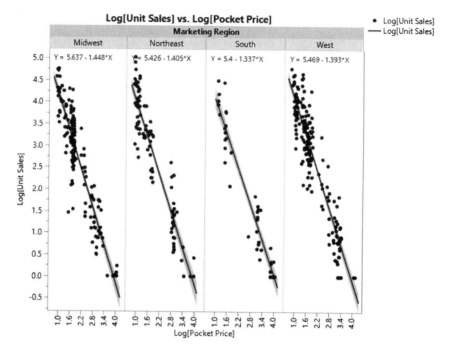

FIGURE 10.5.4 Second version of Figure 10.5.3 with the natural log of sales and the natural log of price. A linear fit was applied to each region, with the OLS equation being shown in each. Since logs are used, the slope of each line is the price elasticity for that region. All regions are moderately elastic.

been giving greater and greater discounts due to competitive pressures. The pocket prices should be declining over time. A time series graph will reveal this. A dynamic visualization tool will allow you to drill down to the components of pocket prices for more detailed analysis. The discounts can be overlaid on the pocket prices to show how both have changed over time.

Figure 10.5.8 shows a time series pattern for the Dealer Discount for the Dining Room China Cabinet and one style sold to stores in the Midwest marketing region. The data were created by first creating a new date variable representing just the month and year of a transaction. This was done by aggregating daily data because they had too much noise and missing dates (there are days in a month when nothing is sold), so monthly numbers are better. Then a set of SQL commands were specified to select the Dealer Discount, Marketing Region, and the new transaction date indicator from the main PDM, average the discounts by region and month, and order the results by region and then date within a region. A time series graph was created and a region filter was applied to study each region specifically. Figure 10.5.8 shows that the Dealer Discount has been rising steadily for almost the last six months of the period, whereas it had been falling for the prior

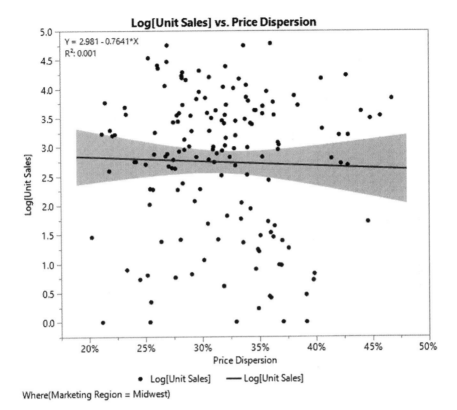

Log[Unit Sales] vs. Price Dispersion

Y = 2.981 - 0.7641*X
R²: 0.001

Where(Marketing Region = Midwest)

FIGURE 10.5.5 The relationship between unit sales and the price dispersion. The sales are scaled using a (natural) log transformation because sales tend to be right skewed. Using a log transformation improves the scatter. The price dispersion is the difference between list and pocket price as a percentage of the list price. An OLS line helps to show the general trend of the data. Clearly, there is a lot of scatter around the line, indicating a very large lack of discipline in pricing.

periods. Compare this to Figure 10.5.9, which is relatively stable. The use of Dealer Discounts is clearly increasing in the Midwest.

10.5.3 Patterns

There is an infinite number of patterns to look for, one of which, of course, is the segments. You can look for:

- Clusters of sales people offering large discounts.
- Sales regions maintaining pocket prices close to list, while others are not.
- A class of SKUs with large rebates.
- Customers who only buy premium items or discounted/sale items.
- Customers who buy infrequently.

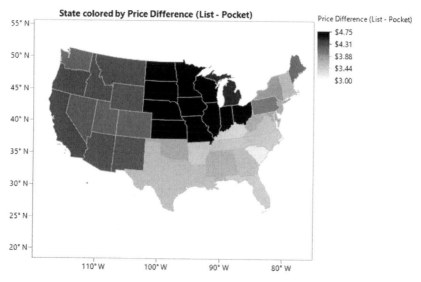

Map shape not found: Baja California.

FIGURE 10.5.6 Map showing total leakages by state for the furniture data.

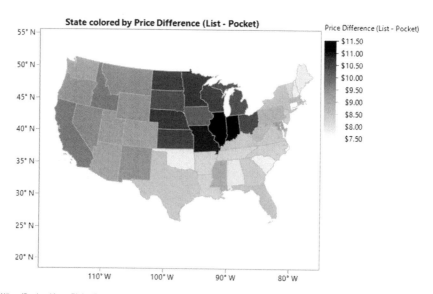

Where(Product Line = Dining Room)
Map shape not found: Baja California.

FIGURE 10.5.7 Map showing total leakages by state, but filtered by dining room furniture.

Where(Marketing Region = Midwest)

FIGURE 10.5.8 Time series plot of one SKU for the average dealer discount for the Midwest marketing region.

Scatterplots, 2D graphs of two variables such as sales by discounts for SKUs in a product category, can reveal clusters of SKUs with high sales but also high discounts. A third variable can be overlaid in the form of a bubble (hence, the chart is called a bubble chart) and even a fourth variable, usually categorical, can be used to color bubbles.

10.5.4 Anomalies

You can learn a lot from distribution charts such as histograms and boxplots. Boxplots are an excellent tool for displaying distributions and especially for identifying aberrant data points, the anomalies. This is clear in Figure 10.5.2. Side-by-side boxplots, such as one plot for each marketing region, can clearly show you which regions have anomalous points needing further study. An example set of boxplots for the pocket prices for a single SKU, DRCCB, by regions is shown in Figure 10.5.10. Notice that price distributions are quite varied and that the

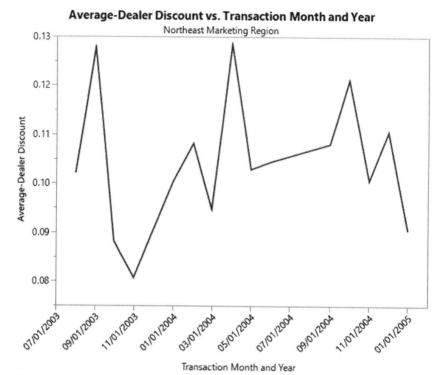

FIGURE 10.5.9 Time series plot of one SKU for the average dealer discount for the Northeast marketing region.

Northeast has the most outliers, indicated by the dots beyond the upper and lower fences. A dynamic visualization tool will allow you to highlight the aberrant points and then link back to the original data, creating a new data table with just those points. You cannot do this with a static tool.

10.6   Software

There are many software packages available for managing large data sets and for data visualization. SAS is probably the most powerful, although it does come with dollar cost as well as a learning curve cost. JMP is a very powerful, user-oriented package for data management, statistical procedures, and visualization capabilities. R is the dominant free statistical package with a wide following; however, it also has a steep learning curve. It requires that you program everything that you want to do, something that could be a drawback for most analysts except those who are trained in programming. Python is in the same category as R and in many respects is passing R in the data sciences area. For JMP, see [57] and [162].

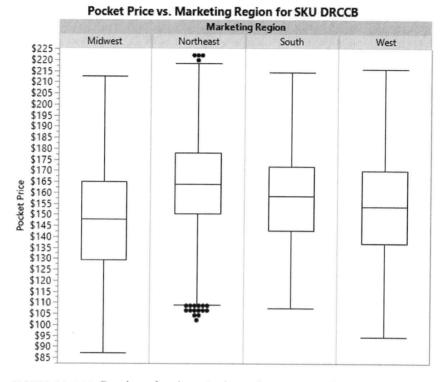

FIGURE 10.5.10 Boxplots of pocket price by marketing regions for the furniture data for one SKU (DRCCB).

10.7 Summary

There are a number of issues associated with using Big Data for pricing research and elasticity development. This chapter presented those issues. Suggestions were made for handling common Big Data problems, including sampling and data visualization. The next chapter will use this one as a background for modeling with Big Data.

Notes

1 See "Analytics: The real-world use of big data. How innovative enterprises extract value from uncertain data." IBM Institute for Business Value.

2 Except for dinosaurs.

3 If you go to the extreme of zero variance for a variable, then there is nothing to estimate since all values are the same.

4 See http://en.wikipedia.org/wiki/Moore%27s_law. Also see www.mckinsey.com/ insights/high_tech_telecoms_internet/moores_law_repeal_or_renewal.

5 See www.kdnuggets.com/2015/09/data-lake-vs-data-warehouse-key-differences.html and https://en.wikipedia.org/wiki/Data_lake for discussions of data lakes and some comparisons to data warehouses.

6 In actual data collection, a time series will have breaks due to weekends, holidays, and exogenous events that disturb market events. In addition, servers go down and cyber-attacks occur that disrupt data collection. This is all different from imposing breaks in a series due to sampling.

7 LOWESS is an acronym for *locally weighted scatterplot smoothing*. It is also sometimes referred to as LOESS for *locally weighted smoothing*. It is a technique for drawing curves through a scatterplot to reveal the general flow or trend of the data. A least squares straight line is a limiting case (see [107] and [106]).

11
BIG DATA PRICING MODELS

I introduce a final approach to pricing analytics in this chapter: econometric modeling using sales or transactions data in a pricing data mart (PDM). Econometric models were used in previous parts of this book, primarily in the discrete choice and segmentation chapters. This chapter, and in fact this whole part of the book, deviates from the previous discussions by a focus on Big Data, primarily PDMs, whereas the previous parts looked at survey-based data.

Some believe that econometric models based on a PDM have limited value because the price variable may have little to no variation over a reasonable period of time. I disagree with this because many just focus on the list price, which I agree often has little variation, and ignore the pocket price, which can have a lot of variation. In addition, they ignore the structure of the PDM, which can have variations because of the panel nature of the data. This structure cannot be ignored and can be used as an advantage, although not without a cost, since the structure introduces complications. I will discuss these below.

This chapter is divided into five sections. Section 1 first presents a Pricing Scenario as a choice situation for pricing strategies. The scenario will be used throughout the chapter. Section 2 discusses a modeling process designed to make working with Big Data easier. This does not mean that all issues with Big Data will disappear; just that the tasks will be simplified if a process is followed. Section 3 just touches on win–loss modeling, an often-overlooked aspect of pricing analysis with Big Data. Too many people concentrate on transactions data, ignoring bids. These, however, are just as important as the transactions. Section 4 discusses software and Section 5 summarizes the chapter.

11.1 Pricing Scenario

The Pricing Scenario for this chapter was introduced in Chapter 10.

11.2   Modeling phases

The previous chapter was devoted to the role and importance of Big Data in pricing analytics. Not all price modeling problems, of course, involve Big Data; some are handled with "small" data as well. Data are very important for any modeling problem; however, they are not the only component of modeling. There are others to be aware of and deal with, which themselves could comprise a whole book. These components are interconnected and interdependent, forming a modeling process that typically is not taught in statistics or econometrics courses, which tend to focus on estimation methods, primarily ordinary least squares (OLS). Some econometric textbooks discuss a research process, but this is usually relegated to the end of the book (e.g., see, [172], Chapter 19). The data issues discussed in Chapter 9 are frequently absent from these courses for a host of reasons. In order to effectively build models for pricing, a holistic approach to modeling is needed, one that emphasizes a process as opposed to just estimation methods.

A schematic illustrating a modeling process is shown in Figure 11.2.1. The process is divided into three blocks:

1.   Data Block;
2.   Modeling Block;
3.   Analysis Block.

These three blocks, working together to accomplish the modeling task, have a logical flow: Data ⇒ Modeling ⇒ Analysis. I will discuss the three blocks in the following subsections.

11.2.1   Data Block

The *Data Block* is at the top of the modeling process chart because without the data, or appropriate data in the correct form and structure, the other two parts of the process will never be accomplished. The data are not only collected and assembled into a PDM in this block, but they are also prepared (i.e., transformed and wrangled into an appropriate form) for the models to be built in the *Modeling Block*.

A rule of thumb (ROT) in the data mining area is that 80% of analytical time is spent collecting, assembling, and preparing the data (see [110]). The activities involve:

•   Importing;
•   Documenting;
•   Grouping;
•   Wrangling;
•   Modifying and transforming.

Whether the actual time is 80% or 60% or some other large number is immaterial; it is the most important time allowance that counts. The *Data Block* consists of three levels:

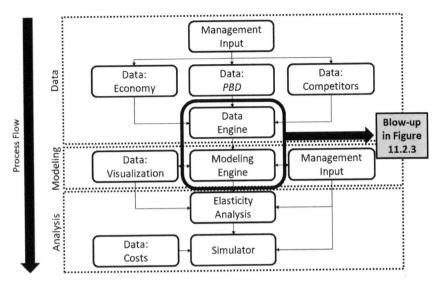

FIGURE 11.2.1 Modeling of sales data does not involve just estimations. There is a series of steps that must be logically followed. These steps constitute a process as illustrated here. The process flow starts at the top and proceeds downward. The data and modeling engines are amplified in Figure 11.2.3.

1. Management input;
2. Data collection;
3. Data engine.

These are explained next.

Management input

An unnoticed part of data collection, assembling, and preparation is management input, although just referring to this as "management input" diminishes its nature and importance. Upper-level management certainly has a role to play in all business activities and decisions, so they should have one to play here. This could be as simple as just stating what is needed or something more complex, such as specifying the corporate objectives that the price modeling must support. This modeling, and the pricing and marketing implications derived from it, cannot be separated from the corporate strategy, the overall plan for the business. Pricing, and all other activities tactical and strategic, must support and be consistent with this strategy. Price modeling must also be part of and interconnected with the major components of a business such as value creation and delivery, market performance, and financial performance, to mention a few. Management develops the strategy and thus, at least by default and indirectly if not directly, plays a role in modeling and specifying the pricing requirements.

Management has input in two places: first, in data specification and acquisition; and second, in the assessment of the relevancy of model results for the major functions and initiatives of the business. Management funds data acquisition, provides guidance, sets head counts and staffing requirements (e.g., skill levels), and establishes and coordinates the myriad set of organizations with a vested interest in price modeling, since marketing is not the sole organization impacted by pricing.

Data collection

The PDM is the dominant part of the data portion of the process. In Chapter 10, I discussed issues associated with it. Two other required parts for the PDM are data on the economy and the competition. Depending on the nature of the business and the type of product(s) sold, the economy can play an important role in determining price impacts. For a pro-cyclical industry, if the economy is doing well, with real GDP rising or remaining high, sales could also do well; if the economy is headed into or is in a recession, then sales will probably suffer. There are industries, of course, that are counter-cyclical. [93] present correlations between real GDP, employment levels, and final demand for a large number of industries. Based on these correlations, they classified industries by how they responded in the past to business cycle behavior.[1] The industry with employment most correlated with real GDP fluctuations happens to be the household furniture industry. So any discussion of price modeling for the Pricing Scenario must include real GDP.

The economy-wide data that can be used vary greatly depending on the industry and product being modeled, as well as the nature of the other data in a PDM. For example, luxury consumer goods would be greatly impacted by real GDP growth. However, if the data in the PDM are on a monthly basis, real GDP would be inappropriate because it is reported on a quarterly basis, so it would be out of sync with the PDM. One solution is to allocate real GDP quarterly numbers to monthly numbers, perhaps by assigning a third of each quarterly number to an appropriate month, but this is not recommended. A better approach is to use a monthly time series that is correlated with real GDP such as the Industrial Production Index or the unemployment rate.

Data on the competition are also important inputs into price modeling simply because very few, if any, businesses sell in a vacuum; they all have competitors. Management should have established a competitive tracking system that at a minimum monitors, captures, and records competitive prices. These price data would be part of Big Data to be used by other parts of the business, but then extracted as needed to a PDM for price modeling.

Data engine

The three disparate types of data (i.e., economy, PDM, and competition) are merged and wrangled in the *data engine*, an extensive and important part of the overall *Data Block* that produces the ultimate modeling data. A magnification of this engine is shown in Figure 11.2.3. This is where the data are cleansed of bad or messy data, outliers are identified, and missing data are at least identified and imputed if possible.

Messy data are highly skewed, sparse, or collinear. Skewed data can distort model estimation by placing undue weight on only a few observations. Sparseness refers to an overabundance of zero values (not missing values), which also distorts estimation. These data are sometimes said to be "zero inflated." Collinearity refers not to the data values per se, but to the relationship between the variables. This is certainly a major problem in a large PDM with many variables. Multivariate data reduction techniques such as principal components can help with this problem by aggregating the variables.

Outliers contribute to the skewness problem, but not all outliers are pernicious; some are innocuous and perhaps evidence of unknown marketing and product development opportunities. For example, sales data distributions may indicate that some products are selling through new distribution channels, so exploring the size and nature of these channels could open new business opportunities. Outliers as well as skewness can be identified using histograms and boxplots.

Missing data are a big problem in price modeling and so the presence of and extent of data missingness must be explored and analyzed. There are two aspects to missing data analysis emphasized by [12]: *missing data patterns* and *missing data mechanisms*. Missing data patterns are descriptions of where the missing data are in the data set; essentially, the location of "holes," as noted by [12]. Some software has tools for producing missing data pattern reports that indicate the holes. Figure 11.2.2 illustrates a report for some furniture data where "holes" were introduced for illustrative purposes only. The first column of the report shows the number of rows with missing values and the second shows the count of missing values in those rows. There are 485 rows without any missing values, while there are 15 rows with missing values. In each of these 15 rows, there is only one missing value. The third to last column shows where the missing values are located using indicator variables. You can see that the 15 missing values are all located in the Dealer Discount column.

Six missing data patterns, briefly outlined by [12], are:

1. Univariate: just one variable for select objects;
2. Unit non-response;
3. Monotone non-response;
4. General: probably the most common, representing a haphazard pattern;
5. Planned;
6. Latent variable.

Count	Number of columns missing	Patterns	List Price	Pocket Price	Price Difference (List - Pocket)	Dealer Discount	Special Competitive Discount	Order Size Discount
485	0	0	0	0	0	0	0	0
15	1	100	0	0	0	1	0	0

FIGURE 11.2.2 This illustrates a missing data pattern report for a random sample of 500 records from the furniture data set and with missing values just randomly inserted for illustration.

[12] then dismisses these because modern imputation methods can handle any of them. This is true, but it ignores the fact that the patterns represent valuable information that still needs to be explored.

The missing data patterns, although informative, do not tell you why there is missingness. The patterns are only half the puzzle; the other half is the reason. [157] described probabilistic reasons for missingness, which are now the ones typically used. There is missing at random (MAR), missing not at random (MNAR), and missing completely at random (MCAR). MAR data occur when the probability of a missing value of a variable depends on other variables, but not the variable in question. MCAR data are unrelated to both the other variables and the variable in question. As noted by [12], this is what analysts normally view as completely haphazard missingness. MNAR data are unrelated to the variable itself.

Once you have identified missing values, you have to decide how to handle them. Options include:

- Imputing missing values using means, medians, or one of a host of statistical techniques.
- Deleting records with any missing data, although this may not be a good solution if it results in deleting a time series component that "breaks up" a time trend.
- Ignoring the missing data.

Most statistical software do list-wise deletion. See [12] for imputation methods.

Finally, you have to wrangle the data into a form needed for modeling. Just because the data are in a data table does not mean the shape of the table is appropriate for statistical or econometric modeling. For example, state unemployment data as well as store-level data by state may be in the PDM. A state unemployment rate would be repeated for each store in that state. If there are, say, 100 store locations in the state, then a single unemployment rate would repeat 100 times, once each store. This is a very inefficient form of data organization. A more efficient one has two data tables: one at the store level and one at the state level. Some software implementations can handle this bi-table structure. See [124] for an illustration.

Wrangling may also involve sorting and joining data tables. Joining is the process of merging two data tables on a common or linking variable present in both tables. This is not as easy as it seems, however. There are many types of joins depending on how the final required data table should be organized and what its composition should be. See [57] for a discussion of joins.

Aggregation of data is an often overlooked aspect of data wrangling. The level of aggregation must be decided upon since it has modeling and interpretation implications. Since aggregation is a data manipulation problem, it is handled in the *data engine*. Aggregation is not a requirement; it is dictated by the problem. In addition, there are multiple ways to aggregate. You could average or sum variables

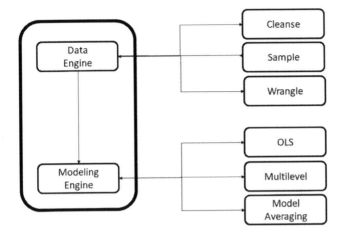

FIGURE 11.2.3 The components of the data and modeling engines are illustrated here.

as well as find the medians, all dependent on the problem and the data type. Nonetheless, there are multiple options if aggregation is required.

The PDM typically has a panel or *longitudinal* structure. It is also a *repeated measures data set*, and an analysis using these data is a *repeated measures analysis*. The "repeated measures" refers to the fact that the same object is measured on multiple measurement instances or *occasions* (i.e., time periods). In the panel, for each individual, or what I generally call an *object* (since the cross-sectional unit could be a person, store, location, etc.), a series of repeated measures is taken or recorded in time, the time being sales or transaction occasions and the measures being sales volume, pocket or transaction price points, sales locations (e.g., stores), and so forth. An example is shown in Table 11.1. In this example, the cross-sectional unit (the object) is the stock keeping unit (SKU), while the time series is the transaction date.

The time periods do not have to be consecutive or of the same length for each object. So if Y_{sit} is sales of SKU s to store i in period t, the periods are indicated as $t = 1,\ldots,T_{si}$. Similarly, the objects do not have to have the same length. So the store for SKU s would be $i = 1,\ldots,N_s$.

It is useful to view a panel structure as time periods nested in or under objects so there are two dimensions.[2] This is illustrated in Figure 11.2.4. You could aggregate across either one. That is, you could either aggregate across time periods within each object for an object-level analysis (i.e., a cross-sectional analysis) or you could aggregate across objects within each time period for a time series analysis.

If P_{sit} is the price of SKU s to store i in period t, the average price over time is

$$\overline{P_{si.}} = \frac{1}{T_{si}} \times \sum_{t=1}^{T_{si}} P_{sit} \tag{122}$$

TABLE 11.1 This is an example of a layout for a panel data set. Three SKUs for one product line and three product classes for the furniture case study are shown. SKU DNCTB is recorded once, while SKU DNDSC (a den desk chair) is recorded three times, each with a different pocket price.

Product line	Product class	SKU	Transaction date	Pocket price
Den	Computer table	DNCTB	01/10/2005	$53.90
Den	Desk chair	DNDSC	01/10/2005	$31.94
Den	Desk chair	DNDSC	01/11/2005	$29.44
Den	Desk chair	DNDSC	01/12/2005	$28.75
Den	Desk	DNDSK	01/11/2005	$57.50
Den	Desk	DNDSK	01/12/2005	$60.23

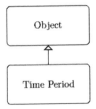

FIGURE 11.2.4 Time periods are nested under the objects, which are macro units. The time periods represent repeated measures for each object. Notice that the flow is upward from the time periods to the object.

where the dot notation indicates that the relevant subscript component is averaged. If you average price over stores, then

$$\overline{P_{s,t}} = \frac{1}{N_s} \times \sum_{i=1}^{N_s} P_{sit} \tag{123}$$

for a time series study.

You could aggregate across time for each object while maintaining the panel structure. For instance, if the panel has daily transactions by SKU at the store location level for several years, you could collapse from daily to monthly transactions by adding the volumes and averaging the prices of each SKU at each store to get a more compact monthly time series. This would make a very large data set with a lot of noise due to random daily fluctuations into a smaller one that is "smoother." In addition, depending on the problem, monthly macroeconomic data (e.g., monthly unemployment rate, monthly Industrial Production Index) could be merged, which would otherwise be impossible with daily data. Dynamic patterns in the daily data, however, would be lost or hidden with monthly aggregates. In some contexts, the dynamic patterns are very important. Airlines, for example, monitor daily and even hourly reservations and adjust prices to optimize load factors on their planes. Monthly aggregates would be far too coarse for their purposes.

Finally, you could average, say, the stores for each time period to produce a smaller data set at the region level and then model regional sales. This is acceptable if you want to focus on the region. However, if the aggregation is done merely to simplify the problem, with results at the region level used to make statements or inferences at the store level, then the *ecological fallacy* would be committed. This fallacy states that a logical error is made when you try to statistically deduce the behavior of individuals from the behavior of their groups. This fallacy is more often committed then realized. See [156] for an initial discussion of the fallacy in statistical analysis.

A problem with any aggregation is that there must be enough observations to support the new level. For example, if you aggregate objects, you must have each time period represented in the resulting time series. A desirable feature of a time series is that it is complete: there should be no missing time periods, so you should not have, say, January followed by February followed by April in a certain year with March missing. In addition, that individual heterogeneity is obscured and you essentially have a "representative agent." Economists have used representative agents as a theoretical modeling tool for a long time, especially in macroeconomic studies. Their use, however, is not without controversy. Aggregating the time level to produce a cross-sectional data set is an acceptable approach if the focus is on the individual objects and the goal is a between-object study. There are several problems with this, however, the primary one being that any time-dynamic patterns are lost in the aggregation. These time patterns may be important in a pricing analysis; for example, seasonality. See [77] and [87] for comments on the use of cross-sectional data in the *FTC v Staples* case involving a proposed merger between Staples and Office Depot.

A common problem for pricing with a PDM is the plethora of SKUs, so that an aggregation of SKUs may be necessary. Unfortunately, it is difficult to aggregate them because they represent different items. One way to deal with this is to create four groups:

Group 1: Price-sensitive SKUs (PSSs)
Group 2: Leadership SKUs
Group 3: Non-price-sensitive SKUs
Group 4: Miscellaneous SKUs

This is the scheme used in the *FTC v Staples* case summarized in [77] as well as in [87]. The reason for the four groupings was to develop price indices for the almost 7000 SKUs involved in the modeling. Nonetheless, it can also be used as a way to group SKUs for any type of analysis.

PSSs are highly elastic, frequently purchased (especially at high volumes), and are most likely bought based on deals such as discounts, rebates, and allowances. The PSSs are highly elastic because they are a large percentage of a purchaser's budget, which should be positively correlated with volume. These are also SKUs that should be price-checked regularly. "Price-check" means that competitive price information is gathered and recorded as in the competitive section of the *Data Block*.

Leadership SKUs are a subset of the PSSs that are low margin and usually low priced with moderate volume or demand that are used as price leaders. Incurring some loss on these is acceptable given their role and function. Non-price-sensitive SKUs are not price-checked and may be elastic, but are not as high volume as the PSSs. They should be included in any analysis, but fewer data are available for them. In addition, they are slightly less important (as determined by management). Miscellaneous or other minor SKUs are low volume and have low margins. An example could be a bushing for a plumbing manufacturer.

Management judgement, with input from subject matter experts and key opinion leaders, *a priori* notions of what goes together, experience, tradition, and industry standards cannot be ignored if this approach to SKU aggregation is used. In addition, management could identify SKUs with the largest contribution, which is revenue minus cost, for each SKU. Finally, you could visually ban or group the SKUs, although this may be impractical with a large number. All of these procedures are subjective.

A second way to group SKUs is with an unsupervised learning algorithm treating the SKUs as variables and then clustering them. Hierarchical and K-means clustering were briefly described in Chapter 8 as ways to create segments. They used variables on consumers (e.g., demographics, preferences, opinions, attitudes, behaviors, lifestyle variables) and clustered the consumers. In both procedures, consumers are assigned to a group based on some amalgamation of the variables. Hierarchical clustering uses different types of data and clusters based on a distance measure. A dendrogram summarizes the clustering, but nothing is said about the variables forming the groups. K-means clustering uses continuous measures and clusters based on the means of these measures. The means of all the variables are reported for further analysis, but this is just a way to profile the groupings. In general for both procedures, objects are grouped or clustered based on variables. This could be reversed to group or cluster the variables. Variable clustering is done in several ways, but the technicalities are not important here. Such clustering is an effective way to reduce a large number of variables to one or a few representative variables that explain most of the variation in the original variables. In the case of SKUs, it may be advantageous to select a few representative SKUs from many. This would be a workable solution to having a large number of SKUs if they tend to behave similarly.

Another method is principal components, a multivariate procedure typically used to reduce a set of variables to a more manageable number derived from the original ones. This is especially useful when the variables are highly collinear, because the new derived variables are orthogonal to each other. The new derived variables are called *components*, which are basically the weighted average of a subset of the original variables. The components can be interpreted as indices. Since SKUs in a product family are most likely highly correlated, doing a principal components analysis accomplishes two things: it creates indices of the SKUs and it provides uncorrelated variables that eliminate any collinearity problem. See [34] for a discussion and derivation of principal components.

Each component accounts for a proportion of the variance among all the original variables. The components are derived in order based on these proportions: the component that accounts for the largest variance is extracted first, followed by the one with the next largest proportion while also being orthogonal to the first, and so on. Only a few are necessary if they account for the majority of the variance of the data. Since components are weighted averages of the variables, they could be used in an analysis.

Two aspects of SKUs are available for clustering: units sold and the associated prices, preferably the pocket prices. My recommendation is that the units sold be the basis for the clustering since the SKUs represent units, perhaps with some standardization as mentioned in Chapter 8.

Once SKU groups are formed, you can combine the associated prices into a price index representing the groups. A weighted average of prices for each SKU in a group for each time period is the price index. Suppose there are G groups of SKUs such as the four mentioned above, so $G = 4$. A price index for group $g \in G$ in period t is

$$P_{.gt} = \sum_{i \in g} \omega_{it} \times P_{igt}$$

where P_{igt} is the price for SKU i in group g at time t and ω_{it} is a weight for SKU i at period t. The weight is a value weight calculated as

$$\omega_{it} = \sum_{i \in g} \frac{P_{igt} \times Q_{igt}}{P_{gt} \cdot Q_{gt}}$$

where the denominator is the dot product of the vector of all prices in set g in period t and the vector of all matching quantities. The dot product is merely the sum of price times quantity of each SKU, hence it gives total revenue in period t for all SKUs. The numerator is the revenue for SKU $i \in g$ in period t. Clearly, $\sum_{i \in g} \omega_{it} = 1.0$.

Just as prices have to be aggregated into a price index, so must the quantities of each SKU, since by definition the units are all different. A quantity index is

$$Q_{st} = \sum_{i \in s} \omega_{it} \times Q_{ist}.$$

An example is shown in Table 11.2 for just two SKUs. See [89] for a technical discussion about index numbers and index number theories. Also see [87] for the use of similar indices in *FTC v Staples*.

In many instance, SKUs are already logically organized into groups such as product lines, product classes, and product styles, with styles subsumed under classes and classes subsumed under lines for a hierarchical structure as in the furniture Pricing Scenario. A SKU is a code representing the hierarchy. This does not mean, however, that you can aggregate unit sales over this hierarchy. For example, a

TABLE 11.2 This is a small example of how to calculate a price and quantity index for two SKUs. The quantity and price of each SKU are multiplied to get the revenue or value of the SKU. The values are then added for a total value. This is used as the base for the value weights. The calculation is done for each record in the data table.

Quantity		Price		Value		Value weight		Index	
SKU_1	SKU_2	SKU_1	SKU_2	SKU_1	SKU_2	SKU_1	SKU_2	Quantity	Price
10	15	$11.91	$12.12	$119.10	$181.80	0.40	0.60	13.0209	12.0369

rectangular colonial kitchen table (line = kitchen, class = table, style = rectangular colonial) cannot be combined with an oval contemporary kitchen table at the line/class levels because they are two different objects. You can, however, form a quantity index of unit sales for this situation. Let Q_{slgit} be SKU s in line l, class c, style j sold to store i in period t for $l = 1,\dots,L$, $c = 1,\dots,C_l$, and $j = 1,\dots,J_{lc}$. Then a quantity index over style is

$$Q_{slc.it} = \sum_{j \in \{lc\}} \omega_{slc.it} \times Q_{slgit} \tag{124}$$

where $\{lc\}$ is the set of SKUs in line l and class c. The quantity weights are

$$\omega_{slc.it} = \sum_{j \in \{lc\}} \frac{P_{slgit} \times Q_{slgit}}{P_{slc.it} \cdot Q_{slc.it}}. \tag{125}$$

You could similarly aggregate prices.

A final data wrangling operation is the division of the data into two or three mutually exclusive and completely exhaustive parts. Sound statistical modeling methodology divides data sets into at least two parts, usually of comparable size, before model estimation. These are a *training data set*, used to fit (i.e., train) a model and to calculate a fit error rate, typically mean square error (MSE), and a *test data set* used to test the performance of the fit and to calculate the validation error rate, typically MSE. Sometimes, depending on the size of the PDM, the data are divided into three parts: *train*, *validation*, and *test*. Either way, the test data set is pristine, unseen by the model and used only when a model passes standard statistical checks (e.g., R^2, Akaike Information Criterion, Bayesian Information Criterion, confusion matrix, area under the receiver operating characteristic curve, etc.). Possible proportions are shown in Figure 11.2.5.

There are two problems with this approach. The first is that the validation error rate is dependent on how the data were split. In most applications, the split is random, although it could still happen that data that normally would give a bad fit appear in the training data set. With a different random split, they could appear in the test data set. This is all by luck of the draw (see [150]). The second problem is that the validation error rate may overestimate the true error rate that would be

Train	Validate	Test
50%	25%	25%

FIGURE 11.2.5 A possible split of the data into training, validation, and testing portions is shown here. Actual divisions and whether or not two or three divisions are used depend on the size of the PDM. If the PDM is not large enough to support a three-way split, then a two-way split of train and test can be used. The test and validation data sets are also sometimes called *holdout samples*.

obtained if the entire data set were used, because models tend to perform worse when fewer observations are used. Cross-validation (CV) is used to avoid these issues. There are two approaches to CV:

1. Leave-one-out CV (LOOCV);
2. k-fold CV.

The steps for the LOOCV are:

1. Set aside the first observation as a validation set.
2. Train a model with the remaining $n - 1$ observations.
3. Repeat steps 1 and 2 for the entire data set iterating over all n, calculating MSE for each iteration. There should be n MSE values.
4. Estimate the validation error rate as $CV_{(n)} = \frac{1}{n} \times \sum_{i=1}^{n} MSE_i$, where

   $MSE_i = (Y_i - \hat{Y}_i)^2$.

The advantage of LOOCV is that it avoids biases. The disadvantage is that it is computationally expensive if n is large, as for most PDMs, since you have to iterate through each case. It has been estimated that LOOCV requires $O(n^2)$ computational time.

The k-fold CV is a generalization of LOOCV since groups of observations are used. For LOOCV as a special case, $k = n$. It has the following steps:

1. Divide the data set into k groups (i.e., *folds*) of approximately equal size. Usually $k = 5$ or $k = 10$.
2. Use the first fold as a validation set.
3. Train a model with the remaining $k - 1$ folds.
4. Repeat steps 2 and 3 for the remaining folds, calculating MSE for each iteration. There should be k of these.
5. Estimate the validation error rate as $CV_{(k)} = \frac{1}{k} \times \sum_{i=1}^{k} MSE_i$, where

   $MSE_i = \sum_{j=1}^{n_i} (Y_{ij} - \hat{Y}_{ij})^2$.

This is a less computationally expensive procedure, but some estimates of computational time are $O(kn^2)$ and $O(n^3)$ for better algorithmic implementations. See [22] and [33] for a discussion on validation. Also see [150] for a discussion of CV in the machine learning area. See [116] and [135] for details on the complexity figures.

11.2.2   Modeling Block

The *Modeling Block*, where econometric models are specified and estimated, is complex, with just a few of the many types of models shown in Figure 11.2.3. The one most often used is OLS. Depending upon the nature of the problem and data availability, this is the fallback methodology because it is the only one most analysts are trained in beginning with a basic statistics course and maybe an introductory econometrics course. Most problems, however, are not simple and the data are likewise not simple. OLS is inappropriate for a panel data set such as a PDM because it is tantamount to estimating a pooled model. A *pooled model* uses all the panel data without regard to their 2D aspect, objects and time. The model is

$$Y_i = \beta_0 + \beta_1 X_i + \varepsilon_i \qquad\qquad (126)$$

where the single subscript refers to the *observation*, not a cross-sectional object or time. Biased estimates will result because the different spatial and temporal groupings of the data are ignored. Figure 11.2.6 shows the possibilities when a completely pooled model is used that ignores these groupings. Figure 11.2.6a shows three groups, each with a positive slope. The pooled OLS line – the heavy black line – also shows a positive slope, but the slope clearly differs from that of the groups. Figure 11.2.6a is more dramatic. Each group has a positive slope, but because of the relationship among the groups, the pooled OLS line has a negative slope, which is counter to the actual patterns. See [132] and [137] for other examples and discussions. See [124] for an extensive discussion of the effects of pooling.

Panel data models, sometimes called *pooled cross-section/time series models, random effects models, linear hierarchical models, longitudinal models,* or *multilevel models,* are more appropriate for panel data because they take into account the heterogeneity among groups. Regardless of the name, they all reflect a nesting structure with time periods nested under objects. Following the terminology of [163], the time measures are *micro* or *level 1* units and the objects are *macro* or *level 2* units, with the micro units nested under the macro units. The nesting structure is depicted in Figure 11.2.4. Also see [139] for similar terminology.

Two econometric panel models – fixed effects and random effects – are based on the objects and time. The dependent variable, Y_{it}, in either model varies by both, hence the double subscript. For a basic OLS problem in a non-panel setting, there is a single dimension, either cross-sectional or time series, so only one subscript is used, and this refers to the observation number. The objective in the basic model is to explain the variation in the dependent variable in this single dimension. In fact,

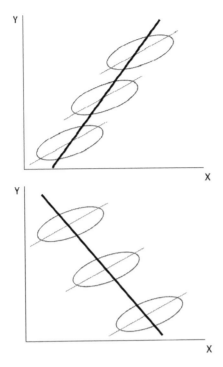

FIGURE 11.2.6 Potential biases from using OLS when the heterogeneity is ignored. (a) Positive slope; (b) negative slope.

in this framework, the well-known and overworked R^2 measures the proportion of the variation in the dependent variable accounted for or explained by the independent variable. In a panel setting, the goal is the same: explain or account for the variation, but now the variation is in two dimensions.

In a basic OLS model, the independent variable must have the same dimension as the dependent variable, otherwise it would be constant or fixed with no impact on the dependent variable. For example, consider a cross-sectional study of consumption that includes real GDP. Real GDP, measured in time, is the same for all cross-sectional units and is thus perfectly collinear with the intercept. This is illustrated in Figure 11.2.7. This means the factor is redundant with the intercept, so its effect is already captured as long as an intercept is part of the model. The factor is not necessary.

Analogously, in a time series study of individual consumption with gender as a factor, gender would be constant over time and also perfectly collinear with the intercept for all female consumers and collinear for all male consumers. Also, in a basic OLS model, the parameters for the independent variables are fixed. These fixed parameters measure the *marginal effect* of the independent variable on the dependent variable. Hence, they are "fixed (marginal) effects" that show the change in Y for a change in X holding the other variables fixed. For instance, a simple model for log sales as a function of log price is $ln(sales) = \beta_0 + \beta_1 ln(price) + \varepsilon$ with β_1 as a "fixed marginal effect."

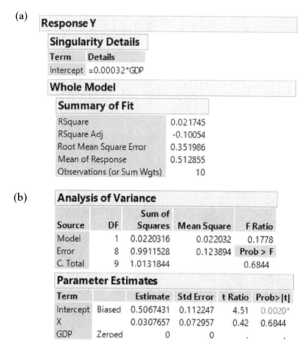

(a) Response Y

Singularity Details

Term	Details
Intercept	=0.00032*GDP

Whole Model

Summary of Fit

RSquare	0.021745
RSquare Adj	-0.10054
Root Mean Square Error	0.351986
Mean of Response	0.512855
Observations (or Sum Wgts)	10

(b) Analysis of Variance

Source	DF	Sum of Squares	Mean Square	F Ratio
Model	1	0.0220316	0.022032	0.1778
Error	8	0.9911528	0.123894	Prob > F
C. Total	9	1.0131844		0.6844

Parameter Estimates

Term		Estimate	Std Error	t Ratio	Prob>|t|
Intercept	Biased	0.5067431	0.112247	4.51	0.0020*
X		0.0307657	0.072957	0.42	0.6844
GDP	Zeroed	0	0	.	.

FIGURE 11.2.7 Two variables were randomly generated: Y as a uniform random number on the 0 to 1 interval and X as a normally distributed random number with mean 0 and variance 1. The GDP number was arbitrarily set at 3141. Ten observations were generated. These are shown in part (a). The OLS results are shown in part (b). Notice the "Singularity Details" report at the top of part (b) that indicates the intercept equals $0.00032 \times GDP$ for perfect multicollinearity, so a GDP marginal effect cannot be estimated as shown in the "Parameter Estimates" report in part (b). The value 0.00032 is the inverse of 3141, so $Intercept = \dfrac{1}{GDP} \times GDP = 1$. (a) Simulated data; (b) OLS results.

Observation number	Y	X	GDP
1	0.17827	0.99775	3141
2	0.94256	-0.73926	3141
3	0.74884	0.35691	3141
4	0.26480	-0.62476	3141
5	0.02057	-1.59023	3141
6	0.69076	2.81575	3141
7	0.39599	2.46702	3141
8	0.77026	1.08908	3141
9	0.21089	-1.36269	3141
10	0.90563	-1.42291	3141

In a panel framework, the situation is more complex. Consider a model

$$Y_{it} = \beta_{1it}X_{it} + \alpha_{it} + \varepsilon_{it}$$

for $i = 1,\ldots,N$ and $t = 1,\ldots,T$ so there are $N \times T$ observations. As noted by [31], there are $2 \times (N \times T)$ parameters to estimate using only $N \times T$ observations. This is impossible. Simplifying assumptions are needed, one of which is that the slopes are all constant and not varying as in this formulation; they are time invariant. This now requires estimating $(N \times T) + 1$ parameters, which is still too much. So not only are the intercepts assumed to be time invariant, but also object variant, so $\alpha_{it} = \alpha_i$. The model then simplifies to

$$Y_{it} = \beta_1 X_{it} + \alpha_i + \varepsilon_{it}$$

with $N + 1 < N \times T$ parameters to estimate as long as $T > 1$ for each object. For a single object, time-invariant factors have an impact, but they are captured by the intercept for that object, so they are not included to avoid redundancy (i.e., collinearity). This is true whether the factors are known or unknown. A simple first step in modeling is to assume that the factors are unknown and reflected in the intercept for the object; that is, in α_i.

When different objects in the panel are considered, the unknown time-invariant factors will have different effects, causing the α_i to vary by object. Why? Because the objects are heterogeneous for the reasons discussed in the segmentation chapters. These object-varying intercepts measure the effect of these unknown factors, but for each object the effect is fixed, since the factors are time invariant for the object. Hence, the intercepts are fixed effects for the objects and a model with such intercepts is a *fixed effects model*.

The fixed effects model (with a single independent variable for simplicity) is written as

$$Y_{it} = \beta_1 X_{it} + \alpha_i + \varepsilon_{it} \tag{127}$$

where

α_i is an unknown intercept for each object that captures the fixed effect of unknown time-invariant factors;

β_1 is the unknown slope, which is the same for all objects;

X_{it} is the independent variable that varies by object and time;

Y_{it} is the dependent variable that varies by object and time;

ε_{it} is the classical disturbance term that varies by object and time.

Consider the estimation of (127). Since the intercepts are unknown for each object, the model can be estimated using dummy or indicator variables, one dummy for each object to represent the object's unknown intercept. The model is

$$Y_{it} = \beta_1 X_{it} + \gamma_1 D_1 + \ldots + \gamma_n D_n + \varepsilon_{it} \tag{128}$$

for $i = 1,\ldots,n$ objects. This model is called a *least squares dummy variable* (LSDV) model.

TABLE 11.3 Perfect multicollinearity with dummy variables.

Obs. #	Object ID	D_1	D_2	D_3	X
1	1	1	0	0	2
2	1	1	0	0	2
3	1	1	0	0	2
4	2	0	1	0	3
5	2	0	1	0	3
6	2	0	1	0	3
7	3	0	0	1	4
8	3	0	0	1	4
9	3	0	0	1	4

Let me expound on the above discussion of time-invariant factors by using the *LSDV* model of (128). If X_{it} is time invariant for object i, so it is really just X_i, then it is collinear with the dummy variables. Consider the three cases shown in Table 11.3. Clearly $X_{it} = \sum_{i=1}^{3} D_{itj} X_{it}$, so this is perfect multicollinearity. Figure 11.2.8 shows an example with randomly generated values for Y and the data in Table 11.3. The singularity report at the top of the example shows the source of the multicollinearity.

With one dummy variable defined for each object in (128), the number of parameters to estimate can quickly become very large. In fact, the total number of parameters could outstrip the number of observations so that estimation is impossible. A "trick" to handle this situation, and to avoid the dummy variables, is to first average both sides of (127) to get

$$\overline{Y_{i.}} = \beta_1 \overline{X_{i.}} + \alpha_i + \overline{\varepsilon_{i.}} \tag{129}$$

where the "dot" subscript indicates that the average is over all time periods for object i and $\overline{X_{i.}} = \dfrac{1}{T_i} \times \sum_{t=1}^{T_i} X_{it}$, where T_i is the number of time periods for object i. Notice that the α_i term is unchanged since it is time invariant. Subtracting (129) from (127), you get

$$Y_{it} - \overline{Y_{i.}} = \beta_1 (X_{it} - \overline{X_{i.}}) + (\varepsilon_{it} - \overline{\varepsilon_{i.}}). \tag{130}$$

The intercept has dropped out, but the slope parameter can be estimated using OLS. The intercept, although not in (130), can be retrieved using $\overline{Y_{i.}} = \hat{\alpha}_i + \hat{\beta}_1 \overline{X_{i.}}$, a basic OLS result, so $\hat{\alpha}_i = \overline{Y_{i.}} - \hat{\beta}_1 \overline{X_{i.}}$. Most software provides this estimate.

A subtle issue with the fixed effects model involves the correlation between the unknown factors absorbed in the α_i term and the X_{it} term. They should not be correlated, otherwise the OLS estimator for the slope coefficient is biased and inconsistent because of the omitted variable bias (OVB) problem. Recall that this problem arises when a relevant explanatory variable is omitted from the model. The effect of this omission depends on the sign of the slope coefficient and the

Response Y

Singularity Details

Term	Details
X	=2*D1 + 3*D2 + 4*D3

Whole Model

Summary of Fit

RSquare	0.040041
RSquare Adj	-0.27995
Root Mean Square Error	0.25432
Mean of Response	0.402482
Observations (or Sum Wgts)	9

Analysis of Variance

Source	DF	Sum of Squares	Mean Square	F Ratio
Model	2	0.01618699	0.008093	0.1251
Error	6	0.38807108	0.064679	**Prob > F**
U. Total	8	0.40425807		0.8846

Tested against reduced model: Y=mean

Parameter Estimates

Term		Estimate	Std Error	t Ratio	Prob>|t|
X	Biased	0.1125833	0.036708	3.07	0.0220*
D1	Biased	0.1847043	0.164163	1.13	0.3035
D2	Biased	0.0094932	0.183539	0.05	0.9604
D3	Zeroed	0	0	.	.

FIGURE 11.2.8 Effect of a time-invariant variable. The dummy variables and the X values are from Table 11.3. The Y values were randomly generated. Notice the "Singularity Details" report at the top. This indicates that X is the sum of the dummies, each multiplied by a value of X, with the sum equaling the original X. This is perfect multicollinearity.

correlation between the included and omitted variables (see [20], [84], and [83] for discussions). In this case, the fixed effects model is unsuitable; however, since the variables are unknown, you cannot determine if there is correlation. Instead, a *random effect* model is more appropriate.

The random effect model, in the simple case, is formulated as

$$Y_{it} = \beta_1 X_{it} + \alpha_i + \varepsilon_{it} \tag{131}$$

where the intercept now varies randomly with the objects. There is confusion in the literature about the "random effect." Some econometric texts state that the random effect is due to a random sampling of the *objects*, whereas the fixed effect is due to a complete enumeration of the objects. Others note that the random effect has nothing to do with a stochastic element, but just the correlation. See [31] for the former and [127] for the latter. Still others state that the intercept is a random draw from a (usually normal) distribution with mean μ and variance σ_α^2. This is the basis for the claim that the intercept represents a sampling from the population, but this should be avoided because it invites confusion concerning the term "population." I advocate interpreting the intercept as a random draw from a distribution. Therefore, I will assume that $\alpha_i \sim \mathcal{N}(\mu, \sigma_\alpha^2)$.

The intercept α_i in a random effect model is the deviation from the mean of the distribution, so it is written as

$$\alpha_i = \mu + u_i \tag{132}$$

where u_i, the *random effect*, is a random disturbance term with the same properties as the OLS disturbance term: $u_i \sim \mathcal{N}(0, \sigma_u^2)$. The random effect model is now written as

$$Y_{it} = \beta_1 X_{it} + \alpha_i + \varepsilon_{it} \tag{133}$$

$$= \mu + \beta_1 X_{it} + (u_i + \varepsilon_{it}) \tag{134}$$

$$= \mu + \beta_1 X_{it} + v_{it}. \tag{135}$$

The last term in parentheses is a composite disturbance term representing the impact of two disturbances. The random effect model is sometimes called an *error components model* because of this composite disturbance term. It is easy to see that $E(u_i + \varepsilon_{it}) = 0$ and $V(u_i + \varepsilon_{it}) = \sigma_u^2 + \sigma_\varepsilon^2$. We usually assume $COV(u_i, \epsilon_{it}) = 0$ and that the u_i terms are uncorrelated with the explanatory variables.

Consider the covariance structure for the composite error term, $v_{it} = u_i + \varepsilon_{it}$. [31] (p. 552) note that there are three cases for the combinations of objects and time subscripts. It is easy to show:

1. Correlation between different objects, same time period: $COV(v_{it}, v_{jt}) = 0$ for $i \neq j$
2. Correlation between same object, different time periods: $COV(v_{it}v_{it'}) = \sigma_u^2$ for $t \neq t'$.
3. Correlation between different objects, different time periods: $COV(v_{it}, v_{jt'}) = 0$ for $i \neq j$ and $t \neq t'$.

Since only the second case has a non-zero covariance, you can find the autocorrelation for object i as

$$\rho = \frac{COV(v_{it}, v_{it'})}{\sqrt{V(v_{it}) \times V(v_{it'})}} \tag{136}$$

$$= \frac{\sigma_u^2}{\sigma_u^2 + \sigma_f^2} \tag{137}$$

Time series analysis can now be done (see [31], p. 553 for more discussion).

Which model (pooled, fixed effect or random effect) to use is difficult to say. There are tests and guidelines to help. The tests are summarized in Table 11.4. The F-test is a basic test of the constancy of the intercepts among the groups. As for all F-tests, the test statistic is

$$F = \frac{(SSE_R - SSE_U)/J}{SSE_U/(N \times T - K)}$$

where SSE_R is the error sum of squares for the restricted model, SSE_U is the error sum of squares for the unrestricted model, J is the difference in the degrees of freedom for the two models,[3] $N \times T$ is the total number of observations, and K is the number of variables plus the constant in the unrestricted model. The restricted model is the one that holds under the null hypothesis and the unrestricted model is the one that holds under the alternative hypothesis. The Breusch–Pagan and Hausman tests are described in [31], [127], and [171].

For the Pricing Scenario, a subset of the data was created for one SKU. The subset consisted of the marketing region, transaction date, units sold, and pocket price. Store-level data were aggregated to the marketing regions by summing the unit sales and averaging the pocket price. Pooled, fixed effect, and random effect models were fit to the data. In addition, a fourth model, called the *between model*, was also estimated. This is a model with the data aggregated over the time periods as described earlier so that estimation is only at the object level. As noted by [31], the estimated parameters of this model are unbiased and consistent, but they do not have minimum variance. The results of the four models are shown in Figure 11.2.9 and summary diagnostics are in Figure 11.2.10.

TABLE 11.4 Several statistical tests for determining which model is applicable to a panel data set.

Test	Null hypothesis	Reject null hypothesis
F-test	Common intercept (α_i all equal)	Fixed effect model is preferred
Breusch–Pagan	$\sigma_u^2 = 0$	Random effect model is preferred*
Hausman	Estimates are consistent	Fixed effect model is preferred**

* Rejecting the null means the random effect model may be better because there is variance in the differences. Not rejecting the null means the pooled model may be better.

** Rejecting the null means the random effect estimates are inconsistent, so the fixed effect model may be better.

Pooled OLS, using 65 observations   Included 4 cross-sectional units
Time-series length: minimum 15, maximum 18

Model Summary

Dependent variable: l_SumUnitSales

Estimate Summary

Variable	Coefficient	Std. Error	t-Ratio	P-Value	LogWorth	
const	9.51241	1.71844	5.53548	6.43e-7	6.19173	
l_AveragePocketPrice	-1.7368	0.63041	-2.755	0.00766	2.11553	

Diagnostic Statistics

Mean dependent var	4.78505	S.D. dependent var	0.78534
Sum squared resid	35.2283	S.E. of regression	0.74778
R-squared	0.10752	Adjusted R-squared	0.09335
F(1, 63)	7.58989	P-value(F)	0.00766
Log-likelihood	-72.324	Akaike criterion	148.647
Schwarz criterion	152.996	Hannan-Quinn	150.363
rho	0.37794	Durbin-Watson	1.20977

Tests

Chow test for structural break at observation %s	.
parameter	.
dfn	2
dfd	61
test statistic	0.89445
p-value	0.41413

FIGURE 11.2.9 Four panel models were estimated: (a) pooled, (b) fixed effects, (c) random effects, and (d) between groups.

Based on the summary in Figure 11.2.10, the F-test for the constancy of the intercepts has a p-value of 0.004, which indicates that the null hypothesis of equal intercepts should be rejected. The fixed effect model is preferred over the pooled model as stated in the note under the F-test report. The Breusch–Pagan test has a p-value of 0.003, which indicates that the random effect model is better. This is supported by the Hausman test. So the random effect model is the one that should be used.

For the *between model*, the estimated model variance is slightly more compli-cated to calculate. It is the between-model variance less the within-model vari-ance divided by the number of time periods. These are shown in the "Variance estimators" portion of the Breusch–Pagan report of Figure 11.2.10: *Between* = 0 .0930311 and *Within* = 0.471223. The within-model variance is from the fixed effects model (Figure 11.2.9b) as the square of the standard error of the regression, or $0.686457^2 = 0.471223$. The between-model variance is

$$\text{Between Variance} = \frac{SSE_{Between}}{N - K_{Between}} - \frac{\text{Within Varaince}}{T}.$$

Fixed-effects, using 65 observations Included 4 cross-sectional units
Time-series length: minimum 15, maximum 18

Model Summary

Dependent variable: l_SumUnitSales

Estimate Summary

Variable	Coefficient	Std. Error	t-Ratio	P-Value	LogWorth	
const	8.44266	1.6357	5.16149	2.92e-6	5.5346	
l_AveragePocketPrice	-1.3438	0.60012	-2.2391	0.02887	1.53961	

Diagnostic Statistics

Mean dependent var	4.78505	S.D. dependent var	0.78534
Sum squared resid	28.2734	S.E. of regression	0.68646
LSDV R-squared	0.28372	Within R-squared	0.07712
LSDV $F(4, 60)$	5.94147	P-value(F)	0.00043
Log-likelihood	-65.176	Akaike criterion	140.352
Schwarz criterion	151.224	Hannan-Quinn	144.641
rho	0.16159	Durbin-Watson	1.53383

Tests

Joint test on named regressors	.
dfn	1
dfd	60
test statistic	5.01377
p-value	0.02887

Test for differing group intercepts	.
dfn	3
dfd	60
test statistic	4.91976
p-value	0.00403

FIGURE 11.2.9 (Cont.)

This is reported as 0.0930311 in Figure 11.2.10. See [31] for a derivation and explanation. Also see [90].

The above discussion was for the simple starting case of an intercept α_i representing unknown factors. A better framework is the *multilevel* or *hierarchical model* framework introduced in Chapter 9. The modeling structure is similar to the fixed effect and random effect models, but with a twist: the intercept can be modeled. There are actually several model structures that can be specified because not only the intercept, but also the slope can be modeled. The following discussion of these models and the notation used with them follows [124] and Chapter 1.

Varying-intercept, constant-slope models

Assume you need to model the sales of a single SKU as a function of its price. This SKU is sold in stores located in J marketing regions so each store maps to a single region.[4] While the sales to a store are a function of price at that store, the economic

Random-effects (GLS), using 65 observations
Included 4 cross-sectional units Time-series length: minimum 15, maximum 18

Model Summary

Dependent variable: l_SumUnitSales

Estimate Summary

Variable	Coefficient	Std. Error	t-Ratio	P-Value	LogWorth	
const	8.69875	1.6383	5.30963	1.1e-7	6.9592	
l_AveragePocketPrice	-1.4438	0.59792	-2.4147	0.01575	1.80279	

Diagnostic Statistics

Mean dependent var	4.78505	S.D. dependent var	0.78534
Sum squared resid	35.3662	S.E. of regression	0.74337
Log-likelihood	-72.451	Akaike criterion	148.901
Schwarz criterion	153.25	Hannan-Quinn	150.617

Tests

'Between' variance	0.09303
'Within' variance	0.47122
mean theta	0.51185
Joint test on named regressors	.
df	1
test statistic	5.83084
p-value	0.01575
Breusch-Pagan test	.
df	1
test statistic	9.05335
p-value	0.00262
Hausman test	.
df	1
test statistic	1.69583
p-value	0.19283

Model 1: Between-groups, using 4 observations

Model Summary

Dependent variable: l_SumUnitSales

Estimate Summary

Variable	Coefficient	Std. Error	t-Ratio	P-Value	LogWorth	
const	24.47	12.42	1.97	0.1877	0.72655	
l_AveragePocketPrice	-7.23	4.56	-1.59	0.2535	0.59605	

Diagnostic Statistics

Mean dependent var	4.75939	S.D. dependent var	0.42899
Sum squared resid	0.24443	S.E. of regression	0.34959
R-squared	0.55729	Adjusted R-squared	0.33593
F(1, 2)	2.51759	P-value(F)	0.25348
Log-likelihood	-0.0855	Akaike criterion	4.17096
Schwarz criterion	2.94355	Hannan-Quinn	1.4775

FIGURE 11.2.9 (Cont.)

Fixed Effects Estimator

Allows for differing intercepts by cross-sectional unit

Parameter Estimates

Variable	Coefficient	Std. Error	P-Value
Constant	8.4427	1.6357	0
l_AveragePocketPrice	-1.3438	0.60012	0.02887

4 group means were subtracted from the data
Residual variance: $28.2734/(65 - 5) = 0.471223$

F-Test

Joint significance of differing group means:
$F(3, 60) = 4.91976$ with p-value 0.00402527
(A low p-value counts against the null hypothesis that the pooled OLS model is adequate, in favor of the fixed effects alternative.)

Units	Mean
Unit 1:	0.13412
Unit 2:	-0.4495
Unit 3:	-0.1803
Unit 4:	0.41375

Breusch-Pagan Test

$LM = 9.05335$ with p-value $=$ prob(chi-square(1) $> 9.05335) = 0.00262214$
(A low p-value counts against the null hypothesis that the pooled OLS model is adequate, in favor of the random effects alternative.)

Variance estimators:
Between $= 0.0930311$
Within $= 0.471223$
Panel is unbalanced: theta varies across units

Random Effects Estimator

Allows for a unit-specific component to the error term

Parameter Estimates

Variable	Coefficient	Std. Error	P-Value
Constant	8.6988	1.6383	0
l_AveragePocketPrice	-1.4438	0.59792	0.01866

Hausman Test

$H = 1.69583$ with p-value $=$ prob(chi-square(1) $> 1.69583) = 0.192834$
A low p-value counts against the null hypothesis that the random effects model is consistent, in favor of the fixed effects model.

FIGURE 11.2.10 The three panel models are summarized.

conditions of the store's geographic area also impact sales. These conditions can be proxied by regional conditions such as the regional median household income. The distribution of this income for 2016 is shown in Figure 11.2.11. For a single store over short time periods, these conditions would be fixed.

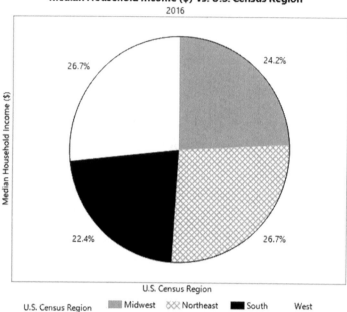

Median Household Income ($) vs. U.S. Census Region
2016

26.7%

24.2%

22.4%

26.7%

U.S. Census Region

U.S. Census Region   Midwest   Northeast   South   West

FIGURE 11.2.11 This shows the median household income for the four US Census regions in 2016. Source: www.census.gov/data/tables/time-series/demo/income-poverty/cps-hinc/hinc-01.html (all races).

Marketing
Region

Individual
Store

FIGURE 11.2.12 The stores are located in marketing regions, with each store location mapped to a single region. There could be several similar stores, perhaps all of the same chain, located in the same region, but a particular store location can only be in one region. The store is nested in a region, the notation for which is $j[i]$.

A store is nested in a region, so there is a hierarchical, multilevel structure to the data. This structure is depicted in Figure 11.2.12. The model for this hierarchical structure is

$$Y_i = \alpha_{j[i]} + \beta X_i + \varepsilon_i, \quad i = 1, \ldots, n \tag{138}$$

$$\alpha_j = a + b Z_j + \gamma_j \quad j = 1, \ldots, J \tag{139}$$

where the subscript i indexes stores and j indexes regions. In the first equation, Y_i is the unit sales of the SKU and X_i is the associated price (perhaps both in log form). The ε_i is the usual disturbance term: $\varepsilon_i \sim \mathcal{N}(0,\sigma_\varepsilon^2)$ and independent, identically distributed (*iid*). The slope, β, is constant for all regions. The intercept's subscript, $j[i]$, indicates that object i is nested under object j. If i is a store and j is a region, then $j[i]$ indicates that store i is nested under region j. Therefore, the intercept varies by region.

The second equation, (139), is a linear model for the intercept in the first equation and shows how the intercept in (138) varies. This is the twist. It says that the intercept, α_j, for level j is itself a function of another intercept and a weighted factor, Z_j, for region j, with b as the weight. The γ_j is a new disturbance term such that $\gamma_j \sim \mathcal{N}(0,\sigma_\alpha^2)$. This is what makes the intercept in the first equation a stochastic factor. The presence of the Z_j term is important because it indicates that some other factor measured at the j level determines the intercept, which in turn determines Y_i. Therefore, Z_j indirectly determines Y_i. As an example, if marketing region is the macro or second level for sales and a store is the micro or first level, then regional income may be a major determinant of sales: a low-income region would be expected to have lower sales than a high-income region. A regional factor could not be included directly in (138) because it would be constant for all stores in that region. This is equivalent to the fixed effects issue for time-invariant factors discussed above. In the two-level model, however, the second-level factor can be included.

Constant-intercept, varying-slope Models

A constant-intercept, varying-slope model is written as

$$Y_i = \alpha + \beta_{j[i]}X_i + \varepsilon_i, \quad i = 1,\dots,n \tag{140}$$

$$\beta_j = a + bW_j + \gamma_j \quad j = 1,\dots, J. \tag{141}$$

This has the same interpretation as above.

Varying-intercept, varying-slope Models

A varying-intercept, varying-slope model is written as

$$Y_i = \alpha_{j[i]} + \beta_{j[i]}X_i + \varepsilon_i, \quad i = 1,\dots,n \tag{142}$$

$$\alpha_j = a + bZ_j + \gamma_{0j} \quad j = 1,\dots, J \tag{143}$$

$$\beta_j = a + bW_j + \gamma_{1j} \quad j = 1,\dots, J. \tag{144}$$

This has the same interpretation as above, but in addition, this is a model that fundamentally has interaction terms (see [124] for a discussion). Of the three possibilities, this last one is the most likely one to be used in a pricing study because you need to know the effect of price by the level 2 factors (e.g., region).

11.2.3 Analysis Block

Once a model is estimated and has been tested/validated against the holdout samples, you have to analyze the results for their applicably to the objectives. The main analysis, of course, is of the elasticities. Do they make economic sense? What are the implications for sales and revenue (based on the elasticity and revenue relationship discussed in Chapter 2)?

For the Pricing Scenario based on the panel models, the price elasticity is −1.4, so the demand is price elastic. This makes intuitive sense since there is competition in the furniture industry, both domestic and foreign. This model, of course, is just illustrative and thus overly simplified. Other explanatory variables need to be included and, because of the OVB problem, the estimated price elasticity is probably biased.

The best way to analyze the effects of model estimation is to use a simulator as discussed in Chapter 5. A simulator is either a specialized software package that allows you to test the impacts of changes in the model variables or a program that can be developed to do this. An example of the former is the Profiler capability in the JMP software.

The simulator can be either simple or complex. A simple simulator will just tell you the impact on sales of a change in the variable such as price. A more complex simulator involves more outside data such as the size of the addressable market (i.e., the number of potential customers) and costs. Knowing the size of the addressable market, the simulator can calculate the total volume of sales. Once the total sales are known, the volume could be multiplied by the price point used in the simulator to calculate revenue. If an average unit cost is also known, then the contribution (= *revenue* − *cost*) and contribution margin (= *contribution/revenue*) can be calculated. Different scenarios, especially relative to a base or most likely case, can be tested, each time changing the price point to determine the best or optimal price point.

11.3 Probability of a win model

The focus until this point has been on a linear model of sales, whether pooled OLS, fixed effect, random effect, or multilevel, although the last is recommended in order for a PDM to make full use of the data structures usually used in these databases to estimate a price elasticity. You are not restricted to a linear model of sales. Suppose the PDM contains data on bids as well as completed sales. The company could operate on a contract basis, so bids are a normal way to make a sale. Contractors, light and heavy construction equipment suppliers, and plumbing/electrical/materials companies are some examples. The PDM would still contain list prices, discounts, date stamps, and so forth, but now it would also contain the bid information, primarily the bid and final agreed price. What should also be maintained is whether or not the bid was won or lost. In many instances, if the bid was won, then it is entered into a PDM, but not if it is lost. A loss is considered a loss and there is no reason to record it. This is unfortunate since the information regarding a loss is just as important as the information regarding a win. Businesses that operate with bids have to track wins–losses because these could be analyzed and modeled for price responses, patterns, and so forth.

A win–loss variable would be a dummy variable: 1 if the bid was won and 0 if the bid was lost. The remaining data are the same. Competitive data would be very valuable because these could help account for the loss and be used in modeling.

An econometric model for a win–loss dummy variable would be a logistic model that specifies the probability of a win as a function of explanatory variables. If the win–loss variable is Y_i for the ith bid, then

$$Logistic = \Pr(Y_i = 1) = \frac{e^{\alpha + \beta X_i}}{1 + e^{\alpha + \beta X_i}}$$

A linear model such as $Y_i = \alpha + \beta X_i$ is inappropriate when Y_i is binary because the disturbance variances are heteroskedastic and there is a chance of predicting outside the range of Y_i, which is just 0 and 1. The logistic cumulative distribution function overcomes these issues. Other distribution functions can be used, but this is the most common in practice. This is the same functional form as for the discrete choice model, but now it is for the binary outcome of a win or a loss. See [20] for details on the inappropriateness of a linear model for this problem.

The logistic model is nonlinear, which is somewhat challenging to estimate. Estimation is simplified by a transformation involving *odds*, which are defined as the ratio of the probability of a win over the probability of a loss. The odds map a probability on a 0–1 scale to a new continuous scale that is 0–∞. The probability is estimated using the log of these odds, called the *log odds* or *logit* (short for *logarithmic transformation*). The logit is the linear function of the independent variables, which is much easier to work with.[5] It turns out that the logistic statement and the logit statement are inverses of each other, so it is sometimes written as

$$Logistic = \Pr(Y_i = 1) = logit^{-1}(\alpha + \beta X_i).$$

The logistic model can be easily extended to a multilevel situation for varying intercepts as

$$Logistic = \Pr(Y_i = 1) = logit^{-1}(\alpha_{j[i]} + \beta X_i)$$

for $i = 1, \ldots, n_j$ and $j = 1, \ldots, J$. A varying-intercept, varying-slope model is

$$Logistic = \Pr(Y_i = 1) = logit^{-1}(\alpha_{j[i]} + \beta_{j[i]} X_i)$$

with

$$\alpha_j = \gamma_0^\alpha + \gamma_1^\alpha Z_j + \varepsilon_j^\alpha$$
$$\beta_j = \gamma_0^\beta + \gamma_1^\beta Z_j + \varepsilon_j^\beta$$

where the Z_j term is an independent variable that affects the intercepts and slopes, but not the win–loss. As an example, in the context of the furniture Pricing Scenario, the Z_j might be the median real household income. This varies by US Census region and would affect household purchase decisions. If the Pricing Scenario is modified to involve bids to the stores, then whether or not a bid is won or lost depends on sales of furniture by the stores. Economic theory states that income is a factor determining demand: the higher the income, the higher the demand. Regions with high income will have a larger demand for furniture, but all stores in the region would be faced with the same level of income, so that there is a hierarchical structure. This equation captures this income effect and structure. See [124] and [163] for reviews of the logistic model in the multilevel context. Also see [20] and [31] for general discussions of the logistic model.

11.4 Software

Panel models can be estimated by most econometric software packages. The three commercial packages Eviews, LimDep, and Stata will handle panels. The freeware econometric software package Gretl is also very good for panel models, especially for the price. I used Gretl for the panel examples in this chapter. R also has the ability to estimate econometric models, including multilevel models. See [124] for many examples using R.

SAS and JMP have procedures for clustering variables. For SAS you would use Proc Varclus and for JMP you would use the *Cluster Variables* platform in the *Analyze/Clustering* main menu option.[6]

11.5 Summary

Modeling with Big Data is not trivial. The data most often have a specific structure – that of a panel. This chapter highlighted panel data modeling, but only skimmed the surface of this topic. Nonetheless, the salient points were presented.

Notes

1 [93] also projected likely responses based on these correlations.
2 I will discuss nesting shortly. For now, just think of it from an intuitive perspective.
3 This is equal to the degrees of freedom in the unrestricted model less those in the restricted model (see [57]).
4 In this context, a "store" is a physical bricks-and-mortar location in, say, a single state and not a chain of stores.
5 For this model, $odds = \left(\dfrac{e^X}{1+e^X}\right) \times \left(\dfrac{1+e^X}{1}\right) = e^X$, where the second ratio is the inverse of the probability of a loss. Then $logit = \ln odds = X$.
6 For JMP Pro 13.

12

BIG DATA AND NONLINEAR PRICES

In the previous chapters, I focused on uniform pricing, either for the market as a whole or for segments. Uniform prices are single price points at which consumers can buy all they wish and are able to do so. For segmentation analysis, this pricing is third-degree price discrimination, a very popular pricing strategy, in which a single uniform price is set for each segment. Another popular approach is second-degree price discrimination, in which prices vary depending on the size of purchases. There is an interaction between price and quantity that goes beyond a simple demand curve relationship. Prices are now nonlinear, being determined by the quantity consumers choose, and are not uniform for either the whole market or submarkets such as segments. The amount consumers choose is a form of segmentation, but one in which they self-select and reveal their segments by the amount they choose to buy. I describe some approaches to this nonlinear pricing situation in the following sections.

This chapter is in Part IV of this book, a part that focuses on Big Data, because the model estimations use historical transactions data on quantities bought and the associated prices. Surveys could provide these data by asking consumers what they bought in some recent past period, how much they bought, and how much they paid per unit (i.e., the uniform price). Unfortunately, consumers tend to have poor memories of the recent past and their memories are very suspect for any activity a year or more in the past. In short, survey data on past purchase behavior may be too dubious. Sometimes, a consumer panel is used to collect diary data. Diaries may be helpful, but they require that the panelists faithfully and accurately record their buying behavior every day. This diligence also may be too much to ask of most consumers. Transactions data are recorded in real time by mechanical or electronic means and do not rely on what consumers have to report. Models fit with this type of data are more reliable.

This chapter has four sections. In the first, I distinguish between linear (or uniform) and nonlinear pricing since this is the first time "nonlinear pricing" is discussed in this book. I then describe several forms of nonlinear pricing in the second section. The most common form is quantity discounts, a form I spend some time discussing. Bundling and product line pricing are also mentioned, but I do not dwell on either since each is worthy of a book unto itself. The third section just mentions some software that could be used to model nonlinear pricing data, while the fourth section is a summary.

12.1   Linear and nonlinear pricing

There are two forms of pricing: linear and nonlinear. The former, sometimes called *uniform, constant, single, market,* or *average pricing,* is the traditional textbook version of a price in the market: all units are sold at one price point. The linearity is due to total revenue (the consumer's total expenditure) rising as the unit sales rise since $TR = P^{*} \times Q$, where P^{*} is the uniform price fixed by the market. Once the price point is set, total revenue is a function only of unit sales, so it is proportional to price. This is depicted in Figure 12.1.1. The more sold, the more earned. How the units are sold is immaterial, meaning that it does not matter if ten people buy one unit each at $2 per unit or one person buys ten units at $2 per unit. Ten units are still sold at one price point, $2, and total revenue is just $2 \times 10 = $20 regardless. The seller should be indifferent to how the units are sold.

This linearity may be puzzling at first because it seems to ignore a price elasticity effect, but this is not incorrect because an elasticity effect reflects the demand curve, which is a schedule of prices or, alternatively, reservation prices or the maximum amounts consumers are willing to pay for one extra unit. The actual market price is just one fixed point on this schedule. Once a particular price point is selected, all units are sold at that single price. The elasticity is only relevant if the price point is changed.

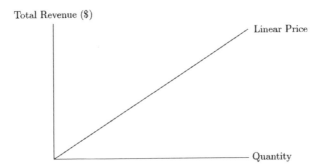

FIGURE 12.1.1 The uniform price is a straight line pricing curve depicted as a ray emanating from the origin. The slope of the ray is the uniform price, P^{*}. It is also the average (and marginal) price per unit purchased.

The linear price is the textbook price as well as one that is used in many real-world market situations. The models in Part II were based on linear pricing. Even Part III had fixed prices, but they were fixed for segments and varied between segments. Price was set for a segment, which is, after all, a mini-market. Within a segment, total revenue will change in proportion to the segment price, which is no different from a non-segmented market.

There are many situations, however, in which the price changes as the quantity changes, sometimes continuously and other times discretely. In most instances, price falls as quantity rises, although there are circumstances in which price rises as quantity rises. These cases involve products or services that are viewed as requiring conservation, such as water and electricity (see [155] for a comment). Barring these cases, which are important in their own right, total revenue changes as the quantity changes because the price changes as well. So there is a *price schedule* with price as a function of quantity reflecting the interaction between price and quantity rather than a linear price. This is the essence of nonlinear pricing. Some special cases are:

- Two-part tariffs that have a fixed amount, usually interpreted as a buy-in or subscription fee for the first unit purchased, and then a constant per unit charge after the first. The second fee is the *marginal price*.
- Three-part tariffs that have a buy-in charge, a flat fee for the first X units purchased, and then a rising fee afterward. If $X = 1$, then the two-part tariff results. In telecommunications, there would be an access fee, a basic fee for X minutes of use, and a fee for each minute over the basic usage allowance (see [91] for a discussion).
- Fixed-price tariffs that have the same flat price regardless of the amount purchased.
- Block tariffs in which prices decline only when a threshold of units is met. Block tariffs are common in electric and water utilities, although the price increases rather than decreases.
- And many more.

A nonlinear price schedule is a general class of situations such that the average price per unit declines as quantity increases. Various nonlinear price schedules are depicted in Figure 12.1.2. The flat fee is just a single charge. The two-part tariff has a basic fee, usually an entry or buy-in fee, and a fee that is uniform for all units once the basic fee is paid. The three-part tariff is similar, with a buy-in fee, a single flat fee for the X units (say the first unit), and then a uniform fee for all succeeding units. The block tariff has a piece-wise linear structure with a different uniform fee for blocks of units.

Nonlinear pricing gives consumers the opportunity to self-select not only the quantity, which is the normal case in basic economic theory, but also the price (see [74]). In basic economic theory with a uniform price in the market, a consumer's sole decision is how much to consume. Based on the discussion in Chapter 2, a consumer would consume up to the point where his/her utility or benefit of an extra unit (i.e., marginal utility) just equals the fixed market price. The marginal

Total Revenue ($)

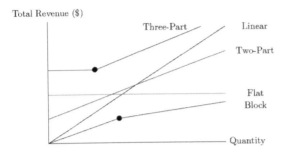

FIGURE 12.1.2 Several cases of more general pricing tariffs are depicted here. The dots at the kinks of the block and three-part tariffs are points of discontinuities in these tariffs. These points are called "knots," as explained in the "Elasticity measurement" section of this chapter. See [74] (p. 5), [91], and [133] for similar graphs.

utility is subjective, but the price is objective, meaning the consumer has no control over it; the price is externally imposed. With nonlinear pricing, however, a consumer does have control over price as well as quantity. A consumer can select not only the quantity as in basic economic theory, but he/she can also, at the same time, select the price point. Intuitively, and in actuality, the more that is bought, the lower the marginal utility and, therefore, the lower the price a consumer would be willing to pay. In nonlinear pricing, the market price is actually lower.

There is a restriction on what a consumer can do regarding the quantity decision. As noted by [85], there is an order to the purchases. Consumers must purchase a lower amount before proceeding to a higher one, even if the lower is implicit in the higher. As an example, consider a nonlinear pricing strategy for cans of tuna as "Buy one for $1.00; two for $1.75." You must buy the first can before the second. The first can of tuna has a price of $1.00. If only one is bought, the total expenditure is $1.00. If two cans are bought, the total expenditure is $1.75. The increment of $0.75 for the second can is less than the price of the first, but this lower price is only realized if the first can is bought. Notice a feature of this nonlinear pricing strategy: the total cost of two cans bought separately at the lower charge (i.e., $1.00 each) is greater than the total cost of two cans bought at once (i.e., $1.75). A restriction on nonlinear pricing is that the total charge for separate purchases must be greater than the total charge for the complete purchase. If the two charges are equal, there is no benefit to the nonlinear pricing strategy: there is only one uniform price. If the total charge for the separate purchases is less than for the complete purchase, then the complete purchase would never occur because it is not to the consumer's benefit to ever buy the complete purchase; the separate purchases always beat the complete purchase.

Consider other examples of sequential purchasing: if there is a coverage charge to enter a nightclub (an access fee), then you must pay that access fee before you can pay a per drink fee inside the club. Similarly, you must pay a fee to access a telephone network as well as meet a target number of minutes of use, with a usage fee per minute, before you can progress to a lower per minute usage fee for more calls.

There are advantages to using a nonlinear pricing schedule. One is profit maximization. For a firm with market power measured by the Lerner Index as a monopolist in the extreme, profits are increased relative to a linear price. I demonstrate this below. Another advantage is that nonlinear pricing not only gives consumers the option to self-select the quantity they will purchase, as in the case of a linear price structure, but it also gives them the option to choose the price they will pay for that quantity, as I noted above. Where they fall on the nonlinear price schedule is up to them. Since consumers are heterogeneous, there will be a distribution of consumers along the price–quantity dimension. Primarily, their placement – the distribution – depends on their price elasticity. If consumers are very heterogeneous, then a nonlinear price schedule is preferred both from an allocative efficiency perspective (economists' major concern) and a profit maximization perspective because the nonlinear price schedule takes advantage of this heterogeneity.

The notion of pricing to different segments discussed in Chapters 8 and 9 is an example of taking advantage of the heterogeneity to maximize profits. This was third-degree price discrimination. In that case, however, consumers did not self-select their segments; they automatically belong to a segment based on their characteristics, the characteristics that define the segments. If an *a priori* segmentation consists of senior citizens and non-senior citizens, then people cannot choose to be a senior; they either are or are not a senior! A business, however, can use the distinction between the two to their advantage if the price elasticities for the two segments differ. If seniors are more price elastic, then they will be charged a per unit price that is less than the one charged to non-seniors.

The notion of heterogeneity speaks to the skewness of the distribution of purchases in the market. Consumers may have a purchase distribution that is right skewed, suggesting that a large proportion of consumers spend small amounts, while relatively smaller proportions spend large amounts. The higher prices deter them more so fewer consumers self-select to be in that category, whereas the lower prices deter fewer people and so more self-select to be in the lower category. This suggests that those who spend the smaller amounts would be more price inelastic and those relatively few who spend in the higher category will be more price elastic. A slight increase in price will drive them into the lower category. So basically this self-selection with nonlinear pricing is segmentation (see [85] and [74]).

Even with nonlinear pricing, price elasticities are still important because they help to determine the degree by which prices are lower for larger quantities. I say more about them in the following subsections.

12.1.1 A simple demand model

To illustrate the benefit of nonlinear pricing, consider the constant elasticity demand function of Chapter 4 shown in (145). As I noted before, this is a popular form for a model. It is modified, however, to handle the fact that with nonlinear pricing there is an interaction between price and quantity. The demand function is

$$N(p,q) = \beta_0 \times p^{\beta_1 \times q} \tag{145}$$

where $N(p, q)$ is the number of customers buying q units at a price of p per unit. This is a *demand profile*, which I discuss in more detail below. Suffice it to say for now that this is the demand.

Now

$$\ln[N(p,q)] = \ln(\beta_0) + \beta_1 \times q \times \ln(p)$$

so $\eta_p^N = \beta_1 \times q < 0$ for $\beta_1 < 0$. The demand elasticity is the product of the price coefficient, β_1, and the quantity. Previously, the elasticity was just β_1. Clearly, as q increases, η_p^N increases in absolute value, so demand becomes more elastic. If $q = 0$, then $\eta_p^N = 0$ and demand is perfectly inelastic. If $q \to \infty$, then $\eta_p^N \to -\infty$ and demand is perfectly elastic.

Recall the inverse pricing rule for pricing from Chapter 3. Then it is easy to show that

$$p = \frac{c \times \beta_1 \times q}{\beta_1 \times q - 1} \tag{146}$$

where c is the average cost. Notice that $\lim_{q \to \infty} p = c$, so price is set at average cost. For any value of β_1, the demand is more elastic the larger is q, so the price will be lower for higher incremental units. For the tuna example, the price for the first unit is $1.00, but the second is $0.75 for a total price of $1.75 for two cans. The second can is more price elastic than the first, so it is priced lower; the second can is discounted from the first. This is *quantity discount pricing*.

The profit from quantity discounting is

$$\pi = \sum_{i=1}^{Q} N(p_i, q_i) \times (p_i - c)$$

where Q is the largest number of units that can be bought. The total units sold is

$$Units = \sum_{i=1}^{Q} \beta_0 \times p_i^{\beta_1 \times q_i}$$
$$= \sum_{i=1}^{Q} N(p_i, q_i).$$

The total number of units is the total demand.

12.2 Forms of nonlinear pricing

[85] observes that the form of nonlinear pricing depends on the number of products and sellers in the market (see Table 12.1). In the following subsections, I will focus

TABLE 12.1 Pricing strategies by seller and product configuration. Source: [85]. Abridged from the original.

	Single product	Multiple products
Single seller	Quantity discounts	Bundle pricing
	Product line pricing	
Multiple sellers	One-stop shopping	Mix-and-match shopping
	Product line pricing	

on quantity discounts with some comments on product-line pricing and bundling. See [85] and [74] for discussions of other methods.

12.2.1 Quantity discounts

Quantity discounts as a form of nonlinear pricing are very popular and important. One reason for this is that they have the potential to increase profits beyond what could be earned using a uniform price. This is a basic result of the price discrimination analysis described in Chapter 3. That framework assumed a monopolist or a firm with sufficient market power so that competition or a competitive fringe was not a concern. In many situations, however, a firm may have market power but competitors are a problem. The firm must deal with other brands. Nonlinear pricing may then provide a competitive advantage by offering more elastic customers lower prices, but without harming the firm's profit position.

Despite their popularity, they have two problems:

1. Devising a discount schedule (i.e., the cut-points or points of discontinuity in the price schedule);
2. Measuring elasticity in each segment of the schedule.

I will discuss these in the following two subsections.

Devising a discount schedule

Quantity discounts are selections from a discrete joint distribution of price and quantity. A simple joint distribution between two variables can be represented as a table. In this context, the columns are the quantities and the rows are the price points. The conditional distribution of quantities given a price point is called a *demand profile* and is represented as $N(p, q)$.[1] An example is shown in Table 12.2. A demand profile shows the number of units bought/ordered/shipped at each selling price. The cells in the profile are the expected or projected number or proportion of customers buying the indicated number of units at the stated price per unit. I recommend proportions since they can be applied to an aggregate count of

TABLE 12.2 Illustrative example of discount determination. Bolded entries correspond to optimal prices. Assumptions: list price = $5; average cost = $1.

Selling price	One unit	Two units	Three units	Four units	Five units	Demand
$2/unit	90	75	55	30	5	255
$3	80	65	**45**	**20**	0	210
$4	**65**	**50**	30	5	0	150
$5	45	30	10	0	0	85

Source: [74].

customers to derive the number of customers per segment. In the following, I will just mention "customers," but the proportions can be used.

An interpretation of the cell values is needed. Recall that in many situations consumers have to buy one quantity of a good before they can purchase another. Extending the tuna example from above, suppose the pricing is "Buy one for $1.00; two for $1.75; three for $2.40," so the increment for the second can is $0.75 and for the third can is $0.65. Consumers have to buy the first can before they can buy the second at the lower price, and they have to buy the second before they can buy the third at a still lower price. They could, of course, buy just one, or just two, or all three; certainly they could buy none. The demand profile table would have three columns, one for each unit, and as many rows as possible price points (the three prices – $1.00, $1.75 and $2.40 – are just specific points). An entry in a cell reflects the potential purchases. The first cell in a row (i.e., at a particular price point) shows the number of customers who would buy that first unit – or more. The qualifier "or more" is important because they could go on to buy the second and third units; the first is just the entry point for buying more. Similarly, the second cell shows the number of customers who would buy the second unit – or more. Finally, the third cell shows the number of customers who buy all three. The difference between the value in the second and first cell is the number of customers who would buy just one unit; the difference between the third and second cell shows the number who would buy just the second; and, of course, the third cell is the number who would buy the third unit. The sum of these three increments is the value in the first cell.

Now consider another example shown in Table 12.2: if the price is $2 per unit, then 90 customers would buy one or more units, 75 would buy two or more units, and 15 would buy just the first (= 90–75). If the price is $5 per unit, 45 people would buy one or more units and 30 would buy two or more units, while none would buy four or five units.

The total demand at a price point (i.e., for a row in the demand profile) is the sum of the entries in a row. This sum is a row marginal given by

$$D(p) = \sum_{i=1}^{Q} (N(p, q_i))$$

TABLE 12.3 Calculations.

	One unit	Two units	Three units	Four units	Five units
Units sold	65	50	45	20	5
Selling price	$4	$4	$3	$3	$2
Revenue	$260	$200	$135	$60	$10
Cost	$65	$50	$45	$20	$5
Contribution	$195	$150	$90	$40	$5
Discount	20%	20%	40%	40%	60%

Source: [74] with modifications.

where the price is unscripted because it is fixed. This is the traditional economics textbook demand. For the first price point of $2 per unit, the total demand is 255 units. Notice that the total demand falls as price rises, as expected.

There are two restrictions on the pricing from the demand profile. The first is the one mentioned above: the total charge for separate purchases must be greater than the total charge for a complete purchase. Another restriction is that the number of customers buying one level for a given price, must be less than the number of customers at the next higher level for that same price (i.e., going across a row in the table), while the number of customers must decrease for a specific level as the price increases (i.e., going down a column). Finally, once the optimal set of price points is determined, the number of customers must decrease as the price points increase. See [74] for a discussion about the restrictions.

The optimal set of prices is determined by calculating the contribution for each price–quantity pair. As an example, the profit contribution for a price of $2 with an average cost of $1 is $90 \times (\$2 - \$1)$, or $90. This is less than the contribution at $4, which is $195 (= $65 \times (\$4 - \$1)$). At $5, the contribution is $45 \times (\$5 - \$1) = \$180$. So $4 is the optimal price point for the first unit for a discount from list price of 20%. This is repeated for each unit. The bolded values in Table 12.2 show the optimal price points. The calculations are summarized in Table 12.3. Notice that the price points fall as the units increase.

Disaggregated data reflecting the heterogeneity of consumers are needed to construct a demand profile. Aggregated data – as for some products, for example, that are purchased once or very infrequently (e.g., cars, boats, homes) – lose information about the heterogeneity because of the aggregation or averaging. These data are too aggregated and would not be sufficient for creating the demand profile table. The table is aggregated in the sense that it has price–quantity pairs, but not so aggregated that variations across quantities and prices are lost. Disaggregated data at the transaction level that preserve these pairs are needed to form the demand profile table. The data could be actual data or data generated or simulated by a model. In the current era of Big Data, transaction data at the individual level maintained in data warehouses and data marts are readily available in most large businesses. The pricing data mart (PDM) would be used to construct the profile.

The type of transaction data could be an issue for the price data rather than the quantity data. There are list and pocket prices where the latter reflect discounts, rebates, and allowances. Clearly, pocket prices should not be used because they already reflect discounts. The price should be uniform prices. List prices are preferred, but they may not have enough variation to be useful for modeling. In any econometric modeling, the data must have sufficient variation for parameter estimation. The needed variation could be induced by converting the list prices, which are nominal, into real prices by dividing by a consumer price index. Economic consumer demand theory, outlined in Chapter 2, states that the prices relevant for consumer choice decisions are relative prices. Using a price index would give these relative prices and also the needed variability.

The demand profile table illustrated above is a nice heuristic for defining an approach for developing a demand profile. The table, however, is overly simplistic and does not do justice to the complexity of the issues involved in creating discounts. A more sophisticated approach recognizes that the table is just a representation of a statistical or econometric model. A statistical model is really behind the table and is preferred for more complex problems. You may be able to build demand models with existing data from a PDM and use the models to generate or simulate the table. The table per se is not actually constructed, but is represented by the model. The type of data, of course, is still an issue.

One possible econometric model for developing a demand profile is a regression model (OLS) with price points as the independent variable and observed quantities as the dependent variable. Depending on the product and market, demographic variables could be included. For the tuna example, there would not be a separate market for tuna along gender, ethnic, educational, or age dimensions because tuna is sold to all-comers. This would be the case for most consumer package goods. Electricity, however, is sold and priced differently based on residential and commercial areas as well as, perhaps, location (e.g., towns). Overall, the regression model would fit a linear line to the data, but such a line would be inappropriate for a nonlinear price schedule because of the nonlinearity of the schedule. A better econometric model is a *spline regression model*. This model, and other possibilities, are explained in the next section, where I discuss elasticity measurement. The same models can be used for both purposes.

Elasticity measurement

Elasticity estimation is more complex for market data that are already based on quantity discounts because of discontinuities in the data due to changes in the price points. Linear econometric models do not capture the nonlinear structure of the prices considered in this chapter. A casual glance at Figure 12.1.2 should be enough to convince you of this. Better models are:

- Polynomial regression;
- Step function regression;

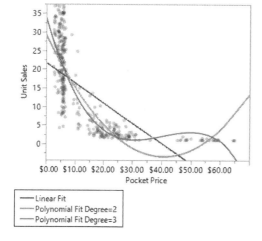

FIGURE 12.2.1 Several values of the degree of a polynomial model. The linear fit is a polynomial with $d = 1$ and is the OLS fit.

- Spline regression;
- Local regression;
- Generalized additive models (GAMs).

This list is in a hierarchical order with polynomial models being the simplest and GAMs being the most complex but also the most flexible and powerful for modeling nonlinearities. See [33], Chapter 7 and [22] for discussions of these models. I will provide summaries since each one is worthy of a book-length treatment.

Polynomial regression models have the basic form of an OLS regression model in that it is linear in the parameters, but it is nonlinear in the variables. For a single explanatory variable, the general model is

$$Y_i = \beta_0 + \beta_1 X_i + \beta_2 X_i^2 + \ldots + \beta_d X_i^d + \varepsilon_i$$

where the degree of the polynomial is d. [33] note that d is usually less than 4, otherwise the model would overfit the data. The nonlinearity in the variables captures the curvature in the data. See Figure 12.2.1 for a comparison of several values of d. This model, because it is still linear in the parameters, could be estimated using OLS. It should be clear that a polynomial regression model is a general case of a linear regression model; the basic linear OLS model is just a polynomial with $d = 1$.

A disadvantage of a polynomial regression is that it can expand quickly if other terms are added and cross-product terms are included. The simple model above only has one explanatory variable, which, of course, means there cannot be a cross-product term. Ignoring the intercept, there is one parameter to estimate. With two explanatory variables, however, one cross-product term can be added. Such a model, written as a quadratic (i.e., $d = 2$), is

$$Y_i = \beta_0 + \beta_1 X_{1i} + \beta_2 X_{2i} + \beta_3 X_{1i}^2 + \beta_4 X_{2i}^2 + \beta_5 (X_{1i} \times X_{2i}) + \varepsilon_i$$

where the last term associated with β_5 is the interaction of the two variables. There are now five parameters to estimate, ignoring the intercept. In general, for p explanatory variables, the number of non-intercept parameters is $2^p + p - 1$. The problem is $O(p^2)$. If the degree of the polynomial is d, then the problem is $O(p^d)$. In short, the complexity increases with the number of explanatory variables and the degree of the polynomial (see [22]).

Despite the smoothness of the estimated curve, the polynomial model may still not be appropriate for nonlinear pricing if the changes in the quantities are sharp, discrete discontinuities. A step function may be more appropriate because it is based on the explanatory variable being discretized into bins, with a different intercept and slope for each bin. In terms of Figure 12.1.2, the increasing block tariff has a single knot, as does the three-part tariff. As noted by [33], the continuous variable X is converted to an ordinal categorical variable with cut-points defining the breaks in X. The "steps" in the function are at the breaks. The bins are coded using either dummy or effects coding, although dummy coding is typical because only shifts relative to a base are needed. As usual, either one dummy is omitted if an intercept is included or all dummies are used if an intercept is excluded.

Splines are a more flexible class of models similar to the polynomial model, but with a polynomial model estimation done for regions of the range of the independent variable.[2] The regions are similar to those of the step function bins. In a spline model, the points where the discontinuities occur are called *knots*; the knots are the X values. A spline regression model with one independent variable and three knots (k_1, k_2, and k_3), and therefore four intervals, is written as[3]

$$Y_i = \beta_0 + \beta_1 (X_i - k_1)_+ + \beta_2 (X_i - k_2)_+ + \beta_3 (X_i - k_3)_+ + \varepsilon_i$$

where

$$(Z)_+ = \begin{cases} Z & \text{if } Z > 0 \\ 0 & \text{if } Z \leq 0. \end{cases}$$

In essence, a low-level polynomial is fit for each region between knots. If there are two regions, there is one knot and two polynomial regression fits, each with separate estimated coefficients. The increasing block tariff in Figure 12.1.2 is an example. If there is one region, there are no knots and therefore there is only one polynomial regression.[4] This would be the case for uniform pricing.

The knots for nonlinear pricing are the points where the price changes. For the tuna example, there is a knot at two cans since the first can of tuna is priced at $1.00 and the second is priced at $1.75. The number of knots and their locations must be specified. One possibility is that they are determined by managerial judgement, input from subject matter experts and key opinion leaders, and knowledge of the market (including competitive pricing). Certainly, comparisons of profit contributions between nonlinear models using different numbers of knots and knot placements and uniform pricing where knots are irrelevant help to determine the points of discontinuities. Another possibility is to use data visualization tools to identify regions of rapid data changes in order to specify a lot of knots in the region. This is recommended by [33] (p. 274) because the polynomial fits are more flexible in those regions. A final possibility also recommended by [33] is to place knots uniformly throughout the range of X, say at the quartiles. Also see [122] (p. 23), who provides a table of equally spaced knots for numbers of knots ranging from three to seven. I recommend the data visualization approach and the use of market knowledge and experience.

Local regressions are models that fit a function using data around a knot. This is a more complicated procedure than it appears at first. See [33] for a description of the methodology. Also see [122] for some discussion of local regressions and especially the locally weighted least squares method (usually abbreviated as LOESS). The GAM is an even higher form of flexible regression model where each explanatory variable is a nonlinear function of the actual explanatory variable. If X is an explanatory variable and $f(X)$ is a nonlinear function of X, then a GAM is

$$Y_i = \beta_0 + f(X_i) + \varepsilon_i.$$

If there are p explanatory variables $X_i, X_2, \ldots, X_p$, then the model is

$$Y_i = \beta_0 + \sum_{j=1}^{p} f(X_{ij}) + \varepsilon_i.$$

The advantage of this approach is that nonlinear relationships in the data are found that a purely linear model would ignore. The disadvantage is that the model is more complex, requiring more specialized software.

An interesting approach for estimating elasticities was proposed by [108] for a study of nonlinear pricing in the health insurance market. The objective in this study was the estimation of price elasticities using data that already reflected nonlinear pricing so there were discontinuities in the data. The problem was compounded by the observation that the nonlinear pricing introduced a selection bias on the part of consumers. The bias existed because consumers can self-select to be above or below the discontinuity point, as I discussed earlier, but the reason for the selection is either unknown or unknowable. The approach developed by [108] used expenditure data in the neighborhood of a discontinuity, both before and after, and then used a local linear regression model in that neighborhood. Different slopes were then estimated before and after the discontinuities and then compared in order to determine the change in the slope at the discontinuities. This procedure would work if the discontinuity points are known and sufficient data are available around them. As [108] notes, however, data far from the discontinuities would not be part of the estimation, so there would be a loss of data. In the era of Big Data, this may not be an issue, but it would certainly be an issue for smaller data set sizes.

Further complications

The existence of brands compounds an already complicated problem. As I noted above, nonlinear pricing can be a competitive advantage for a firm with some market power. The issue here is the modeling of brand choice in the face of nonlinearities. [81] observed that there are three general approaches to modeling brand choice in this situation. The first is to basically ignore pricing discontinuities by creating all brand-size combinations and then modeling these as a function of price. The problem with this approach is that substitutions between quantities and differential elasticities are not possible. The second is to restrict the analyses to products of a certain size so that quantity decisions are ruled out. Finally, another class of approaches uses an average uniform price for all products, which basically negates the nonlinear pricing.

[81] proposed a revealed preference discrete choice model of brand selection with discrete quantities and quantity discounts. The choice probabilities are derived following a two-step procedure:

1. Identify the optimal quantity given that a brand, k, is selected.
2. Identify the probability of the quantity being selected for brand k.

Making the usual stochastic assumption yields a choice probability with a structure similar to the one developed in Chapter 5. This choice probability is a function of the observed purchases for the brands, a budget allotment, and the price of a brand for a package size. This latter factor reflects the quantity discounts. The expected brand demand is then the product of the optimal quantity for the brand times the probability this quantity is purchased.

Another complication is that order sizes may have to be within the bounds of what can be delivered. For instance:

> ... individual buyers may ... prefer to consider ... units for their own convenience in transporting, packaging, handling or storing the product. The constraints on order sizes emanate from these considerations, and they may take the form of upper/lower bounds on the order size, integer multiples of a certain container size or the number of containers that will fit into a transport mode.
>
> *[109]*

This is a constraint on what can be shipped. Shipping beyond a certain amount would reduce the profits that would otherwise be gained by using nonlinear pricing by adding in a transportation cost. These problems would not exist with consumer packaged goods sold in retail outlets because the products are not delivered to consumers, but it does become an issue with products sold to those retailers as well as manufactures who buy raw products used in the manufacturing process. See [109] for an operations research perspective.

12.2.2 *Bundling*

Bundling is considered a special case of quantity discounts. A bundle is usually several products sold as a unit. For example, an airplane reservation may be combined or bundled with a hotel reservation at a vacation destination. Each could be purchased separately, but the bundle may be more attractive if it is priced lower than the two separate reservations. Compared to a quantity discount situation, a bundling situation usually involves two or more distinct products. This is just the condition for quantity discounts discussed above. With quantity discounts, however, the items are usually the same such as cans of tuna. Nonetheless, the concept is the same.

There are three forms of bundling:

1. Pure;
2. Mixed;
3. Complex.

A pure bundle is an offering of the bundle only. The individual components are not available for separate sale. As such, the bundle can be viewed as a single product and therefore it would be priced that way. The pricing would be linear as for any other product. A mixed bundle, on the other hand, is an offering of the bundle, but the individual components can be purchased as stand-alone items, so they do not have to be purchased as a bundle. In most instances, two or more products are combined in a straightforward manner, meaning that if you buy one product, say A, then you must buy a second one, B. For a mixed bundle, a discount is offered on the bundle compared to the single purchase. In this case, the different products can be viewed as being purchased in sequence: you cannot buy the second one without buying the first. In this sense, there is no difference between the bundle case and the quantity discount case. This means that the previous discussions hold for this situation. See [74] for the same perspective.

A complex bundle is different. Consider three examples from [131]:

1. Get a discount on the total sales of one product if a second one is also purchased.
2. Get a discount on one unit of a product if one unit of another is also purchased.
3. Get a discount on the purchase of two or more products, the size of the discount dependent on the proportions of the two products.

[131] point out that these three examples highlight that two (or more) products are involved in some proportion. A subtlety is that the buyer has certain quantity requirements, but is not willing to fill their needs completely by one supplier. They may split their purchase across several suppliers. Any one supplier may then require that a percentage of the total requirement be purchased from it in order to receive a discount. This is a complex bundle because it not only involves a package of products that may be discounted, but also proportions. How the discounts are

offered may have antitrust implication because this has characteristics of predatory pricing by a dominant firm. See [131] for a discussion of the legal issues.

There are obviously three issues with bundling. One is the same as for quantity discounting: *What is the discount?* This was addressed above. The second question is: *What comprises the bundle?* And the third is: *What proportions?* For quantity discounting, there was only one product, just different units. Now there are different products and different proportions, as noted above. This is a more complex issue.

For the bundle composition, subject matter experts, key opinion leaders, and management experience can clearly be useful and informative. *Association analysis,* also called *market basket analysis,* could be used to determine those products that have an affinity for each other in the majority of purchases. This type of analysis relies on transactions data in a Big Data setting. If a business has these data and it wants to form bundles of products to offer, then mining the Big Data using association analysis tools would help. If the products are from other suppliers (e.g., an airline bundling a hotel reservation and a flight reservation), identifying that they might form a bundle requires extensive ideation work (i.e., brainstorming), market needs surveys, and partnering negotiations. The proportions may also follow from these activities. Finally, the composition of a bundle and the proportions may be contract driven in a bid process.

12.2.3 Product line pricing

Product-line pricing involves a collection of several similar products that may vary by package size, color, quality, version, and so forth. If you view the line as variations in package size, the pricing of the line is based on the same demand profile as discussed above. The difference, of course, is that just one item in the line is usually purchased. Nonetheless, the larger-sized item is usually more price elastic, so it will have a lower price. This lower price is on a standardized unit (e.g., ounces, pounds, feet), not on the entire package.

The entire line has to be priced. An issue, however, is possible cannibalization of one product by another in the same line. Cannibalization refers to reducing the sales of one product in the line to benefit another in the same line. Sometimes, firms use a loss-leader pricing strategy in which one product is priced low so that a loss is incurred on it, but the low price will attract customers. Other products sold by the firm will then benefit by the new customers. This is not cannibalization; it is sacrificing.

With a product line, there are own- and cross-price elasticities. There are as many own-price elasticities as there are products in the line, but there are also cross-price elasticities involving all pairs. If there are n products in a line, there are $[n \times (n+1)]/2$ own- and cross-price elasticities.[5] Estimation now becomes an issue for a large product line. You could, of course, ignore the cross-price elasticities and just price each product individually without regard to cannibalization.

On a theoretical level, there is a growing literature asserting that there is little difference to a firm's profit if pricing a product line accounts for the cross-elasticities or just the own-elasticities. In other words, little is gained from multi-product pricing versus single-product pricing. In fact, profits may actually be reduced if the costs of calculating, implementing, managing, and tracking cross-product pricing are included. These tasks are obviously simplified, but not eliminated, with single-product pricing.

The basis for this view that nothing is gained is that, in many instances, a product line consists of a series of products differentiated by quality and the lower-quality product is bundled with a higher-quality one. Consider an example of an economy- and business-class seat on an airplane mentioned in [134]. The business-class seat is the economy-class seat plus an upgrade. Buying a business-class seat requires that you first buy an economy-class seat and then the upgrade, even though only the business-class seat is purchased. Using this perspective, the economy- and business-class seats are neither substitutes nor complements, so there is no cross-price elasticity. The implication is that pricing involves just the economy-class seat and an upgrade price for a better-quality product. If the economy class is eliminated, then the business-class seat is just a pure bundled product as described above. This result may be negated under some (albeit theoretical) conditions, but these may be situations in which offering a product line menu offers little gain to begin with (see [134] for a discussion). For the product line as bundles, also see [85].

12.3 Software

The models listed for the elasticity estimation can be estimated using R functions. See [33] for descriptions of R implementations. JMP and SAS can easily handle polynomial regressions, spline regressions, and local regressions. JMP has a platform for association analysis. Also see Stata for many advanced econometric methods.

12.4 Summary

Most treatments of pricing research deal with uniform or linear prices – usually just a single price point in the market. Nonlinear prices are very common and so they deserve attention. This was the focus of this chapter.

Notes

1 The notion of a "profile" as the conditional row of a contingency table is used in other areas of statistics. See [34] for profiles in correspondence analysis.
2 [122] notes that a spline is a draftsman's tool for drawing curves.
3 The notation follows [122].
4 Some people include a knot at the very beginning and end of the full data range, so if there is one range, then there are two knots.
5 This is the number of elements on the diagonal of a square matrix of order n plus the number of elements in the upper (or lower) triangle of the matrix.

BIBLIOGRAPHY

[1] A. Agresti. *Categorical Data Analysis.* John Wiley & Sons, 2002.

[2] R.E. Bailey. *The Economics of Financial Markets.* Cambridge University Press, 2005.

[3] D.A. Besanko and R.R. Braeutigam. *Microeconomics.* John Wiley & Sons, Fourth edition, 2011.

[4] R.C. Blattberg, B.-D. Kim, and S.A. Neslin. *Database Marketing: Analyzing and Managing Customers.* Springer, 2008.

[5] G.E.P. Box, W.G. Hunter, and J.S. Hunter. *Statistics for Experimenters: An Introduction to Design, Data Analysis, and Model Building.* John Wiley & Sons, 1978.

[6] K. Carroll and D. Coates. Teaching Price Discrimination: Some Clarification. *Southern Economic Journal*, 62(2): 466–480, 1999.

[7] R.G. Chapman and R. Staelin. Exploiting Rank-Ordered Choice Set Data Within the Stochastic Utility Model. *Journal of Marketing Research*, 19: 288–301, 1982.

[8] W.G. Cochrane and G.M. Cox. *Experiment Designs.* John Wiley & Sons, Second edition, 1957.

[9] L.M. Collins and S.T. Lanza. *Latent Class Analysis and Latent Transition Analysis: With Applications in the Social, Behavioral, and Health Sciences.* John Wiley & Sons, 2010.

[10] W.J. Diamond. *Practical Experiment Design for Engineers and Scientists.* Van Nostrand Reinhold, 1989.

[11] P.H. Dybvig and S.A. Ross. Arbitrage. In J. Eatwell, M. Milgate, and P. Newman, editors, *The New Palgrave: A Dictionary of Economics: Finance.* W.W. Norton & Company, Ltd., 1987.

[12] C.K. Enders. *Applied Missing Data Analysis.* The Guilford Press, 2010.

[13] B.S. Everitt, S. Landau, and M. Leese. *Cluster Analysis.* Arnold Publishers, Fourth edition, 2001.

[14] C.E. Ferguson. *Microeconomic Theory.* Richard D. Irwin, Inc., Third edition, 1972.

[15] S. Ferrari and F. Cribari-Neto. Beta Regression for Modelling Rates and Proportions. *Journal of Applied Statistics*, 31(7): 799–815, 2004.

[16] M. Friedman. *Essays in Positive Economics.* The University of Chicago Press, 1953.

[17] M. Friedman. *Price Theory: A Provisional Text.* Aldine Publishing Co., Revised edition, 1962.

[18] J.P. Gould and E.P. Lazear. *Microeconomic Theory.* Irwin, Sixth edition, 1989.

[19] P.E. Green and A.M. Krieger. Individualized Hybrid Models for Conjoint Analysis. *Management Science*, 42: 850–867, 1996.

[20] D.N. Gujarati. *Basic Econometrics*. McGraw-Hill/Irwin, Fourth edition, 2003.

[21] D. Hanlon and D. Luery. The Role of Pricing Eesearch in Assessing the Commercial Potential of New Drugs in Development. *International Journal of Market Research*, 44: 423–447, 2002.

[22] T. Hastie, R. Tibshirani, and J. Friedman. *The Elements of Statistical Learning: Data Mining, Inference, and Prediction*. Springer-Verlag, 2001.

[23] J.A. Hausman and D.A. Wise. A Conditional Probit Model for Qualitative Choice: Discrete Decisions Recognizing Interdependences and Heterogeneous Preferences. *Econometrica*, 46(2): 403–426, 1978.

[24] J.J. Heckman. Sample Selection Bias as a Specification Error. *Econometrica*, 47(1): 153–161, 1979.

[25] J.J. Heckman. The Common Structure of Statistical Models of Truncation, Sample Selection and Limited Dependent Variables and a Simple Estimator for such models. *Annals of Economic and Social Measurement*, 5(4): 475–492, 1976.

[26] A.S. Hedayat, N.J.A. Sloane, and J. Stufken. *Orthogonal Arrays: Theory and Applications*. Springer-Verlag, 1999.

[27] J.M. Henderson and R.E. Quandt. *Microeconomic Theory: A Mathematical Approach*. McGraw-Hill Book Company, Second edition, 1971.

[28] D.A. Hensher, J.M. Rose, and W.H. Greene. *Applied Choice Analysis: A Primer*. Cambridge University Press, 2005.

[29] C.R. Hicks and K.V. Turner. *Fundamental Concepts in the Design of Experiments*. Oxford University Press, 1999.

[30] J.R. Hicks. *Value and Capital: An Inquiry into Some Fundamental Principles of Economic Theory*. Oxford University Press, Second edition, 1946.

[31] R.C. Hill, W.E. Griffiths, and G.C. Lim. *Principles of Econometrics*. John Wiley & Sons, Inc, Fourth edition, 2008.

[32] K. Hinkelmann and O. Kempthorne. *Design and Analysis of Experiments*, Volume 1: Introduction to Experimental Design. John Wiley & Sons, 1994.

[33] G. James, D. Witten, T. Hastie, and R. Tibshirani. *An Introduction to Statistical Learning: With Applications in R*. Springer Science+Business Media, 2013.

[34] J.D. Jobson. *Applied Multivariate Data Analysis*, Volume II: Categorical and Multivariate Methods. Springer-Verlag, 1992.

[35] J.D. Jobson. *Applied Multivariate Data Analysis*, Volume I: Regression and Experimental Design. Springer-Verlag, 1991.

[36] P.W.M. John. *Statistical Design and Analysis of Experiments*. The Macmillan Company, 1971.

[37] B. Jones and C.J. Nachtsheim. Split-Plot Designs: What, Why, and How. *Journal of Quality Technology*, 41(4): 340–361, 2009.

[38] O. Kempthorne. *Design and Analysis of Experiments*. John Wiley & Sons, 1952.

[39] J.M. Keynes. *The General Theory of Employment, Interest, and Money*. Harcourt, Brace & World, First Harbinger Edition, 1964 edition, 1936.

[40] F.S. Koppelman and C. Bhat. A Self Instructing Course in Mode Choice Modeling: Multinomial and Nested Logit Models. U.S. Department of Transportation, Federal Transit Administration, 2006.

[41] W.F. Kuhfeld. *Experimental Design: Efficiency, Coding, and Choice Designs*. The SAS Institute, Inc., 2008.

[42] W.M. Landes and R.A. Posner. Market Power in Antitrust Cases. *Harvard Law Review*, 94(5): 937–996, 1981.

[43] E.P. Lazear. Retail Pricing and Clearance Sales. *American Economic Review*, 76(1): 14–32, 1986.

[44] F. Leisch. Visualizing Cluster Analysis and Finite Mixture Models. In A, Unwin, C. Chen, and W.K. Härdle, editors, *Handbook of Data Visualization*. Springer-Verlag, 2008.

[45] A.P. Lerner. The Concept of Monopoly and the Measurement of Monopoly Power. *Review of Economic Studies*, 1(3): 157–175, 1934.

[46] J.J. Louviere, D.A. Hensher, and J.D. Swait. *Stated Choice Methods: Analysis and Applications*. Cambridge University Press, 2000.

[47] J.J. Louviere, T.N. Flynn, and R.T. Carson. Discrete Choice Experiments Are Not Conjoint Analysis. *Journal of Choice Modelling*, 3(3): 57–72, 2010.

[48] P. Marshall and E.T. Bradlow. A Unified Approach to Conjoint Analysis Models. *Journal of the American Statistical Association*, 459: 674–682, 1997.

[49] E. Jerome McCarthy and W.D. Perreault. *Basic Marketing: A Managerial Approach*. Irwin, Ninth edition, 1987.

[50] A.H. Milley, J.D. Seabolt, and J.S. Williams. Data Mining and the Case for Sampling. *A SAS Institute Best Practices Paper*, 1998.

[51] G.A. Milliken and D.E. Johnson. *The Analysis of Messy Data*, Volume I: DeDesign Experiments. Lifetime Learning Publications, 1984.

[52] L. Mlodinow. *The Drunkard's Walk: How Randomness Rules Our Lives*. Vintage Books, 2008.

[53] K.B. Monroe. *Pricing: Making Profitable Decisions*. McGraw-Hill, Second edition, 1990.

[54] M.D. Morris. *Design of Experiments: An Introduction Based on Linear Models*. CRC Press, 2011.

[55] M.D. Morris. Orthogonal Arrays. Available at mmorris.public.iastate.edu/stat612/OA.pdf.

[56] T.T. Nagle and R.K. Holden. *The Strategy and Tactics of Pricing: A Guide to Profitable Decision Making*. Prentice Hall, Third edition, 2002.

[57] W.R. Paczkowski. *Market Data Analysis Using JMP*. SAS Press, 2016.

[58] A.C. Pigou. *The Economics of Welfare*. Macmillan and Co., Fourth edition, 1932.

[59] D. Raghavarao, J.B. Wiley, and P. Chitturi. *Choice-based Conjoint Analysis: Models and Designs*. Chapman & Hall/CRC, 2011.

[60] P.E. Rossi, G.M. Allenby, and R. McCulloch. *Bayesian Statistics and Marketing*. John Wiley & Sons, 2005.

[61] P.A. Samuelson. A Note on the Pure Theory of Consumers' Behaviour. *Economica*, 5(17): 61–71, 1938.

[62] P.A. Samuelson. *Foundations of Economic Analysis*. Harvard University Press, 1947.

[63] B. Schwartz. *The Paradox of Choice: Why More is Less*. HarperCollins, 2004.

[64] B.R. Shiller. First Degree Price Discrimination Using Big Data. Working Paper, Department of Economics, Brandeis University, 2013.

[65] J.H. Stock and M.W. Watson. *Introduction to Econometrics*. Addison-Wesley, 2011.

[66] H. Theil. *Principles of Econometrics*. John Wiley & Sons, 1971.

[67] J.J. Tirole. *The Theory of Industrial Organization*. The MIT Press, 1988.

[68] E.R. Tufte. *The Visual Display of Quantitative Information*. Graphics Press, 1983.

[69] A. Unwin, C. Chen, and W.K. Härdle. Introduction. In A. Unwin, C. Chen, and W.K. Härdle, editors, *Handbook of Data Visualization*. Springer-Verlag, 2008.

[70] H.R. Varian. Price Discrimination. In R. Schmalensee and R. Willig, editors, *Handbook of Industrial Organization*. Elsevier B.V., 1989.

[71] H.R. Varian. Revealed Preference. In Samuelsonian Economics and the Twenty-First Century. M. Szenberg, L. Ramrattan, and A.A. Gottesman, editors. Oxford University Press, 2006.

[72] P.A.Viton. Mode Choice – The IIA Problem. Available at facweb.knowlton.ohio-state. edu/pviton/courses2/crp5700/mode-choice-iia.pdf.

[73] M. Wedel and W.A. Kamakura. *Market Segmentation: ConConcept and Methodological Foundations*. Kluwer Academic Publishers, 1998.

[74] R.Wilson. *Nonlinear Pricing*. Oxford University Press, 1993.

[75] C.F.J. Wu and M. Hamada. *Experiments: Planning, Analysis, and Parameter Design Optimization*. John Wiley & Sons, 2000.

[76] J.M. Yedlin. Beverage Operations Pricing Strategies. Unpublished Masters Thesis, 2008.

[77] American Bar Association. Econometrics: Legal, Practical, and Technical Issues. ABA Section of Antitrust Law, 2005.

[78] P. McCullagh and J.A. Nelder. *Generalized Linear Models*. Chapman & Hall, Second edition, 1989.

[79] American Bar Association. Market Power Handbook: Competition Law and Economic Foundations. ABA Section of Antitrust Law, 2005.

[80] H.Akaike. Statistical Predictor Identification. *Annals of the Institute Statistical Mathematics*, 22: 203–217, 1973.

[81] G.M. Allenby, T.S. Shively, S.Yang, and M.J. Garratt. A Choice Model for Packaged Goods: Dealing with Discrete Quantities and Quantity Discounts. *Marketing Science*, 23(1): 95–108, 2004.

[82] R.L. Andrews and I.S. Currim. A Comparison of Segment Retention Criteria for Finite Mixture Logit Models. *Journal of Marketing Research*, 40: 235–243, 2003.

[83] J.D.Angrist and J.-S. Pischke. *Mastering 'Metrics: The Path from Cause to Effect*. Princeton University Press, 2015.

[84] J.D.Angrist and J.-S. Pischke. *Mostly Harmless Econometrics: An Empiricist's Companion*. Princeton University Press, 2009.

[85] M.Armstrong. Nonlinear Pricing. *Annual Review of Economics*, 8(1): 583–614, 2016.

[86] M. Armstrong and J.Vickers. Competitive Price Discrimination. *The RAND Journal of Economics*, 32(4): 579–605, 2001.

[87] O. Ashenfelter, D. Ashmore, J.B. Baker, S. Gleason, and D.S. Hosken. Econometric Methods in Staples. Available at harris.princeton.edu/pubs/pdfs/486.pdf.

[88] R.A. Bailey. *Design of Comparative Experiments* of Cambridge Series in Statistical and Probabilistic Mathematics. Cambridge University Press, 2008.

[89] B.M. Balk. *Price and Quantity Index Numbers: Models for Measuring Aggregate Change and Difference*. Cambridge University Press, 2008.

[90] B.H. Baltagi. *Econometric Analysis of Panel Data*. John Wiley & Sons, 1995.

[91] J. Barrientos Marín, D. Tobón Orozco and J.F. Bedoya Marulanda. Three-Part Tariffs and Short-Run Rationality in the Local Fixed Telephone Consumption: Empirical Evidence from Medellín. *Revista Desarrollo y Sociedad*, (65): 147–170, 2010.

[92] R.A. Beck. *Statistical Learning from a Regression Perspective*. Springer, 2008.

[93] J. Berman and J. Pfleeger. Which Industries are Sensitive to Business Cycles? *Monthly Labor Review*, 120(2): 19–25, 1997.

[94] F. deBoer. p-Value Weirdness in a World of Big Data. Available at: https://fredrikdeboer. com/2018/03/13/archives-p-value-weirdness-in-a-world-of-big-data/.

[95] K.A. Bollen. Latent Variables in Psychology and the Social Sciences. *Annual Review of Psychology*, 53: 605–634, 2002.

[96] D.G. Bonett. Sample Size Planning for Behavioral Science Research. Available at: https://people.ucsc.edu/~dgbonett/sample.html.

[97] R.A. Boyles. On the Convergence of the EM Algorithm. *Journal of the Royal Statistical Society, Series B (Methodological)*, 45(1): 47–50, 1983.

[98] L. Breiman, J.H. Friedman, R.A. Olshen, and C.J. Stone. *Classification and Regression Trees.* Wadworth & Brooks, 1984.

[99] K.P. Burnham and D.R. Anderson. *Model Selection and Multimodel Inference: A Practical Information-Theoretic Approach.* Springer-Verlag, Second edition, 2002.

[100] A.C. Cameron and P.K. Trivedi. *Microeconometrics: Methods and Applications.* Cambridge University Press, 2005.

[101] L. Camilleri and L.M. Azzopardi. Market Segmentation through Conjoint Analysis using Latent Class Models. *25th ESM (European Simulation and Modelling),* 2011.

[102] Y. Chen and G. Iyer. Consumer Addressability and Customized Pricing. *Marketing Science,* 21(2): 197–208, 2002.

[103] Y. Chen and M.R. Gupta. EM Demystified: An Expectation-Maximization Tutorial. techreport, UWEETR-2010-0002, Department of Electrical Engineering University of Washington, Department of Electrical Engineering University of Washington Box 352500 Seattle, Washington 98195-2500, 2010.

[104] M.R. Chernick. *Bootstrap Methods: A Practitioner's Guide.* John Wiley & Sons, Inc., 1999.

[105] K. Chrzan. The Options Pricing Model: An Application of Best-Worst Measurement. resreport, Sawtooth Software, 2005.

[106] W.S. Cleveland. LOWESS: A Program for Smoothing Scatterplots by Robust Locally Weighted Regression. *The American Statistician,* 35(1): 54, 1981.

[107] W.S. Cleveland. Robust Locally Weighted Regression and Smoothing Scatterplots. *Journal of the American Statistical Association,* 74(368): 829–836, 1979.

[108] C.M. Dalton. Estimating Demand Elasticities Using Nonlinear Pricing. *International Journal of Industrial Organization,* 37: 178–191, 2014.

[109] C. Das. An Algorithm for Selecting Quantity Discounts from Realistic Schedules. *Journal of the Operational Research Society,* 41(2): 165–172, 1990.

[110] T. Dasu and T. Johnson. *Exploratory Data Mining and Data Cleaning.* John Wiley & Sons, Inc., 2003.

[111] A.C. Davison and D.V. Hinkley. *Bootstrap Methods and Their Applications* of Cambridge Series in Statistical and Probabilistic Mathematics. Cambridge University Press, 1997.

[112] A.P. Dempster and N.M. Laird and D.B. Rubin. Maximum Likelihood from Incomplete Data via the EM Algorithm. *Journal of the Royal Statistical Society, Series B (Methodological),* 39(1): 1–38, 1977.

[113] J.G. Diaz. *Finite Mixture Models: Review, Applications, and Computer Intensive Methods.* Ph.D. Dissertation, Groningen of University, The Netherlands, Research School Systems, Organisation and Management (SOM), 2004.

[114] T.A. Domencich and D. McFadden. *Urban Travel Demand: A Behavioral Analysis.* Elsevier, 1975.

[115] E.J. Dudewicz and S.N. Mishra. *Modern Mathematical Statistics.* John Wiley & Sons, 1988.

[116] R.E. Edwards, H. Zhang, L.E. Parker, and J.R. New. Approximate l-fold Cross-Validation with Least Squares SVM and Kernel Ridge Regression. *12th International Conference on Machine Learning and Applications,* 2013.

[117] L. Einav and J.D. Levin. The Data Revolution and Economic Analysis. Working Paper, 19035, NBER, 2013.

[118] G. Ellison. A Model of Add-on Pricing. *The Quarterly Journal of Economics,* 120(2): 585–637, 2005.

[119] B.S. Everitt and D.J. Hall. *Finite Mixture Distributions* of Applied Probability and Statistics. Chapman and Hall, 1981.

[120] D. Firth. Bias Reduction of Maximum Likelihood Estimates. *Biometrika,* 80: 27–38, 1993.

[121] A.K. Formann. Latent Class Model Diagnostics – A Review and Some Proposals. *Computational Statistics & Data Analysis*, 41: 549–559, 2003.

[122] F.E. Harrell, Jr. *Regression Modeling Strategies: With Applications to Linear Models, Logistic Regression, and Survival Analysis* of Springer Series in Statistics. Springer-Verlag, 2001.

[123] A. Gabor. *Pricing: Concepts and Methods for Effective Marketing*. Gower Publishing, Second edition, 1988.

[124] A. Gelman and J. Hill. *Data Analysis Using Regression and Multilevel/Hierarchical Models*. Cambridge University Press, 2007.

[125] P.I. Good. *Resampling Methods: A Practical Guide to Data Analysis*. Birkhauser, Second edition, 2001.

[126] C.W.J. Granger. Extracting Information From Mega-panels and High-frequency Data. *Statistica Neerlandia*, 52(3): 258–272, 1998.

[127] W.H. Greene. *Econometric Analysis*. Prentice Hall, Fifth edition, 2003.

[128] W.H. Greene and D.A. Hensher. A Latent Class Model for Discrete Choice Analysis: Contrasts with Mixed Logit. *Transportation Research Part B: Methodological*, 37(8): 681–698, 2003.

[129] G. Heinze. The Application of Firth's Procedure to Cox and Logistic Regression. techreport, 10/1999, Section of Clinical Biometrics, Department of Medical Computer Sciences, University of Vienna, 1999. Updated in January 2001.

[130] H.E.T. Holgersson, L. Nordstrom, and O. Oner. Dummy Variables vs. Category-wise Models. *Journal of Applied Statistics*, 41(2): 233–241, 2014.

[131] H.J. Hovenkamp and E. Hovenkamp. Complex Bundled Discounts and Antitrust Policy. *Buffalo Law Review*, 57: 1227–1266, 2009.

[132] H. Cheng. *Analysis of Panel Data*. Cambridge University Press, 1986.

[133] R. Iyengar and S. Gupta. Nonlinear Pricing. In V.R. Rao, editor, *Handbook of Pricing Research in Marketing*. Edward Elgar, 2009.

[134] J.P. Johnson and D.P. Myatt. The Properties of Product Line Prices. *International Journal of Industrial Organization*, 43: 182–188, 2015.

[135] P. Joulani, A. Gyorgy, and C. Szepesvari. Fast Cross-Validation for Incremental Learning. *Proceedings of the Twenty-Fourth International Joint Conference on Artificial Intelligence*, 2015.

[136] L. Kazbare, H.C.M. va Trijp, and J.K. Eskildsen. *A-priori* and *Post-hoc* Segmentation in the Design of Healthy Eating Campaigns. *Journal of Marketing Communications*, 16(1–2): 21–45, 2010.

[137] P. Kennedy. *A Guide to Econometrics*. MIT Press, Fifth edition, 2003.

[138] J. Kmenta. Latent Variables in Econometrics. *Statistica Neerlandica*, 45(2): 73–84, 1991.

[139] I.G.G. Kreft and J. de Leeuw. *Introducing Multilevel Modeling*. SAGE Publications Ltd., First edition, 1998.

[140] W.F. Kuhfeld. *Marketing Research Methods in SAS*. The SAS Institute, Inc., 2010.

[141] P.J. Lenk, W.S. Desarbo, P.E. Green, and M.R. Young. Hierarchical Bayes Conjoint Analysis: Recovery of Partworth Heterogeneity from Reduced Experimental Design. *Marketing Science*, 15(2): 173–191, 1996.

[142] P.S. Levy and S. Lemeshow. *Sampling of Populations: Methods and Applications*. John Wiley & Sons, Inc., Fourth edition, 2008.

[143] D. Lindley and A. Smith. Bayes Estimates for the Linear Model. *Journal of the Royal Statistical Society, Series B (Methodological)*, 34(1): 1–41, 1972.

[144] S.S. Mangiafico. Summary and Analysis of Extension Program Evaluation in R. Version 1.9.0. Available at: http://rcompanion.org/handbook/.

[145] D. McFadden. Conditional Logit Analysis of Qualitative Choice Behavior. In P. Zarembka, editor, *Frontiers in Econometrics*. Academic Press, 1974.

[146] B.B. McShane and D. Gal. Statistical Significance and the Dichotomization of Evidence. *Journal of the American Statistical Association*, 112(519): 885–908, 2017.

[147] S. Michels, M. Kurz-Levin, and C. Schmitz. Off-label Drug Use – Price Analysis for Avastin in Ophthalmology. *International Journal of Pharmaceutical and Healthcare Marketing*, 3(1): 59–73, 2009.

[148] E.R. Morey and J.A. Thacher. Using Choice Experiments and Latent-class Modeling to Investigate and Estimate How Academic Economists Value and Trade Off the Attributes of Academic Positions, 2012.

[149] M. Moseki. Segmenting the Consumer Market. In J. Strydom, editor, *Introduction to Marketing*. Juta and Co., LTD., Third edition, 2004.

[150] A.C. Muller and S. Guido. *Introduction to Machine Learning*. O'Reilly Media Inc., 2017.

[151] J.H. Myers. *Segmentation and Positioning for Strategic Marketing Decisions*. American Marketing Association, 1996.

[152] N. Jun. *Extensions of Hierarchical Bayesian Shrinkage Estimation with Applications to a Marketing Science Problem*. Ph.D. thesis, University of South Carolina, 2007.

[153] Y. Nievergelt. The Concept of Elasticity in Economics. *SIAM Review*, 25(2): 261–265, 1983.

[154] D. Oberski. Mixture Models: Latent Profile and Latent Class Analysis. In J. Robertson and M. Kaptein, editors, *Modern Statistical Methods for HCI* in Human–Computer Interaction Series. Springer International Publishing Switzerland, 2016.

[155] S.S. Oren. Nonlinear Pricing. In Ö. Özer and R. Phillips, editors, *The Oxford Handbook of Pricing Management*. Oxford University Press, 2012.

[156] W.S. Robinson. Ecological Correlations and the Behavior of Individuals. *American Sociological Review*, 15(3): 351–357, 1950.

[157] D.B. Rubin. Inference and Missing Data. *Biometrika*, 63: 581–592, 1976.

[158] Sawtooth. The MaxDiff System Technical Paper. Technical report, Sawtooth Software, Inc., 2013. Version 8.

[159] J. Schepers. On Regression Modelling with Dummy Variables Versus Separate Regressions Per Group: Comment on Holgersson et al. *Journl of Applied Statistics*, 43(4): 674–681, 2016.

[160] G. Schwarz. Estimating the Dimension of a Model. *Annals of Statistics*, 6: 461–464, 1978.

[161] D. Serra. *Implementing TURF Analysis through Binary Linear Programming*. Department of Economics and Business, Universitat Pompeu Fabra, 2012.

[162] G. Shmueli, P.C. Bruce, M.L. Stephens, and N.R. Patel. *Data Mining for Business Analytics: Concepts, Techniques, and Applications with JMP Pro*. John Wiley Sons Inc., 2016.

[163] T.A.B. Snijders and R.J. Bosker. *Multilevel Analysis: An Introduction to Basic and Advanced Multilevel Modeling*. Sage, Second edition, 2012.

[164] L.A. Stole. Price Discrimination and Competition. In M. Armstrong and R. Porter, editors, *Handbook of Industrial Organization*. Elsevier B.V., 2007.

[165] D.B. Suits. Use of Dummy Variables in Regression Equations. *Journal of the American Statistical Association*, 52(280): 548–551, 1957.

[166] K. Train. *Discrete Choice Methods with Simulation*. Cambridge University Press, Second edition, 2009.

[167] R.L. Wasserstein and N.A. Lazar. The ASA's Statement on p-Values: Context, Process, and Purpose. *The American Statistician*, 70: 129–133, 2016.

[168] E.J. Wegman. Huge Data Sets and the Frontier of Computational Feasibility. *Journal of Computational and Graphical Statistics*, 4(4): 281–295, 1995.

[169] P. Van Westendorp. NSS-Price Sensitivity Meter (PSM) – A new approach to study consumer perception of price. *Proceedings of the ESOMAR Congress*, 1976.

[170] P.H. Westfall, R.D. Tobias, D. Rom, R.D. Wolfinger, and Y. Hochberg. *Multiple Comparisons and Multiple Test Using SAS.* The SAS Institute, Inc., 1999.

[171] J.M. Wooldridge. *Econometric Analysis of Cross Section and Panel Data.* MIT Press, 2002.

[172] J.M. Wooldridge. *Introductory Econometrics: A Modern Approach.* South-Western, Fifth edition, 2013.

[173] C.-C. Yang and C.-C. Yang. Separating Latent Classes by Information Criteria. *Journal of Classification*, 24:183–203, 2007.

[174] F.W. Young, P.M. Valero-Mora, and M. Friendly. *Visual Statistics: Seeing Data with Dynamic Interactive Graphics.* John Wiley & Sons, 2006.

[175] D. Zahay, A. Griffin, and E. Fredicks. Sources, Uses, and Forms of Data in the New Product Development Process. *Industrial Marketing Management*, 33:657–666, 2004.

[176] H. Zhang and B. Singer. *Recursive Partitioning in the Health Science.* Springer-Verlag, 1999.

[177] S.T. Ziliak and D.N. McCloskey. *The Cult of Statistical Significance: How the Standard Error Costs Us Jobs, Justice, and Lives (Economics, Cognition, and Society).* University of Michigan Press, First edition, 2008.

INDEX

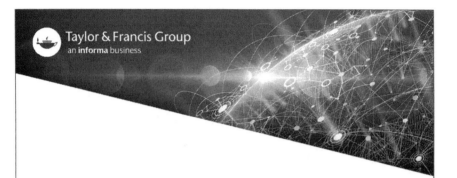